Suzuki LT-Z400
Kawasaki KFX400
Arctic Cat DVX400

Service and Repair Manual

by Alan Ahlstrand

Models covered

Suzuki LT-Z400, 2003 through 2009
Kawasaki KFX400, 2003 through 2006
Arctic Cat DVX400, 2004 through 2008

ABCDE
FGHIJ
KLMNO
PQRST

ISBN-13: **978-1-56392-910-6**
ISBN-10: **1-56392-910-4**

Library of Congress Control Number: 2011930176
Printed in the USA

Haynes Publishing
Sparkford, Nr Yeovil, Somerset BA22 7JJ, England

Haynes North America, Inc
861 Lawrence Drive, Newbury Park, California 91320, USA 11-208

A book in the **Haynes Service and Repair Manual Series**

Contents

LIVING WITH YOUR ATV

Introduction

Daily (pre-ride) checks

MAINTENANCE

Routine maintenance and servicing

Contents

REPAIRS AND OVERHAUL

Engine, transmission and associated systems

Chassis and bodywork components

REFERENCE

Suzuki
Every Which Way

by Julian Ryder

From Textile Machinery to Motorcycles

Suzuki were the second of Japan's Big Four motorcycle manufacturers to enter the business, and like Honda they started by bolting small two-stroke motors to bicycles. Unlike Honda, they had manufactured other products before turning to transportation in the aftermath of World War II. In fact Suzuki has been in business since the first decade of the 20th-Century when Michio Suzuki manufactured textile machinery.

The desperate need for transport in post-war Japan saw Suzuki make their first motorized bicycle in 1952, and the fact that by 1954 the company had changed its name to Suzuki Motor Company shows how quickly the sideline took over the whole company's activities. In their first full manufacturing year, Suzuki made nearly 4500 bikes and rapidly expanded into the world markets with a range of two-strokes.

Suzuki didn't make a four-stroke until 1977 when the GS750 double-overhead-cam across-the-frame four arrived. This was several years after Honda and Kawasaki had established the air-cooled four as the industry standard, but no motorcycle epitomizes the era of what came to be known as the Universal Japanese motorcycle better than

The T500 two-stroke twin

One of the later GT750 'kettle' models with front disc brakes

the GS. So well engineered were the original fours that you can clearly see their genes in the GS500 twins that are still going strong in the mid-1990s. Suzuki's ability to prolong the life of their products this way means that they are often thought of as a conservative company. This is hardly fair if you look at some of their landmark designs, most of which have been commercial as well as critical successes.

Two-stroke Success

Early racing efforts were bolstered by the arrival of Ernst Degner who defected from the East German MZ team at the Swedish GP of 1961, bringing with him the rotary-valve secrets of design genius Walter Kaaden. The new Suzuki 50 cc racer won its first GP on the Isle of Man the following year and winning the title easily. Only Honda and Ralph Bryans interrupted Suzuki's run of 50 cc titles from 1962 to 1968.

The arrival of the twin-cylinder 125 racer in 1963 enabled Hugh Anderson to win both 50 and 125 world titles. You may not think 50 cc racing would be exciting - until you learn that the final incarnation of the thing had 14 gears and could do well over 100 mph on fast circuits. Before pulling out of GPs in 1967 the 50 cc racer won six of the eight world titles chalked up by Suzuki during the 1960s as well as providing Mitsuo Itoh with the distinction of being the only Japanese rider to win an Isle of Man TT. Mr. Itoh still works for Suzuki, he's in charge of their racing program.

Europe got the benefit of Suzuki's two-stroke expertise in a succession of air-cooled twins, the six-speed 250 cc Super Six being the most memorable, but the arrival in 1968 of the first of a series of 500 cc twins which were good looking, robust and versatile marked the start of mainstream success.

So confident were Suzuki of their two-stroke expertise that they even applied it to the burgeoning Superbike sector. The GT750 water-cooled triple arrived in 1972. It was big, fast and comfortable although the handling and stopping power did draw some comment. Whatever the drawbacks of the road bike, the engine was immensely successful in Superbike and Formula 750 racing. The roadster has its devotees, though, and is now a sought-after bike on the classic Japanese scene. Do not refer to it as the Water Buffalo in such company. Joking aside, the later disc-braked versions were quite civilized, but the audacious idea of using a big two-stroke motor in what was essentially a touring bike was a surprising success until the fuel crisis of the mid-'70s effectively killed off big strokers.

The same could be said of Suzuki's only real lemon, the RE5. This is still the only mass-produced bike to use the rotary (or Wankel) engine but never sold well. Fuel consumption in the mid-teens allied to frightening complexity and excess weight meant the RE5 was a non-starter in the sales race.

Suzuki's GT250X7 was an instant hit in the popular 250 cc 'learner' sector

The GS400 was the first in a line of four-stroke twins

Development of the Four-stroke range

When Suzuki got round to building a four-stroke they did a very good job of it. The GS fours were built in 550, 650, 750, 850, 1000 and 1100 cc sizes in sports, custom, roadster and even shaft-driven touring forms over many years. The GS1000 was in on the start of Superbike racing in the early 1970s and the GS850 shaft-driven tourer was around nearly 15 years later. The fours spawned a line of 400, 425, 450 and 500 cc GS twins that were essentially the middle half of the four with all their reliability. If there was ever a criticism of the GS models it was that with the exception of the GS1000S of 1980, colloquially known as the ice-cream van, the range was visually uninspiring.

They nearly made the same mistake when they launched the four-valve-head GSX750 in 1979. Fortunately, the original twin-shock version was soon replaced by the 'E'-model with Full-Floater rear suspension and a full set of all the gadgets the Japanese industry was then keen on and has since forgotten about, like 16-inch front wheels and anti-dive forks. The air-cooled GSX was like the GS built in 550, 750 and 1100 cc versions with a variety of half, full and touring fairings, but the GSX that is best remembered is the Katana that first appeared in 1981. The power was provided by an 1000 or 1100 cc GSX motor, but wrapped around it was the most outrageous styling package to come out of Japan. Designed by Hans Muth of Target Design, the Katana looked like nothing seen before or since. At the time there was as much anti feeling as praise, but now it is rightly regarded as a classic, a true milestone in motorcycle design. The factory have even started making 250 and 400 cc fours for the home market with the same styling as the 1981 bike.

Just to remind us that they'd still been building two-strokes for the likes of Barry Sheene, in 1986 Suzuki marketed a road-going version of their RG500 square-four racer which had put an end to the era of the four-stroke in 500 GPs when it appeared in 1974. In 1976 Suzuki not only won their first 500 title with Sheene, they sold RG500s over the counter and won every GP with them - with the exception of the Isle of Man TT which the works riders boycotted. Ten years on, the RG500 Gamma gave road riders the nearest experience they'd ever get to riding a GP bike. The fearsome beast could top 140 mph and only weighed 340 lb - the other alleged GP replicas were pussy cats compared to the Gamma's man-eating tiger.

The RG only lasted a few years and is already firmly in the category of collector's item; its four-stroke equivalent, the GSX-R, is still with us and looks like being so for many years. You have to look back to 1985 and its launch to realize just what a revolutionary step the GSX-R750 was: quite simply it was the first race replica. Not a bike dressed up to look like a race bike, but a genuine racer with lights on, a bike that could be taken straight to the track and win.

The first GSX-R, the 750, had a completely new motor cooled by oil rather than water and an aluminium cradle frame. It was sparse, a little twitchy and very, very fast. This time Suzuki got the looks right, blue and white bodywork based on the factory's racing colors and endurance-racer lookalike twin headlights. And then came the 1100 - the big GSX-R got progressively more brutal as it chased the Yamaha EXUP for the heavyweight championship.

The GS750 led the way for a series of four cylinder models

Later four-stroke models, like this GSX1100, were fitted with 16v engines

And alongside all these mould-breaking designs, Suzuki were also making the best looking custom bikes to come out of Japan, the Intruders; the first race replica trail bike, the DR350; the sharpest 250 Supersports, the RGV250; and a bargain-basement 600, the Bandit. The Bandit proved so popular they went on to build 1200 and 750 cc versions of it. I suppose that's predictable, a range of four-stroke fours just like the GS and GSXs. It's just like the company really, sometimes predictable, admittedly - but never boring.

It's a V-twin Jim, but not as we know it

The late 1990s was a time when Honda and Suzuki decided it was time to keep up with their Italian neighbors at Ducati and build a V-twin. Both built a softer, road orientated version and a harder-edged model to register for Superbike racing. Honda's bike was uncontroversial, and did exactly what it said on the tin. Suzuki's didn't.

Everybody agreed the TL1000S had a great engine that felt just like a big V-twin should and that in the days before the R1 it was as quick as you could want. Then rumors started circulating about some nasty habits. Some reports in specialist magazines said the TL was prone to vicious tank-slappers; others equally vehemently said the rumors were rubbish. It was enough to persuade the British importer to retro-fit steering dampers, and suspicion centred on the rear suspension system and its innovative (or weird, depending on which camp you were in) rotary damper. After some unpleasant accidents and subsequent court cases, things quieted down. The steering damper certainly helped and fuel-injection tweaks that smoothed out the power delivery on later models helped riders keep the bike under control. However, the model's reputation was seriously damaged and a lot of people fought shy of the TL - which means second-hand examples are satisfyingly cheap for those in the know.

The R-model isn't just a modified version of the S, it's a completely different machine. This was the bike that was supposed to take on Ducati on the tracks and take over Suzuki's racing efforts from the aging and now out-gunned GSX-R750. It didn't happen. The R was still high, long and, at nearly 200 kg dry, heavy. They did turn up on race tracks but never made it to the World Superbike grid. The Alstare Corona organization that ran the works World Superbike effort secretly developed a race-ready TL1000R with multiple World Superbike winner and World Endurance Champion Stephane Mertens of Belgium as the test rider. However, even the team that kept the old 750 competitive well after its sell-by date couldn't get the big twin competitive.

The motor did win a race though, but in a Bimota chassis.

Aussie wild child Anthony Gobert rode a Bimota SB8 with TL1000 motor for the first part of the 2000 season. He scored points in race two of the opening round of the year in South Africa then with an inspired tyre gamble on a drying Phillip Island track at home in Oz he won the first race of round two and followed it up with ninth place in the second race. Next time out in Japan, it blew up spectacularly, flinging Gobert down the track and following him into the barriers. Even the Go-Show admitted it was a crash that scared him severely as well as giving him a collection of minor fractures and burns. The team folded soon afterwards, citing lack of funds. The whole episode summed up the TL's relationship with the race track.

Nothing daunted, Suzuki took another cue from Honda and put their V-twin in a giant trailbike, and again just like Honda they gave it a very strange name, the V-Strom (that is

Suzuki's GSX-R range represented their cutting edge sports bikes

The TL1000S-W

The TL1000R-K1

The DL1000-K2 V-Strom

not a misprint). Pushing peak power down to produce more midrange and bottom end made for a very nice motor which suited the chassis brilliantly. The V-Strom, along with its compatriots in the giant trailbike class, is sadly under-rated by those obsessed with sports bikes, but it's the sort of machine on which you can load two people and their luggage and set off to travel on anything from motorways to dirt tracks and enjoy it.

It would be a shame to consign such a great motor to an early grave so unappreciated, so Suzuki went back to the original TL, the S, and re-invented the bike as a budget sportster in the SV range. It may wear a different designation, but the SV has all the DNA of the TL. With the exception of that strange damper.

Suzuki's first major success in the V-twin cruiser market came with the 750 Intruder in 1985. Using a liquid-cooled engine with a 45-degree angle between the cylinders, twin-shock rear suspension and shaft drive, the bike gave Suzuki a credible entry in the category.

Displacement was reduced to 700cc (and the model designation changed to VS700) for US models in 1986 and 1987. This was in response to a tariff on Japanese bikes over 700cc, which was designed to protect Harley-Davidson, at that time in severe financial peril. The tariff was rescinded at HD's request as their business picked up, and displacement on US models was returned to 750cc in 1988.

The VZ800 Marauder added some styling variety to Suzuki's cruiser line, beginning in 1997. The bike was mechanically almost the same as the Intruder, with chain drive being the most important difference.

The VL800 Volusia, added to the line in 2001, was more of a cruiser than a chopper. It used a single carburetor, rather than the dual carbs of the Intruder and Marauder. The fuel tank was wide, the fenders swoopy, and the front forks made to look plump with the addition of trim covers on the upper fork legs.

The Intruder was renamed the Boulevard S50 (as in 50 cubic inches of piston displacement) for 2005. Mechanically, it's almost unchanged from the Intruder.

The Marauder was renamed the Boulevard M50 for 2005. Its carburetors were replaced by a dual-throttle fuel injection system.

The Volusia was renamed the Boulevard C50 for 2005 and equipped with the same fuel injection system as the M50.

The LT-Z400 was a significant addition to Suzuki's sport ATV line, beginning in 2003. It featured a DOHC engine, adjustable front and rear shocks, and disc brakes at front and rear. Kawasaki and Arctic cat both produced versions of the vehicle, the Kawasaki KFX400 and Arctic Cat DVX400. In 2009, the LT-Z400 was equipped with fuel injection instead of a carburetor, and the front and rear suspensions were modified.

Acknowledgements

Our thinks to GP Sports of Santa Clara and San Jose, California, for supplying the ATVs used the photographs throughout this manual; To David Guy, service manager, for arranging the teardown and fitting the project into his shop's busy schedule; to Tony Correa, service technician, for doing the mechanical work; and to Tony and to Kevin Wood for providing valuable technical information.

About this manual

The aim of this manual is to help you get the best value from your ATV. It can do so in several ways. It can help you decide what work must be done, even if you choose to have it done by a dealer; it provides information and procedures for routine maintenance and servicing; and it offers diagnostic and repair procedures to follow when trouble occurs.

We hope you use the manual to tackle the work yourself. For many simpler jobs, doing it yourself may be quicker than arranging an appointment to get the vehicle into a dealer and making the trips to leave it and pick it up. More importantly, a lot of money can be saved by avoiding the expense the shop must pass on to you to cover its labor and overhead costs. An added benefit is the sense of satisfaction and accomplishment that you feel after doing the job yourself.

References to the left or right side of the vehicle assume you are sitting on the seat, facing forward.

We take great pride in the accuracy of information given in this manual, but motorcycle manufacturers make alterations and design changes during the production run of a particular motorcycle of which they do not inform us. No liability can be accepted by the authors or publishers for loss, damage or injury caused by any errors in, or omissions from, the information given.

Engine and frame numbers

The frame serial number is stamped into the left side of the frame. The engine number is stamped into the crankcase and is visible from the right side of the machine. Both of these numbers should be recorded and kept in a safe place so they can be given to law enforcement officials in the event of a theft.

The frame serial number and engine serial number should also be kept in a handy place (such as with your driver's license) so they are always available when purchasing or ordering parts for your machine.

Buying spare parts

Once you have found all the identification numbers, record them for reference when buying parts. Since the manufacturers change specifications, parts and vendors (companies that manufacture various components on the machine), providing the ID numbers is the only way to be reasonably sure that you are buying the correct parts.

Whenever possible, take the worn part to the dealer so direct comparison with the new component can be made. Along the trail from the manufacturer to the parts shelf, there are numerous places that the part can end up with the wrong number or be listed incorrectly.

The two places to purchase new parts for your ATV – the accessory store and the franchised dealer – differ in the type of parts they carry. While dealers can obtain virtually every part for your ATV, the accessory dealer is usually limited to normal high wear items such as shock absorbers, tune-up parts, various engine gaskets, cables, chains, brake parts, etc. Rarely will an accessory outlet have major suspension components, cylinders, transmission gears, or cases.

Used parts can be obtained for considerably less than new ones, but you can't always be sure of what you're getting. Once again, take your worn part to the salvage yard for direct comparison.

Whether buying new, used or rebuilt parts, the best course is to deal directly with someone who specializes in parts for your particular make.

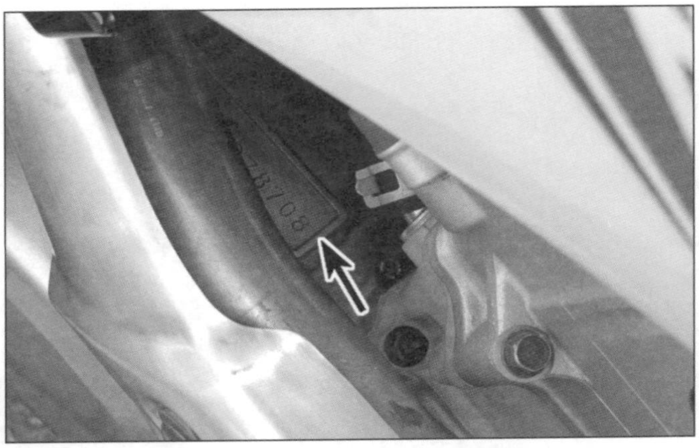

The engine number is stamped into the right side of the crankcase

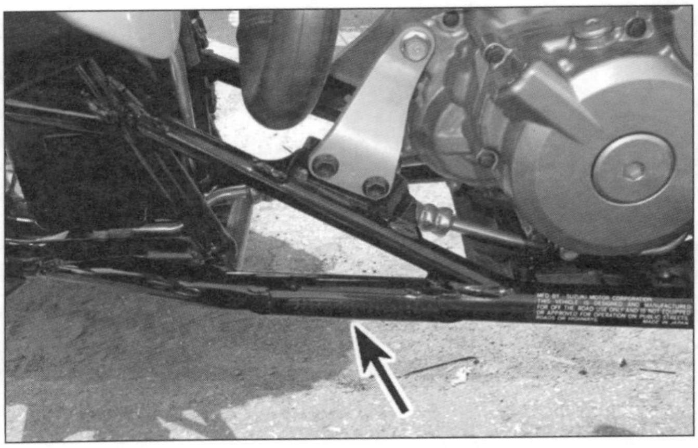

The frame serial number is stamped into the left frame rail forward of the footrest

Professional mechanics are trained in safe working procedures. However enthusiastic you may be about getting on with the job at hand, take the time to ensure that your safety is not put at risk. A moment's lack of attention can result in an accident, as can failure to observe simple precautions.

There will always be new ways of having accidents, and the following is not a comprehensive list of all dangers; it is intended rather to make you aware of the risks and to encourage a safe approach to all work you carry out on your bike.

Asbestos

- Certain friction, insulating, sealing and other products - such as brake pads, clutch linings, gaskets, etc. - contain asbestos. Extreme care must be taken to avoid inhalation of dust from such products since it is hazardous to health. If in doubt, assume that they do contain asbestos.

Fire

- Remember at all times that gasoline is highly flammable. Never smoke or have any kind of naked flame around, when working on the vehicle. But the risk does not end there - a spark caused by an electrical short-circuit, by two metal surfaces contacting each other, by careless use of tools, or even by static electricity built up in your body under certain conditions, can ignite gasoline vapor, which in a confined space is highly explosive. Never use gasoline as a cleaning solvent. Use an approved safety solvent.
- Always disconnect the battery ground terminal before working on any part of the fuel or electrical system, and never risk spilling fuel on to a hot engine or exhaust.
- It is recommended that a fire extinguisher of a type suitable for fuel and electrical fires is kept handy in the garage or workplace at all times. Never try to extinguish a fuel or electrical fire with water.

Fumes

- Certain fumes are highly toxic and can quickly cause unconsciousness and even death if inhaled to any extent. Gasoline vapor comes into this category, as do the vapors from certain solvents such as trichloro-ethylene. Any draining or pouring of such volatile fluids should be done in a well ventilated area.
- When using cleaning fluids and solvents, read the instructions carefully. Never use materials from unmarked containers - they may give off poisonous vapors.
- Never run the engine of a motor vehicle in an enclosed space such as a garage. Exhaust fumes contain carbon monoxide which is extremely poisonous; if you need to run the engine, always do so in the open air or at least have the rear of the vehicle outside the workplace.

The battery

- Never cause a spark, or allow a naked light near the vehicle's battery. It will normally be giving off a certain amount of hydrogen gas, which is highly explosive.
- Always disconnect the battery ground terminal before working on the fuel or electrical systems (except where noted).
- If possible, loosen the filler plugs or cover when charging the battery from an external source. Do not charge at an excessive rate or the battery may burst.
- Take care when topping up, cleaning or carrying the battery. The acid electrolyte, even when diluted, is very corrosive and should not be allowed to contact the eyes or skin. Always wear rubber gloves and goggles or a face shield. If you ever need to prepare electrolyte yourself, always add the acid slowly to the water; never add the water to the acid.

Electricity

- When using an electric power tool, inspection light etc., always ensure that the appliance is correctly connected to its plug and that, where necessary, it is properly grounded. Do not use such appliances in damp conditions and, again, beware of creating a spark or applying excessive heat in the vicinity of fuel or fuel vapor. Also ensure that the appliances meet national safety standards.
- A severe electric shock can result from touching certain parts of the electrical system, such as the spark plug wires (HT leads), when the engine is running or being cranked, particularly if components are damp or the insulation is defective. Where an electronic ignition system is used, the secondary (HT) voltage is much higher and could prove fatal.

Remember...

✗ **Don't** start the engine without first ascertaining that the transmission is in neutral.

✗ **Don't** suddenly remove the pressure cap from a hot cooling system - cover it with a cloth and release the pressure gradually first, or you may get scalded by escaping coolant.

✗ **Don't** attempt to drain oil until you are sure it has cooled sufficiently to avoid scalding you.

✗ **Don't** grasp any part of the engine or exhaust system without first ascertaining that it is cool enough not to burn you.

✗ **Don't** allow brake fluid or antifreeze to contact the machine's paintwork or plastic components.

✗ **Don't** siphon toxic liquids such as fuel, hydraulic fluid or antifreeze by mouth, or allow them to remain on your skin.

✗ **Don't** inhale dust - it may be injurious to health (see Asbestos heading).

✗ **Don't** allow any spilled oil or grease to remain on the floor - wipe it up right away, before someone slips on it.

✗ **Don't** use ill-fitting wrenches or other tools which may slip and cause injury.

✗ **Don't** lift a heavy component which may be beyond your capability - get assistance.

✗ **Don't** rush to finish a job or take unverified short cuts.

✗ **Don't** allow children or animals in or around an unattended vehicle.

✗ **Don't** inflate a tire above the recommended pressure. Apart from overstressing the carcass, in extreme cases the tire may blow off forcibly.

✓ **Do** ensure that the machine is supported securely at all times. This is especially important when the machine is blocked up to aid wheel or fork removal.

✓ **Do** take care when attempting to loosen a stubborn nut or bolt. It is generally better to pull on a wrench, rather than push, so that if you slip, you fall away from the machine rather than onto it.

✓ **Do** wear eye protection when using power tools such as drill, sander, bench grinder etc.

✓ **Do** use a barrier cream on your hands prior to undertaking dirty jobs - it will protect your skin from infection as well as making the dirt easier to remove afterwards; but make sure your hands aren't left slippery. Note that long-term contact with used engine oil can be a health hazard.

✓ **Do** keep loose clothing (cuffs, ties etc. and long hair) well out of the way of moving mechanical parts.

✓ **Do** remove rings, wristwatch etc., before working on the vehicle - especially the electrical system.

✓ **Do** keep your work area tidy - it is only too easy to fall over articles left lying around.

✓ **Do** exercise caution when compressing springs for removal or installation. Ensure that the tension is applied and released in a controlled manner, using suitable tools which preclude the possibility of the spring escaping violently.

✓ **Do** ensure that any lifting tackle used has a safe working load rating adequate for the job.

✓ **Do** get someone to check periodically that all is well, when working alone on the vehicle.

✓ **Do** carry out work in a logical sequence and check that everything is correctly assembled and tightened afterwards.

✓ **Do** remember that your vehicle's safety affects that of yourself and others. If in doubt on any point, get professional advice.

- If in spite of following these precautions, you are unfortunate enough to injure yourself, seek medical attention as soon as possible.

1 Engine/transmission oil level check

> ⚠ ***Warning: On models with an oil level dipstick, never remove the dipstick to check oil level immediately after hard or high-speed riding. Hot oil could spurt out and cause burns. Let the engine cool to approximately 70-degrees C (150-degrees F) before removing the dipstick.***

Before you start:

✔ The engine and transmission share a common oil supply, which is checked through the oil tank filler plug/dipstick.

✔ Park the vehicle in a level position, then start the engine and allow it to reach normal operating temperature.

Caution: Do not run the engine in an enclosed space such as a garage or shop.

✔ Stop the engine and allow the machine to sit undisturbed in a level position for about five minutes.

Vehicle care:

● If you have to add oil frequently, you should check whether you have any oil leaks. If there is no sign of oil leakage from the joints and gaskets the engine could be burning oil (see *Troubleshooting*).

The correct oil

● Modern, high-revving engines place great demands on their oil.
It is very important that the correct oil for your ATV is used.

● Always top up with a good quality oil of the specified type
and viscosity and do not overfill the engine.

Oil type

API grade meeting JASO standard MA - the MA standard is required to prevent clutch slippage. See Chapter 1 for viscosity ratings.

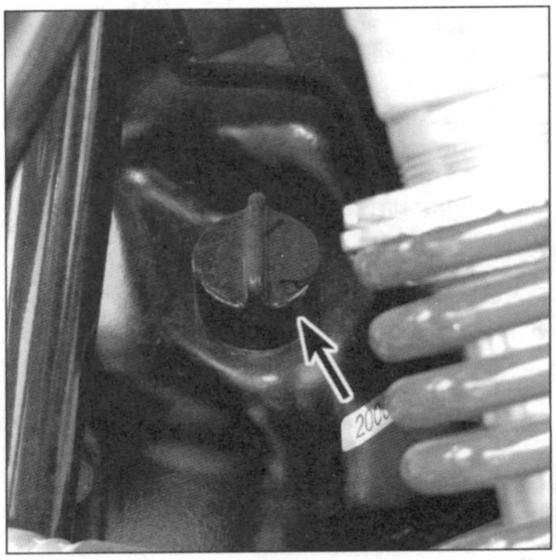

1 Warm the engine to normal operating temperature, let it idle for a few minutes, shut it off and let the oil settle for three minutes. Remove the dipstick from the oil tank (arrow), wipe it with a clean rag and put it back in the tank (don't screw it in - just let it rest on the threads). Pull the dipstick out and check the oil level on the dipstick scale. If the oil level is low, add oil through the dipstick hole. Add enough oil of the specified grade and type to bring the level on the dipstick up to the upper mark. Do not overfill.

2 Coolant level check

Before you start:

✔ Make sure you have a supply of coolant available (a mixture of 50% distilled water and 50% corrosion inhibited ethylene glycol antifreeze is needed). Keep in mind that many brands of coolant are pre-mixed, so be sure to check the container. Do not add water to pre-mixed coolant.

✔ Always check the coolant level when the engine is cold.

Caution: Do not run the engine in an enclosed space such as a garage or workshop.

✔ Make sure the vehicle is on level ground.

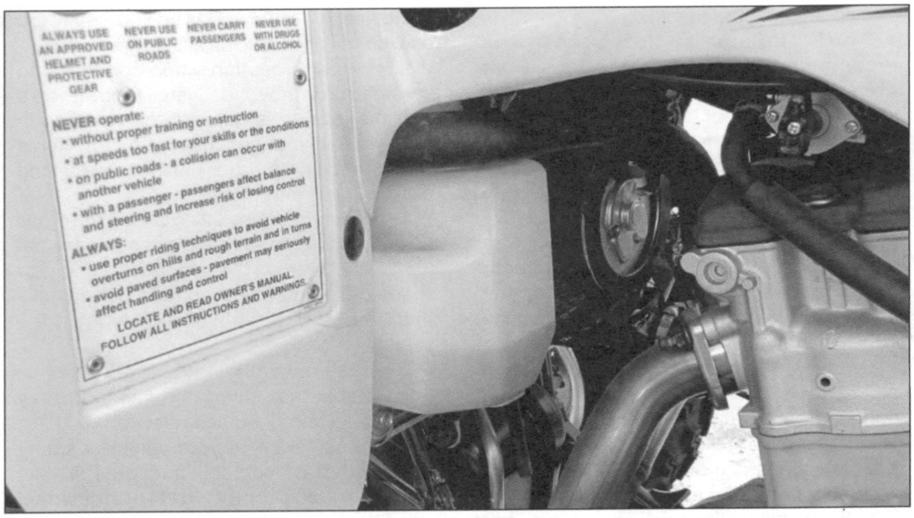

1 Check coolant level in the reservoir under the left front fender. It should between the Low and Full marks with the engine warmed up. If it's low, remove the cap, top off the reservoir with a 50/50 mixture of ethylene glycol-based antifreeze and distilled water, then reinstall the cap.

3 Brake fluid level check

1 With the front brake fluid reservoir as level as possible, check that the fluid level is above the LOWER level line on the inspection window. If the level is below the LOWER level line, remove the cover screws (arrows) and lift off the cover and diaphragm. Top up fluid to the upper level line; don't overfill the reservoir, and take care to avoid spills (see WARNING above). Compress the diaphragm, reinstall the diaphragm and cover and tighten the screws securely.

Warning: Brake fluid can harm your eyes and damage painted or some plastic surfaces, so use extreme caution when handling and pouring it and cover surrounding surfaces with rag. Do not use fluid that has been standing open for some time, as it absorbs moisture from the air which can cause a dangerous loss of braking effectiveness.

Before you start:

✔ Make sure the vehicle is on level ground.
✔ Make sure you have the correct brake fluid. DOT 4 is recommended. Never reuse old fluid.

✔ Wrap a rag around the reservoir to ensure that any spillage does not come into contact with painted surfaces.

Vehicle care:

- The fluid in the front master cylinder reservoir will drop slightly as the brake pads wear down.
- If the fluid reservoir requires repeated topping-up this is an indication of a hydraulic leak somewhere in the system, which should be investigated immediately.
- Check for signs of fluid leakage from the hydraulic hoses and components – if found, rectify immediately.
- Check the operation of the front brakes before taking the machine on the road; if there is evidence of air in the system (spongy feel to lever), it must be bled as described in Chapter 7.

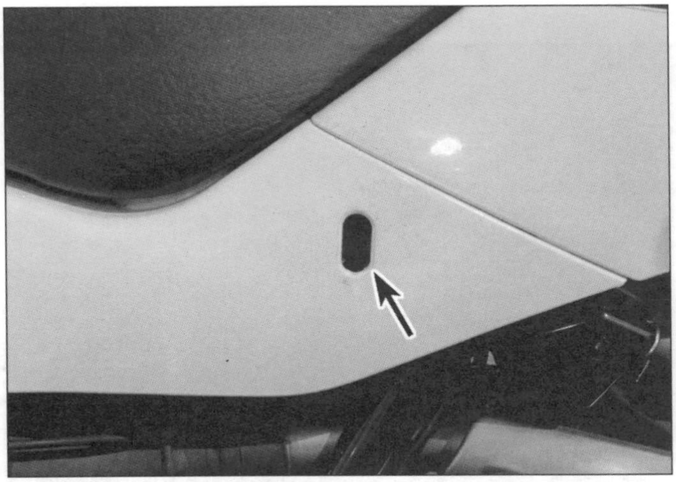

2 The rear brake fluid level can be seen through this viewing port in the right bodywork.

3 Check rear brake fluid level through the translucent reservoir. It should be between the upper and lower lines. If it's low, remove the seat and right side cover for access to the reservoir cap. Unscrew the cap and lift it off. Add the specified brake fluid until the level is up to the upper line on the reservoir, then install the cap and tighten it securely.

4 Tire checks

The correct pressures:

● The tires must be checked when **cold**, not immediately after riding. Note that low tire pressures may cause the tire to slip on the rim or come off. High tire pressures will cause abnormal tread wear and unsafe handling.
● Use an accurate pressure gauge.
● Proper air pressure will increase tire life and provide maximum stability and ride comfort.

Tire care:

● Check the tires carefully for cuts, tears, embedded nails or other sharp objects and excessive wear. Operation of the vehicle with excessively worn tires is extremely hazardous, as traction and handling are directly affected.
● Check the condition of the tire valve and ensure the dust cap is in place.
● Pick out any stones or nails which may have become embedded in the tire tread. If left, they will eventually penetrate through the casing and cause a puncture.
● If tire damage is apparent, or unexplained loss of pressure is experienced, seek the advice of a tire fitting specialist without delay.

Tire tread depth:

The minimum tread depth for these vehicles is 4 mm (5/32 inch) for all models. To maintain good performance and handling, check the profile of the knobs on the tires as well as the tread depth. When the knobs begin to get excessively rounded on their edges, the tire should be replaced.

Tire pressures

2004 through 2008	
Front	4.4 psi (30 kPa)
Rear	4.0 psi (27.5 kPa)
2009 and later	
Front	4.4 psi (30 kPa)
Rear	4.4 psi (30 kPa)

1 Unscrew the cap from the tire valve and measure air pressure with a gauge designed for the low pressures used in ATV tires

2 Measure tread depth with a depth gauge or tape measure

Service record

Date	Mileage	Work performed

Notes

Chapter 1
Tune-up and routine maintenance

Contents

Degrees of difficulty

Easy, suitable for novice with little experience	**Fairly easy,** suitable for beginner with some experience	**Fairly difficult,** suitable for competent DIY mechanic	**Difficult,** suitable for experienced DIY mechanic	**Very difficult,** suitable for expert DIY or professional

Specifications

Engine

Spark plug	
Type	NGK CR7E or Denso U22ESR-N
Gap	0.7 to 0.8 mm (0.028 to 0.031 inch)
Valve clearance	
Intake	0.10 to 0.20 mm (0.004 to 0.008 inch)
Exhaust	0.20 to 0.30 mm (0.008 to 0.012 inch)
Engine idle speed	
Carbureted models	1500 +/- 100 rpm
Fuel injected models	1600 +/- 100 rpm

Specifications (continued)

Chassis

Brake pad thickness (limit)	To wear groove or 0.030 inch (1.0 mm)
Front brake lever freeplay	Not specified
Rear brake pedal height	0 to 10 mm (0 to 0.4 inch) below footpeg
Throttle lever freeplay	3 to 5 mm (0.12 to 0.20 inch)
Clutch lever freeplay	8 to 13 mm (0.31 to 0.51 inch)
Drive chain slack	30 to 40 mm (1.2 to 1.6 inches)
Speed limiter screw setting	Do not back out more than 12 mm (0.47 inch)
Minimum tire tread depth	See *Daily (pre-ride) checks*
Tire pressures (cold)	See *Daily (pre-ride) checks*
Front wheel toe setting	
Toe-in (2008 and earlier)	5 +/- 4 mm (0.20 +/- 0.16 inch)
Toe-out (2009 and later)	6 +/- 4 mm (0.24 +/- 0.16 inch)

Torque specifications

Coolant drain bolt	6 Nm (54 inch-lbs)
Oil drain bolts	
Crankcase	21 Nm (15 ft-lbs)
Oil tank	12 Nm (100 inch-lbs)
Oil filter cover bolts	Not specified
Spark plugs	11 Nm (96 inch-lbs)
Tie rod locknuts	29 Nm (21 ft-lbs)
Spark arrester bolts	13 Nm (114 inch-lbs)

Recommended lubricants and fluids

Engine oil	
Type	API Service SF/SG or SH/SJ, meeting JASO Standard MA* **The JASO MA standard is required to avoid clutch slippage*
Viscosity	SAE 10W-40
Capacity	
At oil change (with filter replacement)	2.1 liters (2.2 quarts)
At oil change (without filter replacement)	2.0 liters (2.1 quarts)
After engine overhaul	2.2 liters (2.3 quarts)
Recommended fuel	87 pump octane (91 Research octane), maximum 10 percent ethanol
Air filter oil	10W-30 engine oil
Cooling system	
Recommended coolant	50/50 mixture of ethylene glycol-based antifreeze and water*
Capacity	
2008 and earlier (engine and reservoir)	1.2 liters (1.3 quarts)
2009 and later	
Engine	0.9 liter (1.0 quart)
Reservoir tank	0.25 liter (0.3 quart)
Miscellaneous	
Wheel bearings	Medium weight, lithium-based multi-purpose grease
Swingarm pivot bearings	Medium weight, lithium-based multi-purpose grease
Steering shaft bushings	Medium weight, lithium-based multi-purpose grease
Cables and lever pivots	Medium weight, lithium-based multi-purpose grease
Brake pedal/shift lever/throttle lever pivots	Medium weight, lithium-based multi-purpose grease

**Many brands of antifreeze do not require mixing with water. Check the instructions on the container carefully.*

1 LT-Z400/KFX400/DVX400 Routine maintenance intervals

Note: *The pre-ride inspection outlined in the owner's manual covers checks and maintenance that should be carried out on a daily basis. It's condensed and included here to remind you of its importance. Always perform the pre-ride inspection at every maintenance interval (in addition to the procedures listed). The intervals listed below are the shortest intervals recommended by the manufacturer for each particular operation during the model years covered in this manual. Your owner's manual may have different intervals for your model.*

Daily or before riding

- ☐ Check the operation of both brakes - check the brake lever and pedal for correct freeplay
- ☐ Check the throttle for smooth operation and correct freeplay
- ☐ Make sure the engine kill switch works correctly
- ☐ Check the tires for damage, the presence of foreign objects and correct air pressure
- ☐ Check the engine oil level
- ☐ Check the engine coolant level*
- ☐ Check the fuel level and inspect for leaks
- ☐ Check the air cleaner drain tube and clean it if necessary
- ☐ If the drain tube is clogged, clean the air filter element
- ☐ Inspect the drive chain
- ☐ Make sure the steering operates smoothly
- ☐ Verify that the headlight and taillight are operating satisfactorily
- ☐ Check all fasteners, including wheel nuts and axle nuts, for tightness
- ☐ Check the underbody for mud or debris that could start a fire or interfere with vehicle operation

**Replace the coolant every two years.*

Every three months

- ☐ Clean the air filter element and replace it if necessary (1)
- ☐ Check the exhaust system for leaks and check fastener tightness
- ☐ Check the throttle for smooth operation and correct freeplay
- ☐ Check choke operation (carbureted models)
- ☐ Inspect the fuel tap (carbureted models) and fuel line (all models) (2)
- ☐ Check idle speed and adjust it if necessary
- ☐ Check brake operation and brake lever and pedal freeplay
- ☐ Check brake fluid level in the front and rear master cylinder (3)
- ☐ Check steering system operation and freeplay
- ☐ Check all chassis fasteners for tightness
- ☐ Lubricate the steering shaft and front suspension
- ☐ Lubricate and inspect the drive chain, sprockets and rollers

(1) More often in dusty or wet conditions.
(2) Replace the fuel line every four years.
(3) Replace the brake fluid every two years

Every six months

- ☐ Change the engine oil and filter
- ☐ Inspect the engine oil tank and hoses
- ☐ Clean, gap and, if necessary, replace the spark plug (1)
- ☐ Clean the spark arrester
- ☐ Inspect the throttle body (fuel injected models)
- ☐ Check the valve clearance and adjust it if necessary
- ☐ Check the clutch for smooth operation and correct lever freeplay
- ☐ Inspect the radiator hoses (2)
- ☐ Inspect the front and rear brake pads and discs
- ☐ Inspect the wheels and tires
- ☐ Check the wheel bearings for looseness or damage
- ☐ Inspect the front and rear suspension
- ☐ Check the skid plates for looseness or damage

(1) Replace the spark plug every 18 months.
(2) Replace the radiator hoses every four years.

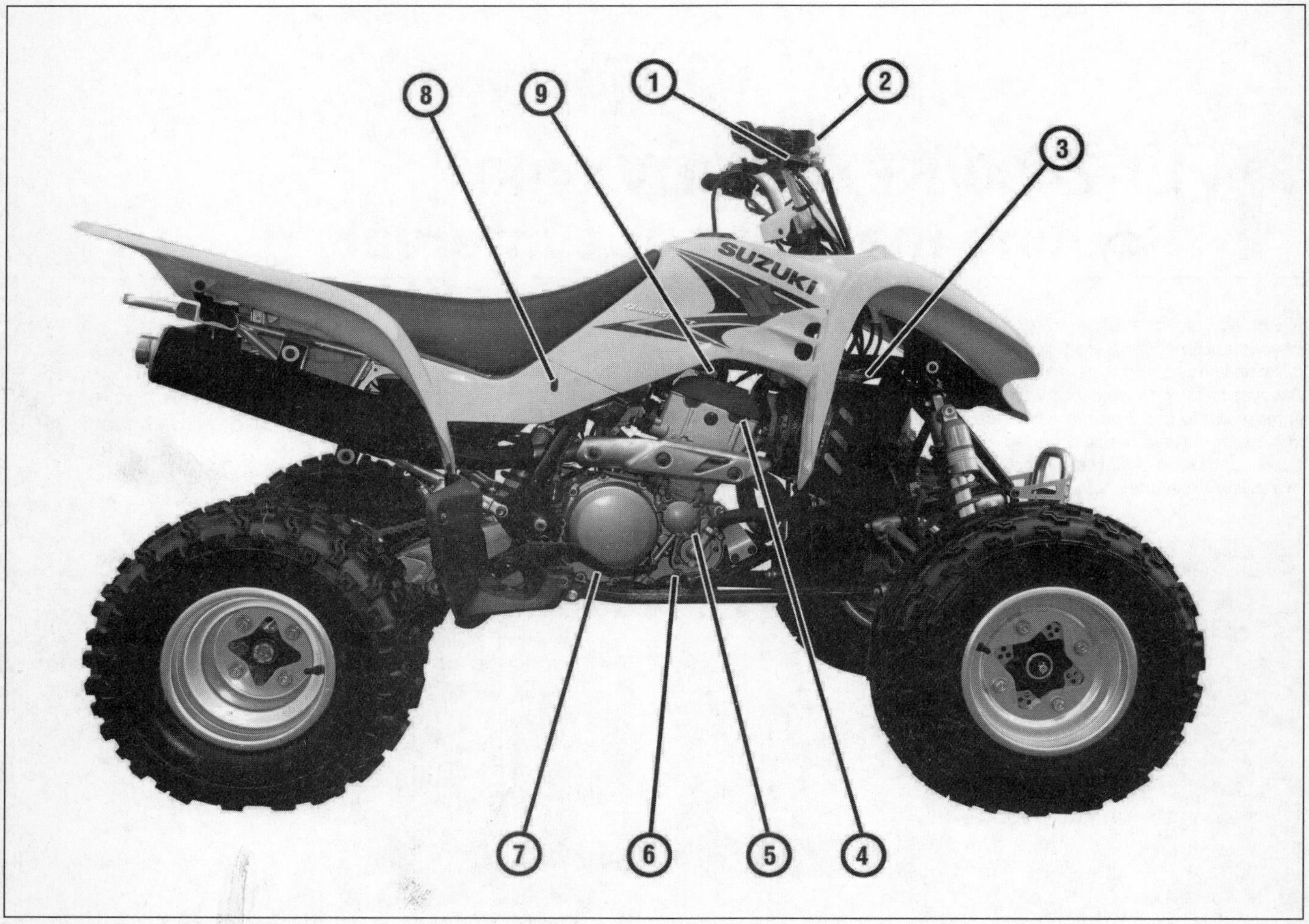

Right side maintenance points

1 Throttle lever
2 Front brake fluid reservoir
3 Radiator cap
4 Valves (under valve cover)
5 Engine oil filter
6 Coolant drain plug
7 Brake pedal
8 Rear brake fluid reservoir viewing port
9 Spark plug (in center of valve cover)

Left side maintenance points

1. *Air filter (under seat)*
2. *Battery (under seat)*
3. *Air cleaner housing drain tube*
4. *Idle speed screw (carburetor shown; fuel injection throttle body similar)*
5. *Oil tank drain plug*
6. *Oil tank filler plug*
7. *Coolant reservoir filler cap*
8. *Parking brake lever*
9. *Choke lever*
10. *Clutch lever*

2.1 Decals on the vehicle include maintenance and safety information

4.3 Remove the wheel to check the front brake pad lining. If the lining has worn down to the wear indicators (the small notches in the pad material), replace the pads

2 Introduction to tune-up and routine maintenance

This Chapter covers in detail the checks and procedures necessary for the tune-up and routine maintenance of your vehicle. Section 1 includes the routine maintenance schedule, which is designed to keep the machine in proper running condition and prevent possible problems. The remaining Sections contain detailed procedures for carrying out the items listed on the maintenance schedule, as well as additional maintenance information designed to increase reliability. Maintenance information is also printed on decals, which are mounted in various locations on the vehicle **(see illustration)**. Where information on the decals differs from that presented in this Chapter, use the decal information.

Since routine maintenance plays such an important role in the safe and efficient operation of your vehicle, it is presented here as a comprehensive check list. These lists outline the procedures and checks that should be done on a routine basis.

Deciding where to start or plug into the routine maintenance schedule depends on several factors. If you have a vehicle whose warranty has recently expired, and if it has been maintained according to the warranty standards, you may want to pick up routine maintenance as it coincides with the next mileage or calendar interval. If you have owned the machine for some time but have never performed any maintenance on it, then you may want to start at the nearest interval and include some additional procedures to ensure that nothing important is overlooked. If you have just had a major engine overhaul, then you may want to start the maintenance routine from the beginning. If you have a used machine and have no knowledge of its history or maintenance record, you may desire to combine all the checks into one large service initially and then settle into the maintenance schedule prescribed.

The Sections that describe the inspection and maintenance procedures are written as step-by-step comprehensive guides to the actual performance of the work. They explain in detail each of the routine inspections and maintenance procedures on the check list. References to additional information in applicable Chapters is also included and should not be overlooked.

Before beginning any actual maintenance or repair, the machine should be cleaned thoroughly, especially around the oil filler plug, spark plug, engine covers, carburetor or throttle body, etc. Cleaning will help ensure that dirt does not contaminate the engine and will allow you to detect wear and damage that could otherwise easily go unnoticed.

3 Fluid levels - check

Check, and if necessary, top up, the front brake fluid, rear brake fluid, engine oil and coolant as described in *Daily (Pre-ride) checks* at the front of this manual.

4 Brake system - general check

1 A routine general check will ensure that brake problems are discovered and remedied before they become dangerous.

2 Inspect the brake lever and pedal for loose pivots, excessive play, bending, cracking and other damage. Replace any damaged parts (see Chapter 7). Make sure all brake fasteners are tight.

3 Jack-up the front of the vehicle and remove the wheels. Check the brake pads by looking at the ends of the calipers **(see illustration)**. If the pad material has been worn down so that the wear indicators touch the disc - or are getting close to the disc - it's time for new pads (see Chapter 7).

4 The rear brake caliper is located at the right side of the swingarm **(see illustration)**. Again, if the pad material is worn down so that the indicators are at or near the disc, install new pads (see Chapter 7).

5 If you have difficulty determining whether the pads are excessively worn because the wear indicator is hard to see (or you have aftermarket pads that don't have any kind of indicator), remove the pads (see Chapter 7), measure the thickness of the pads and compare your measurements to the pad thickness limits listed in this Chapter's Specifications.

4.4 Check the thickness of the outer pad lining of the rear brake. If the lining has worn down to the wear indicator (small notch) replace the pads

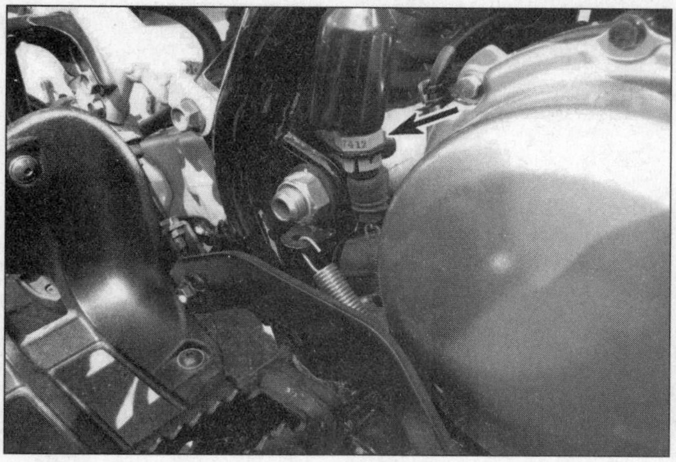

4.7 The brake light switch is adjusted by turning the adjusting nut

5.4 Measure brake pedal height from the top of the footpeg to the top of the pedal

6 Verify that the parking brake system will hold the vehicle on an incline. If it won't, adjust the parking brake (see Chapter 7).

7 These vehicles are equipped with a brake light which is activated by a brake light switch **(see illustration)** at the rear brake pedal. Make sure that the brake light works when the rear brake pedal is applied (it should come on just before the brake light begins to work). If it doesn't, hold the body of the brake light switch so that it doesn't turn, and rotate the switch adjusting nut as necessary.

5 Brake levers and pedal - check and adjustment

Front brake lever freeplay

1 Operate the brake lever and measure freeplay at the tip of the lever; there shouldn't be any (zero freeplay). If there is freeplay, bleed the front brakes (see Chapter 7). If this doesn't work, check the master cylinder and calipers for wear and check the brake lines for leaks (see Chapter 7). Front brake freeplay is not adjustable.

2 The position of the front brake lever can be adjusted to suit rider preference. To make the adjustment, loosen the adjuster locknut while pushing the brake lever toward the front of the vehicle. While holding pressure on the lever, turn the adjusting bolt until the lever is where you want it to be.

3 Tighten the adjuster locknut securely and recheck the lever position.

Rear brake pedal height

4 The upper side of the rear brake pedal should be the specified distance (listed in this Chapter's Specifications) below the top of the footpeg **(see illustration)**.

5 If the pedal height is incorrect, loosen the locknut on the adjusting bolt **(see illustration)**. Turn the adjusting bolt to obtain the correct pedal height, then tighten the locknut.

Caution: The distance between the locknut and the hex on the adjusting bolt must not exceed the value listed in this Chapter's Specifications. If it does, check the master cylinder and pedal for wear.

6 After making the adjustment, jack up the rear of the vehicle, spin the rear wheels and check for brake drag. If the brake drags, repeat the height adjustment.

Parking brake lever

7 Loosen the locknut and adjuster bolt at the parking brake lever on the rear caliper **(see illustration)**.

8 Locate the cable adjuster in the parking

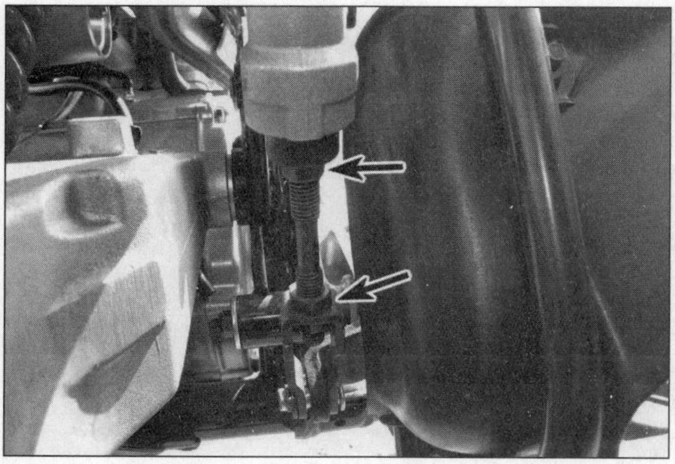

5.5 Loosen the locknut (lower arrow) and rotate the master cylinder pushrod with the hex (upper arrow)

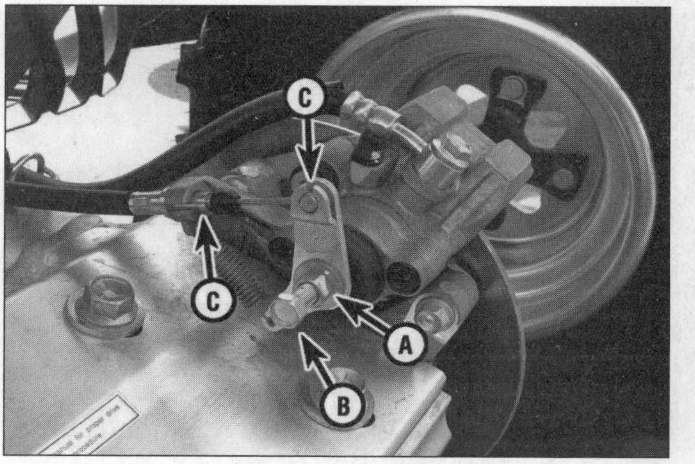

5.7 Parking brake cable details

A Adjusting bolt locknut
B Adjusting bolt
C Cable length measurement points

5.8a Pull back the rubber cover to expose the adjuster

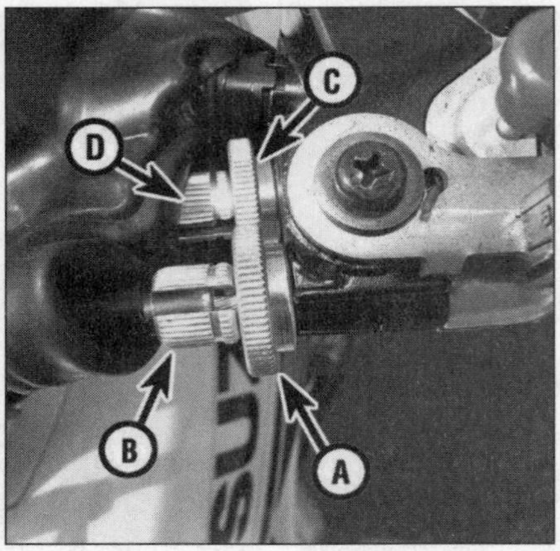

5.8b The parking brake and clutch cable adjusters are located in the cables at the left handlebar

A *Parking brake cable locknut*
B *Parking brake cable adjuster*
C *Clutch cable locknut*
D *Clutch cable adjuster*

brake cable at the left handlebar **(see illustrations)**. Pull the cover off to expose the adjuster. Loosen the adjuster locknut, turn the adjuster to obtain the specified cable length at the caliper **(see illustration 5.7)**, then tighten the locknut.

9 At the caliper, turn the adjusting bolt in until it feels tight, then back it out 1/8 to 1/4 turn and tighten the locknut.

10 At the handlebar cable adjuster, slide the cover back over the adjuster.

6 Steering system - inspection and toe adjustment

Inspection

1 These vehicles are equipped with bearings at the upper and lower ends of the steering shaft. These can become dented, rough or loose during normal use. In extreme cases, worn or loose parts can cause steering wobble that is potentially dangerous.

2 To check, block the rear wheels so the vehicle can't roll, jack up the front end and support it securely on jackstands.

3 Point the wheels straight ahead and slowly move the handlebar from side-to-side. Dents or roughness in the bearing will be felt and the bars will not move smoothly. **Note:** *Make sure any hesitation in movement is not being caused by the cables and wiring harnesses that run to the handlebar.*

4 If the handlebar doesn't move smoothly, or if it has excessive lateral play, remove and inspect the steering shaft bushings (see Chapter 6).

5 Look at the tie-rod ends (inner and outer) while slowly turning the handlebar from side-to-side. If there's any vertical movement in the tie-rod balljoints, replace them (see Chapter 6).

Toe adjustment

6 Roll the vehicle forward onto a level surface and stop it with the front wheels pointing straight ahead.

7 Make a mark at the front and center of each tire, even with the centerline of the front hub.

8 Measure the distance between the marks with a toe gauge or steel tape measure.

9 Have an assistant push the vehicle backward while you watch the marks on the tires. Stop pushing when the tires have rotated exactly one-half turn, so the marks are at the backs of the tires.

10 Again, measure the distance between the marks. Subtract the rear measurement from the front measurement to get toe-in (2008 and earlier) or toe-out (2009).

11 If toe-in or toe-out is not as specified in this Chapter's Specifications, hold each tie-rod with a wrench on the flats and loosen the locknuts **(see illustrations)**. Turn the tie-rods an equal amount to change toe-in or toe-out. When the setting is correct, tighten the locknuts to the torque listed in this Chapter's Specifications.

7 Suspension - check

1 The suspension components must be maintained in top operating condition to ensure rider safety. Loose, worn or damaged suspension parts decrease the vehicle's stability and control.

2 Lock the front brake and push on the handlebars to compress the front shock absorbers several times. See if they move up-and-down smoothly without binding. If binding is felt, the shocks should be inspected as described in Chapter 6.

3 Check the tightness of all front suspen-

6.11a Loosen the locknuts at the tie rod inner ends . . .

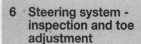

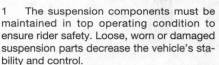

6.11b . . . and at the outer ends (left arrow); use a wrench on the flat (right arrow) to hold and turn the tie rod

8.4a Loosen the bolts on top of the axle housing

8.4b Turn the adjusting nuts (early models) or single nut (later models, shown) to set drive chain tension

sion nuts and bolts to be sure none have worked loose.

4 Inspect the rear shock absorber for fluid leakage and tightness of the mounting nuts and bolts. If leakage is found, the shock should be replaced.

5 Raise the rear of the vehicle and support it securely on jackstands. Grab the swingarm on each side, just ahead of the axle. Rock the swingarm from side to side - there should be no discernible movement at the rear. If there's a little movement or a slight clicking can be heard, make sure the swingarm pivot shaft is tight. If the pivot shaft is tight but movement is still noticeable, the swingarm will have to be removed and the bearings replaced as described in Chapter 6.

6 Inspect the tightness of the rear suspension nuts and bolts.

8 Drive chain and sprockets - check, adjustment and lubrication

Check and adjustment

Note: *Always replace the chain and sprockets as a set.*

1 A neglected drive chain won't last long and can quickly damage the sprockets. Routine chain adjustment isn't difficult and will ensure maximum chain and sprocket life.

2 To check the chain, support the vehicle securely on jackstands with the rear wheels off the ground. Place the transmission in neutral. If you're working on a 2008 or earlier model, remove the rear brake caliper, leaving the brake hose connected (see Chapter 7).

3 Check the entire length of the chain for damaged rollers or O-rings, loose links and loose pins.

4 Loosen the axle housing bolts and turn the chain adjuster nuts (2003) or single nut (2004 and later) just enough to remove all slack from the chain **(see illustrations)**. Mark a pin in one of the chain links, then count 20 additional pins and mark the twenty-first pin. Measure the distance between the two marked pins and compare it to the maximum chain length listed in this Chapter's Specifications. If it's beyond the maximum, refer to Chapter 6 and replace the chain and sprockets as a set.

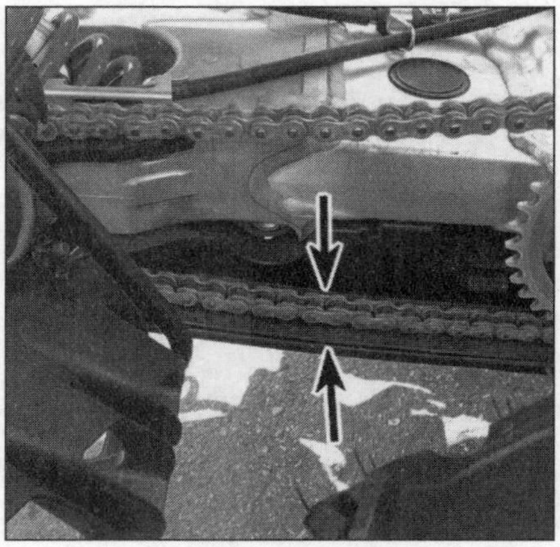

8.5 Measure drive chain slack along the bottom chain run

5 Loosen the chain adjusting bolt. Push down and pull up on the bottom run of the chain and measure the slack midway between the two sprockets **(see illustration)**, then compare the measurements to the value listed in this Chapter's Specifications. As wear occurs, the chain will actually stretch, which means adjustment is necessary to remove some slack from the chain. In some cases where lubrication has been neglected, corrosion and galling may cause the links to bind and kink, which effectively shortens the chain's length. If the chain is tight between the sprockets, rusty or kinked, it's time to replace it with a new one. **Note:** *Repeat the chain slack measurement along the length of the chain - ideally, every inch or so. If you find a tight area, mark it with felt pen or paint and repeat the measurement after the machine has been ridden. If the chain's still tight in the same areas, it may be damaged or worn. Because a tight or kinked chain can damage the transmission countershaft bearing, it's a good idea to replace it.*

8.7 Inspect the front sprocket teeth for excessive wear through the holes in the cover; make sure there's no play in the sprocket

6 Loosen or tighten the chain adjusting bolt to get the correct amount of slack in the chain, then tighten the axle housing bolts **(see illustrations 8.4b and 8.4a)**.

7 Look through the slots in the engine sprocket cover and inspect the engine sprocket **(see illustration)**. Check the teeth on the engine sprocket and the rear sprocket for wear (see Chapter 6). Refer to Chapter 6 for the sprocket replacement procedure if the sprockets appear to be worn excessively.

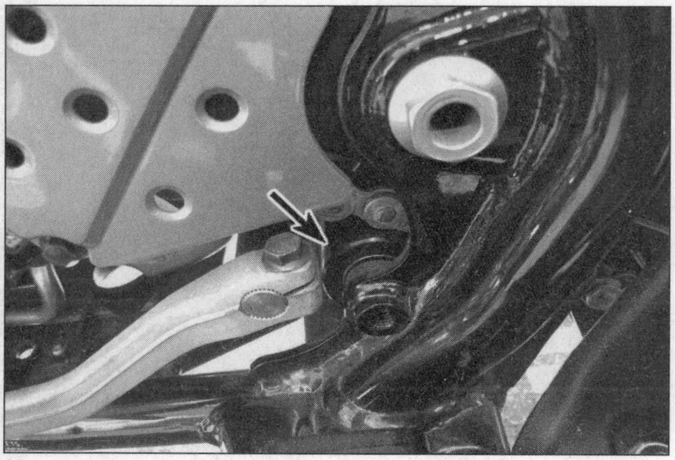

8.8a Check the chain roller . . .

8.8b . . . and the upper and lower contact surfaces of the slider for wear or damage

9.4 Check tire pressure with a gauge that will accurately read the low pressures used in ATV tires

9.5a Be sure the directional arrow (if there is one) points in the forward rotating direction of the tire

9.5b Some tires have the words THIS SIDE FACING OUTWARD molded in the sidewall; this side of the tire faces away from the vehicle

8 Check the chain roller and slider **(see illustrations)**. If a roller or slider is worn, replace it (see Chapter 6).

Lubrication

Note: *If the chain is dirty, it should be removed and cleaned before it's lubricated (see Chapter 6).*

9 The best time to lubricate the chain is after the vehicle has been ridden. When the chain is warm, the lubricant will penetrate the joints between the side plates to provide lubrication. The manufacturers of these vehicles specify using heavyweight engine oil only; do not use chain lube, which may contain solvents that can damage the chain's rubber O-rings. Apply the oil to the area where the side plates overlap - not to the middle of the rollers.

HAYNES HiNT ***Apply the lubricant along the top of the lower chain run, so that when the machine is ridden, centrifugal force will move the lubricant into the chain, rather than throwing it off.***

10 Roll the rear wheels forward to place a new section of chain on the bottom of the run, then lubricate that section. Repeat this until the entire chain has been lubricated.

11 After applying the lubricant, let it soak in a few minutes before wiping off any excess.

9 Tires/wheels - general check

1 Routine tire and wheel checks should be made with the realization that your safety depends to a great extent on their condition.

2 Check the tires carefully for cuts, tears, embedded nails or other sharp objects and excessive wear. Operation of the vehicle with excessively worn tires is extremely hazardous, as traction and handling are directly affected. Measure the tread depth at the center of the tire and replace worn tires with new ones when the tread depth is less than that listed in *Daily (pre-ride) checks*.

3 Repair or replace punctured tires as soon as damage is noted. Do not try to patch a torn tire, as wheel balance and tire reliability may be impaired.

4 Check the tire pressures when the tires are cold **(see illustration)** and keep them properly inflated (see *Daily (pre-ride) checks* at the front of this manual). Proper air pressure will increase tire life and provide maximum stability and ride comfort. Keep in mind that low tire pressures may cause the tire to slip on the rim or come off, while high tire pressures will cause abnormal tread wear and unsafe handling.

Caution: ATV tires operate at very low pressures. Over-inflation may rupture them.

5 Make sure the tires are installed on the correct side of the vehicle. ATV tires are directional; that is, they are designed to rotate in only one forward direction. The direction of forward rotation is indicated either by an arrow molded into the tire sidewall or by the words SIDE FACING OUTWARDS **(see illustrations)**.

6 The wheels used on these machines are maintenance free, but they should be kept clean and checked periodically for cracks, bending and rust. Never attempt to repair damaged wheels; they must be replaced with new ones.

7 Check the valve stem locknuts to make sure they're tight. Also, make sure the valve stem caps are in place and tight. If any of them are missing, install a new one made of metal or hard plastic.

10 Front wheel bearings - check

1 Raise the front of the vehicle and support it securely on jackstands.

2 Spin the front wheels by hand. Listen for noise, which indicates dry or worn wheel bearings.

3 Grasp the top and bottom of the tire and try to rock it back-and-forth. If there's more than a very small amount of play, the wheel bearings are in need of adjustment or replacement. Refer to Chapter 7 for service procedures.

11 Lubrication - general

1 Since the controls, cables and various other components of an ATV are exposed to the elements, they should be lubricated periodically to ensure safe and trouble-free operation.

2 The throttle lever, brake levers and brake pedal should be lubricated frequently. Multi-purpose lithium grease is recommended for cable ends and other lubrication points, such as suspension and steering bushings. In order for the lubricant to be applied where it will do the most good, the component should be disassembled. However, if chain and cable lubricant is being used, it can be applied to the pivot joint gaps and will usually work its way into the areas where friction occurs. If motor oil or light grease is being used, apply it sparingly as it may attract dirt (which could cause the controls to bind or wear at an accelerated rate). **Note:** *One of the best lubricants for the control lever pivots is a dry-film lubricant (available from many sources by different names).*

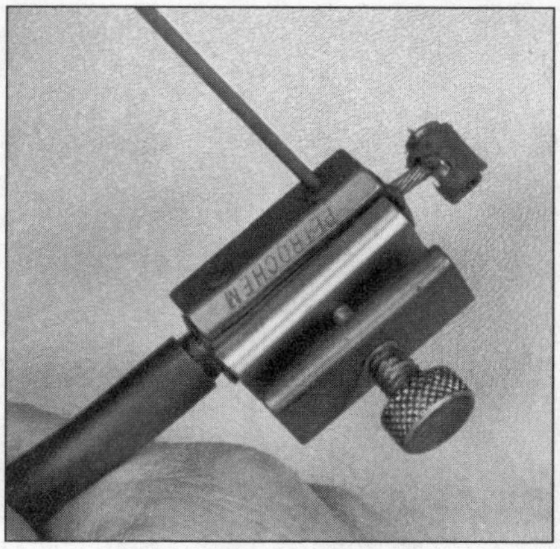

11.3 Lubricating a cable with a pressure lube adapter (make sure the tool seats around the inner cable)

3 The throttle and clutch cables should be removed and treated with a commercially available cable lubricant which is specially formulated for use on ATV control cables. Small adapters for pressure lubricating the cables with spray can lubricants are available and ensure that the cable is lubricated along its entire length **(see illustration)**. When attaching a cable to its handlebar lever, be sure to lubricate the barrel-shaped fitting at the end with multi-purpose grease.

4 To lubricate the cables, disconnect one end, then lubricate the cable with a pressure lube adapter **(see illustration 11.3)** (clutch cable, see Chapter 2; throttle cable, see Chapter 4).

11.7a Lubricate the rear suspension fittings with a grease gun at the cushion rod-to-swingarm pivot. . .

5 Refer to Chapter 6 for the following lubrication procedures:

a) Steering shaft bushings
b) Swingarm bearings and dust seals

6 Refer to Chapter 7 for the following lubrication procedures:

a) Rear brake pedal pivot
b) Front wheel bearings

7 Using a grease gun, lubricate the rear suspension bushings through the grease nipples **(see illustrations)**. Lubrication of the front suspension bushings requires that the pivot bolts be removed (see Chapter 6).

12 Fasteners - check

1 Since vibration of the machine tends to loosen fasteners, all nuts, bolts, screws, etc. should be periodically checked for proper

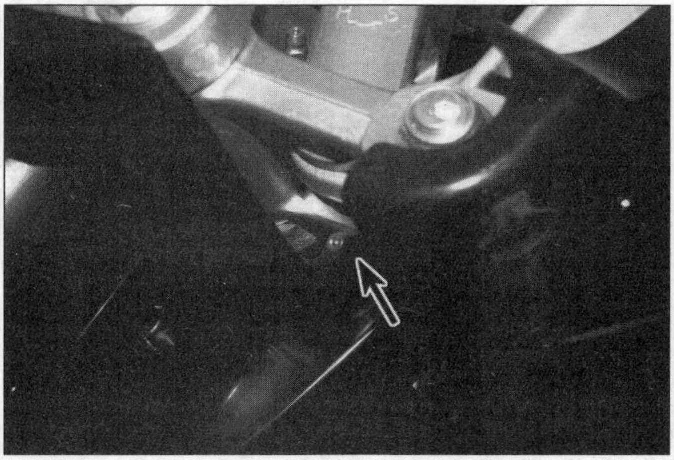

11.7b . . . at the cushion lever connection to the lower end of the cushion rod . . .

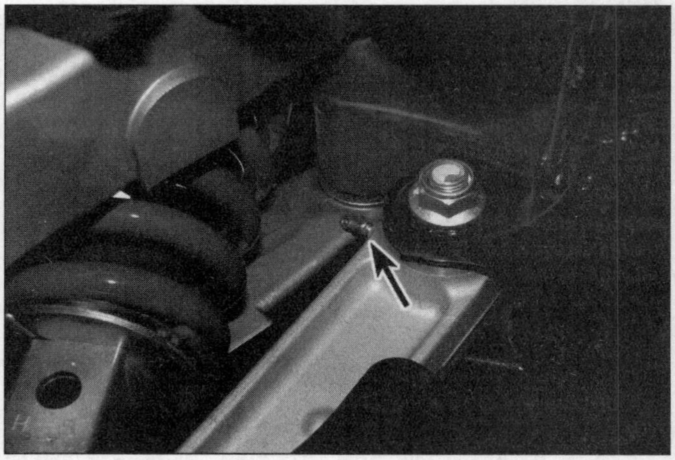

11.7c . . . and at the connection of the cushion lever upper end to the frame

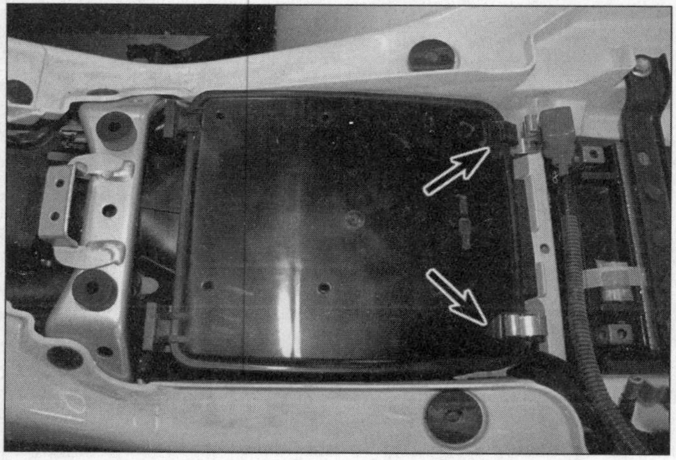

14.2 To remove the air cleaner cover, release these clips (arrows), lift the rear edge of the cover and slide it rearward to disengage the tabs at the front

14.3a Remove the screw . . .

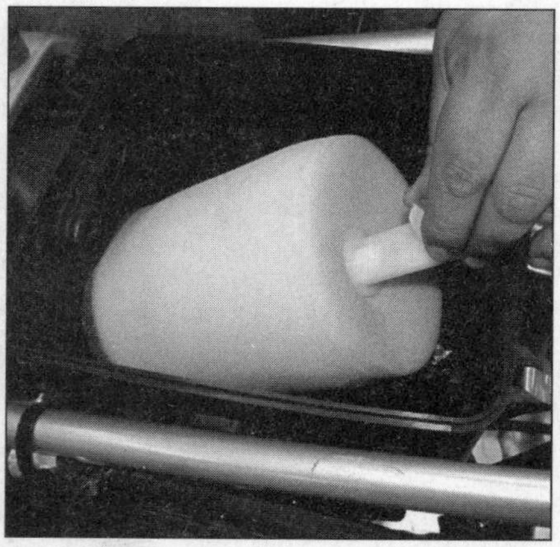

14.3b . . . and lift the air filter out of the air cleaner housing

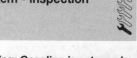

14.3c Separate the foam filter element from the plastic guide inside it

tightness. Also make sure all cotter pins or other safety fasteners are correctly installed.

2 Pay particular attention to the following:

Spark plug(s)
Engine oil drain plug
Gearshift pedal
Brake pedal
Footpegs
Engine mount bolts
Shock absorber mount bolts
Front axle nuts
Rear axle nuts
Skid plate bolts

3 If a torque wrench is available, use it along with the torque specifications at the beginning of this, or other, Chapters.

13 Skid plates - check

1 Check the skid plates under the vehicle for damage (see Chapter 8). Have damaged plates repaired, or replace them.

2 Make sure the skid plate fasteners are all in position and tightly secured.

14 Air filter element and drain tube - cleaning

Element cleaning

1 Remove the seat (see Chapter 8).

2 Pull back the cover clips and open the air filter housing cover **(see illustration)**.

3 Remove the air filter element and separate the element from the element guide **(see illustrations)**.

4 Clean the element and guide in a high flash point solvent, squeeze the solvent out of the foam and let the guide and element dry completely.

5 Soak the foam element in the clean engine oil, then squeeze it firmly to remove the excess oil. Don't wring it out or the foam may be damaged. The element should be thoroughly oil-soaked, but not dripping.

6 Reassemble the element and guide.

7 Installation is the reverse of removal.

Drain tube cleaning

8 Check the air cleaner housing drain tube for accumulated water and oil. If oil or water has built up in the tube, squeeze its clamp, remove the tube from the air cleaner housing and clean it out. Install the drain tube on the housing and secure it with the clamp. **Note:** *A drain tube that's full indicates the need to clean the filter element and the inside of the case.*

15 Fuel system - inspection

Warning: Gasoline is extremely flammable, so take extra precautions when you work on any part of the fuel system. Don't smoke or allow open flames or bare light bulbs near the work area, and don't work in a garage where a gas-type appliance (such as a water heater or clothes dryer) is present. Since gasoline is carcinogenic, wear latex gloves when there's a possibility of being exposed to fuel, and if you spill any fuel on your skin, rinse it off immediately with soap and water. Mop up any fuel spills immediately and do not store fuel-soaked rags where they could ignite. When you perform any kind of work on the fuel system, wear safety glasses and have a fire extinguisher suitable for class B type fires (flammable liquids) on hand.

15.1 Inspect the fuel tap, fuel line and float chamber seam for leaks

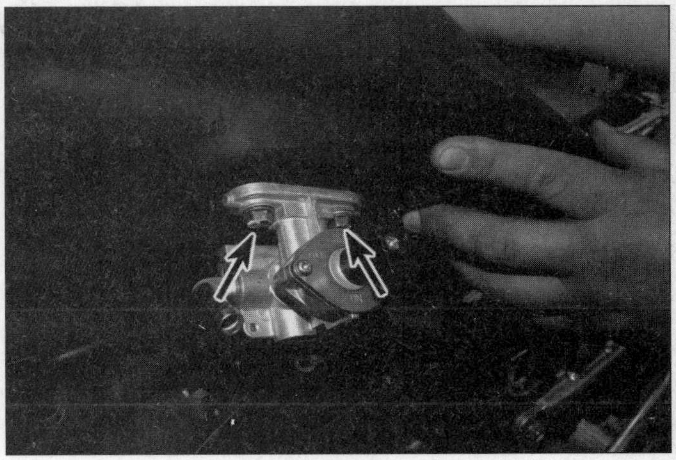

15.5 Remove the fuel tap screws and separate the tap and strainer from the tank

Carbureted models

1 Check the fuel tank, the fuel tap, the fuel line and the carburetor for leaks and evidence of damage **(see illustration)**.

2 If carburetor gaskets are leaking, the carburetor should be disassembled and rebuilt (see Chapter 4).

3 If the fuel tap is leaking, tightening the screws may help. If leakage persists, the tap should be disassembled and repaired or replaced with a new one.

4 If the fuel line is cracked or otherwise deteriorated, replace it with a new one.

5 Place the fuel tap lever in the Off position. Remove and drain the fuel tank. Remove the screws and detach the tap from the tank **(see illustration)**.

6 Clean the strainer with solvent and let it dry.

7 Installation is the reverse of removal. Be sure to use a new O-ring. Hand-tighten the screws firmly, but don't overtighten them. If you do, the O-ring will be distorted, which will result in fuel leaks.

8 After installation, run the engine and check for fuel leaks.

9 Any time the vehicle is going to be stored for a month or more, remove and drain the fuel tank. Also remove the float chamber drain plug (in the bottom of the carburetor on the left-hand side) and drain the fuel from the carburetor.

10 Inspect the condition of the crankcase breather hose. Replace it if it's cracked, torn or deteriorated.

Fuel injected models

11 Remove the fuel tank cover (see Chapter 8).

12 Check the fuel line that runs from the fuel valve on the bottom of the tank to the throttle body for leaks and evidence of damage. If problems are visible, refer to Chapter 4 and replace the line.

Warning: Refer to precautions in Chapter 4 regarding disconnecting of fuel injection system lines before disconnecting the fuel line.

13 Check the fuel tank breather hose that runs from the fuel filler cap to the handlebar. Replace it if it's cracked or deteriorated.

14 Inspect the condition of the crankcase breather hose. Replace it if it's cracked, torn or deteriorated.

16 Spark plug - inspection, cleaning and gapping

1 Remove the front fender and fuel tank lower cover (see Chapters 8 and 4).

2 Twist the spark plug cap to break the seal, then pull it off the spark plug **(see illustrations)**.

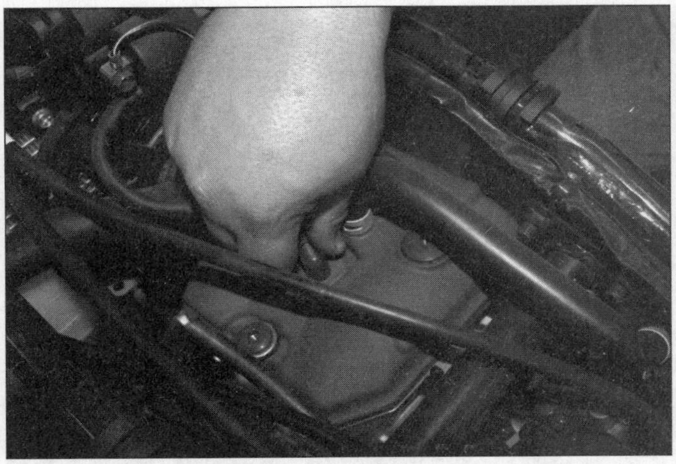

16.2a Twist and pull the spark plug boot to free it from the cylinder head, but don't use pliers or a screwdriver . . .

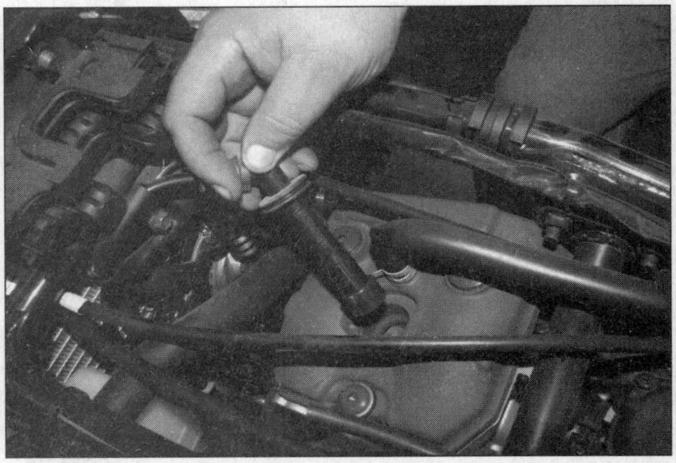

16.2b . . . and pull the boot out of the spark plug well in the valve cover and cylinder head

16.3a Unscrew the spark plug with a short extension and a 5/8-inch spark plug socket

16.3b The plug socket should have a rubber insert that grips the plug so you can lift it out

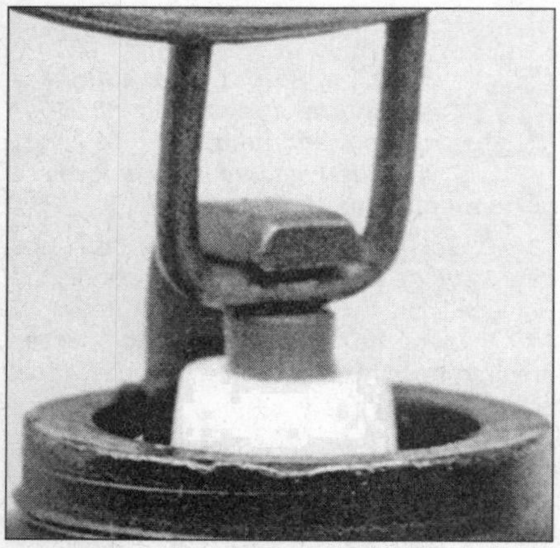

16.7a Spark plug manufacturers recommend using a wire type gauge when checking the gap - if the wire doesn't slide between the electrodes with a slight drag, adjustment is required

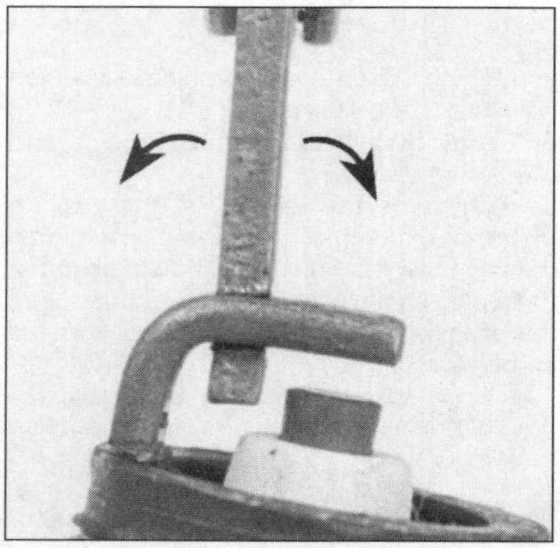

16.7b To change the gap, bend the side electrode only, as indicated by the arrows, and be very careful not to crack or chip the ceramic insulator surrounding the center electrode

3 If available, use compressed air to blow any accumulated debris from around the spark plug. Remove the plug with a spark plug socket **(see illustrations)**.

4 Inspect the electrodes for wear. Both the center and side electrodes should have square edges and the side electrode should be of uniform thickness. Look for excessive deposits and evidence of a cracked or chipped insulator around the center electrode. Compare your spark plugs to the color spark plug reading chart on the inside back cover. Check the threads, the washer and the ceramic insulator body for cracks and other damage.

5 If the electrodes are not excessively worn, and if the deposits can be easily removed with a wire brush, the plug can be regapped and reused (if no cracks or chips are visible in the insulator). If in doubt about the condition of the plug, replace it with a new one, as the expense is minimal.

6 Cleaning the spark plug by sandblasting is permitted, provided you clean the plug with a high flash-point solvent afterwards.

7 Before installing a new plug, make sure it is the correct type and heat range. Check the gap between the electrodes, as it is not preset. For best results, use a wire-type gauge rather than a flat gauge to check the gap **(see illustration)**. If the gap must be adjusted, bend the side electrode only and be very careful not to chip or crack the insulator nose **(see illustration)**. Make sure the washer is in place before installing the plug.

8 Since the cylinder head is made of aluminum, which is soft and easily damaged, thread the plug into the head by hand. Slip a short length of hose over the end of the plug to use as a tool to thread it into place. The hose will grip the plug well enough to turn it, but will start to slip if the plug begins to cross-thread in the hole - this will prevent damaged threads and the accompanying repair costs.

9 Once the plug is finger tight, the job can be finished with a socket. If a torque wrench is available, tighten the spark plug to the torque listed in this Chapter's Specifications. If you do not have a torque wrench, tighten the plug finger tight (until the washer bottoms on the cylinder head) then use a spark plug socket to tighten it an additional 1/4 turn. Regardless of the method used, do not over-tighten it.

10 Take a look at the drain hole for the spark plug well, located in the side of the cylinder head **(see illustration)**. If oil has been

16.10 If oil has been running out of the drain hole for the spark plug well, the valve cover gasket is leaking oil and should be checked

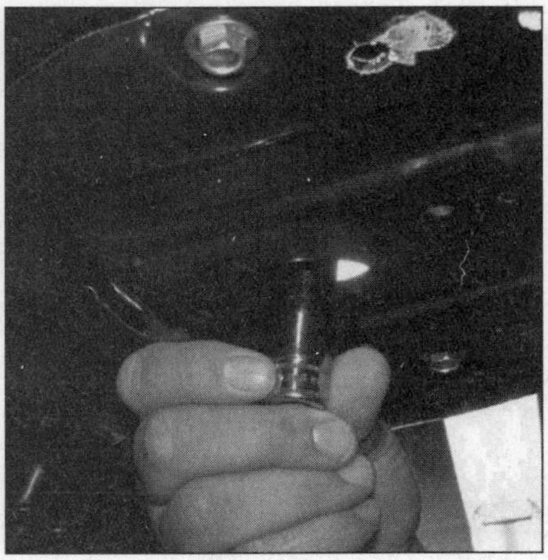

17.3a Insert a socket through the hole in the skid plate and unscrew the engine drain plug

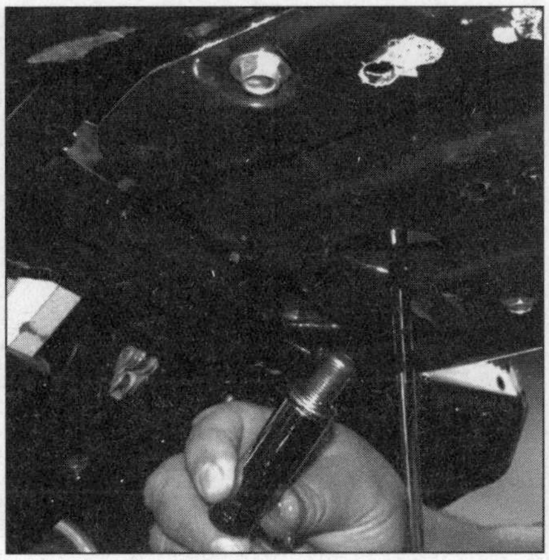

17.3b Allow the oil to drain into a pan

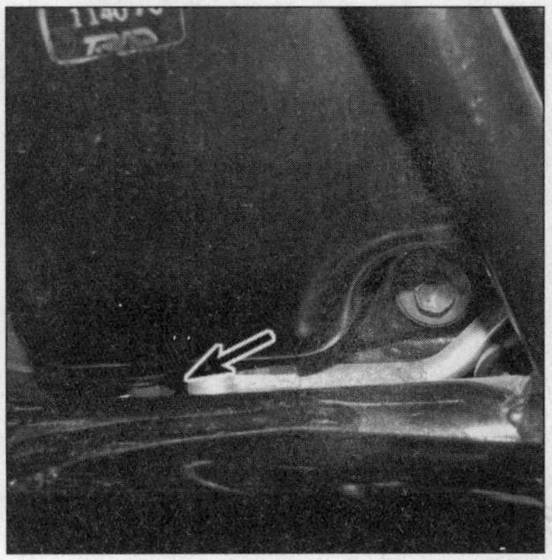

17.3c Remove the drain plug from the oil tank and allow it to drain into a pan

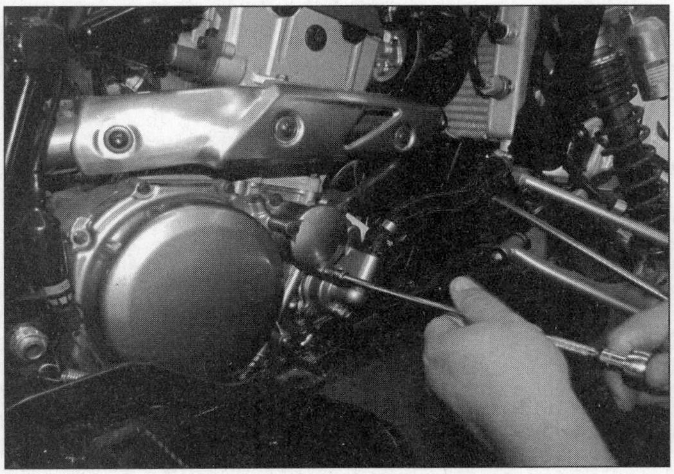

17.6a Remove the oil filter cover bolts

17.6b Place the drain pan to catch oil that drips as the bolts are loosened - on installation, the arrow mark should point upward

running out of the hole, the valve cover gasket is probably leaking oil into the spark plug well. Try tightening the valve cover bolts to the torque listed in the Chapter 2 Specifications. If the bolts aren't loose, refer to Chapter 2 and replace the valve cover gasket with a new one.

17 Engine oil and filter change

1 Consistent routine oil and filter changes are the single most important maintenance procedure you can perform on a vehicle. The oil not only lubricates the internal parts of the engine, transmission and clutch, but it also acts as a coolant, a cleaner, a sealant and a protectant. Because of these demands, the oil takes a terrific amount of abuse and should be replaced often with new oil of the recommended grade and type.

2 Before changing the oil and filter, warm up the engine by running it for several minutes so the oil will drain easily. Be careful when draining the oil, as the exhaust pipe, the engine and the oil itself can cause severe burns.

3 Place a clean drain pan under the vehicle, positioned underneath the engine and oil tank drain plugs **(see illustrations)**.

4 Remove the dipstick from the oil tank to vent the crankcase and act as a reminder that there is no oil in the engine.

5 Remove the drain plugs from the engine and oil tank **(see illustrations 17.3a, 17.3b and 17.3c)** and allow the oil to drain into the pan.

6 Remove the oil filter cover bolts **(see illustrations)**. Take the cover off, being sure not to lose the spring inside it **(see illustration)**.

17.6c Take the cover off, together with its O-ring - be careful not to lose the spring inside the cover

17.7a Remove the filter element, noting that the closed side faces outward . . .

17.7b . . . and the open side faces inward . . .

17.7c . . . and remove the inner O-ring

7 Remove the filter element and the inner O-ring **(see illustrations)**. If additional maintenance is planned for this time period, check or service another component while the oil is allowed to drain completely.

8 Wipe any remaining oil out of the filter housing area of the crankcase and make sure the oil passage is clear.

9 Check the condition of the drain plug threads. Replace the O-rings with new ones whenever the filter is removed.

10 Coat a new inner O-ring with clean engine oil and install it in the filter housing **(see illustration 17.7c)**. Install the filter element with its closed end facing out **(see illustration 17.7a)**.

Caution: The filter must be installed facing the correct direction or oil starvation may cause severe engine damage.

11 Coat a new cover O-ring with clean engine oil. Install the cover and O-ring with the and tighten the bolts to the torque listed in this Chapter's Specifications.

12 Install the oil strainer, spring and engine drain plug, using a new O-ring if the old one is worn or damaged. Tighten the plug to the torque listed in this Chapter's Specifications. Avoid overtightening, as damage to the engine case will result.

13 Before refilling the engine, check the old oil carefully. If the oil was drained into a clean pan, small pieces of metal or other material can be easily detected. If the oil is very metallic colored, then the engine is experiencing wear from break-in (new engine) or from insufficient lubrication. If there are flakes or chips of metal in the oil, then something is drastically wrong internally and the engine will have to be disassembled for inspection and repair.

14 If there are pieces of fiber-like material in the oil, the clutch is experiencing excessive wear and should be checked.

15 If the inspection of the oil turns up nothing unusual, refill the crankcase to the proper level with the recommended oil and install the dipstick/filler cap.

16 Start the engine and let it run for two or three minutes. Shut it off, wait a few minutes, then check the oil level. If necessary, add more oil to bring the level up to the upper level mark on the dipstick. Check around the drain plug and filter cover for leaks.

17 The old oil drained from the engine cannot be reused in its present state and should be disposed of. Check with your local refuse disposal company, disposal facility or environmental agency to see if they will accept the oil for recycling. Don't pour used oil into drains or onto the ground. After the oil has cooled, it can be drained into a suitable container (capped plastic jugs, topped bottles, milk cartons, etc.) for transport to one of these disposal sites.

18 Cooling system - inspection and coolant change

Inspection

1 The cooling system should be carefully inspected at the recommended intervals. Look for evidence of leaks, check the condition of the coolant, check the radiator for clogged fins and damage and make sure the fan operates when required.

2 Examine each of the rubber coolant hoses along its entire length. Look for swelling, cracks, abrasions and other damage. Squeeze each hose at various points. They should feel firm, yet pliable, and return to their original shape when released. If they are dried out or hard, replace them.

3 Look for leaks at each cooling system joint. Tighten the hose clamps carefully to halt minor leaks. If a hose is seriously cracked or torn at a hose clamp, tightening the clamp won't stop the leak; it might even accelerate it. If a hose leaks after tightening the hose clamp, drain the coolant (see Section 18), loosen the clamp, pull off the hose and inspect it closely. If the damage is close to the end of the hose, cut off the damaged end and reattach the hose. If the damage is too far from the end of the hose, cutting off the end of the hose is not an option; replace the hose.

4 Check for leaks at the water pump **(see illustration)**. The weep hole, which is designed to let coolant drip if the water pump seals are worn, isn't directly visible while the water pump is mounted on the engine. However, a leak will cause coolant residue to accumulate on the frame below the water pump. Also check for leaks at the coolant drain plug. Replace water pump or drain plug gaskets if they've been leaking. If coolant has been leaking from the weep hole, it's time for a new water pump seal (see Chapter 3).

5 Inspect the radiator for evidence of leaks and other damage. Radiator leaks usually produce tell-tale deposits or stains on the surface of the core below the leak. If the radiator is leaking, remove it (see Chapter 3) and have it repaired by a radiator shop or replace it.

Caution: Do NOT use a liquid leak-stopping compound to try to repair leaks.

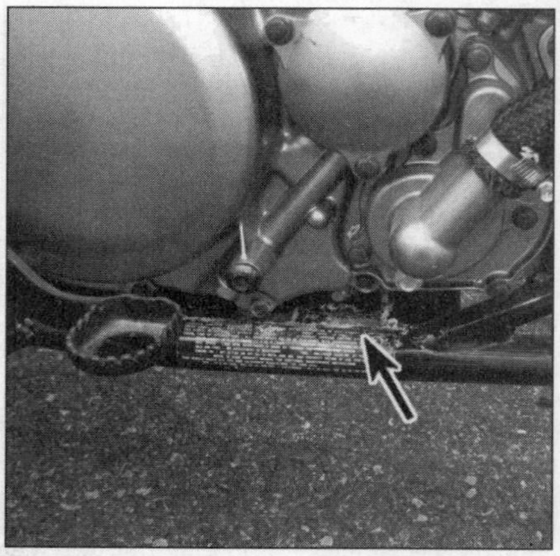

18.4 If coolant has been leaking from the water pump weep hole, there will be residue on the frame below the water pump

18.14 18.14 With the engine completely cool, remove the radiator cap to relieve any residual pressure in the cooling system, then reinstall it temporarily

18.15a Remove the drain bolt and sealing washer . . .

6 Inspect the radiator cooling fins for mud, dirt and insects. Debris stuck in the fins can impede the flow of air through the radiator. If the fins are dirty, force water or low-pressure compressed air through the fins from the backside of the radiator. If any of the fins are bent or distorted, straighten them carefully with a screwdriver.

7 Remove the right side cover (see Chapter 8).

8 Remove the radiator cap as follows: Turn it counterclockwise until it reaches the first detent. If you hear a hissing sound (indicating there is still pressure in the system), wait until it stops. Then press down on the cap and continue turning it counterclockwise until it's free.

9 Inspect the condition of the coolant in the radiator. If it's rust-colored, or if accumulations of scale are visible in the radiator, drain, flush and refill the system with new coolant. Inspect the cap gaskets for cracks and other damage. Have the cap tested by a dealer service department or replace it with a new one. Install the cap by turning it clockwise until it reaches the first detent, then push down on the cap and continue turning it until it stops.

10 Analyze the condition of the antifreeze in the coolant with an antifreeze hydrometer. Sometimes coolant may look like it's in good condition, but might be too weak to offer adequate protection. If the hydrometer indicates a weak mixture, flush and refill the cooling system (see Section 18).

11 Start the engine and let it reach normal operating temperature, then check for leaks again. As the coolant temperature increases, the fan should come on automatically and the temperature should begin to drop. If it doesn't, check the fan and fan circuit (see Chapter 3).

12 If the coolant level is constantly low, but there is no evidence of leaks, have the system pressure checked by a dealer service department, motorcycle repair shop or service station.

Coolant change

⚠ ***Warning: Don't allow antifreeze to come into contact with your skin or with painted surfaces of the vehicle. Rinse off spills immediately with plenty of water. Antifreeze is highly toxic if ingested. Never leave antifreeze in an open container or in puddles on the floor; children and pets are attracted by its sweet odor and may drink it. Check with local authorities regarding the proper disposal of used antifreeze. Many communities have collection centers that can dispose of antifreeze safely. Finally, antifreeze is combustible, so don't store it or put it near open flames.***

⚠ ***Warning: Let the engine cool completely before performing this Step. Opening the radiator cap while the engine is hot will allow scalding coolant to spray out.***

Draining

13 Remove the right side cover if you haven't already done so (see Chapter 8).

14 Put a shop rag over the radiator cap **(see illustration)**. Slowly rotate the cap counterclockwise to the first detent and allow any residual pressure to escape. When the hissing sound ceases, push down on the cap, turn it counterclockwise again and remove it (this will ensure that all pressure in the cooling system has been relieved). Reinstall the radiator cap.

15 Place a large, clean drain pan under the water pump, remove the drain plug, then remove the radiator cap and drain the coolant into the container **(see illustrations)**.

HAYNES HiNT ***The coolant will rush out with considerable force, so be prepared to quickly readjust the position of the drain pan.***

16 Remove the coolant reservoir (see Chapter 3) and drain it. Wash out the reservoir with clean water. Install the reservoir.

18.15b . . . then remove the radiator cap and allow the coolant to drain into a container

Flushing

17 Flush the system with clean tap water by inserting a garden hose into the radiator filler neck. Allow the water to run through the system until it is clear when it exits the drain bolt hole. If the radiator is extremely corroded, remove it (see Chapter 3) and have it cleaned by a radiator shop.

18 Using a new gasket, install the drain bolt and tighten it to the torque listed in this Chapter's Specifications.

19 Fill the cooling system with clean water mixed with a flushing compound. Make sure the flushing compound is compatible with aluminum, and follow the manufacturer's instructions carefully.

20 Start the engine and allow it to reach normal operating temperature. Let it run for about ten minutes.

21 Stop the engine. Let the machine cool for awhile, then cover the radiator cap with a heavy rag and turn it counterclockwise to the first stop, releasing any pressure that may be present in the system. Once the hissing

18.29 Remove the filler cap from the reservoir tank

19.2 Measure clutch lever freeplay at the lever tip

20.3 Adjust the idle speed with the throttle stop screw (carbureted models) or idle air screw (fuel injected models) (carburetor shown)

stops, push down on the cap and remove it completely.

22 Drain the system.

23 Fill the system with clean water, then repeat Steps 17 and 18.

Refilling and air bleeding

24 Fill the system with the correct coolant mixture (listed in this Chapter's Specifications). Fill the system to the top of the radiator cap filler neck, but leave the radiator cap off for now. Fill the reservoir to the FULL mark and install the reservoir cap.

25 Rock the vehicle from side to side to free trapped air. As the coolant level drops in the radiator, top it off with fresh coolant.

26 Start the engine and let it idle. Run the engine for several minutes so trapped air can make its way to the radiator, then shut the engine off. Top up the coolant.

27 Repeat Step 26 several times, until the coolant level in the radiator stops dropping. Once this happens, install the radiator cap. Top up the coolant reservoir to the FULL mark.

28 Run the engine for several minutes with the radiator cap on and check for leaks.

29 Warm the engine up, then shut it off and let it cool down. Recheck the level in the reservoir. Top up as needed through the reservoir filler cap **(see illustration)**.

30 Repeat Step 29 until the coolant level in the reservoir is at the FULL mark after the engine has cooled down.

19 Clutch lever freeplay - check and adjustment

1 The clutch cable is adjusted at the clutch lever. Clutch freeplay can also be adjusted at the crankcase end of the clutch cable if adjustment at the handlebar doesn't bring freeplay within the specified range.

2 Operate the clutch lever and check freeplay at the lever tip **(see illustration)**.

3 If freeplay isn't within the range listed in this Chapter's Specifications, pull back the adjuster cover and loosen the locknut **(see illustration 5.8b)**. Turn the adjuster to set freeplay and tighten the locknut. Slide the cover back over the adjuster.

20 Idle speed - check and adjustment

1 Before adjusting the idle speed, make sure the spark plug gap is correct (see Section 16). Also, turn the handlebars back-and-forth and note whether the idle speed changes. If it does, the throttle cable may be incorrectly routed. Be sure to correct this problem before proceeding.

2 Start the engine and warm it up to its normal operating temperature. Make sure the transmission is in Neutral, then hook up an inductive-type tachometer.

3 Turn the throttle stop screw (carbureted models) or idle air adjustment screw (fuel injected models) to bring the idle speed within the range listed in this Chapter's Specifications **(see illustration)**. Turning the screw in increases the idle speed; backing it out decreases the idle speed.

4 Snap the throttle open and shut a few times, then recheck the idle speed. If necessary, repeat the adjustment procedure.

5 If a smooth, steady idle can't be achieved, the fuel/air mixture may be incorrect. Refer to Chapter 4 for additional carburetor or fuel injection system information.

21 Throttle cable and speed limiter - check and adjustment

Throttle cable

1 Before proceeding, check and, if necessary, adjust the idle speed (see Section 20).

2 Make sure the throttle lever moves easily from fully closed to fully open with the front wheel turned at various angles. The lever should return automatically from fully open to fully closed when released. If the throttle sticks, check the throttle cable for cracks or kinks in the housing. Also, make sure the inner cable is clean and well-lubricated.

3 Measure freeplay at the throttle lever **(see illustration)**. If it's within the range listed in this Chapter's Specifications, no adjustment is necessary. If not, adjust it as follows.

4 Pull back the rubber boot to expose the throttle cable adjuster **(see illustration)**. Loosen the adjuster locknut. Turn the adjuster to set freeplay, then tighten the locknut.

5 Reposition the rubber boot over the adjuster.

Speed limiter

6 The speed limiter **(see illustration)** can be used to restrict maximum throttle

21.3 Check throttle lever freeplay at the lever tip

21.4 Slide the rubber boot (arrow) off the adjuster, loosen the locknut and turn the adjuster

21.6 To adjust the speed limiter, loosen the locknut (left arrow) and turn the screw (right arrow)

opening. Turning the screw in reduces the maximum throttle opening; backing it out increases maximum throttle opening.

7 To change the speed limiter screw setting, loosen the locknut, turn the screw in or out as necessary and tighten the locknut. Screw length is measured from the underside of the screw head to the throttle housing.

Warning: Do NOT back out the speed limiter screw farther than the maximum setting listed in this Chapter's Specifications; doing so will affect throttle lever operation.

22 Choke (carbureted models) - operation check

1 Operate the choke lever **(see illustration)** and note whether it operates smoothly.

2 If the choke lever doesn't operate smoothly, inspect the choke system (see Chapter 4).

23 Battery - check

1 All models use a sealed, maintenance-free battery. Periodic checking of the electrolyte specific gravity is not possible. Inspect the battery as described in Chapter 5.

2 If the vehicle will be stored for an extended time, fully charge the battery, then remove it. Disconnect the negative cable and remove the battery retainer strap. Disconnect the positive cable and vent tube and lift the battery out.

Warning: Always disconnect the negative cable first and reconnect it last to avoid sparks which could cause a battery explosion.

3 Store the battery in a cool dark place. Check open circuit voltage (see Chapter 5) at least once a month and recharge the battery if it's low.

24 Valve clearance - check and adjustment

Check

1 The engine must be cool to the touch for this maintenance procedure, so if possible let the machine sit overnight before beginning.

2 Remove the seat and fuel tank cover (see Chapter 8). On 2008 and earlier models, remove the side covers. On 2009 models, remove the front fender.

3 Remove the fuel tank (see Chapter 4).

4 Disconnect the crankcase breather hose and oil tank breather hose **(see illustration)**.

5 Remove the spark plug (see Sec-

22.1 Check the choke lever for smooth operation

24.4 Disconnect the hoses from the valve cover

24.7 Unscrew the crankshaft bolt cover and the timing hole cover directly above it

24.8a Align the timing mark next to the T mark (upper arrows) with the notch (lower arrow) - if the piston is on the compression stroke . . .

tion 16). This will make it easier to turn the crankshaft.

6 Remove the valve cover (see Chapter 2).

7 Unscrew the crankshaft end plug and timing hole access plug **(see illustration)**.

8 Make sure the transmission is in Neutral. Using a socket on the crankshaft rotation bolt, turn the engine to position the piston at Top Dead Center on the compression stroke. **Note:** *Rotate the crankshaft counterclockwise.* When this occurs, the timing mark on the rotor will align with the notch in the crankcase cover **(see illustration)**. To make sure the piston is on the compression stroke, not the exhaust stroke, check the camshaft position. The camshaft lobes should point away from each other **(see illustration)**. If the camshaft lobes are out of position, rotate the crankshaft one full turn, so the crankshaft timing mark again aligns with the notch.

9 With the engine in this position, all four valve clearances can be checked.

10 Insert a feeler gauge of the same thickness as the valve clearance listed in this Chapter's Specifications between each of the cam lobes and the lifter beneath it **(see illustration).**

11 Pull the feeler gauge out slowly - you should feel a light drag. If there's no drag, the clearance is too loose. If there's a heavy drag, the clearance is too tight.

12 Record the locations of any valves with incorrect clearances. Recheck the clearances of these valves, trying different feeler gauges until you find the thickness that fits correctly (a light drag). Once you do, write this thickness down - you'll need this information later to select a new valve adjusting shim.

13 If any of the clearances need to be adjusted, go to Step 14. If all of the clearances are within the Specifications, go to Step 20.

Adjustment

14 Remove the camshaft (see Chapter 2). Remove the lifter and shim for each of the valves that need to be adjusted.

15 Determine the thickness of the shim that was removed. It should be marked on the top of the shim **(see illustration)**, but the ideal way is to measure it with a micrometer or vernier caliper (refer to *Tools and Workshop Tips* at the end of this manual). **Note:** *If the number on the shim does not end with zero or 5, round it off to the nearest zero or 5. For example, if the number on the shim is 238, round it off to 240. If it's 244, round it off to 245.*

16 If the clearance (measured in Steps 10 and 11 and recorded in Step 12) was too large, you need a thicker shim. If it was too small, you need a thinner shim.

17 If the measured valve clearance in Steps 10 and 11 was too great, subtract the mid-range specified clearance from the measured clearance. Write this number down, then add it to the thickness of the adjusting shim you removed. This will give you the thickness of the needed new shim. For example:

Measured clearance: 0.20 mm
Specified clearance: 0.10 to 0.15 mm

24.8b . . . the cam lobes will point away from each other like this (if they don't, rotate the crankshaft another full turn)

24.10 Slip the feeler gauge between the cam lobe and lifter to measure the clearance

24.15 The shim thickness is marked on the shim, but it should also be checked with a vernier caliper or micrometer

25.4 The spark arrester is secured by three bolts

Mid-range desired clearance: 0.12 mm
Measured clearance minus desired clearance: 0.08 mm

So if the existing shim is numbered 230 (2.30 mm thick), the new shim should be 2.38 mm thick. The closest to this is a 240 (2.40 mm thick). This is the thickness of the new shim that you will need for that valve.

18 Select new shims for any remaining valves that are not within the Specifications.

19 Install the new shims and their lifters (see Chapter 2).

20 The remainder of installation is the reverse of the removal steps. After the camshafts are reinstalled, recheck the valve clearances to make sure they're within the Specifications.

25 Exhaust system - inspection

1 Periodically, inspect the exhaust system for leaks and loose fasteners.

2 The exhaust pipe flange nuts at the cylinder head are especially prone to loosening, which could cause damage to the head (see Chapter 4). Check them frequently and keep them tight. If tightening the flange nuts fails to stop the leak, replace the gasket (see Chapter 4).

3 The spark arrester should be removed and cleaned at the specified intervals.

Warning: To avoid burns, be sure the exhaust system has cooled down before you start this procedure.

Warning: To avoid carbon monoxide poisoning, run the engine in a well-ventilated area.

4 Unbolt the spark arrester. Remove three bolts from the rear end of the tailpipe **(see illustration)**.

5 Pull the spark arrester out of the muffler. Tap it lightly with a soft-faced mallet to loosen any deposits, then clean the deposits off with a wire brush. Also clean any deposits from the inside of the muffler, again using a wire brush.

6 Reinstall the spark arrester and tighten the bolt(s) to the torque listed in this Chapter's Specifications.

26 Engine oil hoses - inspection

1 Locate the oil hoses that run from the oil tank to the engine **(see illustration)**.

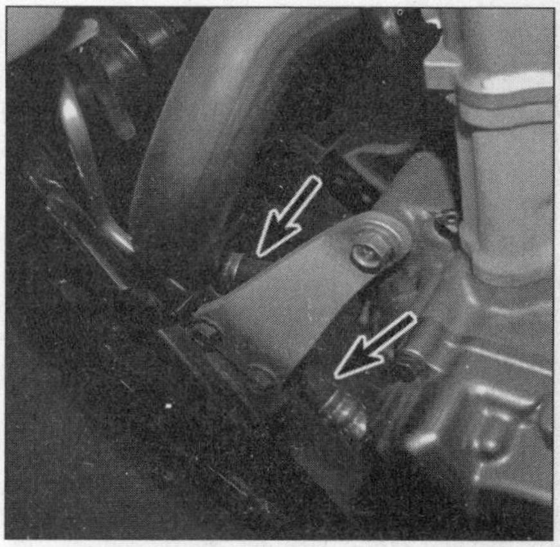

26.1 Check the oil hoses and metal lines for cracks, damage or loose connections

2 Check the flexible hoses for cracks or deterioration. Check the metal lines for cracks, corrosion and damage caused by an impact. If any problems are found, replace the hoses or lines. It's a good idea to replace the clamps with new ones whenever you replace a hose or line.

Notes

Chapter 2
Engine, clutch and transmission

Contents

Degrees of difficulty

Easy, suitable for novice with little experience	**Fairly easy,** suitable for beginner with some experience	**Fairly difficult,** suitable for competent DIY mechanic	**Difficult,** suitable for experienced DIY mechanic	**Very difficult,** suitable for expert DIY or professional

Specifications

General

Bore	90 mm (3.546 inches)
Stroke	62.6 mm (2.465 inches)
Displacement	398 cc
Cylinder compression (automatic compression release actuated)	142 psi (1000 kPa)
Oil pressure at 3000 rpm, 140-degrees F (60-degrees C)	2.8 to 8.5 psi (20 to 60 kPa)

General (continued)

Camshaft	
Lobe height (intake)	
Standard	36.320 to 36.370 mm (1.4299 to 1.4319 inches)
Limit	36.020 mm (1.4181 inches)
Lobe height (exhaust)	
Standard	35.200 to 35.250 mm (1.3858 to 1.3878 inches)
Limit	34.900 mm (1.3740 inches)
Runout limit	0.10 mm (0.004 inch)
Bearing oil clearance	
Standard	0.019 to 0.053 mm (0.0007 to 0.0021 inch)
Limit	0.150 mm (0.006 inch)

Cylinder head, valves and valve springs

Cylinder head warpage limit	0.05 mm (0.002 inch)
Valve cover warpage limit	0.05 mm (0.002 inch)
Valve stem runout	0.01 mm (0.0004 inch)
Valve stem diameter	
Intake	
Standard	4.975 to 4.990 mm (0.1959 to 0.1965 inch)
Limit	Not specified
Exhaust	
Standard	4.955 to 4.970 mm (0.1951 to 0.1957 inch)
Limit	Not specified
Valve guide inside diameter (intake and exhaust)	
Standard	5.000 to 5.012 mm (0.1969 to 0.1973 inch)
Limit	Not specified
Stem-to-guide clearance	
Intake	
Standard	0.010 to 0.037 mm (0.0004 to 0.0015 inch)
Limit	Not specified
Exhaust	
Standard	0.030 to 0.057 mm (0.0012 to 0.0022 inch)
Limit	Not specified
Valve seat width (intake and exhaust)	
Standard	0.9 to 1.1 mm (0.0354 to 0.0433 inch)
Limit	Not specified
Valve margin thickness limit (intake and exhaust)	0.5 mm (0.2 inch)
Valve spring free length limit (intake and exhaust)	38.8 mm (1.53 inches)
Valve spring bend limit	Not specified

Cylinder

Bore diameter	
Standard	90.000 to 90.015 mm (3.5460 to 3.5466 inches)
Limit	Not specified
Top surface warpage limit	0.05 mm (0.002 inch)
Out-of-round limit	Not specified
Taper limit	Not specified
Measuring point	Top, center and bottom of bore, parallel and crosswise to crankshaft centerline

Piston

Diameter	89.965 to 89.980 mm (3.5446 to 3.5452 inches)
Measuring point	15.0 mm (0.6 inch) from bottom of skirt
Piston-to-cylinder clearance	
Standard	0.030 to 0.040 mm (0.0012 to 0.0016 inch)
Limit	0.120 mm (0.0047 inch)
Piston pin bore	
Standard	20.002 to 20.008 mm (0.7881 to 0.7883 inch)
Limit	20.030 mm (0.7891 inch)
Piston pin outer diameter	
Standard	19.995 to 20.000 mm (0.7878 to 0.7879 inch)
Limit	19.980 mm (0.7872 inch)
Piston pin-to-piston clearance	Not specified
Piston ring groove width	
Top ring	0.78 to 0.80 mm (0.0307 to 0.0315 inch)
Second ring	1.30 to 1.32 mm (0.0512 to 0.0520 inch)
Oil ring	2.01 to 2.03 mm (0.0791 to 0.0799 inch)

Piston

Ring side clearance limit	
Top ring	0.180 mm (0.007 inch)
Second ring	0.150 mm (0.006 inch)
Oil ring	Not specified
Ring end gap (not installed in engine)	
Top ring	
Standard (approximate)	6.9 mm (0.27 inch)
Limit	5.5 mm (0.22 inch)
Second ring (approximate)	
Standard	11.5 mm (0.45 inch)
Limit	9.2 mm (0.36 inch)
Oil ring	Not specified
Ring end gap (installed in engine)	
Top and second rings	
Standard	0.08 to 0.20 mm (0.003 to 0.008 inch)
Limit	0.5 mm (0.02 inch)
Oil ring	Not specified
Ring thickness	
Top ring	0.71 to 0.76 mm (0.028 to 0.030 inch)
Second ring	1.08 to 1.10 mm (0.0425 to 0.0433 inch)
Oil ring	Not specified

Clutch

Spring free length limit	49.9 mm (1.96 inches)
Metal plate thickness	Not specified
Friction plate thickness	
Standard	2.92 to 3.08 mm (0.115 to 0.121 inch)
Limit	2.62 mm (0.103 inch)
Metal plate warpage limit	0.1 mm (0.004 inch)

Transmission

Shift fork clearance in grooves	
Standard	0.1 to 0.3 mm (0.004 to 0.012 inch)
Limit	0.05 mm (0.002 inch)
Shift fork thickness	4.8 to 4.9 mm (0.189 to 0.193 inch)
Shift fork groove width	5.0 to 5.1 mm (0.197 to 0.201 inch)

Crankshaft, connecting rod and balancer

Runout limit	0.08 mm (0.003 inch)
Assembly width	62 +/- 1.0 mm (2.441 +/- 0.004 inch)
Connecting rod big-end side clearance	
Standard	0.30 to 0.65 mm (0.012 to 0.026 inch)
Limit	1.0 mm (0.040 inch)
Connecting rod small end inside diameter	
Standard	20.010 to 20.018 mm (0.7884 to 0.7887 inch)
Limit	20.040 mm (0.7896 inch)

Torque specifications

Valve cover bolts	14 Nm (120 inch-lbs)
Cylinder head small bolts	10 Nm (86 inch-lbs)
Cylinder head main bolts (1)	
Step 1	25 Nm (18 ft-lbs)
Step 2	46 Nm (33.5 ft-lbs)
Oil hose union bolt (to crankcase)	23 Nm (16.5 ft-lbs)
Oil hose mounting bolts (to oil tank and engine)	Not specified
Oil tube bracket bolt (outside of right crankcase)	Not specified
Camshaft bearing cap bolts	10 Nm (86 inch-lbs) (2)
Cam chain guide bolt	10 Nm (86 inch-lbs)
Cam chain tensioner body bolts	10 Nm (86 inch-lbs)
Cam chain tensioner cap bolt	30 Nm (21.5 ft-lbs)
Cylinder base bolts	10 Nm (86 inch-lbs)
Crankcase bolts	11 Nm (96 inch-lbs)
Crankcase cover bolts	Not specified
Oil pump mounting screws	Not specified (3)
Oil pump assembly screw	Do not remove
Clutch boss nut	70 Nm (50.5 ft-lbs) (4)
Clutch spring bolts	Not specified

Torque specifications (continued)

Gearshift cam driven gear bolt	24 Nm (17.5 ft-lbs)
External shift linkage stopper	19 Nm (168 in-lbs) (3)
External shift linkage pawl lifter screws	Not specified (3)
Shift pedal pinch bolt	Not specified
Primary drive gear nut	140 Nm (101.5 ft-lbs) (4)
Balancer driven gear nut	50 Nm (36 ft-lbs) (4)
Engine mounting bolts/nuts	
Brackets to frame	26 Nm (19 ft-lbs)
Through-bolts and nuts	66 Nm (47.5 ft-lbs)

1 Apply clean engine oil to the threads, bolt seating surfaces and upper and lower sides of the washers. Install the washers with the rounded sides upward.

2 Make sure the piston at Top Dead Center on the compression stroke before tightening these bolts.

3 Apply non-permanent thread locking agent to the threads.

4 Use a new lockwasher.

1 General information

The engine/transmission unit is of the liquid-cooled, single-cylinder four-stroke design.

All models have four valves (two intake and two exhaust). The valves are operated by dual overhead camshafts, which are chain driven off the crankshaft.

The engine/transmission assembly is constructed from aluminum alloy. The crankcase is divided vertically.

The crankcase incorporates a dry sump, pressure-fed lubrication system which uses a gear-driven rotor-type oil pump and an oil filter. All models have an external oil tank, mounted in front of the engine.

On all models, a wet, multi-plate clutch connects the crankshaft to the transmission. Engagement and disengagement of the clutch is controlled by a lever on the left handlebar through a cable. Engagement of reverse gear is controlled by a knob and cable.

The transmission has five forward gears and one reverse gear.

2 Operations possible with the engine in the frame

The components and assemblies listed below can be removed without having to remove the engine from the frame. If, however, a number of areas require attention at the same time, removal of the engine is recommended.

Starter motor (if equipped)
Starter reduction gears
Starter clutch
Alternator rotor and stator
Clutch
External shift mechanism
Cam chain tensioner and chain
Camshafts and lifters
Cylinder head
Cylinder and piston
Oil pump
Balancer gears

3 Operations requiring engine removal

It is necessary to remove the engine/transmission assembly from the frame and separate the crankcase halves to gain access to the following components:

Crankshaft and connecting rod
Transmission shafts
Shift drum and forks

4 Major engine repair - general note

1 It is not always easy to determine when or if an engine should be completely overhauled, as a number of factors must be considered.

2 High mileage is not necessarily an indication that an overhaul is needed, while low mileage, on the other hand, does not preclude the need for an overhaul. Frequency of servicing is probably the single most important consideration. An engine that has regular and frequent oil and filter changes, as well as other required maintenance, will most likely give many miles of reliable service. Conversely, a neglected engine, or one which has not been broken in properly, may require an overhaul very early in its life.

3 Exhaust smoke and excessive oil consumption are both indications that piston rings and/or valve guides are in need of attention. Make sure oil leaks are not responsible before deciding that the rings and guides are bad. Refer to Section 5 and perform a cylinder compression check to determine for certain the nature and extent of the work required.

4 If the engine is making obvious knocking or rumbling noises, the connecting rod and/or main bearings are probably at fault.

5 Loss of power, rough running, excessive valve train noise and high fuel consumption rates may also point to the need for an overhaul, especially if they are all present at the same time. If a complete tune-up does not remedy the situation, major mechanical work is the only solution.

6 An engine overhaul generally involves restoring the internal parts to the specifications of a new engine. During an overhaul the piston rings are replaced and the cylinder walls are bored and/or honed. If a rebore is done, then a new piston is also required. Generally the valves are serviced as well, since they are usually in less than perfect condition at this point. While the engine is being overhauled, other components such as the carburetor and the starter motor (if equipped) can be rebuilt also. The end result should be a like-new engine that will give as many trouble-free miles as the original.

7 Before beginning the engine overhaul, read through all of the related procedures to familiarize yourself with the scope and requirements of the job. Overhauling an engine is not all that difficult, but it is time consuming. Plan on the vehicle being tied up for a minimum of two weeks. Check on the availability of parts and make sure that any necessary special tools, equipment and supplies are obtained in advance.

8 Most work can be done with typical shop hand tools, although a number of precision measuring tools are required for inspecting parts to determine if they must be replaced. Often a dealer service department or repair shop will handle the inspection of parts and offer advice concerning reconditioning and replacement. As a general rule, time is the primary cost of an overhaul so it doesn't pay to install worn or substandard parts.

9 As a final note, to ensure maximum life and minimum trouble from a rebuilt engine, everything must be assembled with care in a spotlessly clean environment.

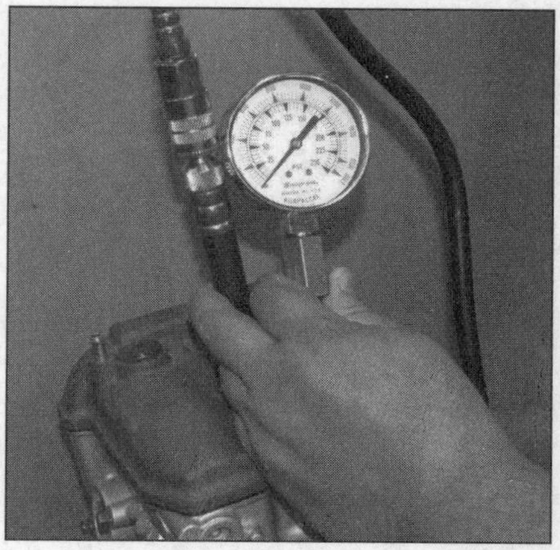

5.5 A compression gauge that screws into the spark plug hole is preferable to the type that's pressed against the opening

5 Cylinder compression - check

1 Among other things, poor engine performance may be caused by leaking valves, incorrect valve clearances, a leaking head gasket, or worn piston, rings and/or cylinder wall. A cylinder compression check will help pinpoint these conditions and can also indicate the presence of excessive carbon deposits in the cylinder head.

2 The only tools required are a compression gauge and a spark plug wrench. Depending on the outcome of the initial test, a squirt-type oil can may also be needed.

3 Check valve clearances and adjust if necessary (see Chapter 1). Start the engine and allow it to reach normal operating temperature, then remove the spark plug (see Chapter 1). Work carefully - don't strip the spark plug hole threads and don't burn your hands.

4 Disable the ignition by disconnecting the primary (low tension) wires from the coil (see Chapter 5). Be sure to mark the locations of the wires before detaching them.

5 Install the compression gauge in the spark plug hole **(see illustration)**. Hold or block the throttle wide open.

6 Crank the engine over a minimum of four or five revolutions (or until the gauge reading stops increasing) and observe the initial movement of the compression gauge needle as well as the final total gauge read-

6.3 Unscrew the main oil gallery plug and thread an oil pressure gauge into the hole

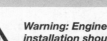

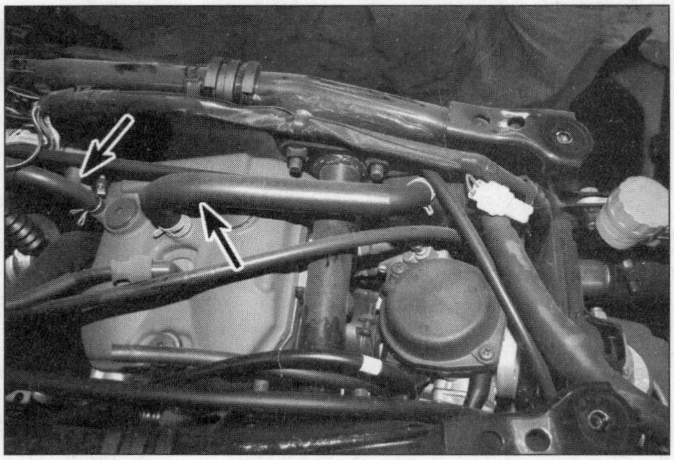

7.16a Disconnect the oil hose (left arrow) and breather hose (right arrow) from the valve cover

ing. Compare the results to the value listed in this Chapter's Specifications.

7 If the compression built up quickly and evenly to the specified amount, you can assume the engine upper end is in reasonably good mechanical condition. Worn or sticking piston rings and a worn cylinder will produce very little initial movement of the gauge needle, but compression will tend to build up gradually as the engine spins over. Valve and valve seat leakage, or head gasket leakage, is indicated by low initial compression which does not tend to build up.

8 To further confirm your findings, add a small amount of engine oil to the cylinder by inserting the nozzle of a squirt-type oil can through the spark plug hole. The oil will tend to seal the piston rings if they are leaking.

9 If the compression increases significantly after the addition of the oil, the piston rings and/or cylinder are definitely worn. If the compression does not increase, the pressure is leaking past the valves or the head gasket. Leakage past the valves may be due to insufficient valve clearances, burned, warped or cracked valves or valve seats or valves that are hanging up in the guides.

10 If compression readings are considerably higher than specified, the combustion chamber is probably coated with excessive carbon deposits. It is possible (but not very likely) for carbon deposits to raise the compression enough to compensate for the effects of leakage past rings or valves. Remove the cylinder head and carefully decarbonize the combustion chamber (see Section 12).

6 Engine oil pressure - check

1 You'll need a tune-up tachometer and a mechanical oil pressure gauge for this procedure.

2 Connect a tachometer to the engine, following the manufacturer's instructions.

3 Unscrew the main oil gallery plug **(see illustration)** and thread an oil pressure gauge into the hole.

4 If the engine is cold, run it at 2000 rpm to warm it up. In warm weather, run the engine for 10 minutes; in cold weather, run it for 20 minutes.

5 Raise engine speed to 3000 rpm and note the reading on the oil pressure gauge. If it's too low, the problem may be a dirty oil filter, defective O-ring, worn oil pump or a leaky O-ring. If it's too high, the oil may be too high a viscosity (refer to Chapter 1 for oil viscosity specifications). If the viscosity is correct and oil pressure is too high, an obstructed oil passage may be the cause.

7 Engine - removal and installation

Warning: Engine removal and installation should be done with the aid of an assistant to avoid damage or injury that could occur if the engine is dropped.

Removal

1 Remove the seat and engine skid plate (see Chapter 8).

2 Disconnect the negative cable from the battery (see Chapter 5).

3 Remove the fuel tank and exhaust system (see Chapter 4).

4 Drain the engine oil and coolant (see Chapter 1).

5 Disconnect the radiator hoses from the engine (see Chapter 3). Remove the radiator lower mounting bolts and push the bottom of the radiator far enough forward to provide removal clearance for the engine. Remove the thermostat.

6 Remove the carburetor or throttle body (see Chapter 4).

7 Unbolt the clutch cable bracket from the valve cover and disconnect the clutch cable from the engine (see Section 20).

8 Disconnect the spark plug wire (see Chapter 1).

9 Disconnect the oil hoses. Remove the oil tank and oil return tank (see Section 18).

10 Remove the drive sprocket from the engine, together with the chain (see Chapter 6).

11 Disconnect the breather hose(s) from the valve cover **(see illustration 7.16a)**.

12 Label and disconnect the following wires (see Chapter 5 for component locations if necessary):

Alternator
Starter motor
Neutral switch
Engine ground wire **(see illustration 12.5 in Chapter 5)**

13 If you're working on a fuel injected model, label and disconnect the following wires (see Chapter 4 for component locations if necessary):

Intake air pressure sensor
Intake air temperature sensor
Engine coolant temperature sensor
Crankshaft position sensor

14 Remove the reverse cable bracket and cable (see Section 24).

15 Support the engine securely from below.

16 Remove the engine mounting bolts, nuts and brackets at the lower front and upper rear **(see illustrations)**.

17 Remove the swingarm pivot bolt partway (see Chapter 6).

HAYNES HiNT ***The swingarm pivot bolt acts as an engine mounting bolt. Pull out the bolt just far enough to free the engine, but leave it in far enough to support one side of the swingarm.***

18 Have an assistant help you support the engine. Remove it from the left side.

19 Slowly lower the engine to a suitable work surface.

7.16b Detach the upper mount from the engine (lower arrow) and frame (upper arrows)

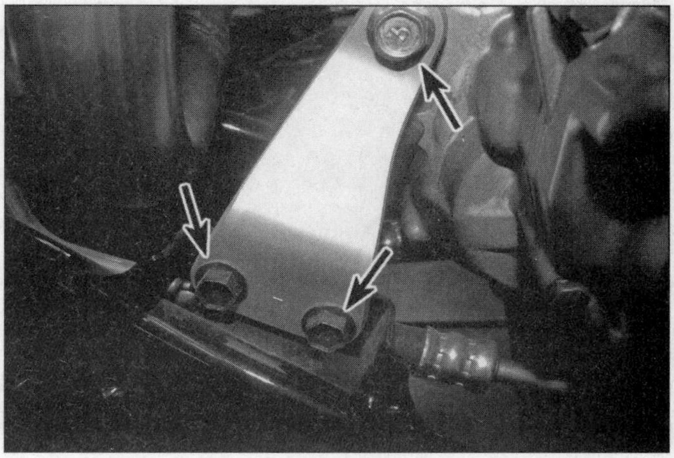

7.16c Remove the bolts from the left mounting bracket . . .

Installation

20 Check the engine supports for wear or damage and replace them if necessary before installing the engine.

21 Make sure the vehicle is securely supported so it can't be knocked over during the remainder of this procedure.

22 With the help of an assistant, lift the engine up into the frame. Install the mounting nuts and bolts at the rear, front and top. Be sure the mount brackets are installed on the correct sides of the bike (refer to their L and R marks). Finger-tighten the mounting bolts, but don't tighten them to the specified torque yet.

23 Tighten the engine mounting bolts and nuts evenly to the torques listed in this Chapter's Specifications.

24 The remainder of installation is the reverse of removal, with the following additions:

a) Use new gaskets at all exhaust pipe connections.

b) Adjust the throttle cable and clutch cable (see Chapter 1).

7.16d . . . and from the right mounting bracket - the left and right mounting brackets are labeled L and R

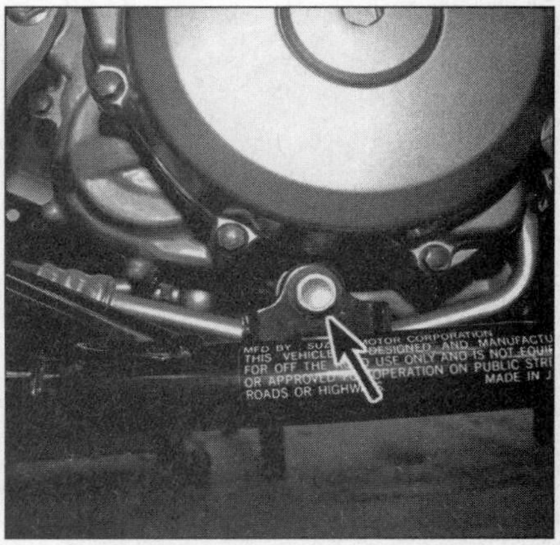

7.16e Unscrew the nut from the lower through-bolt, then remove the through-bolt and spacers

c) Fill the engine with oil and coolant (see Chapter 1). Run the engine and check for oil, coolant and exhaust leaks.

d) Check engine idle speed and adjust it if necessary (see Chapter 1).

7.16f It's a good idea to put the mounting hardware back on the frame, so you can remember how it goes during installation

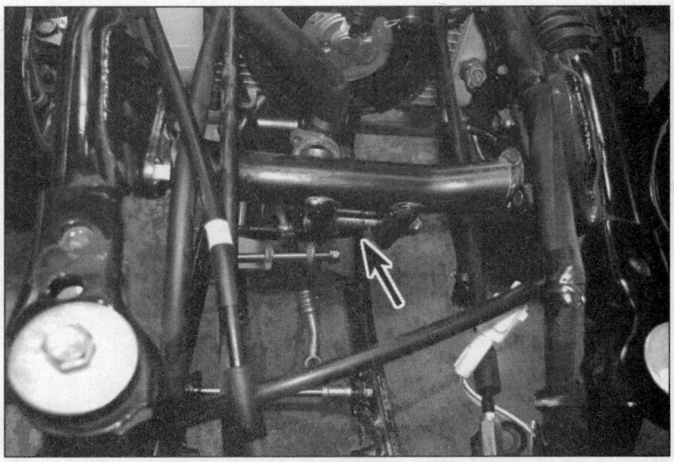

7.16g Upper mounting bracket through-bolt location

8.3 An engine stand can be made from short lengths of lumber and lag bolts or nails

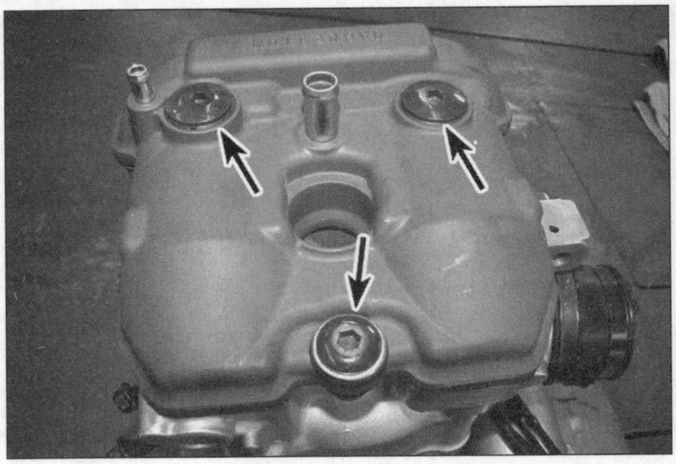

9.4a Remove the valve cover bolts

8 Engine disassembly and reassembly - general information

1 Before disassembling the engine, clean the exterior with a degreaser and rinse it with water. A clean engine will make the job easier and prevent the possibility of getting dirt into the internal areas of the engine.

2 In addition to the precision measuring tools mentioned in *Tools and Workshop Tips* at the end of this manual, you will need a torque wrench, a valve spring compressor, oil gallery, a piston ring removal and installation tool and a piston ring compressor. Some new, clean engine oil of the correct grade and type, some engine assembly lube (or moly-based grease) and a tube of RTV (silicone) sealant will also be required.

3 An engine support stand made from short lengths of 2 x 4's bolted together will facilitate the disassembly and reassembly procedures **(see illustration)**. If you have an automotive-type engine stand, an adapter plate can be made from a piece of plate, some angle iron and some nuts and bolts.

4 When disassembling the engine, keep "mated" parts together (including gears, rocker arms and shafts, etc.) that have been in contact with each other during engine operation. These "mated" parts must be reused or replaced as an assembly.

5 Engine/transmission disassembly should be done in the following general order with reference to the appropriate Sections.

Remove the cam chain tensioner
Remove the camshafts and lifters
Remove the cylinder head
Remove the cylinder
Remove the piston
Remove the clutch
Remove the balancer gears
Remove the oil pump
Remove the external shift mechanism
Remove the alternator rotor
Remove the starter reduction gears
Separate the crankcase halves
Remove the shift drum and forks
Remove the transmission gears and shafts
Remove the crankshaft and connecting rod

6 Reassembly is the reverse of disassembly.

9 Valve cover - removal and installation

1 Remove the seat, fuel tank and both side covers (see Chapters 4 and 8).

2 Remove the spark plug (see Chapter 1).

3 Disconnect the cylinder head breather hose from the valve cover.

4 Loosen the valve cover mounting bolts in several stages, in a criss-cross pattern, then remove them **(see illustrations)**.

5 Lift the valve cover off the cylinder head.

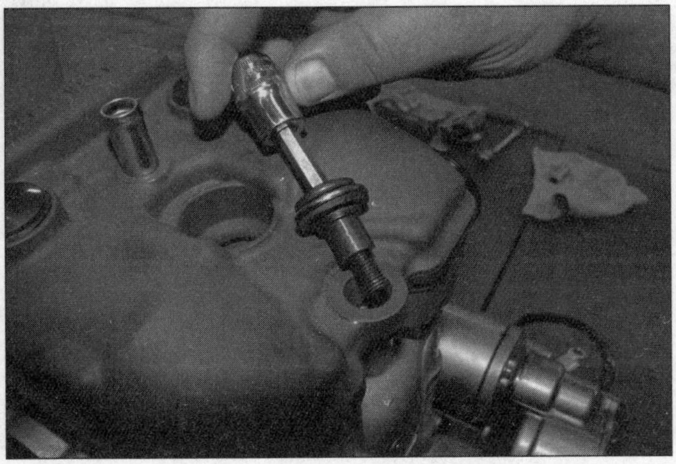

9.4b Front bolt collar and sealing washer locations

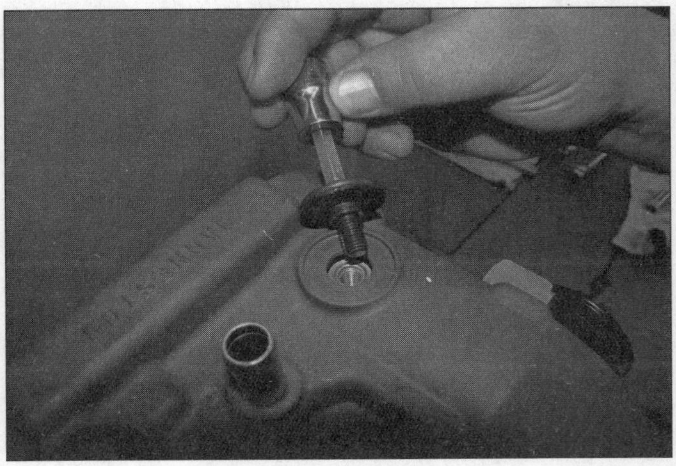

9.4c Rear bolt locations

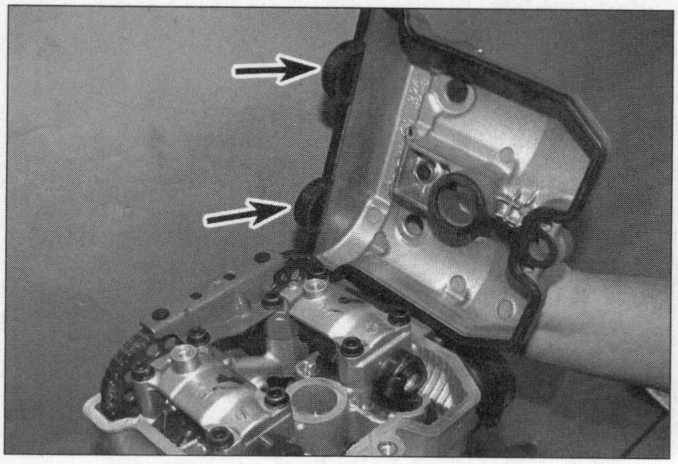

9.8 Apply non-hardening sealant to the semicircular portions of the gasket

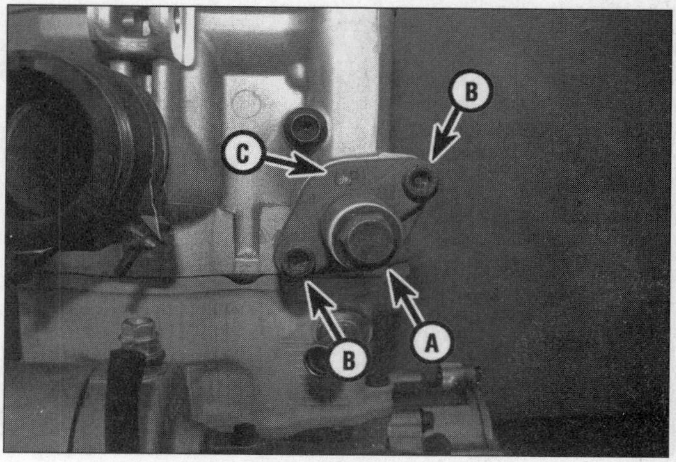

10.1 Cam chain tensioner details

A Cap bolt and washer
B Mounting bolts
C UP mark

If it's stuck, don't attempt to pry it off - tap around the sides of it with a plastic hammer to dislodge it. Remove the sealing washers if they didn't come off with the bolts.

6 Work the gasket free of the cylinder head and remove it.

7 Check the valve cover gasket for damage or deterioration and replace it as needed. It's a good idea to replace the bolt sealing washers whenever they're removed.

8 Installation is the reverse of removal, with the following additions:

a) Use non-hardening sealer to coat the area of the valve cover gasket that fits into the cylinder head cutouts **(see illustration).**

b) Install new sealing washers and tighten the valve cover bolts evenly to the torque listed in this Chapter's Specifications.

10 Cam chain tensioner - removal, inspection and installation

Removal

Caution: Once you start to remove the tensioner bolts you must remove the tensioner all the way and reset it before tightening the bolts. The tensioner extends and locks in place, so if you loosen the bolts partway and then tighten them, the tensioner or cam chain will be damaged.

1 Loosen the tensioner cap bolt **(see illustration)**.

2 Remove the tensioner mounting bolts and detach the tensioner from the cylinder **(see illustration)**. Remove the cap bolt, the sealing washer and spring **(see illustration)**.

Installation

3 Clean all old gasket material from the tensioner body and engine.

4 Place a new gasket on the tensioner body.

5 Pull back the tensioner pushrod latch with a finger and press the pushrod all the way in, then release to latch to lock the pushrod in the retracted position **(see illustration 10.2b and the accompanying illustration)**.

6 Position the tensioner body on the cylinder, making sure the UP mark is upward **(see illustration 10.1)**. Install the bolts, tightening them to the torque listed in this Chapter's Specifications.

7 Install the spring and cap bolt, using a new sealing washer **(see illustration 10.1)**. Tighten the cap bolt to the torque listed in this Chapter's Specifications.

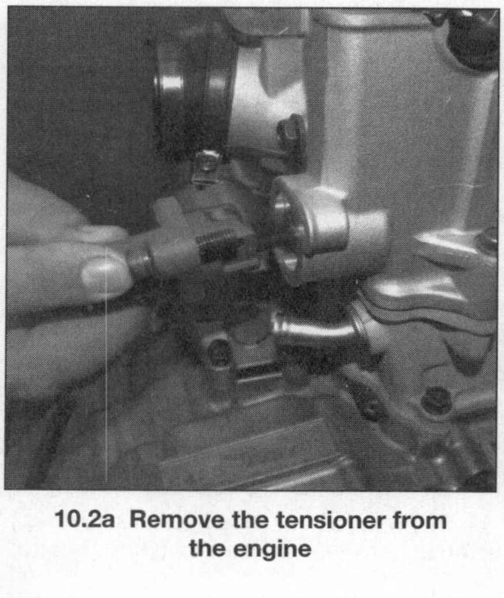

10.2a Remove the tensioner from the engine

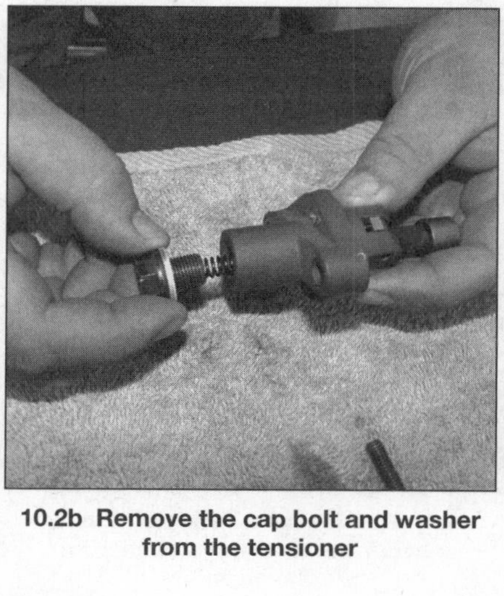

10.2b Remove the cap bolt and washer from the tensioner

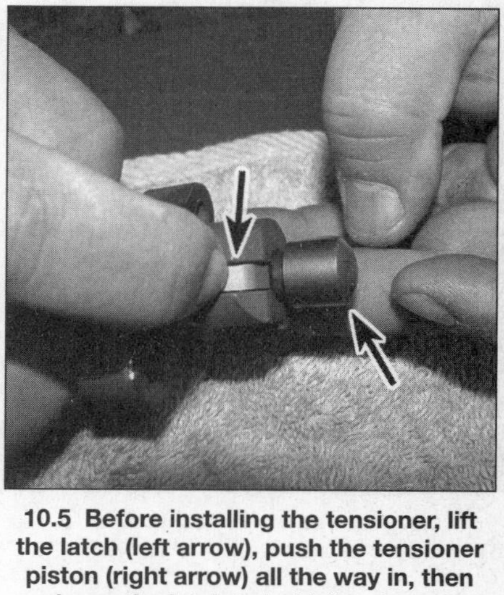

10.5 Before installing the tensioner, lift the latch (left arrow), push the tensioner piston (right arrow) all the way in, then release the latch to hold the piston in

11.5a Loosen the camshaft cap bolts in a criss-cross pattern . . .

11.5b . . . two of the bolts secure the upper chain guide

11.5c Lift the caps and locate the dowels on the intake side . . .

11 Camshafts and lifters - removal, inspection and installation

Removal

Camshafts

1 Remove the valve cover (see Section 9).

2 Place the engine at top dead center on the compression stroke (see Chapter 1, Section 24).

3 Remove the cam chain tensioner (see Section 10).

4 Tie the cam chain up with wire so it can't fall into the chain cavity.

5 Loosen the camshaft cap bolts in several stages, in a criss-cross pattern **(see illustration)**. Unbolt the upper cam chain guide and lift it out **(see illustration)**. Lift the caps off the camshafts and locate the dowels **(see illustrations)**. Put the dowels in a safe place so they won't drop into the engine. **Note:** *The caps are marked IN (intake) and EX (exhaust). If the marks aren't visible, make your own marks.*

6 Lift the intake camshaft out of its saddles and disengage the sprocket from the chain **(see illustration)**. Remove the exhaust camshaft in the same way. Unscrew the face bolt from the side of the cylinder head and remove it, together with its sealing washer **(see illustration)**.

HAYNES HiNT ***If you're removing the camshafts to adjust the valves, don't remove them all the way - you can just roll them out of their saddles (one at a time), leaving them attached to the chain. That way, you won't need to realign the timing marks when you install the camshafts.***

11.5d . . . and on the exhaust side

11.6a Roll the camshafts out of their saddles and disengage them from the chain

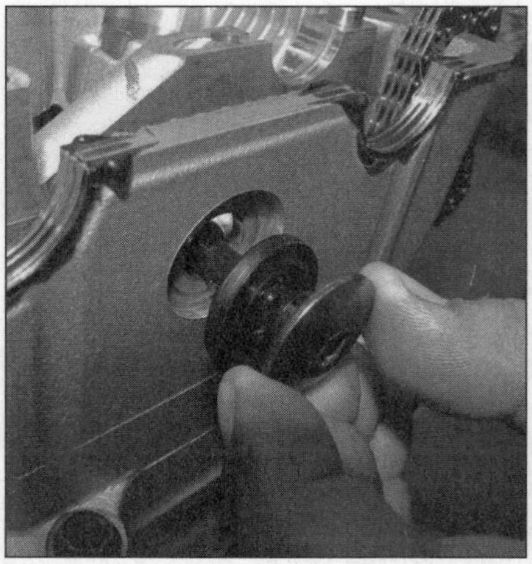

11.6b Remove the face bolt and sealing washer from the side of the cylinder head

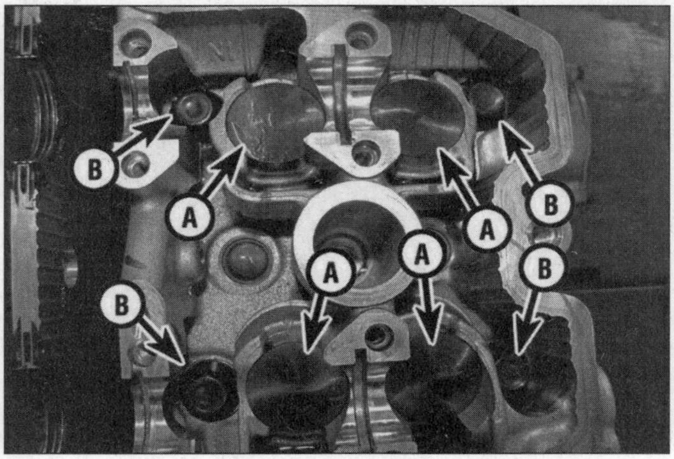

11.10a Lifter (A) and main head bolt (B) locations

11.10b Pull the lifters out of their bores with a magnet

Lifters

7 Stuff a clean shop rag into the timing chain cavity so the valve adjusting shims can't fall into it when they're removed.

8 Remove the camshafts (see Steps 1 through 6). Be sure to keep tension on the cam chain.

9 Make a holder for each lifter and its adjusting shim (an egg carton or box will work). Label the sections according to whether the lifter belongs with the intake or exhaust camshaft, and left or right valve. The lifters from a wear pattern with their bores and must be returned to their original locations if reused.

10 Label each lifter and pull each lifter out of the bore, using a magnet or suction cup **(see illustrations)**. The shims may stay with their lifters or remain on the valve stems. The shims are inside the lifters, so if they come out with the lifters, be careful not to let them fall as you lift the lifters out **(see illustration)**.

Cam chain and guides

11 The rear (intake side) chain guide is bolted at the bottom, so the right crankcase cover and clutch will have to be removed for access if the guide or the cam chain need to be removed. See Sections 19 and 21 for these procedures.

12 Stuff clean rags into the cam chain opening so dirt, small parts or tools can't fall into it.

Inspection

Camshaft, chain and guides

Note: *Before replacing camshafts or the cylinder head because of damage, check with local machine shops specializing in ATV engine work. In the case of the camshaft, it may be possible for cam lobes to be welded, reground and hardened, at a cost far lower than that of a new camshaft. If the bearing surfaces in the cylinder head are damaged, it may be possible for them to be bored out to accept bearing inserts. Due to the cost of a new cylinder head, it is recommended that all options be explored before condemning it as trash!*

13 Check the camshaft lobes for heat discoloration (blue appearance), score marks, chipped areas, flat spots and spalling. Measure the height of each lobe with a micrometer and compare the results to the minimum lobe height listed in this Chapter's Specifications. If damage is noted or wear is excessive, the camshaft must be replaced. Check the bearing surfaces for scoring or wear. Also, be sure to check the condition of the lifters (see Step 22).

14 Except in cases of oil starvation, the camshaft chain wears very little. If the chain has stretched excessively, which makes it difficult to maintain proper tension, replace it with a new one. To remove the chain from the crankshaft sprocket, remove the clutch (see Section 20).

15 Check the sprockets for wear, cracks and other damage, replacing it if necessary. If a sprocket is worn, the chain is also worn,

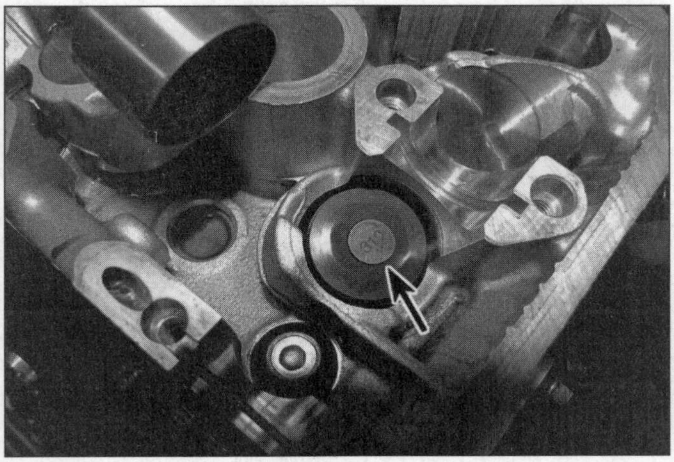

11.10c The valve adjusting shims may stay on top of the valves, as shown here . . .

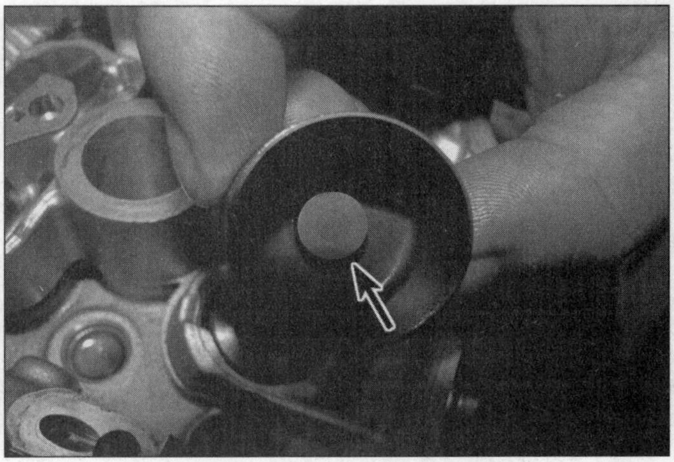

11.10d . . . or come off with the lifters

11.16 Check the chain guides for wear or damage

11.21 Check the contact surface of the compression release for wear or damage

and possibly the sprocket on the crankshaft. If wear this severe is apparent, the entire engine should be disassembled for inspection. The sprockets are permanently attached to the camshafts, so if the sprockets must be replaced, the camshafts must be replaced as well. The crankshaft sprocket can be removed if necessary (see Section 22).

16 Check the chain guides for wear or damage, especially along the friction surfaces **(see illustration)**. Use a flashlight to look down the cam chain tunnel at the intake side chain guide. If they are worn or damaged, replace them (see Section 21).

17 Check the camshaft bearing oil clearances with Plastigage, referring to *Tools and Workshop Tips* at the end of this manual.

18 Compare the results to this Chapter's Specifications.

19 If oil clearance is greater than specified, measure the diameter of the cam bearing journal with a micrometer. If the journal diameter is less than the specified limit, replace the camshaft with a new one and recheck the clearance.

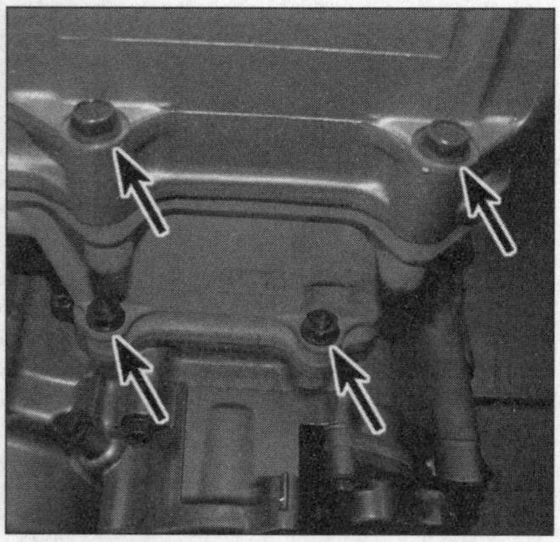

12.5 Cylinder head small bolt (upper arrows) and cylinder base nut (lower arrows) locations

20 If the clearance is still too great, replace the cylinder head and bearing caps with new parts (see the **Note** that precedes Step 13).

21 Check the automatic compression release in the left camshaft **(see illustration)**. Operate the lever on the sprocket end of the camshaft by hand. It should move smoothly, causing the plunger in the camshaft to extend. When released, it should return by itself. Also check the contact surface for wear. If the compression release doesn't work properly, replace the camshaft.

Lifters

22 Check the lifters and their bores for wear, scuff marks, scratches and other damage. Check the camshaft contact surface, as well as the outer surface that rides in the bore. Replace the lifters if they're visibly worn or damaged.

Installation

23 Make sure the piston is still at Top Dead Center on the compression stroke (refer to the valve adjustment procedure in Chapter 1 if necessary).

24 Coat the lifters and their bores with clean engine oil. Apply a small amount of moly-based grease to the shims and stick them to their respective valve stems with the thickness number upward.

25 Slide the lifters into their bores, taking care not to knock the valve shims out of position. When the lifters are correctly installed, it should be possible to rotate them with a finger.

26 Coat the camshaft contact surfaces of the lifters and the bearing surfaces of the camshafts with moly-based grease.

27 Install the exhaust camshaft, then the intake camshaft in the cylinder head, engaging the sprocket with the chain as you do so, and make sure the sprockets are in the correct positions (see Chapter 1). Install the cap dowels in their holes (if they were removed).

28 Install the camshaft bearing caps. Tighten the cap bolts in stages, in a criss-cross pattern, to the torque listed in this Chapter's Specifications.

Caution: The caps must be tightened in the proper sequence with an accurate torque wrench, or the camshafts may seize.

29 Install the cam chain tensioner (see Section 10). Release the tensioner so its piston presses against the chain.

30 Recheck the crankshaft timing mark in the timing hole cover and the match marks on both camshafts. If they are not still aligned, stop and find out why before continuing.

Caution: Don't run the engine with the marks misaligned or the valves may strike the pistons, bending the valves.

31 Rotate the crankshaft two full turns and make sure the timing marks still line up correctly.

32 Check the valve clearances (see Chapter 1). This is necessary to make sure none of the shims has slipped out of position.

33 Change the engine oil (see Chapter 1).

34 The remainder of installation is the reverse of removal.

12 Cylinder head - removal, inspection and installation

Removal

1 Drain the cooling system (see Chapter 1).

2 Remove the seat, side covers and fuel tank cover (see Chapter 8).

3 Remove the fuel tank, carburetor or throttle body and exhaust system (see Chapter 4).

4 Remove the valve cover and camshafts (see Sections 9 and 11).

5 Remove the two bolts that secure the left-hand side of the cylinder head **(see illustration)**.

6 Loosen the four main head bolts in several stages, in a criss-cross pattern, until they're completely loose **(see illustration 11.10a)**. Lift out the bolts and their washers **(see illustration)**.

7 Lift the cylinder head off the cylinder **(see illustration)**. If it's stuck, don't attempt to pry it off - tap around the sides of it with a plastic hammer to dislodge it.

8 Locate the dowels **(see illustration 12.7)**. There are two of them, one in each of the head bolt holes nearest the timing chain. The dowels may be in the cylinder or they may have come off with the head.

9 Remove the old head gasket from the cylinder or head.

12.6 Remove the head bolts and their washers

12.7 Locate the dowels

Inspection

10 Check the cylinder head gasket and the mating surfaces on the cylinder head and cylinder for leakage, which could indicate warpage.

11 Check the flatness of the cylinder head (see Section 14).

12 Clean all traces of old gasket material from the cylinder head and cylinder. Be careful not to let any of the gasket material fall into the crankcase, the cylinder bore or the bolt holes.

Installation

13 Install the two dowel pins, then place the new head gasket on the cylinder **(see illustration 12.7)**. Never reuse the old gasket and don't use any type of gasket sealant.

HAYNES HiNT ***The head gasket will line up almost exactly with the coolant passages and bolt holes if it's installed upside down. Make sure the coolant passages and bolt holes line up exactly.***

14 Install the exhaust side cam chain guide, fitting the lower end and the middle guide into their notches **(see illustration 21.1)**.

HAYNES HiNT ***Don't forget to install the chain guide at this point. It won't be possible to install it once the cylinder head is installed.***

15 Carefully lower the cylinder head over the dowels, guiding the cam chain through the slot in the cylinder head. It's helpful to have an assistant support the cam chain with a piece of wire so it doesn't fall and become kinked or detached from the crankshaft. When the head is resting on the cylinder, wire the cam chain to another component to keep tension on it.

16 Lubricate the threads and seating surfaces of the four main cylinder head bolts with clean engine oil. Lubricate the upper and lower sides of the head bolt washers with the same grease.

17 Install the washers on the four main head bolts and install the bolts finger-tight. Tighten the four bolts in a criss-cross pattern, in several stages, to the initial torque listed in this Chapter's Specifications.

18 Loosen the bolts all the way, again in a criss-cross pattern. Retighten them to the second-step torque setting listed in this Chapter's Specifications, then tighten them exactly 1/2 turn further.

19 After the main nuts or bolts are tightened, tighten the two Allen bolts to the torque listed in this Chapter's Specifications.

20 The remainder of installation is the reverse of removal.

13 Valves/valve seats/valve guides - servicing

1 Because of the complex nature of this job and the special tools and equipment required, servicing of the valves, the valve seats and the valve guides (commonly known as a valve job) is best left to a professional.

2 The home mechanic can, however, remove and disassemble the head, do the initial cleaning and inspection, then reassemble and deliver the head to a dealer service department or properly equipped vehicle repair shop for the actual valve servicing. Refer to Section 14 for those procedures.

3 The dealer service department will remove the valves and springs, recondition or replace the valves and valve seats, replace the valve guides, check and replace the valve springs, spring retainers and keepers (as necessary), replace the valve seals with new ones and reassemble the valve components.

4 After the valve job has been performed, the head will be in like-new condition. When the head is returned, be sure to clean it again very thoroughly before installation on the engine to remove any metal particles or abrasive grit that may still be present from the valve service operations. Use compressed air, if available, to blow out all the holes and passages.

14 Cylinder head and valves - disassembly, inspection and reassembly

1 As mentioned in the previous Section, valve servicing and valve guide replacement should be left to a dealer service department or other repair shop. However, disassembly, cleaning and inspection of the valves and related components can be done (if the necessary special tools are available) by the home mechanic. This way no expense is incurred if the inspection reveals that service work is not required.

2 To properly disassemble the valve components without the risk of damaging them, a valve spring compressor is absolutely necessary. If the special tool is not available, have a dealer service department or vehicle repair shop handle the entire process of disassembly, inspection, service or repair (if required) and reassembly of the valves.

Disassembly

3 Before the valves are removed, scrape away any traces of gasket material from the head gasket sealing surface. Work slowly and do not nick or gouge the soft aluminum of the head. Gasket removing solvents, which work very well, are available at most motorcycle shops and auto parts stores.

4 Carefully scrape all carbon deposits out of the combustion chamber area. A hand held wire brush or a piece of fine emery cloth can be used once most of the deposits have been scraped away. Do not use a wire brush mounted in a drill motor, or one with extremely stiff bristles, as the head material is soft and may be eroded away or scratched by the wire brush.

5 Before proceeding, arrange to label and store the valves along with their related components so they can be kept separate and reinstalled in the same valve guides they are removed from (plastic bags work well for this).

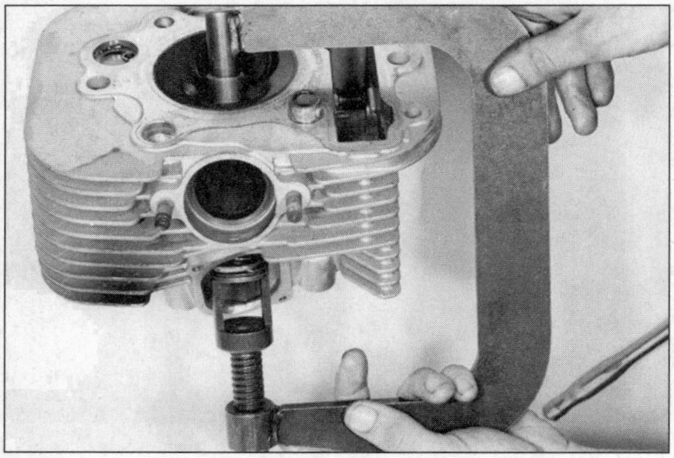

14.6a Compress the valve springs with a valve spring compressor

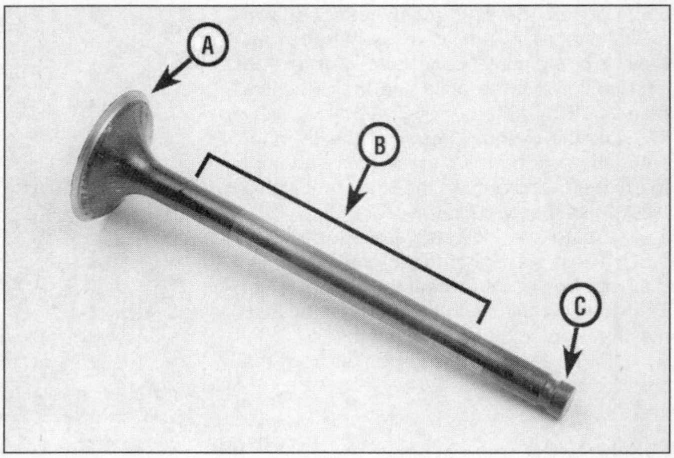

14.6b Check the valve face (A), stem (B) and keeper groove (C) for wear and damage

6 Compress the valve spring(s) on the first valve with a spring compressor, then remove the keepers and the retainer from the valve assembly **(see illustration)**. Do not compress the spring(s) any more than is absolutely necessary. Carefully release the valve spring compressor and remove the spring(s), spring seat and valve from the head. If the valve binds in the guide (won't pull through), push it back into the head and deburr the area around the keeper groove with a very fine file or whetstone **(see illustration)**.

7 Repeat the procedure for the remaining valve. Remember to keep the parts for each valve together so they can be reinstalled in the same location.

8 Once the valves have been removed and labeled, pull off the valve stem seals with pliers and discard them (the old seals should never be reused).

9 Next, clean the cylinder head with solvent and dry it thoroughly. Compressed air will speed the drying process and ensure that all holes and recessed areas are clean.

10 Clean all of the valve springs, keepers, retainers and spring seats with solvent and dry them thoroughly. Clean the parts from one valve at a time so that no mixing of parts between valves occurs.

11 Scrape off any deposits that may have formed on the valve, then use a motorized wire brush to remove deposits from the valve heads and stems. Again, make sure the valves do not get mixed up.

Inspection

12 Inspect the head very carefully for cracks and other damage. If cracks are found, a new head will be required. Check the cam bearing surfaces for wear and evidence of seizure. Check the camshaft for wear as well (see Section 9).

13 Using a precision straightedge and a feeler gauge, check the head gasket mating surface for warpage as described in *Tools and Workshop Tips* at the end of this manual. If the head is warped, it must either be machined or, if warpage is excessive (see this Chapter's Specifications), replaced with a new one.

14 Examine the valve seats in each of the combustion chambers. If they are pitted, cracked or burned, the head will require valve service that is beyond the scope of the home mechanic. Measure the valve seat width and compare it to this Chapter's Specifications. If it is not within the specified range, or if it varies around its circumference, valve service work is required.

15 Clean the valve guides to remove any carbon buildup, then measure the inside diameters of the guides (at both ends and the center of the guide) as described in *Tools and Workshop Tips* at the end of this manual. Record the measurements for future reference. The guides are measured at the ends and at the center to determine if they are worn in a bell-mouth pattern (more wear at the ends). If they are, guide replacement is an absolute must.

16 Carefully inspect each valve face for cracks, pits and burned spots. Check the valve stem and the keeper groove area for cracks **(see illustration 14.6b)**. Rotate the valve and check for any obvious indication that it is bent. Check the end of the stem for pitting and excessive wear and make sure the bevel is the specified width. The presence of any of the above conditions indicates the need for valve servicing.

17 Measure the valve stem diameter with a micrometer. If the diameter is less than listed in this Chapter's Specifications, the valves will have to be replaced with new ones. Also check the valve stem for bending. Set the valve in a V-block with a dial indicator touching the middle of the stem. Rotate the valve and look for a reading on the gauge (which indicates a bent stem). If the stem is bent, replace the valve.

18 Check the end of each valve spring for wear and pitting. Measure the free length **(see illustration)** and compare it to this Chapter's Specifications. Any springs that are shorter than specified have sagged and should not be reused. Stand the spring on a flat surface and check it for squareness **(see illustration)**.

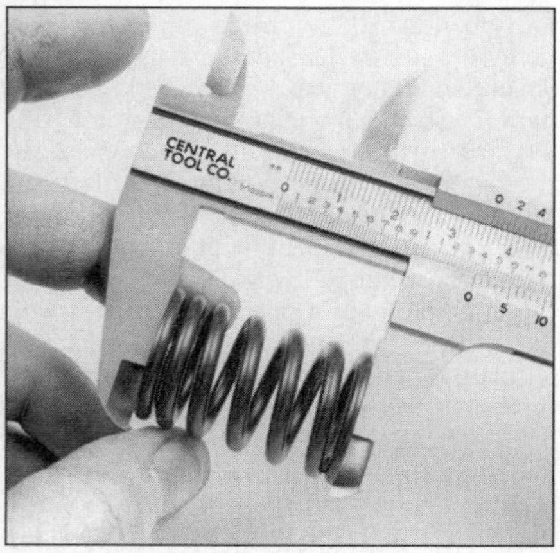

14.18a Measuring the free length of the valve springs

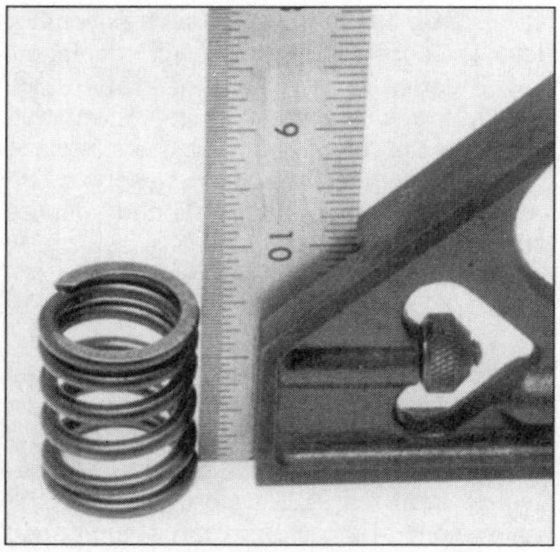

14.18b Checking the valve springs for squareness

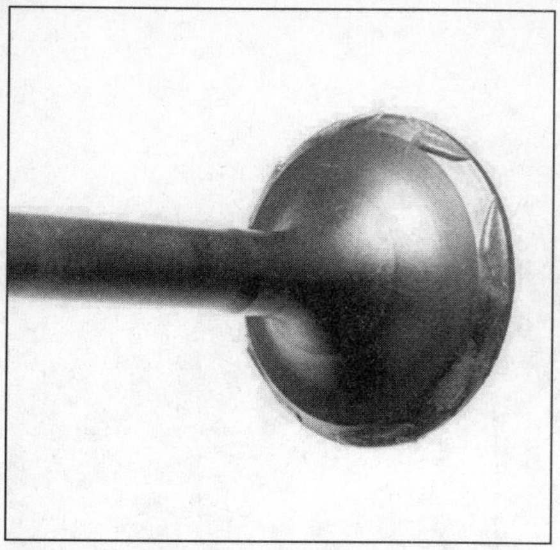

14.22 Apply the lapping compound very sparingly, in small dabs, to the valve face

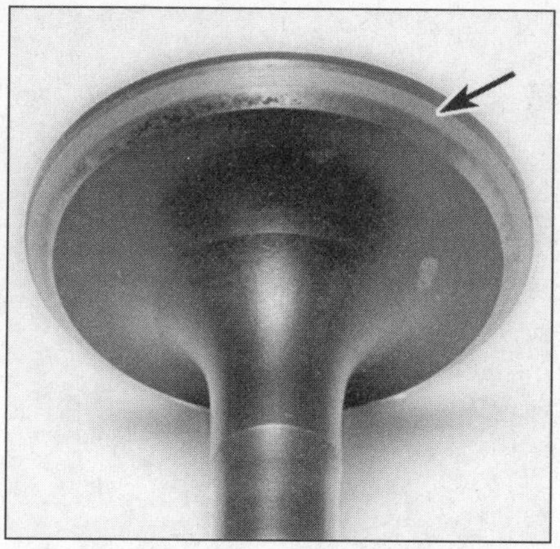

14.23 After lapping, the valve face should have a uniform, unbroken contact pattern (arrow)

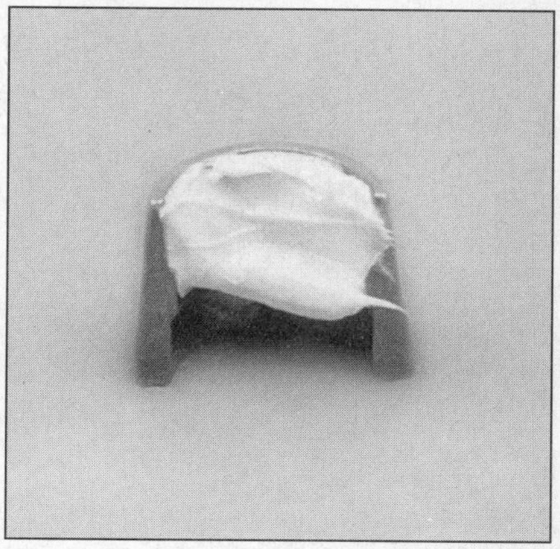

14.26 A small dab of grease will help hold the keepers in place on the valve while the spring compressor is released

19 Check the spring retainers and keepers for obvious wear and cracks. Any questionable parts should not be reused, as extensive damage will occur in the event of failure during engine operation.
20 If the inspection indicates that no service work is required, the valve components can be reinstalled in the head.

Reassembly

21 If the valve seats have been ground, the valves and seats should be lapped before installing the valves in the head to ensure a positive seal between the valves and seats. This procedure requires coarse and fine valve lapping compound (available at auto parts stores) and a valve lapping tool. If a lapping tool is not available, a piece of rubber or plastic hose can be slipped over the valve stem (after the valve has been installed in the guide) and used to turn the valve.
22 Apply a small amount of coarse lapping compound to the valve face **(see illustration)**, then slip the valve into the guide. **Note:** *Make sure the valve is installed in the correct guide and be careful not to get any lapping compound on the valve stem.*
23 Attach the lapping tool (or hose) to the valve and rotate the tool between the palms of your hands. Use a back-and-forth motion rather than a circular motion. Lift the valve off the seat and turn it at regular intervals to distribute the lapping compound properly. Continue the lapping procedure until the valve face and seat contact area is of uniform width and unbroken around the entire circumference of the valve face and seat **(see illustration)**. Once this is accomplished, lap the valves again with fine lapping compound.
24 Carefully remove the valve from the guide and wipe off all traces of lapping compound. Use solvent to clean the valve and wipe the seat area thoroughly with a solvent soaked cloth. Repeat the procedure for the remaining valves.
25 Lay the spring seat in place in the cylinder head, then install new valve stem seals on both of the guides. Use an appropriate size deep socket to push the seals into place until they are properly seated. Don't twist or cock them, or they will not seal properly against the valve stems. Also, don't remove them again or they will be damaged.
26 Coat the valve stems with assembly lube or moly-based grease, then install one of them into its guide. Next, install the spring seat, springs and retainers, compress the springs and install the keepers. **Note:** *Install the springs with the tightly wound coils at the bottom (next to the spring seat).* When compressing the springs with the valve spring compressor, depress them only as far as is absolutely necessary to slip the keepers into place. Apply a small amount of grease to the keepers **(see illustration)** to help hold them in place as the pressure is released from the springs. Make certain that the keepers are securely locked in their retaining grooves.
27 Support the cylinder head on blocks so the valves can't contact the workbench top, then very gently tap each of the valve stems with a soft-faced hammer. This will help seat the keepers in their grooves.
28 Once all of the valves have been installed in the head, check for proper valve sealing by pouring a small amount of solvent into each of the valve ports. If the solvent leaks past the valve(s) into the combustion chamber area, disassemble the valve(s) and repeat the lapping procedure, then reinstall the valve(s) and repeat the check. Repeat the procedure until a satisfactory seal is obtained.

15 Cylinder - removal, inspection and installation

Removal

1 Remove the cylinder head (see Section 12). Make sure the crankshaft is positioned at Top Dead Center (TDC).
2 Lift out the cam chain front guide **(see illustrations 21.3a and 21.3b)**.
3 Remove the nuts securing the base of the cylinder to the crankcase **(see illustration 12.5)**.
4 Lift the cylinder straight up to remove it **(see illustration)**. If it's stuck, tap around its perimeter with a soft-faced hammer. Don't

15.4 Lift the cylinder off the piston

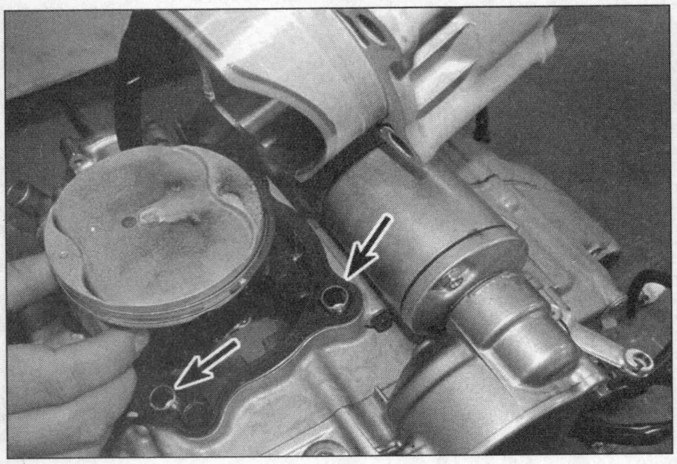

15.5a Locate the dowels

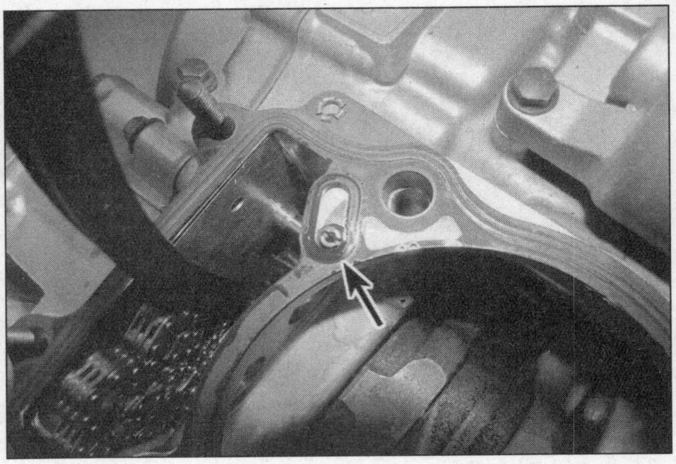

15.5b Check the oil jet for clogging - it's a good idea to remove and clean it

attempt to pry between the cylinder and the crankcase, as you'll ruin the sealing surfaces.

5 Locate the dowel pins (they may have come off with the cylinder or still be in the crankcase) **(see illustration)**. There are two dowels, located opposite the timing chain cavity. Be careful not to let these drop into the engine. Stuff rags around the piston and remove the gasket and all traces of old gasket material from the surfaces of the cylinder and the crankcase. Do not let anything block the cylinder oil jet in the crankcase **(see illustration)**.

Inspection

6 Don't attempt to separate the liner from the cylinder.

7 Check the cylinder walls carefully for scratches and score marks. The manufacturers don't specify a maximum bore limit, but if scratches and score marks are so deep they can't be removed without honing the cylinder beyond the upper diameter listed in this Chapter's Specifications, the cylinder should be replaced with a new one.

8 Using the appropriate precision measuring tools, check the cylinder's diameter. Measure parallel to the crankshaft axis and across the crankshaft axis, at the depth from the top of the cylinder listed in this Chapter's Specifications. Average the two measurements and compare the results to this Chapter's Specifications. If the cylinder walls are tapered, out-of-round, worn beyond the specified limits, or badly scuffed or scored, have the cylinder rebored and honed by a dealer service department or a motorcycle repair shop. If a rebore is done, an oversize piston and rings will be required as well. Check with your dealer service department about available oversizes.

9 As an alternative, if the precision measuring tools are not available, a dealer service department or repair shop will make the measurements and offer advice concerning servicing of the cylinder.

10 If it's in reasonably good condition and not worn to the outside of the limits, and if the piston-to-cylinder clearance can be maintained properly, then the cylinder does not have to be rebored; honing is all that is necessary.

11 To perform the honing operation, you will need the proper size flexible hone with fine stones as shown *in Maintenance techniques, tools and working facilities* at the front of this book, or a bottle brush type hone, plenty of light oil or honing oil, some shop towels and an electric drill motor. Hold the cylinder block in a vise (cushioned with soft jaws or wood blocks) when performing the honing operation. Mount the hone in the drill motor, compress the stones and slip the hone into the cylinder. Lubricate the cylinder thoroughly, turn on the drill and move the hone up and down in the cylinder at a pace which will produce a fine crosshatch pattern on the cylinder wall with the crosshatch lines intersecting at approximately a 60-degree angle. Be sure to use plenty of lubricant and do not take off any more material than is absolutely necessary to produce the desired effect. Do not withdraw the hone from the cylinder while it is running. Instead, shut off the drill and continue moving the hone up and down in the cylinder until it comes to a complete stop, then compress the stones and withdraw the hone. Wipe the oil out of the cylinder and repeat the procedure on the remaining cylinder. Remember, do not remove too much material from the cylinder wall. If you do not have the tools, or do not desire to perform the honing operation, a dealer service department or vehicle repair shop will generally do it for a reasonable fee.

12 Next, the cylinder must be thoroughly washed with warm soapy water to remove all traces of the abrasive grit produced during the honing operation. Be sure to run a brush through the bolt holes and flush them with running water. After rinsing, dry the cylinder thoroughly and apply a coat of light, rust-preventative oil to all machined surfaces.

Installation

13 Lubricate the cylinder bore with plenty of clean engine oil. Apply a thin film of moly-based grease to the piston skirt.

14 Install the dowel pins (and O-ring on the large dowel), then slip a new cylinder base gasket over them **(see illustration 15.5a)**.

15 Attach a piston ring compressor to the piston and compress the piston rings. A large hose clamp can be used instead - just make sure it doesn't scratch the piston, and don't tighten it too much.

16 Install the cylinder and carefully lower it down until the piston crown fits into the cylinder liner **(see illustration 15.4)**. While doing this, pull the camshaft chain up, using a hooked tool or a piece of stiff wire. Push down on the cylinder, making sure the piston doesn't get cocked sideways, until the bottom of the cylinder liner slides down past the piston rings. A wood or plastic hammer handle can be used to gently tap the cylinder down, but don't use too much force or the piston will be damaged.

17 Remove the piston ring compressor or hose clamp, being careful not to scratch the piston.

18 The remainder of installation is the reverse of removal.

16 Piston - removal, inspection and installation

1 The piston is attached to the connecting rod with a piston pin that's a slip fit in the piston and rod.

2 Before removing the piston from the rod, stuff a clean shop towel into the crankcase hole, around the connecting rod. This will prevent the snap-rings from falling into the crankcase if they are inadvertently dropped.

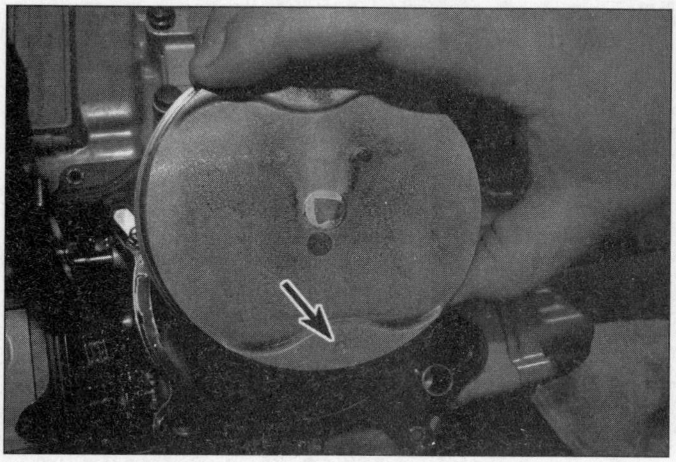

16.3a There should be a punch mark to indicate the exhaust side of the piston - if not, make your own mark

16.3b Wear eye protection and remove the snap-ring from its groove with snap-ring pliers

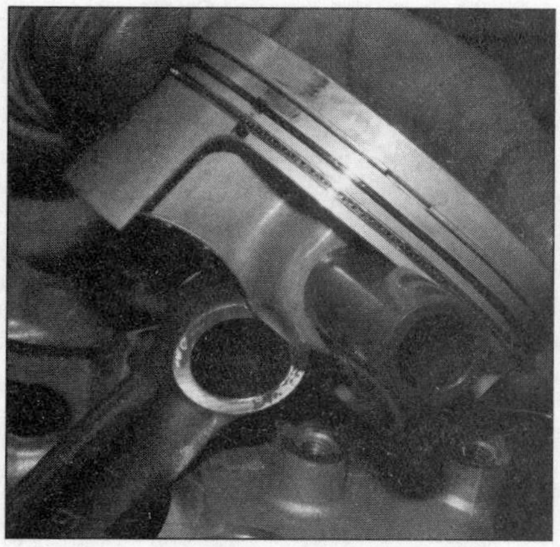

16.4 The piston pin should come out with hand pressure - if it doesn't, a drawbolt-type removal tool can be fabricated from readily available parts

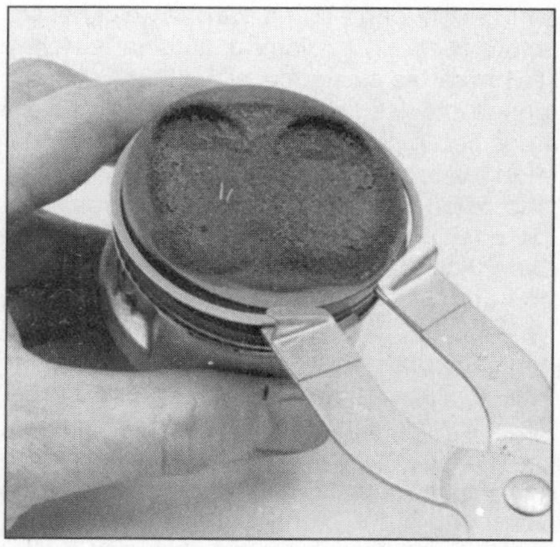

16.6 Remove the piston rings with a ring removal and installation tool

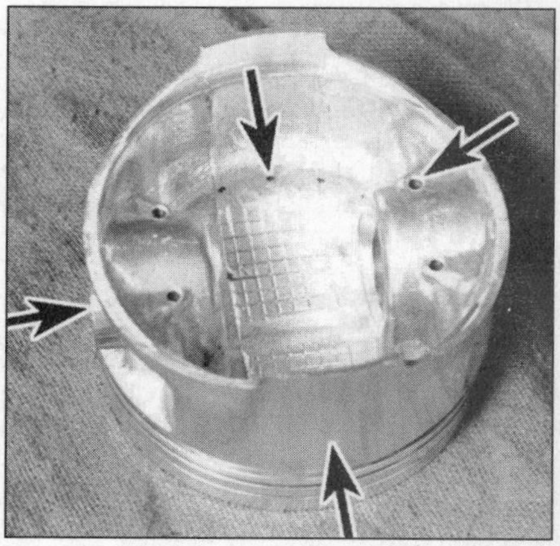

16.11 Check the piston pin bore and the piston skirt for wear, and make sure the internal holes are clear

Removal

3 The piston should have a punch mark on its crown toward the exhaust (front) side of the engine **(see illustration)**. If this mark is not visible due to carbon buildup, make your own mark with a felt pen or sharp punch. Support the piston and remove the snap-ring with snap-ring pliers **(see illustration)**.

4 Push the piston pin out from the opposite end to free the piston from the rod **(see illustration)**. You may have to deburr the area around the groove to enable the pin to slide out (use a triangular file for this procedure). If the pin won't come out, you can fabricate a drawbolt piston pin removal tool from a long bolt, a nut, a piece of tubing and washers (refer to *Tools and Workshop Tips* at the end of this manual).

Inspection

5 Before inspection can be carried out, the piston must be cleaned and the old piston rings removed.

6 Using a piston ring removal and installation tool, carefully remove the rings from the piston **(see illustration)**. Do not nick or gouge the piston in the process.

7 Scrape all traces of carbon from the top of the piston. A hand-held wire brush or a piece of fine emery cloth can be used once the majority of the deposits have been scraped away. Do not, under any circumstances, use a wire brush mounted in a drill motor to remove deposits from the piston; the piston material is soft and will be eroded away by the wire brush.

8 Use a piston ring groove cleaning tool to remove any carbon deposits from the ring grooves. If a tool is not available, a piece broken off the old ring will do the job. Be very careful to remove only the carbon deposits. Do not remove any metal and do not nick or gouge the sides of the ring grooves.

9 Once the deposits have been removed, clean the piston with solvent and dry it thoroughly. Make sure the oil return holes below the oil ring grooves are clear.

10 If the piston is not damaged or worn excessively and if the cylinder is not rebored, a new piston will not be necessary. Normal piston wear appears as even, vertical wear on the thrust surfaces of the piston and slight looseness of the top ring in its groove. New piston rings, on the other hand, should always be used when an engine is rebuilt.

11 Carefully inspect each piston for cracks around the skirt, at the pin bosses and at the ring lands **(see illustration)**.

12 Look for scoring and scuffing on the thrust faces of the skirt, holes in the piston crown and burned areas at the edge of the crown. If the skirt is scored or scuffed, the engine may have been suffering from overheating and/or abnormal combustion, which caused excessively high operating temperatures. The oil pump should be checked thoroughly. A hole in the piston crown, an extreme to be sure, is an indication that abnormal combustion (pre-ignition) was occurring. Burned areas at the edge of the piston crown are usually evidence of spark

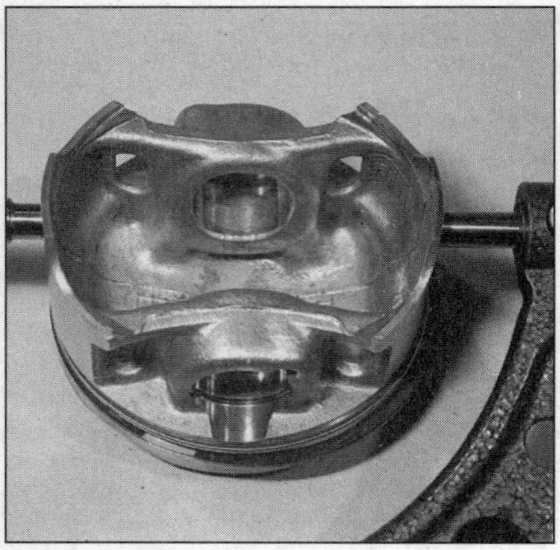

16.14 Measure the piston diameter with a micrometer

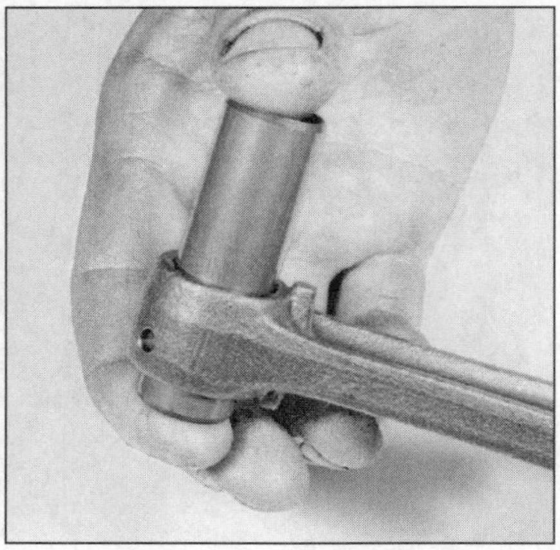

16.16 Slip the piston pin into the connecting rod and check for looseness

knock (detonation). If any of the above problems exist, the causes must be corrected or the damage will occur again.

13 Measure the piston ring-to-groove clearance (side clearance) by laying a new piston ring in the ring groove and slipping a feeler gauge in beside it. Check the clearance at three or four locations around the groove. Be sure to use the correct ring for each groove; they are different. If the clearance is greater then specified, a new piston will have to be used when the engine is reassembled.

14 Check the piston-to-bore clearance by measuring the bore (see Section 15) and the piston diameter **(see illustration)**. Measure the piston across the skirt on the thrust faces at a 90-degree angle to the piston pin, at the specified distance up from the bottom of the skirt. Subtract the piston diameter from the bore diameter to obtain the clearance. If it is greater than specified, the cylinder will have to be rebored and a new oversized piston and rings installed. If the appropriate precision measuring tools are not available, the piston-to-cylinder clearance can be obtained, though not quite as accurately, using feeler gauge stock. Feeler gauge stock comes in 12-inch lengths and various thicknesses and is generally available at auto parts stores. To check the clearance, slip a piece of feeler gauge stock of the same thickness as the specified piston clearance into the cylinder along with appropriate piston. The cylinder should be upside down and the piston must be positioned exactly as it normally would be. Place the feeler gauge between the piston and cylinder on one of the thrust faces (90-degrees to the piston pin bore). The piston should slip through the cylinder (with the feeler gauge in place) with moderate pressure. If it falls through, or slides through easily, the clearance is excessive and a new piston will be required. If the piston binds at the lower end of the cylinder and is loose toward the top, the cylinder is tapered, and if tight spots are encountered as the piston/feeler gauge is rotated in the cylinder, the cylinder is out-of-round. Be sure to have the cylinder and piston checked by a dealer service department or a repair shop to confirm your findings before purchasing new parts.

15 Apply clean engine oil to the pin, insert it into the piston and check for freeplay by rocking the pin back-and-forth. If the pin is loose, a new piston and possibly new pin must be installed.

16 Repeat Step 15, this time inserting the piston pin into the connecting rod **(see illustration)**. If the pin is loose, measure the pin diameter and the pin bore in the rod (or have this done by a dealer or repair shop). A worn pin can be replaced separately; if the rod bore is worn, the rod and crankshaft must be replaced as an assembly.

17 Refer to Section 17 and install the rings on the piston.

Installation

18 Install the piston with its punch mark toward the exhaust side (front) of the engine. Lubricate the pin and the rod bore with moly-based grease. Install a new snap-rings in the groove in one side of the piston (don't reuse the old snap-rings). Push the pin into position from the opposite side and install another new snap-ring. Compress the snap-rings only enough for them to fit in the piston. Make sure the snap-rings are properly seated in the grooves **(see illustration)**.

17 Piston rings - installation

1 Before installing the new piston rings, the ring end gaps must be checked.

2 Insert the top (No. 1) ring into the bottom of the first cylinder and square it up with the cylinder walls by pushing it in with the top of the piston. The ring should be about one-half inch above the bottom edge of the cylinder. To measure the end gap, slip a feeler gauge between the ends of the ring **(see illustration)** and compare the measurement to the Specifications.

3 If the gap is larger or smaller than specified, double check to make sure that you have the correct rings before proceeding.

16.18 Make sure both piston pin snap-rings are securely seated in the piston grooves

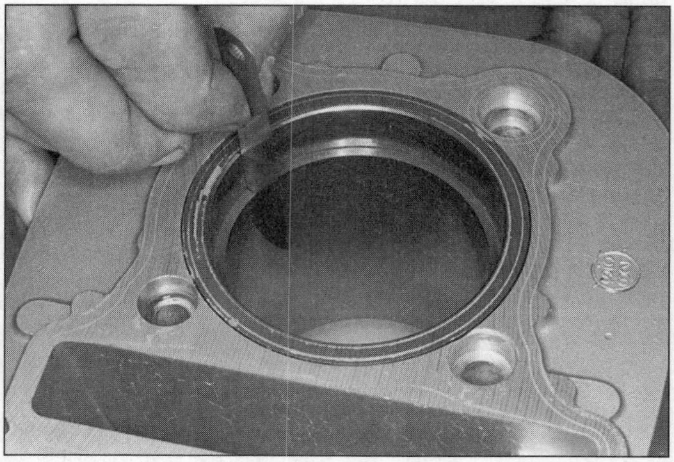

17.2 Check the piston ring end gap with a feeler gauge at the bottom of the ring travel area

17.4 If the end gap is too small, clamp a file in a vise and file the ring ends (from the outside in only) to enlarge the gap slightly

17.7a Installing the oil ring expander - make sure the ends don't overlap

4 If the gap is too small, it must be enlarged or the ring ends may come in contact with each other during engine operation, which can cause serious damage. The end gap can be increased by filing the ring ends very carefully with a fine file **(see illustration)**. When performing this operation, file only from the outside in.

5 Repeat the procedure for the second compression ring (ring gap is not specified for the oil ring rails or spacer).

6 Once the ring end gaps have been checked/corrected, the rings can be installed on the piston.

7 The oil control ring (lowest on the piston) is installed first. It is composed of three separate components. Slip the spacer into the groove, then install the upper side rail **(see illustrations)**. Do not use a piston ring installation tool on the oil ring side rails as they may be damaged. Instead, place one end of the side rail into the groove between the spacer expander and the ring land. Hold it firmly in place and slide a finger around the piston while pushing the rail into the groove (taking care not to cut your fingers on the sharp edges). Next, install the lower side rail in the same manner.

Caution: Be sure the ends of the oil ring spacer butt against each other and don't overlap.

8 After the three oil ring components have been installed, check to make sure that both the upper and lower side rails can be turned smoothly in the ring groove.

9 Install the no. 2 (middle) ring next with its identification mark facing up **(see illustration)**. Do not mix the top and middle rings; their profiles are slightly different, but the difference can be hard to see. The most important indicator is the ring thickness. The top ring is thicker than the second ring. On a new piston, the top ring will not fit into the second ring's groove. If you're not sure which ring is which, measure their thicknesses with a micrometer.

10 To avoid breaking the ring, use a piston ring installation tool and make sure that the identification mark is facing up. Fit the ring into the middle groove on the piston. Do not expand the ring any more than is necessary to slide it into place.

11 Finally, install the no. 1 (top) ring in the same manner. Make sure the identifying mark is facing up. Be very careful not to confuse the top and second rings.

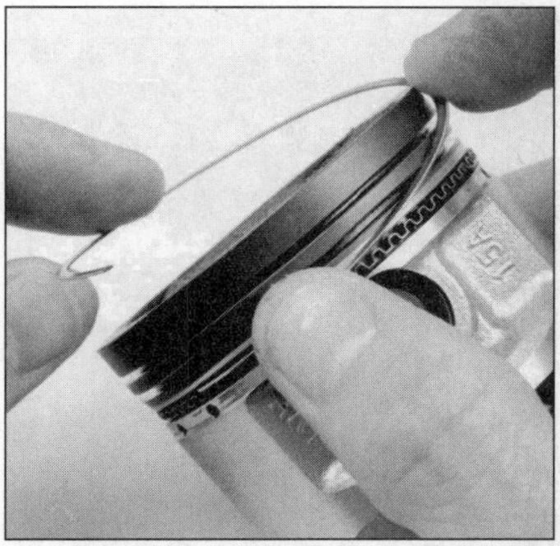

17.7b Installing an oil ring side rail - don't use a ring installation tool to do this

12 Once the rings have been properly installed, stagger the end gaps, including those of the oil ring side rails **(see illustration)**.

17.9 Install the middle ring with its identification mark up

17.12 Arrange the ring gaps like this

A *Oil ring spacer*
B *Oil ring upper rail*
C *Oil ring lower rail*
D *Second compression ring*
E *Top compression ring*

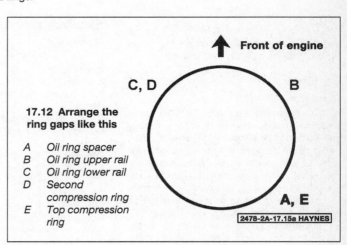

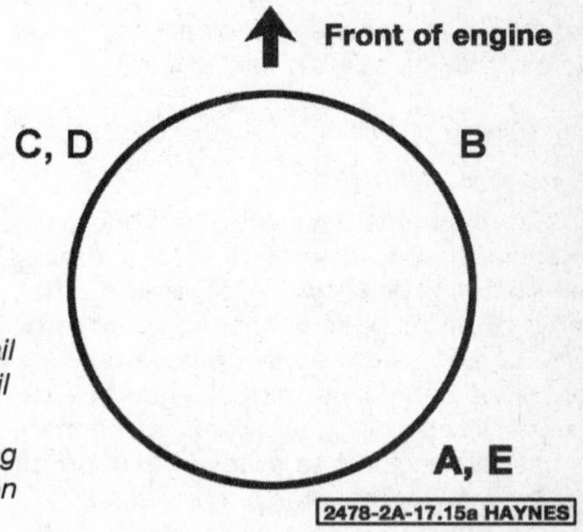

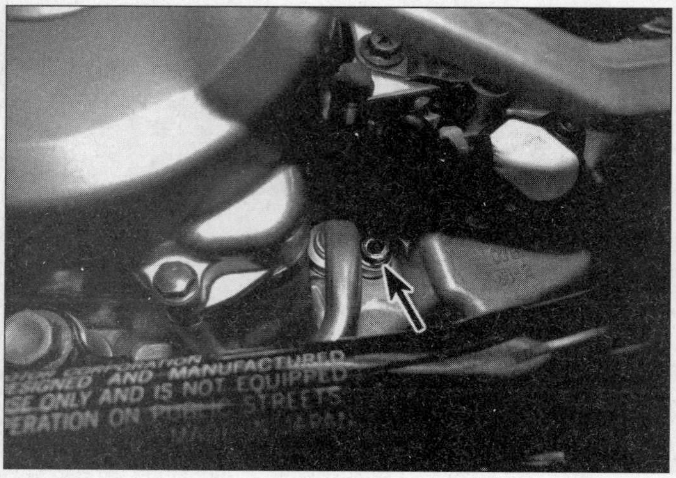

18.2a Remove the oil line bolt

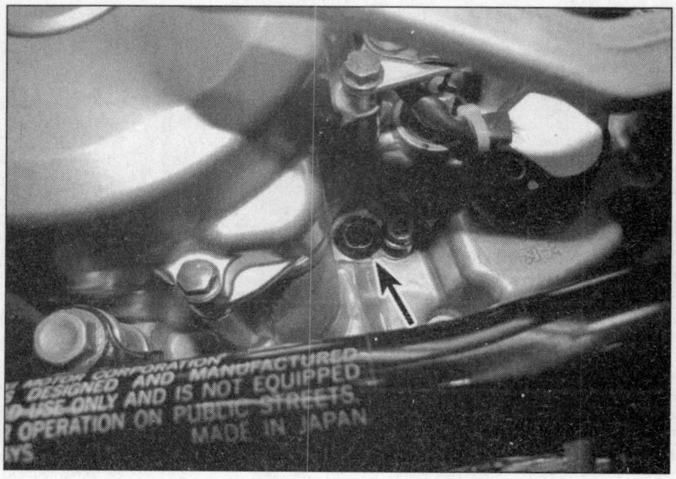

18.2b Disconnect the oil line from the engine and remove the O-ring

18.2c Remove the oil line union bolt from the underside of the engine

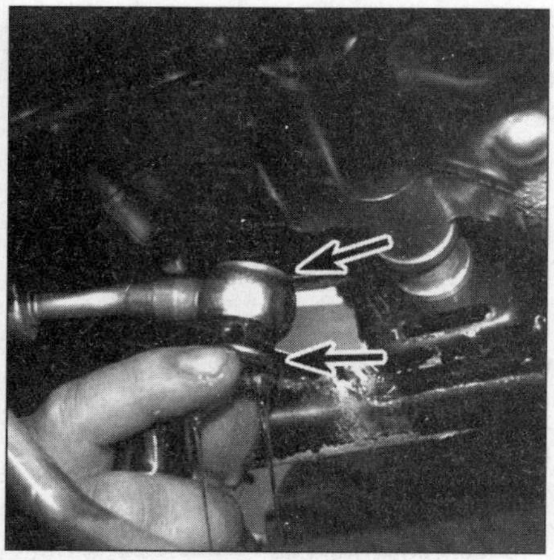

18.2d Disconnect the oil line - there's a sealing washer on each side of the fitting

18.8a Remove the mounting bolt at the front of the oil tank . . .

18 External oil tank and lines - removal and installation

1 All models have an external oil tank on the frame forward of the engine and a combined oil pipe/hose on each side of the engine.

Oil lines

Removal

2 To disconnect an oil pipe/hose from engine, remove its mounting bolt (upper hose) or union bolt (lower hose) **(see illustrations)**. Both oil hose connections at the oil tank, as well as the upper oil hose connection at the engine, have a dowel and O-ring **(see illustrations)**. The lower hose connection to the engine has a dowel, banjo bolt and sealing washers **(see illustrations)**.

3 To disconnect the oil tank vent hose, loosen its clamps and carefully pry it off the fittings.

Installation

4 Installation is the reverse of removal. Replace the O-rings whenever they are removed.

External oil tank

Removal

5 Remove the front fender and radiator (see Chapters 8 and 3).

6 Drain the oil tank (see Chapter 1).

7 Disconnect the hoses from the tank (see Step 2).

8 Remove the tank mounting bolts and lift the tank off the frame **(see illustrations)**.

nstallation

9 Check the mounting bolt bushings for damage or deterioration and replace them as needed.

10 Position the tank on the frame and tighten the mounting bolts. Connect the hoses as described above.

11 Change the engine oil (see Chapter 1).

Oil return tank

12 The oil return tank is mounted behind the engine on the right side of the vehicle **(see illustration)**.

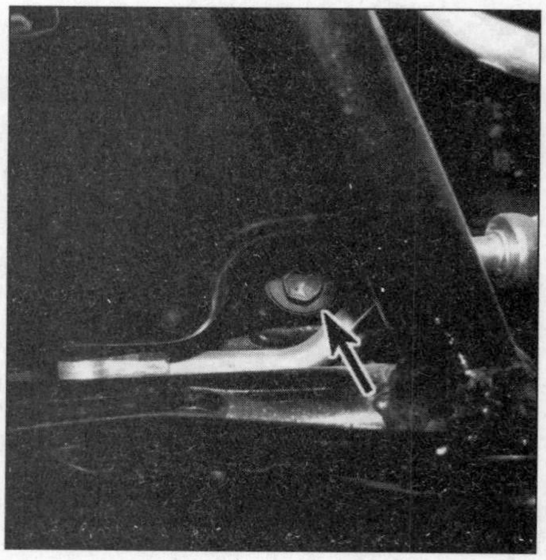

18.8b . . . and at the rear

18.12 Remove the bolt and disconnect the hose to remove the oil return tank

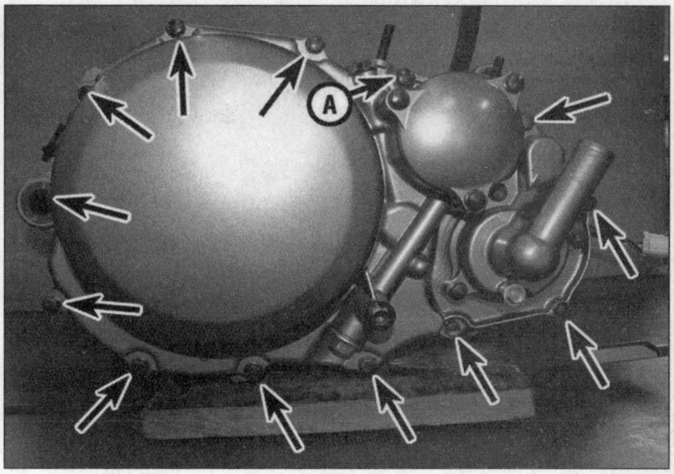

19.2 Right crankcase cover bolt locations - Bolt A has a washer

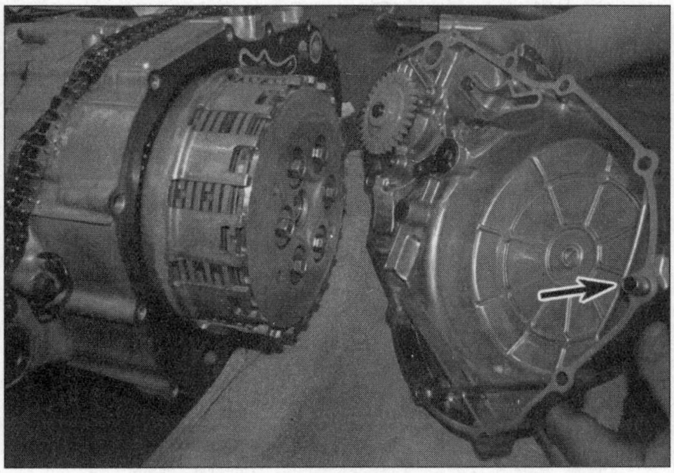

19.3a Remove the cover - the dowels may come off with the cover . . .

19.3b . . . or stay in the engine

13 To remove the tank, squeeze the hose clamps and slide them down the hose. Remove the mounting bolt, lift the tank out and disconnect the hose.
14 Installation is the reverse of removal.

19 Crankcase covers - removal and installation

Right crankcase cover

1 Drain the engine oil (see Chapter 1).
2 Remove the water pump bolts (see Chapter 3) and the cover mounting bolts **(see illustration)**.
3 Tap the cover gently with a soft-faced mallet to free it and take it off the engine. Locate the dowels and remove the old gasket **(see illustrations)**.
4 Check the condition of the oil check valve **(see illustration)**. If its condition is in doubt, pull the bushing out of the cover, then remove the ball and spring.

Installation

5 If the oil check valve was removed, install it with the rubber part of the bushing facing out of the bore.
6 Installation is the reverse of removal. Use a new gasket, coated on both sides with gasket sealer. Be sure the dowels and O-rings are installed.
7 Tighten the cover bolts evenly to the torque listed in this Chapter's Specifications.

Left crankcase cover

Removal

8 Drain the engine oil (see Chapter 1).
9 Remove the starter drive gear (see Chapter 5).
10 Follow the alternator wiring harness to the electrical connector and disconnect it (see Chapter 5).

19.4 Remove the oil check valve, spring and ball - reinstall it with the rubber side of the check valve outward (toward the center of the engine)

20.1 Rotate the cable out of the slot (arrow), then lower the end plug out of the clutch lever

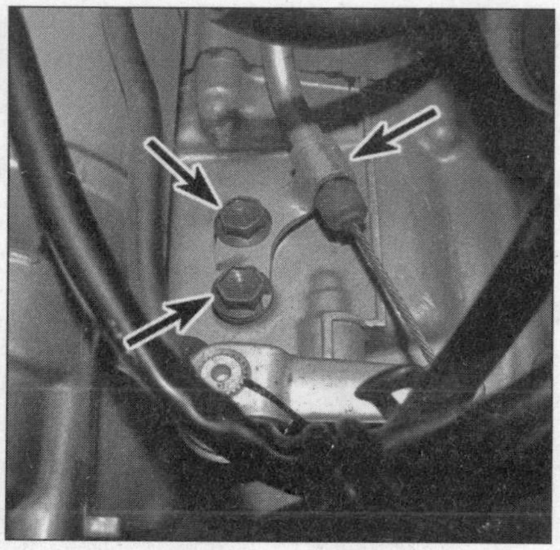

20.2 Either remove the bracket bolts (left arrows) or pull the cable back and slide it out of the slot in the underside of the bracket (right arrow)

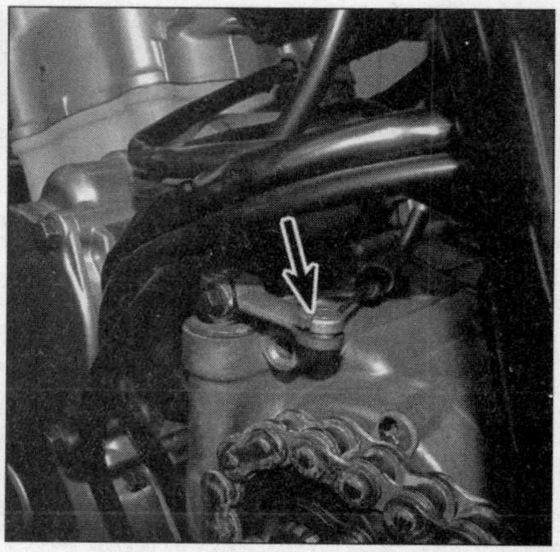

20.3 Rotate the cable out of the release lever, then lift it up out of the slot

11 Remove the cover bolts **(see illustration 19.2)**. Loosen the bolts evenly in a criss-cross pattern, then remove them.

12 Pull the cover off. Tap it with a rubber mallet if it won't come easily. Don't pry the cover off or the gasket surfaces will be damaged.

13 Locate the cover dowels **(see illustration 19.3a)**. They may have stayed in the crankcase or come off with the cover.

14 Remove all traces of the old gasket from the cover and crankcase.

Installation

15 Installation is the reverse of removal. Use a new gasket, coated on both sides with gasket sealer. Be sure the dowels are installed. Don't forget to refill the engine oil (see Chapter 1).

16 Tighten the cover bolts evenly to the torque listed in this Chapter's Specifications.

20 Clutch and release mechanism - removal, inspection and installation

Cable and lever

Removal

1 Loosen the handlebar cable adjuster all the way to create slack (see Chapter 1). Rotate the cable so the inner cable aligns with the slot in the lever, then slip the cable and fitting out of the lever **(see illustration)**.

2 Either unbolt the lever bracket from the top of the crankcase, or disengage the cable housing from the bracket **(see illustration)**.

3 Rotate the exposed end of the cable so it aligns with the slot in the lever, then lift the cable end upward out of the lever **(see illustration)**.

4 Take the cable bracket off the vehicle, together with the cable if you haven't already separated them **(see illustration 20.2)**. Separate the cable from the bracket.

5 To remove the lever from the handlebar, undo the clamp screws from the rear side of the lever bracket and take the lever off.

6 At the crankcase, disconnect the cable as described above, then remove the lever pinch bolt all the way **(see illustration)**. Slide the lever off the release shaft **(see illustration)**.

7 Remove the screw that secures the retaining washer **(see illustration 20.6a)**. Take the washer off to expose the seal **(see illustration)**. Pry the seal out, taking care not to damage the bore. Lift the pivot shaft and bearings out of the crankcase.

Inspection

8 Slide the inner cable back and forth in the housing and make sure it moves freely. If it doesn't, try lubricating it as described in Chapter 1. If that doesn't help, replace the cable.

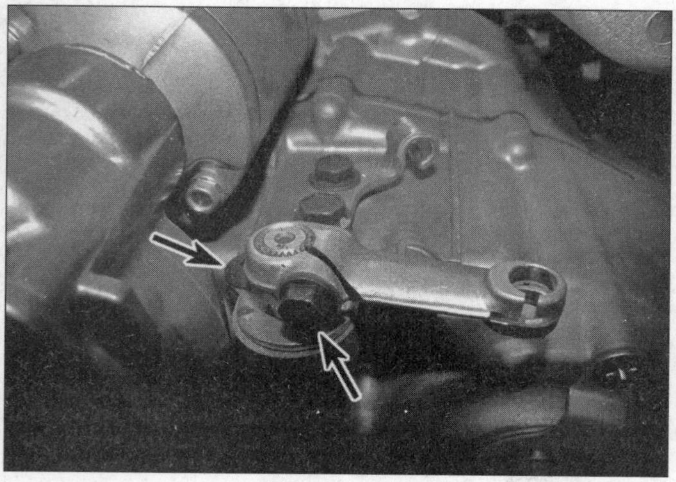

20.6a Remove the pinch bolt (right arrow) all the way, lift the lever off the shaft, then remove the retaining screw (left arrow)

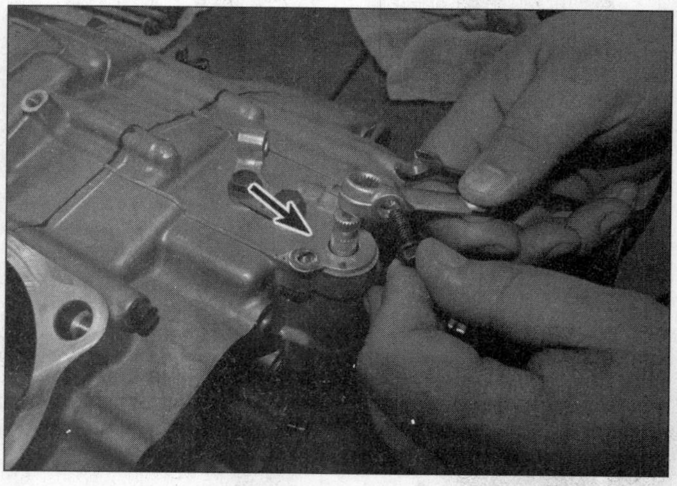

20.6b Remove the washer

20.7 Pry the seal out of its bore

20.12a Loosen the clutch cover bolts in a criss-cross pattern . . .

20.12b . . . then remove the bolts and springs

20.12c Remove the clutch cover and release bearing as an assembly

20.12d Remove the push piece from the clutch center . . .

Installation

9 Installation is the reverse of removal. Install the pivot shaft to the notch on its lower end faces toward the right side of the engine. Refer to Chapter 1 and adjust clutch freeplay.

Clutch

Removal

10 Remove the right crankcase cover (see Section 19).

11 Hold the clutch from turning with a holding tool. You can make your own holding tool from steel strap if you don't have one. **Note:** *If you've removed the right crankcase cover, you can wedge a copper washer or penny between the primary drive gear and clutch housing driven gear to keep the clutch housing from turning while you loosen the clutch spring bolts and clutch housing nut.*

12 Refer to the accompanying illustrations to remove the clutch **(see illustrations)**.

20.12e . . . and place it in the release bearing for storage - on installation, the long end (arrow) goes into the clutch center

20.12f The pushrod is located in the transmission countershaft

20.12g Pull the pushrod out with a magnet . . .

20.12h . . . and place it in the push piece for storage

20.12i Bend back the lockwasher with a hammer and chisel

20.12j Remove the metal plates and friction plates (except for the innermost friction plate), then hook the damper spring with a pick or similar tool . . .

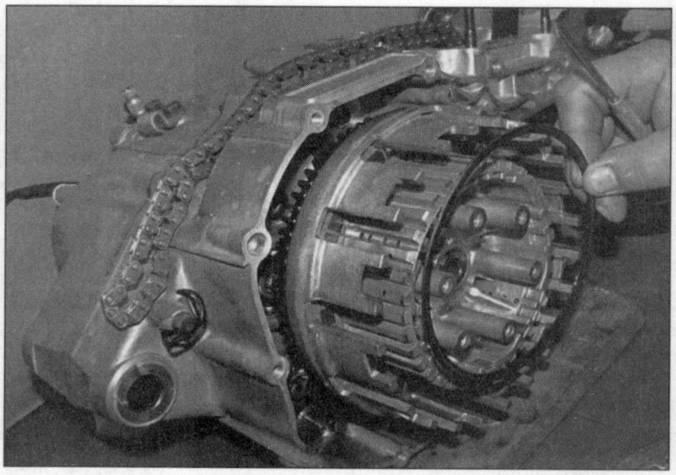

20.12k . . . and pull it out - the concave side faces away from the engine

20.12l Remove the innermost friction plate - it's narrower than the others

20.12m Use a clutch holding tool or wedge the primary gears with a copper washer, then unscrew the clutch nut

20.12n Remove the splined washer

20.12o Pull off the clutch center . . .

20.12p . . . and the clutch housing . . .

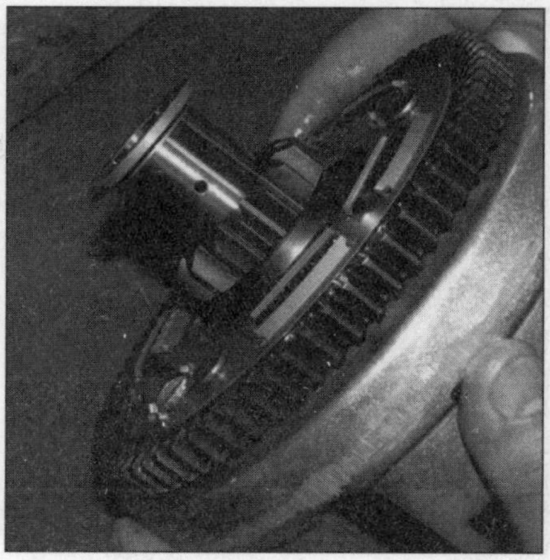

20.12q . . . if the collar comes off with the clutch housing, pull it out

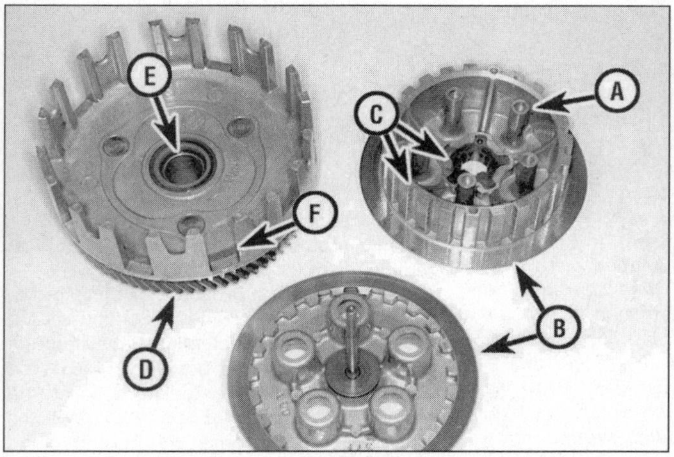

20.14a Clutch inspection points

A Spring posts
B Friction surfaces
C Splines
D Primary driven gear
E Clutch housing bushing
F Clutch housing slots

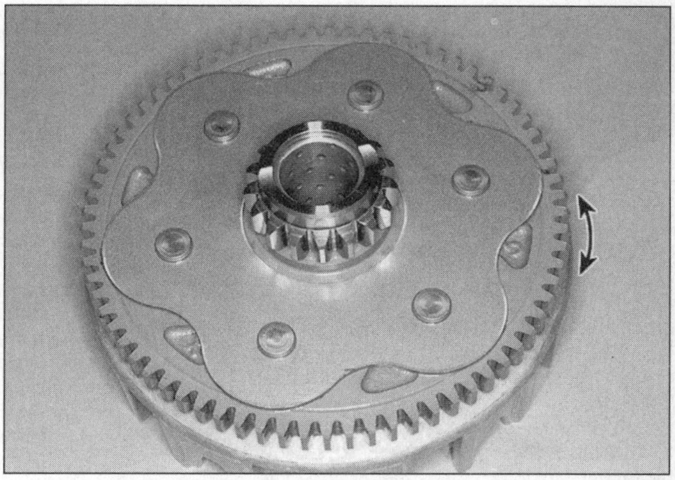

20.14b Grip the clutch housing and try to rotate the primary gear; if there's play, replace the housing

Inspection

13 Check the bolt posts and the friction surface on the pressure plate for damaged threads, scoring or wear. Replace the pressure plate if any defects are found.

14 Check the edges of the slots in the clutch housing for indentations made by the friction plate tabs **(see illustration)**. If the indentations are deep they can prevent clutch release, so the housing should be replaced with a new one. If the indentations can be removed easily with a file, the life of the housing can be prolonged to an extent. Check the bushing surface in the center of the clutch housing for score marks, scratches and excessive wear. Also, check the driven gear teeth for cracks, chips and excessive wear. If the bushing or gear is worn or damaged, the clutch housing must be replaced with a new one. Check the primary driven gear for play **(see illustration)**. If there is any, replace the clutch housing.

15 Check the splines of the clutch boss for indentations made by the tabs on the metal plates. Check the clutch boss friction surface for wear or scoring. Replace the clutch boss if problems are found.

16 Measure the free length of the clutch springs **(see illustration)** and compare the results to this Chapter's Specifications. If the springs have sagged, or if cracks are noted, replace them with new ones as a set.

17 If the lining material of the friction plates smells burnt or if it is glazed, new parts are required. If the metal clutch plates are scored or discolored, they must be replaced with new ones. Measure the thickness of the

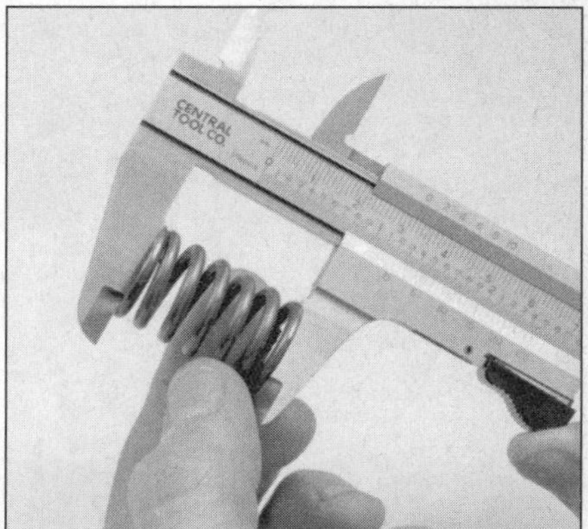

20.16 Measure the clutch spring free length

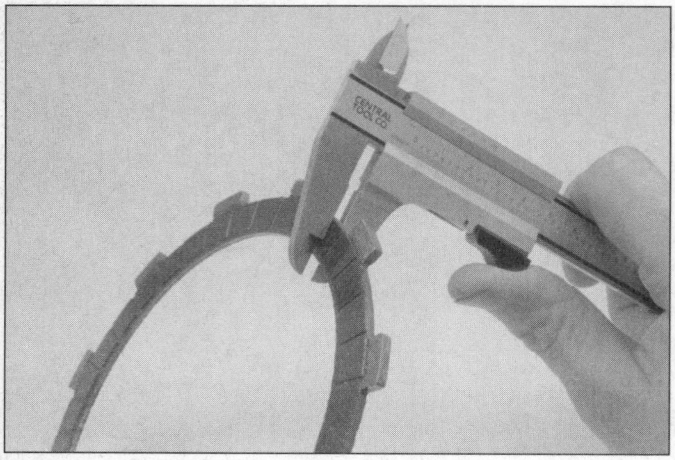

20.17 Measure the friction plate thickness

20.18 Use a feeler gauge to check for warpage

friction plates **(see illustration)**. Compare the measurements to the values listed in this Chapter's Specifications and replace with new parts any friction plates that are worn.

18 Lay the metal plates, one at a time, on a perfectly flat surface (such as a piece of plate glass) and check for warpage by trying to slip a feeler gauge between the flat surface and the plate **(see illustration)**. The feeler gauge should be the same thickness as the maximum warp listed in this Chapter's Specifications. Do this at several places around the plate's circumference. If the feeler gauge can be slipped under the plate, it is warped and should be replaced with a new one.

19 Check the tabs on the friction plates for excessive wear and mushroomed edges. They can be cleaned up with a file if the deformation is not severe, but the width must be at least the minimum listed in this Chapter's Specifications. Check the friction plates for warpage.

20 Check the thrust washer for score marks, heat discoloration and evidence of excessive wear.

Installation

21 Installation is the reverse of removal, with the following additions:

a) *Install a new lockwasher and position its tabs between the ribs of the clutch center. Tighten the clutch nut to the torque listed in this Chapter's Specifications, then bend the lockwasher tabs against one of the flats on the nut.*

b) *Coat the friction plates with clean engine oil before you install them.*

c) *Install the narrower friction plate first, then a metal plate, then alternate the remaining metal and friction plates until they're all installed. Friction plates go on first and last, so the friction material contacts the metal surfaces of the clutch center and the pressure plate. Be sure the narrower friction plate goes on first* **(see illustration)**. *The last friction plate should be installed with its tab one notch offset from the tabs of the other friction plates* **(see illustration)**.

d) *Apply grease to the ends of the clutch pushrod, the steel ball and the end of the adjuster rod.*

21 Camshaft chain and guides - removal and installation

1 If inspection procedures in Section 11 indicate problems with the chain or guides, remove them for further inspection.

2 To remove the exhaust side chain guide, remove the cylinder head (see Section 12). Lift the guide out of its pocket **(see illustration)**.

3 To remove the intake side guide or the chain, remove the left crankcase cover and clutch (see Sections 19 and 20). Unbolt the guide and slip the chain off the crankshaft sprocket **(see illustrations)**.

4 If you need to remove the crankshaft sprocket, refer to Section 22 and remove the primary drive gear, then slide the sprocket off the crankshaft.

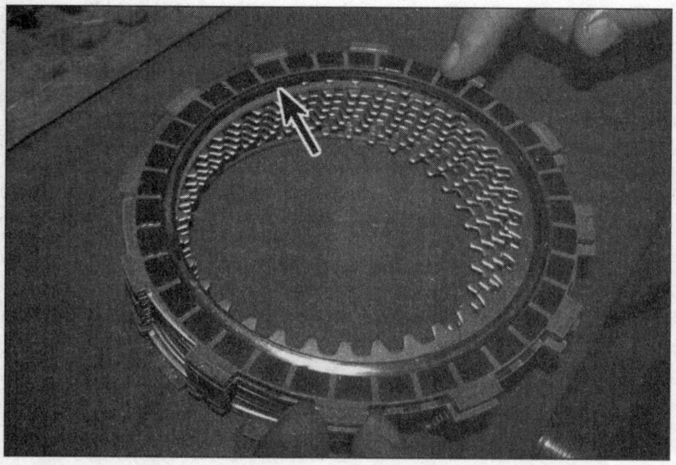

20.21a The damper spring fits inside the innermost friction plate

20.21b The tabs of the outermost friction plate (lower arrow) are offset from the other friction plate tabs (upper arrow) by one notch

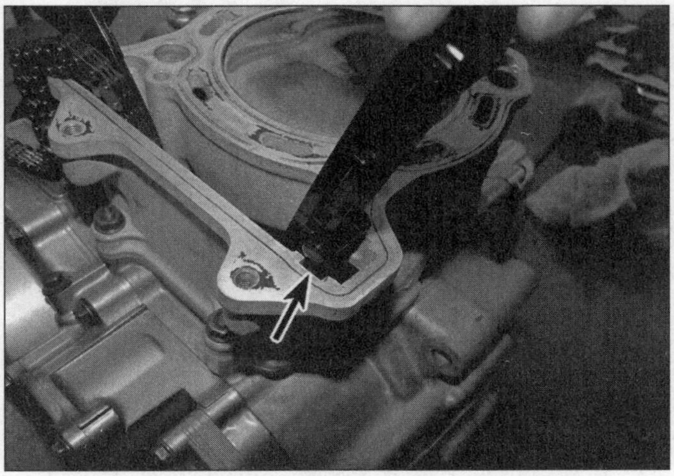

21.2 Lift the exhaust side chain guide out of its notch

21.3a Unscrew the Allen bolt that secures the intake side chain guide . . .

21.3b . . . and pull it out

21.3c Disengage the chain guide from the sprocket

5 Installation is the reverse of removal. Be sure the screw holding the metal tab that forms the outer side pocket for the intake chain guide is tightened securely **(see illustration)**. If you removed the crankshaft sprocket, install the Woodruff key, then slip the sprocket onto the crankshaft.

22 Primary drive gear, crankshaft sprocket and balancer gears - removal, inspection and installation

Removal

1 If you're just planning to remove the gears, remove the right crankcase cover and clutch (see Sections 19 and 20). If you're planning to remove the balancer weight or

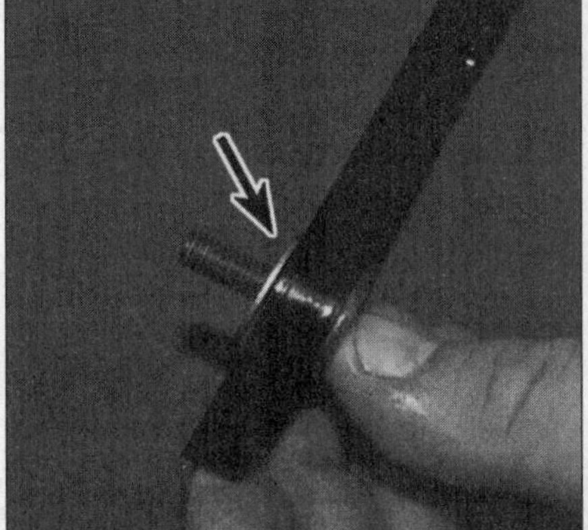

21.3d Remove the washer from the inner side of the chain guide

21.5 Be sure the screw that holds the chain guide pocket tab is tight

22.2 The punch marks on the balancer drive and driven gears must be aligned like this when the gears are installed

22.5a The drive gear nut has left-hand threads (turn clockwise to loosen); remove the lockwasher (arrow)

shaft, remove the engine and disassemble the crankcase halves (see Section 25).

2 Turn the crankshaft so the match marks on the balancer drive and driven gears align **(see illustration)**.

3 Bend back the tab on the balancer drive gear lockwasher.

4 Wedge a copper washer or penny between the teeth of the balancer drive and driven gears to prevent them from turning. Loosen the driven gear nut. If you plan to remove the primary drive gear or balancer drive gear, wedge the gears from the other side and loosen the primary drive gear nut.

5 Unscrew the nuts and remove the lockwashers **(see illustrations)**. **Note:** *The primary drive gear nut has left-hand threads (unscrews clockwise).*

6 Slide off the primary drive gear, then the crankshaft sprocket, then the balancer drive gear **(see illustrations)**. Remove the Woodruff key from the crankshaft and remove the drive pins from the crankshaft and balancer shaft **(see illustrations)**.

22.5b Unscrew the driven gear nut . . .

22.5c . . . and remove the washer

22.6a Remove the gear and pull the Woodruff key out of its slot

22.6b Remove the cam chain sprocket

22.6c Remove the driven gear from the balancer shaft - the shouldered side of the gear (shown) faces the engine on installation

22.6d Pull the driven gear pin out of the shaft with a magnet

Inspection

7 Check the gears for worn or damaged teeth and replace them as a set if problems are found. The driven gear can be separated into its components - gear, hub, springs and pins - if necessary for inspection. Before you disassemble it, make sure the alignment marks on gear and hub are visible. If not, make your own marks.

8 Check the ball bearings for wear, looseness or rough movement. If any problems are found, replace the bearings as described in Section 26.

9 Check the remaining components for wear and damage and replace any worn or damaged parts. Replace the lockwasher with a new one whenever it's removed.

10 Inspect the balancer and crankshaft ball bearings. If wear, looseness or roughness can be detected, the crankcase will have to be disassembled to replace the bearings.

Installation

11 If you took the balancer driven gear apart, reassemble it. Note that two of the springs have pins inside them and two of the springs don't have pins. The pins go opposite each other when the gear is assembled.

22.6e Slide the drive gear off the crankshaft . . .

22.6f . . . and remove the drive pin with a magnet

12 Install the drive pins in the balancer shaft and crankshaft **(see illustration 22.6f)**. Install the balancer drive and driven gears over the pins so their match marks align with each other **(see illustration 22.2)**.

13 Install the Woodruff key in the crankshaft, then install the cam chain sprocket and primary drive gear.

14 Install the lockwashers and nuts on the balancer shaft and crankshaft.

15 Wedge the gears as described in Step 4 and tighten the nuts to the torque listed in this Chapter's Specifications. **Note:** *The primary drive gear nut has left-hand threads (tightens counterclockwise).* Bend the lockwasher tab to secure the nuts.

16 The remainder of installation is the reverse of removal.

23.2 Remove the bolt and pull the oil pipe out of the crankcase

23 Oil pump and pipe - removal, inspection and installation

Oil pipe

Removal

1 Remove the clutch (see Section 20).

2 Remove the oil pipe bolt and pull the oil pipe out of the crankcase **(see illustration)**.

3 Take the O-rings off the oil pipe.

23.7a Remove the snap-ring and remove the oil pump idler gear from its shaft - the shouldered side (arrow) faces the engine on installation

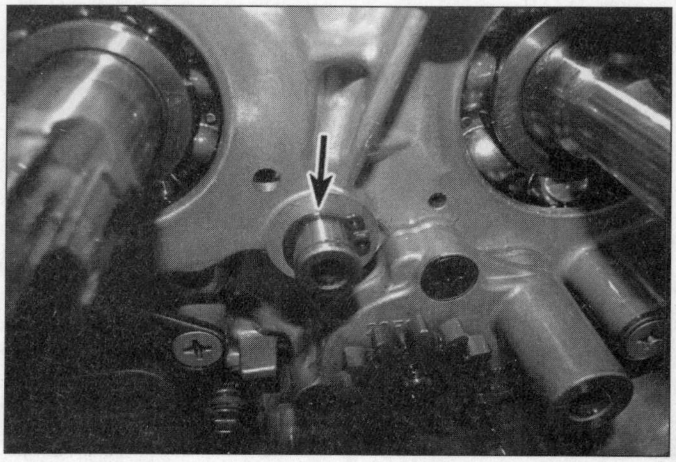

23.7b DO NOT remove the idler shaft snap-ring - if the idler shaft slides into the crankcase, you'll have to separate the case halves to get it out

Installation

4 Apply clean engine oil to new O-rings and install them on the pipe.

5 Push the pipe into the engine and secure it with the bolt.

Oil pump

Removal

6 Remove the right crankcase cover and clutch (see Sections 19 and 20).

7 Remove the snap-ring and take the oil pump idler gear off its shaft **(see illustration)**.

Caution: Don't remove the snap-ring from the idler gear shaft after removing the gear (see illustration). The shaft might fall into the crankcase. If this happens, the crankcase will have to be disassembled to reinstall the shaft.

8 Remove the snap-ring from the oil pump drive gear, pull the gear off and remove its drive pin **(see illustration)**.

9 Remove the oil pump mounting screws and remove the pump from the engine **(see illustration 23.7a and the accompanying illustration)**.

10 Locate the pump dowel(s). They may have come off with the pump or stayed in the engine.

Inspection

11 Remove the outer rotor, inner rotor and drive pin.

12 The assembly screw that secures the cover to the oil pump body is secured with permanent-type thread locking agent, so it can't be removed without damaging it. The screw, cover and pump body are not available separately. If inspection shows any problems, replace the oil pump as a unit.

13 Wash all the components in solvent, then dry them off. Check the pump body, the rotors and the cover for scoring and wear. If any damage or uneven or excessive wear is evident, replace the pump. If you are rebuilding the engine, it's a good idea to install a new oil pump.

14 Reassemble the pump by reversing the disassembly steps, with the following additions:

- *a) Before installing the cover, pack the cavities between the rotors with petroleum jelly - this will ensure the pump develops suction quickly and begins oil circulation as soon as the engine is started.*
- *b) Make sure the drive pin is in position.*
- *c) Install the outer rotor in the crankcase with its punch mark facing away from the pump body.*

Installation

15 Installation is the reverse of removal, with the following additions:

- *a) Make sure the pump dowels are in position.*
- *b) Tighten the oil pump mounting screws to the torque listed in this Chapter's Specifications.*

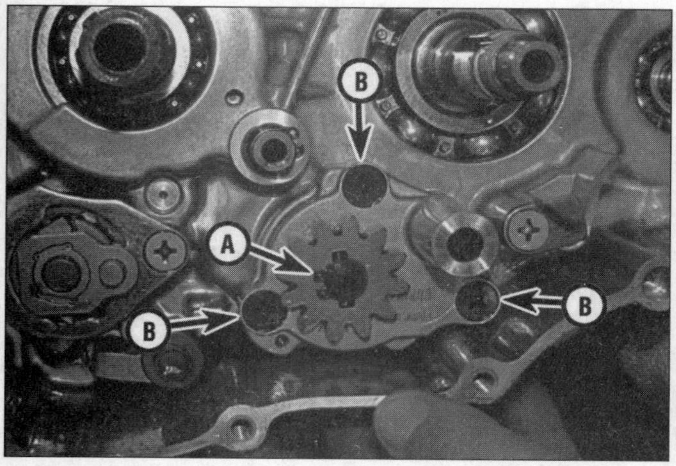

23.8 Remove the snap-ring (A), the oil pump gear and its drive pin, and the pump screws (B) to remove the pump from the engine

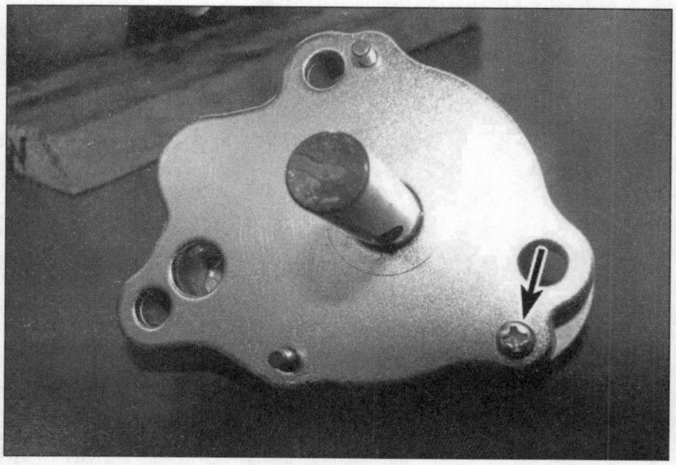

23.9 This screw can't be removed without damaging it

24.1 Remove the pinch bolt all the way, then slide the shift pedal off the shaft

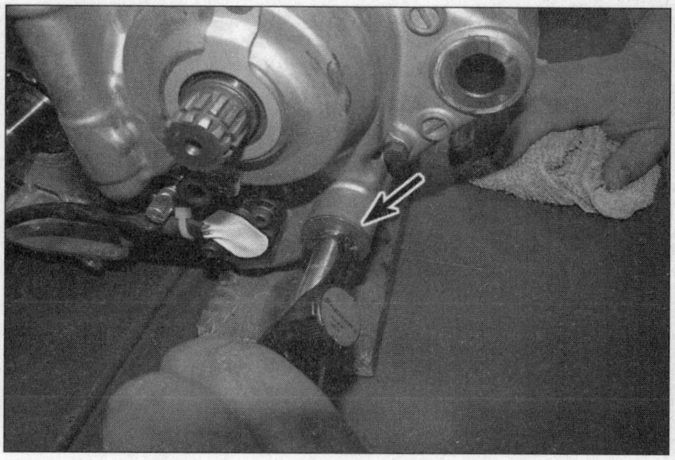

24.7a On the left-hand side of the engine, remove the snap-ring and washer from the shift shaft

24.7b On the right-hand side of the engine, pull the shift shaft out . . .

24.7c . . . and remove the bushing from the post on the pawl assembly

24.7d Remove the screws and remove the pawl assembly

24 External shift mechanism - removal, inspection and installation

Shift pedal

Removal

1 Look for alignment marks on the end of the shift pedal and shift shaft **(see illustration)**. If they aren't visible, make your own marks with a felt pen or sharp punch. Remove the shift pedal pinch bolt completely (it fits in a groove) and slide the pedal off the shaft.

Inspection

2 Check the shift pedal for wear or damage such as bending. Check the splines on the shift pedal and shaft for stripping or step wear. Replace the pedal or shaft if these problems are found.

3 Check the shift shaft seal in the alternator cover for signs of leakage. If the seal has been leaking, remove the left crankcase cover (see Section 19). Pry the seal out of the cover, then tap in a new one with a seal driver or socket the same diameter as the seal.

Installation

4 Install the shift pedal or shift arm. Line up its punch marks and tighten the pinch bolt to the torque listed in this Chapter's Specifications.

External shift linkage

Removal

5 Remove the shift pedal as described above.

6 Remove the right crankcase cover and the clutch (see Sections 19 and 20).

7 Refer to the accompanying illustrations to remove the linkage **(see illustrations)**.

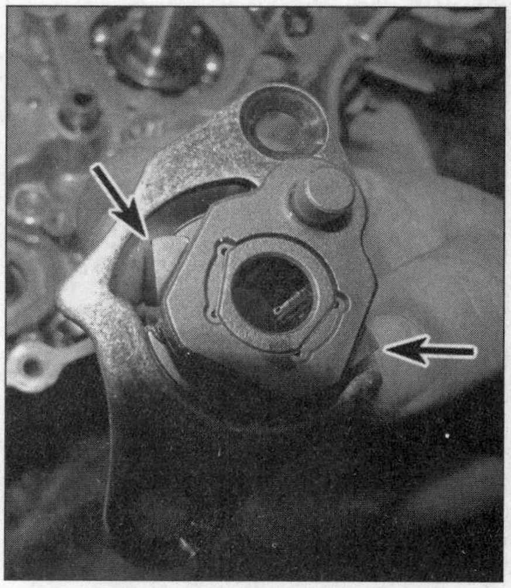

24.7e Note how the pawls fit in the unit . . .

24.7f . . . then disassemble it for inspection

24.7g Remove the bolt and remove the stopper arm and spring

24.7h Remove the center bolt from the shift drum driven gear

24.7i Remove the gear - its notch engages the pin on installation

Inspection

8 Check the shift shaft for bends and damage to the splines. If the shaft is bent, you can attempt to straighten it, but if the splines are damaged it will have to be replaced. Check the condition of the return spring, shift arm and the pawl spring. Replace the shift shaft if they're worn, cracked or distorted.

Installation

9 Installation is the reverse of removal, with the following additions:

a) *Apply non-permanent thread locking agent to the return spring pin and tighten it securely.*
b) *Apply non-permanent thread locking agent to the gearshift cam driven gear bolt and tighten it to the torque listed in this Chapter's Specifications.*
c) *Check the engine oil level and add some, if necessary (see Chapter 1).*

25 Crankcase - disassembly and reassembly

1 To examine and repair or replace the balancer shaft, crankshaft, connecting rod, bearings and transmission components, the crankcase must be split into two parts.

Disassembly

2 Remove the engine from the vehicle (see Section 7).

3 Remove the alternator and starter clutch (see Chapter 5).

4 Remove the right crankcase cover and clutch (see Sections 19 and 20).

5 Remove the external shift mechanism (see Section 24).

6 Remove the valve cover, cam chain tensioner, camshafts, cylinder head, cylinder, piston and crankcase oil pipe (see Sections 9, 10, 11, 12, 15, 16 and 23).

7 Remove the timing chain and intake side guide (see Section 21).

8 Remove the oil pump (see Section 23).

9 Remove the balancer gears (see Section 22).

10 Check carefully to make sure there aren't any remaining components that attach the upper and lower halves of the crankcase together.

11 Loosen the crankcase bolts in two or three stages, in a criss-cross pattern **(see illustrations)**.

12 Place the engine on blocks so the transmission shafts and crankshaft can extend

25.11a Left side crankcase bolt locations (upper left bolt hidden)

25.11b Right side crankcase bolt locations (four lower right bolts hidden)

25.12a Set up a puller like this to separate the crankcase halves

25.12b The halves will separate like this - if they don't separate evenly as shown, make sure you've removed all the bolts, reposition the puller and try again

downward. Set up a three-legged puller against the end of the crankshaft so it can pull the upper case half off the crankshaft **(see illustration)**. Tap gently on the ends of the transmission shafts, balancer shaft and crankshaft as the case halves are being separated. Make sure the case halves separate evenly **(see illustration)**. Carefully pry the crankcase apart at the pry points. Don't pry against the mating surfaces or they'll develop leaks.

13 Lift the right crankcase half off the left half.

14 Locate the crankcase dowels **(see illustrations)**. If they aren't secure in their holes, remove them and set them aside for safekeeping.

15 Refer to Sections 26 through 29 for information on the internal components of the crankcase.

Reassembly

16 Remove all traces of old gasket and sealant from the crankcase mating surfaces with a sharpening stone or similar tool. Be careful not to let any fall into the case as this is done and be careful not to damage the mating surfaces.

17 Check to make sure the dowel pins are in place in their holes in the mating surface of the crankcase **(see illustrations 25.14a and 25.14b)**.

18 Coat both crankcase mating surfaces with Three Bond sealant 0636-070 (or equivalent).

19 Pour some engine oil over the transmission gears, balancer shaft and crankshaft bearing surfaces and the shift drum. Don't get any oil on the crankcase mating surfaces.

20 Carefully place the removed crankcase half onto the other crankcase half. While doing this, make sure the transmission shafts, shift drum, crankshaft and balancer shaft fit into their bearings in the upper crankcase half.

21 Install the crankcase half bolts or screws in the correct holes and tighten them so they are just snug. Then tighten them in two or three stages, in a criss-cross pattern, to the torque listed in this Chapter's Specifications.

22 Turn the transmission shafts to make sure they turn freely. Also make sure the crankshaft and balancer shaft turn freely.

23 The remainder of installation is the reverse of removal.

26 Crankcase components - inspection and servicing

1 Separate the crankcase and remove the following:

a) Transmission shafts and gears
b) Crankshaft and main bearings
c) Shift drums and forks
d) Balancer shaft

2 Clean the crankcase halves thoroughly with new solvent and dry them with compressed air. All oil passages should be blown

25.14a This case dowel stayed in the left side of the crankcase . . .

25.14b . . . and this one stayed in the right side

26.3 Check the bearings inside the case for wear and for rough or noisy movement

26.4a Unbolt the oil strainer

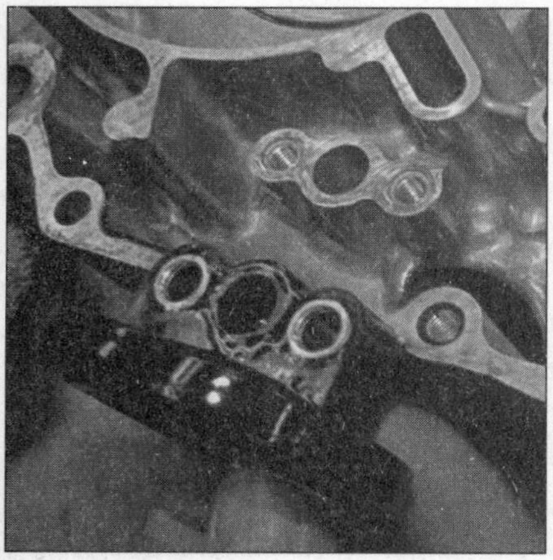

26.4b Remove the strainer and check the screen and passages for clogging

27.2 Rotate the balancer weight (arrow) out of the crankshaft slot, then pull the balancer shaft out of the crankcase

out with compressed air and all traces of old gasket sealant should be removed from the mating surfaces.

Caution: Be very careful not to nick or gouge the crankcase mating surfaces or leaks will result. Check both crankcase sections very carefully for cracks and other damage.

3 Check the bearings in the case halves **(see illustrations 25.14a and the accompanying illustration)**. If they don't turn smoothly, replace them, referring to *Tools and Workshop Tips* at the end of this manual.

4 Check the oil strainer screen for clogging or damage. If problems are found, remove the screen for cleaning or replacement **(see illustration)**. It's a good idea to remove the screen and check its oil passage in the crankcase whenever the crankcase is disassembled **(see illustration)**. When you reinstall the screen, make sure the oil passages in the screen and crankcase line up exactly.

5 Pull out the oil jet and remove its O-ring. Make sure the jet is clear by blowing through it with compressed air or aerosol carburetor cleaner. Coat a new O-ring with engine oil, install it on the jet, and push the jet back into its passage in the crankcase.

6 If any damage is found that can't be repaired, replace the crankcase halves as a set.

7 Assemble the case halves (see Section 25) and check to make sure the crankshaft and the transmission shafts turn freely.

27 Balancer shaft - removal and installation

1 Separate the crankcase halves (see Section 25).

2 Lift the balancer shaft out of its bearing in the left case half **(see illustration)**.

3 Installation is the reverse of removal.

28 Transmission shafts and shift drum - removal, inspection and installation

Note: *When disassembling the transmission shafts, place the parts on a long rod or thread a wire through them to keep them in order and facing the proper direction.*

Removal

1 Remove the engine, then separate the case halves (see Sections 7 and 25). The transmission components remain in one case half when the case is separated.

2 Remove the shift drum, shift forks and transmission shafts from the crankcase **(see illustrations)**.

28.2a Here's how the transmission gears look when they're fully assembled

28.2b There are two forks on one fork shaft - their pins engage the shift drum grooves like this

28.2c The pin of the fork on the reverse lock shaft engages the shift drum like this

28.2d Remove the collar (lower arrow) and washer (upper arrow) from their shafts

28.2e Lift out the fork shaft, disengage the forks and reinstall them on the shaft to keep them in order

28.2f Lift the shift drum out of the crankcase

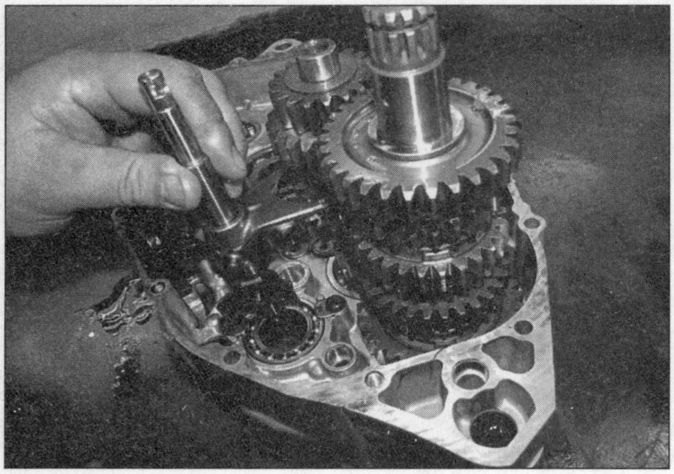

28.2g Lift out the reverse lock shaft and its fork

28.2h Remove the countershaft as a unit

28.2i Remove the reverse idler gear and shaft

28.2j Remove the washer from the reverse idler shaft

28.2k Remove the bushing from inside the gear

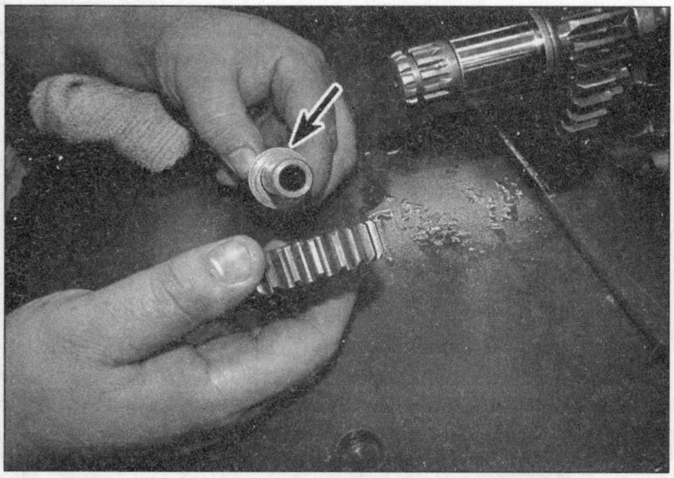

28.2l Remove the gear from the shaft, noting which way the beveled edge faces, then remove the washer (arrow) and the snap-ring behind it

28.2m Remove the mainshaft as a unit

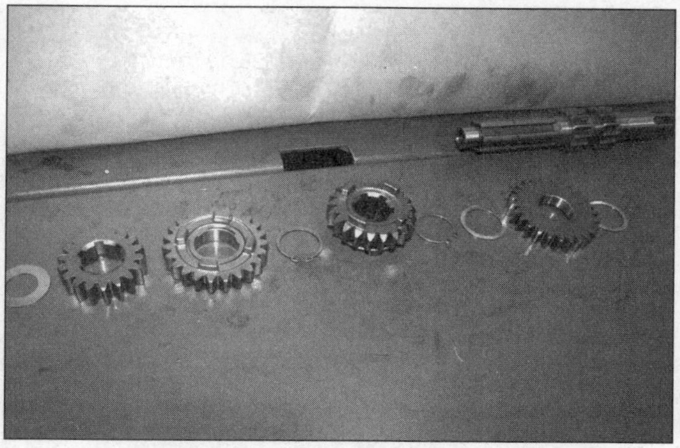
28.4a Countershaft details - the side of each gear facing upward goes onto the shaft first

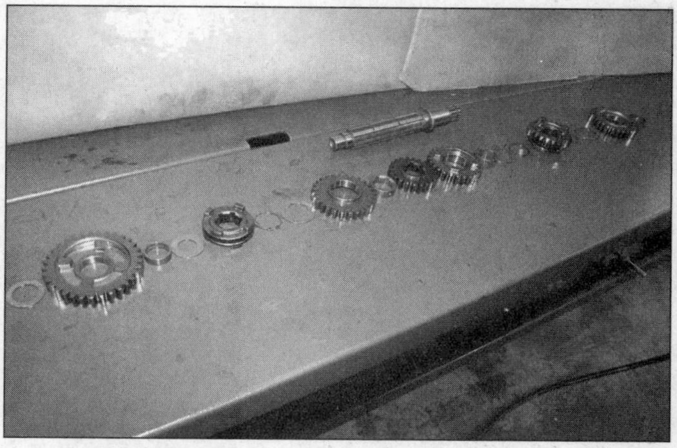
28.4b Mainshaft details - the side of each gear facing upward goes onto the shaft first

28.14a The assembled mainshaft and countershaft should look like this when they're installed

28.14b Install the fork shafts and forks like this, then install the shift drum

3 Using snap-ring pliers, remove the snap-rings and take the gears off the shafts.

4 Place the gears in order on a coat hanger or dowel so they won't be mixed up. Alternatively, as the gears come off the shafts, set them on the workbench, all facing the same direction **(see illustrations)**.

Inspection

5 Wash all of the components in clean solvent and dry them off.

6 Inspect the shift fork grooves in the gears. If a groove is worn or scored, replace the affected part and inspect its corresponding shift fork.

7 Check the shift forks for distortion and wear, especially at the fork ears. If they are discolored or severely worn they are probably bent. Inspect the guide pins for excessive wear and distortion and replace any defective parts with new ones.

8 Check the shift fork guide bars evidence of wear, galling and other damage. Make sure the shift forks move smoothly on the guide bars. If the shafts are worn or bent, replace them with new ones.

9 Check the edges of the grooves in the shift drums for signs of excessive wear.

10 Hold the inner race of the shift drum bearing with fingers and spin the outer race. Replace the bearing if it's rough, loose or noisy. Replace the shift drum driven gear if it's worn or damaged (see Section 24).

11 Check the gear teeth for cracking and other obvious damage. Check the bushing surface in the inner diameter of the freewheeling gears for scoring or heat discoloration. Replace damaged parts.

12 Inspect the engagement dogs and dog holes on gears so equipped for excessive wear or rounding off. Replace the paired gears as a set if necessary.

13 Check the transmission shaft bearings in the crankcase for wear or heat discoloration and replace them if necessary (see Section 26).

Installation

14 Installation is the reverse of removal, noting the following points:

a) *Use new snap-rings. Install the snap-rings with their rounded edges facing the direction of thrust (toward the component they're securing). Refer to Tools and Workshop Tips at the end of this manual if necessary.*
b) *Lubricate the components with engine oil before assembling them.*
c) *Install the shift forks, making sure they face in the proper direction* **(see illustration)**.
d) *After assembly, check the gears to make sure they're installed correctly* **(see illustration 28.2a and the accompanying illustration)**. *Move the shift drum through the gear positions and rotate the gears to make sure they mesh and shift correctly.*

29 Crankshaft and connecting rod - removal, inspection and installation

Note: *The procedures in this section require special tools. If you don't have the necessary equipment or suitable substitutes, have the crankshaft removed and installed by a dealer.*

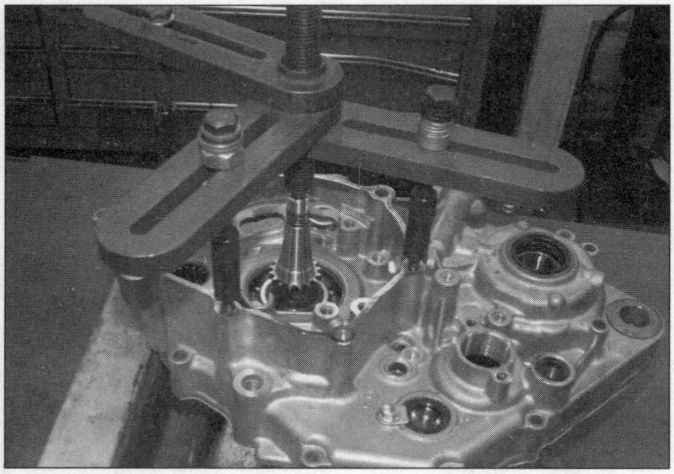

29.2 Use a puller like this to push the crankshaft out of the case half

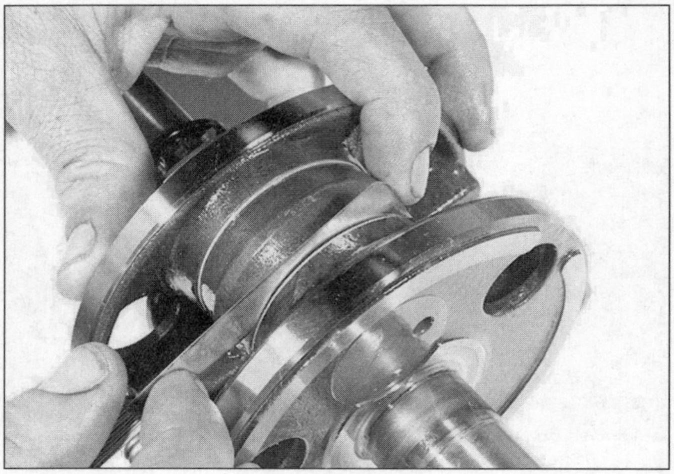

29.3 Measure the gap between the connecting rod and the crankshaft with a feeler gauge

29.5 Check the cam chain sprocket and the ball bearing on the end of the crankshaft

Removal

1 Remove the engine and separate the crankcase halves (see Sections 7 and 25). The transmission shafts need not be removed.

2 The crankshaft may be loose enough in its bearing that you can lift it out of the left crankcase half. If not, push it out with a crankshaft puller **(see illustration)**.

Inspection

3 Measure the side clearance between connecting rod and crankshaft with a feeler gauge **(see illustration)**. If it's more than the limit listed in this Chapter's Specifications, it may be possible to have the crankshaft rebuilt. However, this is a specialized job that should be done by a dealer service department or qualified machine shop.

4 Set up the crankshaft in V-blocks with a dial indicator contacting the big end of the connecting rod. Move the connecting rod side-to-side against the indicator pointer and compare the reading to the value listed in this Chapter's Specifications. If it's beyond the limit, the crankshaft can be disassembled and the needle roller bearing replaced. However, this is a specialized job that should be done by a dealer service department or qualified machine shop.

5 Check the crankshaft splines, the ball bearing at the sprocket end of the crankshaft and the bearing journals for visible wear or damage **(see illustration)**. Replace the crankshaft if any of these conditions are found.

6 Set the crankshaft in a lathe or a pair of V-blocks, with a dial indicator contacting each end **(see illustration)**. Rotate the crankshaft and note the runout. If the runout at either end is beyond the limit listed in this Chapter's Specifications, replace the crankshaft and connecting rod as an assembly.

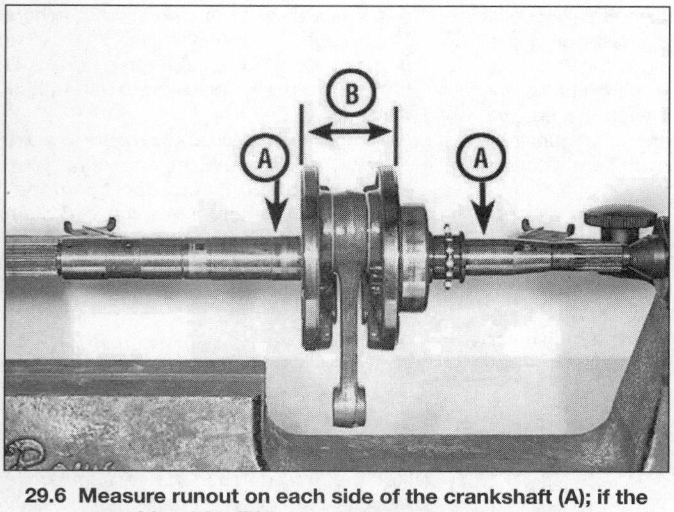

29.6 Measure runout on each side of the crankshaft (A); if the assembly width (B) is greater than specified, replace the crankshaft

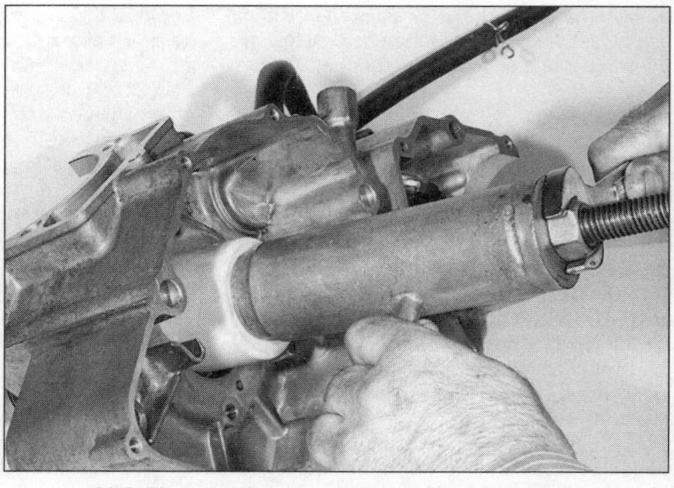

29.8 These tools are used to pull the crankshaft into the crankcase

7 Measure the assembly width of the crankshaft (from the outside of one crank throw to the outside of the other crank throw). If it exceeds the limit listed in this Chapter's Specifications, replace the crankshaft.

Installation

8 Start the crankshaft into the case half. If it doesn't go in easily, pull it in the rest of the way with a crankshaft puller such as manufacturer tools 09919-32812, 09910-32820 and 09911-11310 **(see illustration)**.

Caution: Do not tap the crankshaft in with a mallet, even a soft-faced one. This can cause misalignment of the crankshaft and subsequent engine damage.

9 The remainder of installation is the reverse of removal.

30 Initial start-up after overhaul

1 Make sure the engine oil level is correct, then remove the spark plug from the engine. Place the engine kill switch in the Off position and unplug the primary (low tension) wires from the coil.

2 Crank the engine over with the starter several times to build up oil pressure. Reinstall the spark plug, connect the wires and turn the switch to On.

3 Make sure there is fuel in the tank, then operate the choke.

4 Once you've made sure that there is oil pressure, allow the engine to run at a moderately fast idle until it reaches operating temperature.

5 Check carefully for oil leaks and make sure the transmission and controls, especially the brakes, function properly before road testing the machine. Refer to Section 31 for the recommended break-in procedure.

6 Upon completion of the road test, and after the engine has cooled down completely, recheck the valve clearances (see Chapter 1).

31 Recommended break-in procedure

1 Any rebuilt engine needs time to break in, even if parts have been installed in their original locations. For this reason, treat the machine gently for the first few miles to make sure oil has circulated throughout the engine and any new parts installed have started to seat.

2 Even greater care is necessary if the cylinder has been rebored or a new crankshaft has been installed. In the case of a rebore, the engine will have to be broken in as if the machine were new. This means greater use of the transmission and a restraining hand on the throttle for the first few operating days. There's no point in keeping to any set speed limit - the main idea is to vary the engine speed, keep from lugging (laboring) the engine and to avoid full-throttle operation. These recommendations can be lessened to an extent when only a new crankshaft is installed. Experience is the best guide, since it's easy to tell when an engine is running freely.

3 If a lubrication failure is suspected (oil doesn't seep from the check bolt, or the engine makes noise), stop the engine immediately and try to find the cause. If an engine is run without oil, even for a short period of time, irreparable damage will occur.

Notes

Chapter 3
Cooling system

Contents

Degrees of difficulty

Easy, suitable for novice with little experience	**Fairly easy,** suitable for beginner with some experience	**Fairly difficult,** suitable for competent DIY mechanic	**Difficult,** suitable for experienced DIY mechanic	**Very difficult,** suitable for expert DIY or professional

Specifications

General

Radiator cap relief pressure	108 to 137 kPa (15.6 to 19.9 psi)
Thermostat opening temperature	
Carbureted models	73.5 to 76.5-degrees C (164 to 170-degrees F)
Fuel injected models	Approximately 76.5-degrees C (170-degrees F)
Thermostat valve lift	
Carbureted models	6 mm (0.24 inch) or more at 90-degrees C (194-degrees F)
Fuel injected models	4.5 mm (0.18 inch) or more at 90-degrees C (194-degrees F)
Fan switch operating temperature	
Carbureted models	82 to 88-degrees C (180 to 190-degrees F)
Fuel injected models	93 to 98-degrees C (199 to 208-degrees F)

Torque specifications

Cooling fan switch to radiator (carbureted models)	20 Nm (174 inch-lbs)
Water pump cover bolts	10 Nm (84 inch-lbs)

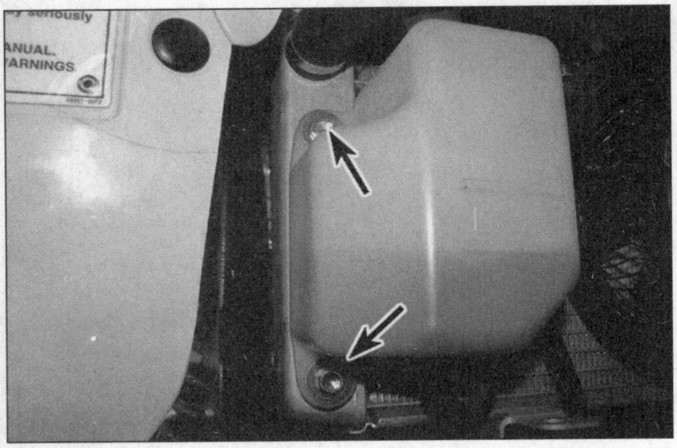

3.1 Remove the mounting bolts (arrows), pull the reservoir tank partway out and disconnect the siphon hose

4.2a The upper radiator hose runs from the upper left corner of the radiator . . .

1 General information

The vehicles covered by this manual are equipped with a liquid cooling system which utilizes a water/antifreeze mixture to carry away excess heat produced during combustion. The combustion chamber and cylinder are surrounded by a water jacket, through which the coolant is circulated by the water pump. The pump is mounted to the right side of the crankcase near the front and is driven by a gear. The radiator is mounted at the front of the frame. The coolant is pumped upward through the cylinder water jacket and cylinder head, then flows from the cylinder head to the radiator where it is cooled, then flows through the radiator bottom hose and water pump, then back into the engine. A thermostat, mounted in the cylinder head, regulates coolant flow. When the engine is cold, the thermostat closes and coolant circulates through the water pump, thermostat by-pass hole, coolant hoses and radiator. As the engine warms up, the thermostat opens, allowing coolant to be circulated through the engine coolant passages.

The cooling system includes a temperature warning light and fan, but does not include a thermostat. All models have a reservoir tank. As the coolant heats up, it expands and flows into the reservoir tank. As it cools, the coolant is pulled back into the cooling system.

2 Radiator cap - check

If problems such as overheating or loss of coolant occur, check the entire system as described in Chapter 1. The radiator cap opening pressure should be checked by a dealer service department or service station equipped with the special tester required to do the job. If the cap is defective, replace it with a new one.

3 Coolant reservoir - removal and installation

1 Locate the coolant reservoir **(see illustration)**.

2 Remove the tank mounting bolts and lift the tank off. Disconnect the siphon hose from the tank.

3 Installation is the reverse of removal.

4 Coolant hoses - removal and installation

1 The coolant hoses are all secured by screw-type clamps to fittings on the engine and radiator. The water pump hose runs to the bottom of the radiator and another hose runs from the top of the radiator to the engine.

2 To remove a hose, loosen its clamp and carefully pry it off the fitting **(see illustrations)**.

4.2b . . . to the thermostat housing on the cylinder head

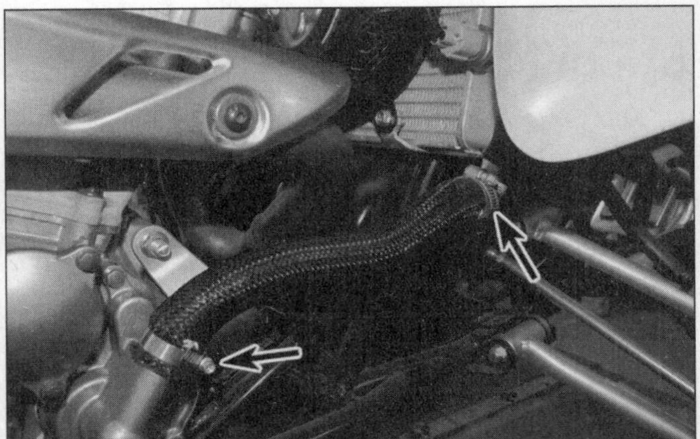

4.2c The lower radiator hose connects the lower right corner of the radiator to the water pump

3 If the hose is stuck, pry the edge up slightly with a pointed tool and spray brake or electrical contact cleaner into the gap. Work the tool around the fitting, lifting the edge of the hose and spraying into the gap until the hose comes free of the fitting.

4 In extreme cases, you may have to slit the hose and cut it off the fitting with a knife. Make sure you can get a replacement hose before doing this.

5 Cooling fan and circuit - check and replacement

Check

1 Check the battery to make sure it's fully charged (see Chapter 5).

2 If the engine is overheating and the cooling fan isn't coming on, disconnect the fan motor connector and connect the fan motor directly to a fully charged 12-volt battery using a pair of jumper wires. The fan motor should run. If it doesn't run, replace the fan motor with a new one.

3 Check the main fuse (2003 carbureted models) or the fan fuse (2004 and later carbureted models and all fuel injected models) (see Chapter 5). If the fuse is blown, check the fan circuit for a short to ground (see the *Wiring diagrams* at the end of this book).

Fuel injected models

4 If the fuses are good on a fuel injected model, remove the front fender (see Chapter 8) and locate the fan motor relay (it can be identified by its wiring colors, shown in the wiring diagram at the end of this manual). Disconnect the relay from the wiring harness.

5 Using a pair of jumper wires, connect a 12-volt battery (the vehicle's battery will do if it's fully charged) to the relay terminals (not the wiring harness terminals) as follows:

a) *Battery positive to terminal 3*
b) *Battery negative to terminal 4*

6 With the battery connected to the relay, connect an ohmmeter between relay terminals 1 and 2 **(see illustration)**. The ohmmeter should show continuity (little or no resistance). If it doesn't, replace the relay with a new one.

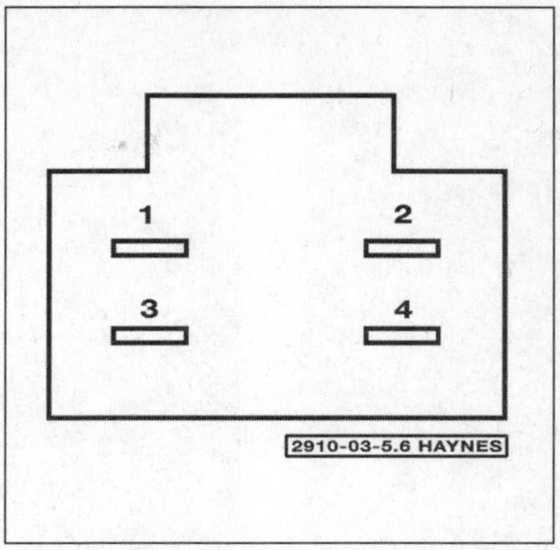

5.6 Fan motor relay terminal identification

7 Disconnect the battery from the relay and recheck continuity between terminals 1 and 2. The ohmmeter should show no continuity (infinite resistance). If it doesn't, replace the relay with a new one.

All models

8 If the fan motor runs when connected directly to the battery, disconnect the electrical connector from the fan thermoswitch. On carbureted models, it's mounted in the radiator.

9 Connect a short jumper wire between the terminals of the fan thermoswitch connector in the wiring harness (not between the terminals of the switch itself). With the ignition key in the ON position, the fan should run. If it does, replace the thermoswitch with a new one.

Switch replacement

10 Drain the cooling system (see Chapter 1).

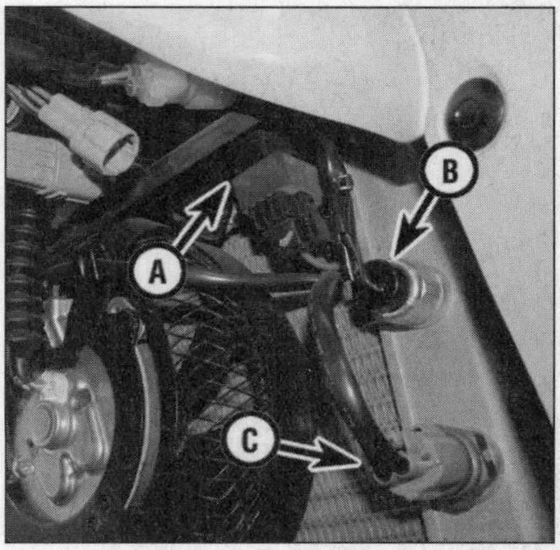

5.12 On carbureted models, the fan fuse box (2004 and later), coolant temperature sensor and fan switch are located on the right rear of the radiator

A *Fuse box*
B *Coolant temperature sensor*
C *Fan switch*

11 If you haven't already done so, disconnect the electrical connector from the thermoswitch.

12 Unscrew the thermoswitch from the radiator **(see illustration)**.

13 If the thermoswitch uses a gasket, install a new one. If it doesn't, coat the threads with silicone sealant.

14 Tighten the thermoswitch to the torque listed in this Chapter's Specifications.

Fan and motor replacement

15 If you haven't already done so, disconnect the wiring connectors for the fan and switch(es).

16 Remove the three screws that secure the fan to the radiator **(see illustrations)**. Lift off the fan, together with the fan motor (and the fan fuse box on 2004 and later models).

17 To remove the fan from the motor, unscrew its mounting nut and take it off.

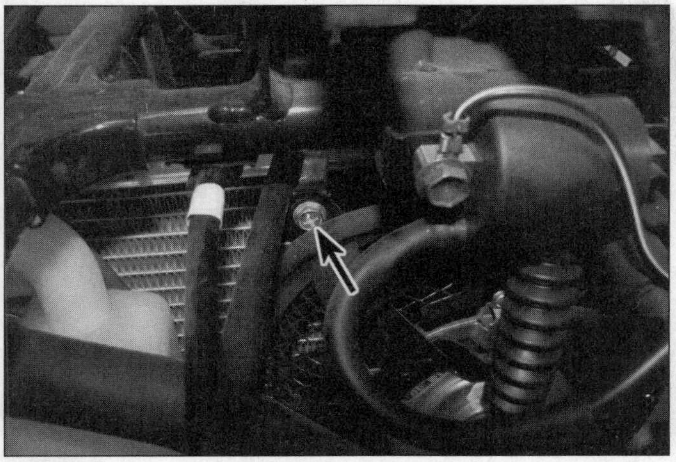

5.16a There's a fan mounting screw at the upper left . . .

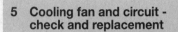

5.16b . . . and two mounting screws on the right side

6.4a Remove the radiator mounting bolts at the upper left . . .

6.4b . . . upper right . . .

18 If necessary, remove three screws that secure the motor to the fan and take it off.
19 Installation is the reverse of removal.

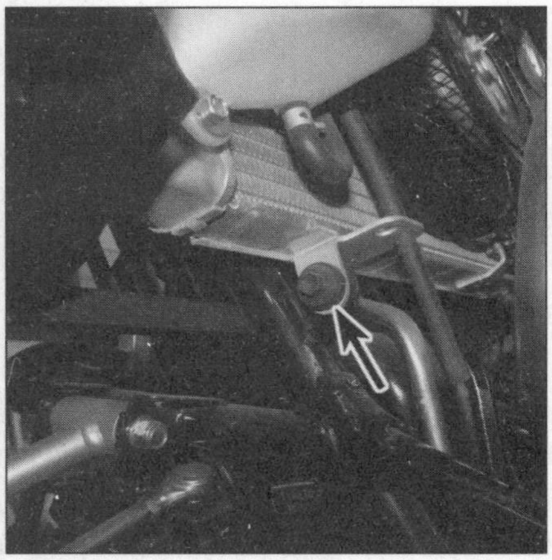

6.4c . . . and the bottom of the radiator (bottom left bolt shown)

6 Radiator - removal and installation

Warning: *The engine must be completely cool before beginning this procedure.*

1 Remove the seat, side covers, radiator grilles and front fender (see Chapter 8). Drain the cooling system (see Chapter 1).
2 Disconnect the electrical connectors for the fan motor, fan switch and temperature warning light switch.
3 Disconnect the radiator hoses (see Section 4).
4 Remove the radiator mounting bolts **(see illustrations)**.
5 Lift the radiator away from the frame, together with the cooling fan and reservoir tank. Inspect the mounting bolt grommets and replace them if they're worn or deteriorated.
6 Installation is the reverse of removal, with the following additions:

a) Tighten the mounting bolts securely, but don't overtighten them and distort the grommets.
b) Fill the cooling system (see Chapter 1).
c) Run the engine and check for coolant leaks.

7 Thermostat - removal, check and installation

Removal

1 Drain the cooling system below the level of the thermostat (see Chapter 1).
2 Place rags beneath the thermostat housing to catch any residual coolant that drips out, then unbolt the thermostat housing from the front of the cylinder head (carbureted models) or the left side (fuel injected models) **(see illustration)**.
3 Take the thermostat out of the cylinder head **(see illustration)**.

7.2 The thermostat housing on carbureted models (shown) is in the front of the cylinder head - on fuel injected models, it's in the left side of the cylinder head

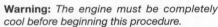

7.3 Pull the thermostat out of the head

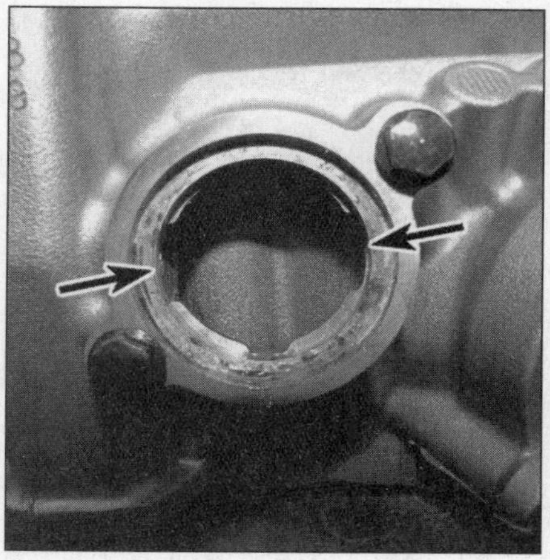

7.11 These flat spots align the thermostat in the correct orientation to the hole

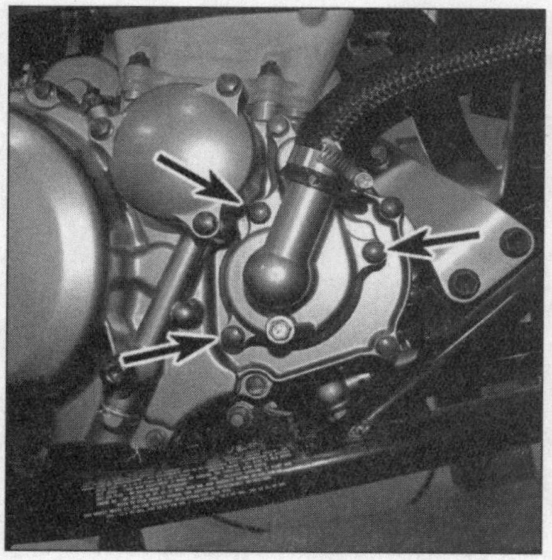

8.4 Loosen and remove the water pump bolts while the crankcase cover is still bolted to the engine

8.7a Remove the drive gear snap-ring . . .

Check

4 Remove any coolant deposits, then visually check the thermostat for corrosion, cracks and other damage. If it was open when it was removed, the thermostat is defective.

5 To check the thermostat operation, submerge it in a container of the specified coolant (50/50 mix of antifreeze and water) along with a thermometer. The thermostat should be suspended so it does not touch the sides of the container.

Warning: Antifreeze is poisonous. Do not use a cooking pan to test the thermostat.

6 Gradually heat the water in the container with a hot plate or stove and check the temperature when the thermostat just starts to open.

7 Compare the opening temperature to the values listed in this Chapter's Specifications.

8 Continue heating the water until the valve is fully open.

9 Measure how far the thermostat valve has opened and compare to this Chapter's Specifications.

10 It these specifications are not met, or if the thermostat doesn't open while the coolant is heated, replace it with a new one.

Installation

11 Apply clean coolant to the rubber seal on the thermostat and install the thermostat into the cylinder head. There's a flat spot on each side of the thermostat recess that only allows the thermostat to be installed in the correct orientation **(see illustration)**.

12 Install the thermostat housing and tighten its bolts securely, but don't overtighten them and strip the threads.

13 Fill and bleed the cooling system (see Chapter 1).

14 The remainder of installation is the reverse of removal.

8 Water pump - removal, inspection and installation

Removal and disassembly

Note: *The following procedure describes removing the water pump completely. If you're only planning to remove the cover so you can inspect the impeller, ignore that steps that don't apply.*

1 Drain the engine oil and cooling system (see Chapter 1).

2 Disconnect the spring from the brake pedal and unbolt the rear master cylinder (see Chapter 7). Leave the fluid line connected to the master cylinder.

3 Disconnect the spring from the brake light switch (see Chapter 5).

4 Disconnect the coolant hose from the water pump **(see illustration)**.

5 Remove the pump cover bolts **(see illustration 8.4)**. The bolts are different lengths, so tag them for reinstallation. Don't try to remove the pump cover yet - the reason to remove the bolts now is that they are easier to loosen while the pump is still attached to the engine.

6 Refer to Chapter 2 and remove the right crankcase cover from the engine together with the water pump. This is necessary because the pump cover is secured to the pump body from the inner side by two screws, and the only way to get at them is to remove the crankcase cover together with the water pump, then remove the drive gear and pull the pump body out of the crankcase cover.

7 The impeller and shaft are one piece. To remove them, remove the snap-ring, drive gear, pin and washer from the inner end of the shaft **(see illustrations)**. Pull the water pump body out of the crankcase cover.

8 Remove the pump cover O-ring and screws, then remove the cover from the

8.7b . . . the drive gear and pin . . .

8.7c . . . and the washer

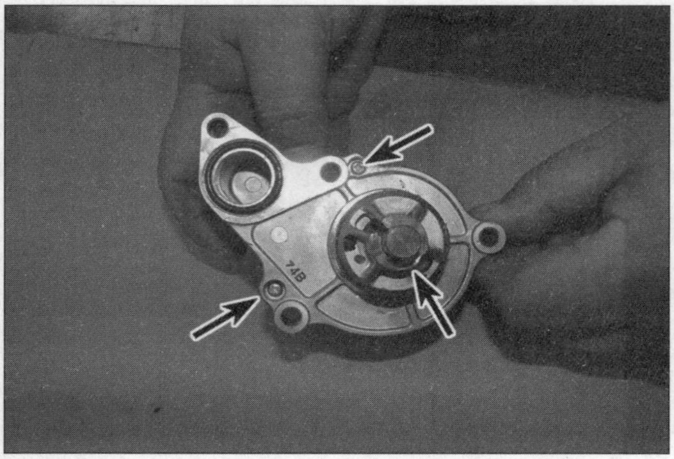

8.8a Remove the cover screws and impeller snap-ring

8.8b Take the cover off the pump and remove the O-ring

8.8c Remove the O-ring from the pump body and pull the impeller out, together with its shaft

9.1a Remove the Teflon seal from the impeller shaft and pry the rubber seal out of the impeller

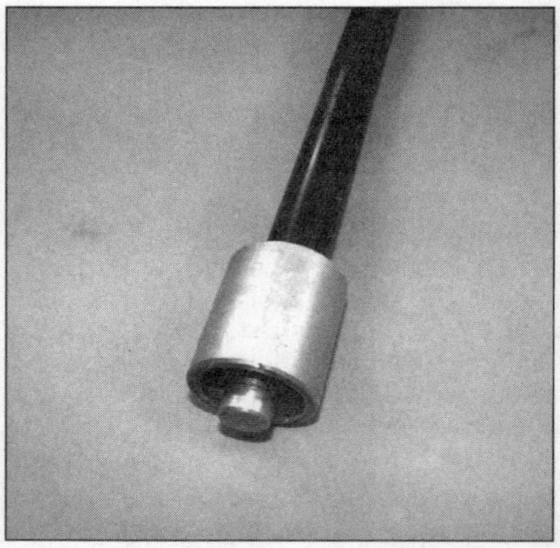

9.1b To install a new mechanical seal, you'll need a tool like this one

pump body **(see illustrations)**. Take the remaining snap-ring off the inner end of the shaft, then pull the impeller and shaft out of the pump body **(see illustration)**.

Inspection

9 Check the oil seal and mechanical seal for wear or damage. These seals separate the coolant from the engine oil. If the oil is milky or foamy, coolant may have been leaking into it past the seals. Refer to Section 9 to replace the seals.

10 The pump O-rings should be replaced whenever the pump is disassembled

Installation

11 Installation is the reverse of removal, with the following additions:

- a) *Use a new O-ring.*
- b) *Engage the impeller shaft pin with the drive gear.*
- c) *Tighten the water pump bolts to the torque listed in this Chapter's Specifications.*
- d) *Fill and bleed the cooling system and fill the engine oil (see Chapter 1).*
- e) *Run the engine and check for coolant leaks.*

9 Water pump seals - replacement

1 If coolant has been leaking from the weep hole, the water pump seals need to be replaced. There are four seals: a rubber seal inside the impeller, a Teflon seal next to the rubber seal, a conventional rubber seal inside the water pump body and a mechanical seal, which is spring-loaded to rub against the Teflon seal. **Note:** *The mechanical seal can't be removed without destroying it. Be sure you have a new one before you remove it from the pump.*

HAYNES HiNT ***If the Teflon seal inside the impeller is worn and is not included with a new mechanical seal, you can turn the old one over and put it back in the impeller so its other surface is exposed to the mechanical seal (see illustration).***

TOOL TiP ***To drive the new seal in, you'll need a tool that bears on the flange of the mechanical seal, and also fits in the recess of the pump body. It should also have a center protrusion that fits inside the seal to keep it from collapsing as it's being installed (see illustration).***

2 Remove and disassemble the water pump (see Section 8).

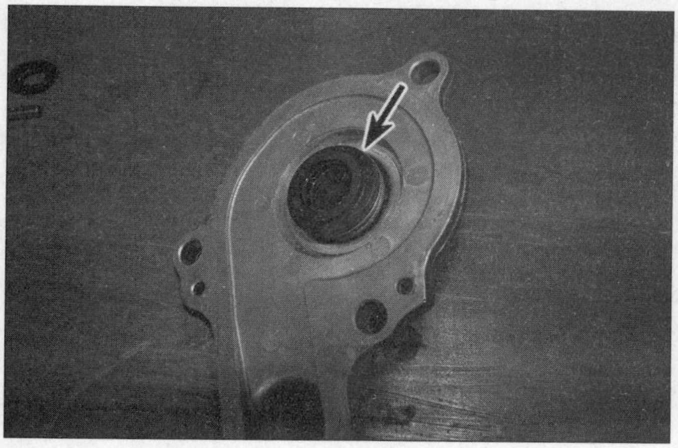

9.3a Pry out the rubber portion of the seal - you'll have to destroy the seal to remove it, so make sure you can get a new one

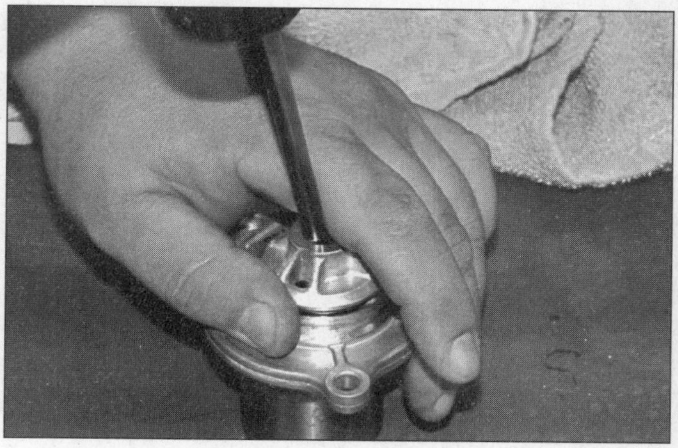

9.3b Insert a punch through the pump body to drive the metal part of the mechanical seal out of its bore

9.3c Remove the mechanical seal once it's loose - use Loctite 518 or equivalent on the sides of the metal portion

9.3d Once the mechanical seal is out, pry the rubber seal out of the pump body

3 Carefully start the seals from their bores with a screwdriver, being careful not to gouge the crankcase cover or impeller **(see illustrations)**. Finish removal of the mechanical seal and the conventional seal behind it by inserting a screwdriver into the access holes in the water pump body,

4 Tap in new seals, using a driver tool **(see illustration 9.1b)**. If the new mechanical seal is not coated with sealant on the outer edge, coat it with Loctite 518 or equivalent.

Notes

Chapter 4 Part A
Fuel and exhaust systems (carbureted models)

Contents

Degrees of difficulty

Easy, suitable for novice with little experience	**Fairly easy,** suitable for beginner with some experience	**Fairly difficult,** suitable for competent DIY mechanic	**Difficult,** suitable for experienced DIY mechanic	**Very difficult,** suitable for expert DIY or professional

Specifications

Carburetor

2003 and 2004 models	
Type	Mikuni BRS-36
ID mark	
US (except California) and Canada	07G0
California	07G1
Main jet	130
Needle/clip position	5E26-1
Pilot jet	22.5
Standard pilot screw setting	
US (except California) and Canada	2-1/4 turns out
California	Not specified
Float height	13.0 +/- 1.0 mm (0.51 +/- 0.04 inch)
2005 and later models	
Type	Mikuni BRS-37
ID mark	
US (except California), Canada, EU	07G2
California	07G3
Main jet	130
Needle/clip position	5E26-1
Pilot jet	22.5
Standard pilot screw setting	
US and Canada	1-1/2 turns out
California	Not specified
Float height	13.0 +/- 1.0 mm (0.51 +/- 0.04 inch)

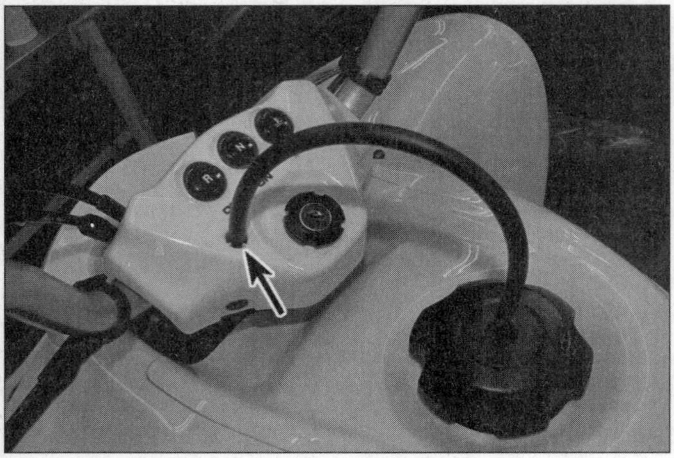

2.1 Pull the fuel tank vent hose out of its hole in the handlebar cover

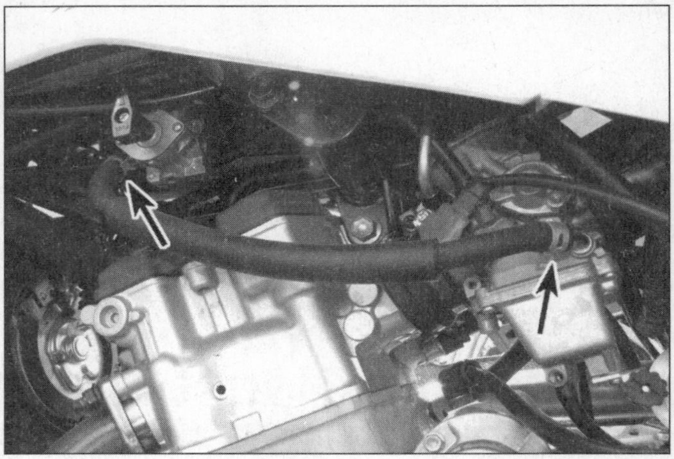

2.2 Disconnect the fuel line at the tank (left arrow) or carburetor (right arrow)

2.4a Remove the mounting bolts at the rear of the tank

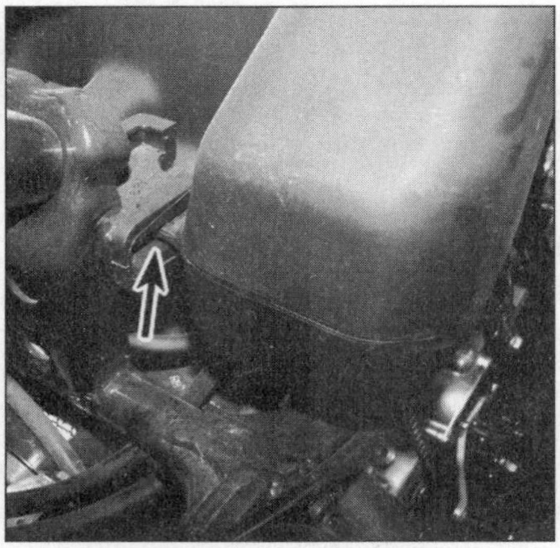

2.4b Pull the tank rearward to clear the front mounting bracket . . .

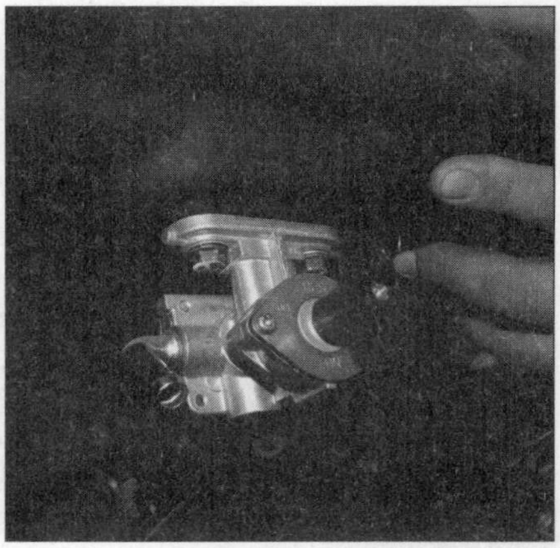

2.4c . . . and lift the tank off

1 General information

2008 and earlier models use a constant-vacuum Mikuni BRS carburetor with a butterfly-type throttle valve. For cold starting, a choke plunger is actuated by a knob. The carburetor on 2005 through 2008 models is equipped with a throttle position sensor.

The exhaust system consists of a pipe and muffler with a removable spark arrester.

2 Fuel tank - removal and installation

Warning: Gasoline is extremely flammable, so take extra precautions when you work on any part of the fuel system. Don't smoke or allow open flames or bare light bulbs near the work area, and don't work in a garage where a gas-type appliance (such as a water heater or clothes dryer) is present. Since gasoline is carcinogenic, wear fuel-resistant gloves when there's a possibility of being exposed to fuel, and, if you spill any fuel on your skin, rinse it off immediately with soap and water. Mop up any spills immediately and do not store fuel-soaked rags where they could ignite. When you perform any kind of work on the fuel system, wear safety glasses and have an extinguisher suitable for a class B type fire (flammable liquids) on hand.

Removal

1 Remove the seat and fuel tank side covers (see Chapter 8). Disconnect the fuel tank breather hose from the handlebar cover **(see illustration)**.

2 Turn the fuel tap to Off and disconnect the fuel line **(see illustration)**.

3 Remove the cover from the air cleaner intake duct (see Section 10).

4 Remove the mounting bolts at the rear of the tank. Pull the tank backward to clear the mounting bracket at the front and lift it off, together with the fuel tap **(see illustrations)**.

Installation

5 Before installing the tank, check the condition of the rubber mounting isolator at the front, the bushings at the two rear bolt holes and the fuel line to the carburetor - if they're hardened, cracked, or show any other signs of deterioration, replace them.

6 Installation is otherwise the reverse of removal. Make sure the tank does not pinch any wires. Tighten the tank mounting bolts securely, but don't overtighten them and strip the threads.

3 Carburetor overhaul - general information

1 Poor engine performance, hesitation, hard starting, stalling, flooding and backfiring are all signs that major carburetor maintenance may be required.

2 Keep in mind that many so-called carburetor problems are really not carburetor problems at all, but mechanical problems within the engine or ignition system malfunc-

4.3 Loosen the clamping bands at the front and rear of the carburetor and disconnect the throttle position sensor's wiring harness

4.5 Work the carburetor free of the bands and take it partway out for access to the throttle and choke cables

tions. Try to establish for certain that the carburetor is in need of maintenance before beginning a major overhaul.

3 Check the fuel tap and its strainer screen, the fuel lines, the intake manifold clamps, the O-ring between the intake manifold and cylinder head, the vacuum hoses, the air filter element, the cylinder compression, crankcase vacuum and compression, the spark plug and the ignition timing before assuming that a carburetor overhaul is required. If the vehicle has been unused for more than 24 hours, drain the float chamber and refill the tank with fresh fuel.

4 Most carburetor problems are caused by dirt particles, varnish and other deposits which build up in and block the fuel and air passages. Also, in time, gaskets and O-rings shrink or deteriorate and cause fuel and air leaks which lead to poor performance.

5 When the carburetor is overhauled, it is generally disassembled completely and the parts are cleaned thoroughly with a carburetor cleaning solvent and dried with filtered, unlubricated compressed air. The fuel and air passages are also blown through with compressed air to force out any dirt that may have been loosened but not removed by the solvent. Once the cleaning process is complete, the carburetor is reassembled using a new top gasket, O-rings and, generally, a new inlet needle valve and seat.

6 Before disassembling the carburetor, make sure you have the necessary gasket, O-rings and other parts, some carburetor cleaner, a supply of rags, some means of blowing out the carburetor passages and a clean place to work.

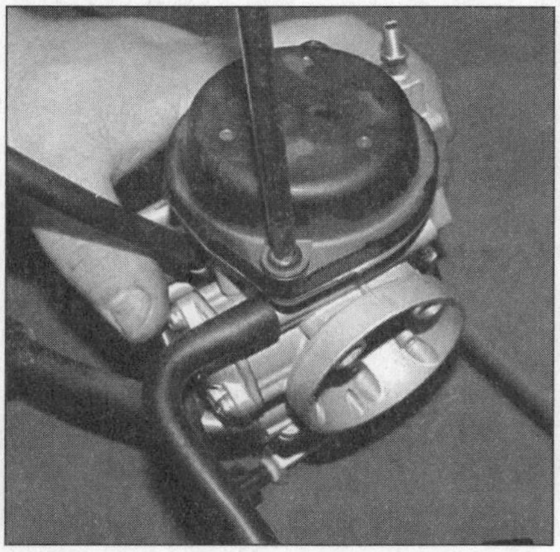

5.3a Remove the screws that secure the cap

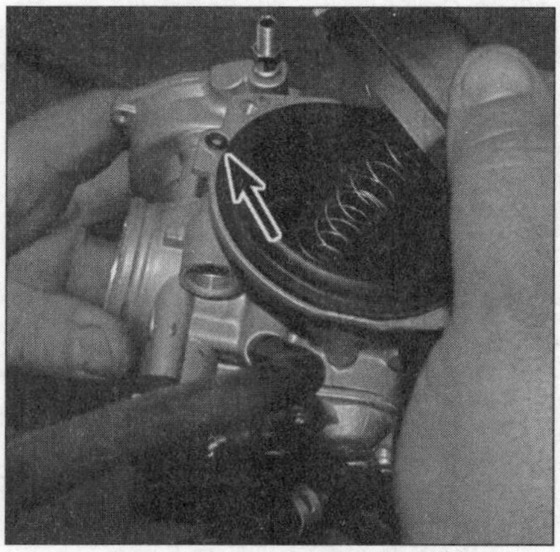

5.3b Lift off the cap, noting the position of the small O-ring on the carburetor body

4 Carburetor - removal and installation

1 Remove the left fuel tank side cover (see Chapter 8).

2 Disconnect the fuel line from the carburetor (see Section 2).

3 Loosen the clamping bands at the front and rear of the carburetor **(see illustration)**.

4 On 2005 and later models, disconnect the wiring connector for the throttle position sensor **(see illustration 4.3)**.

5 Free the carburetor from the intake tube and the air cleaner tube **(see illustration)**.

6 Remove the carburetor partway and disconnect the throttle and choke cables (see Section 7).

7 Note how the hoses are routed and free them from the retainer. Remove the carburetor.

8 Installation is the reverse of the removal steps, with the following additions:

a) Adjust the throttle freeplay (see Chapter 1).

b) Adjust the idle speed (see Chapter 1).

5 Carburetor - disassembly, cleaning and inspection

Warning: Gasoline is extremely flammable, so take extra precautions when you work on any part of the fuel system. See the Warning in Section 2.

Disassembly

1 Remove the carburetor (see Section 4).

2 Set the carburetor on a clean working surface. Take note of how the vent hoses are routed, including locations of hose retainers. On 2005 and later models, remove the throttle position sensor (see Section 9).

3 To disassemble the carburetor, refer to the accompanying illustrations **(see illustrations)**.

Cleaning

Caution: Use only a carburetor cleaning solution that is safe for use with plastic parts (be sure to read the label on the container).

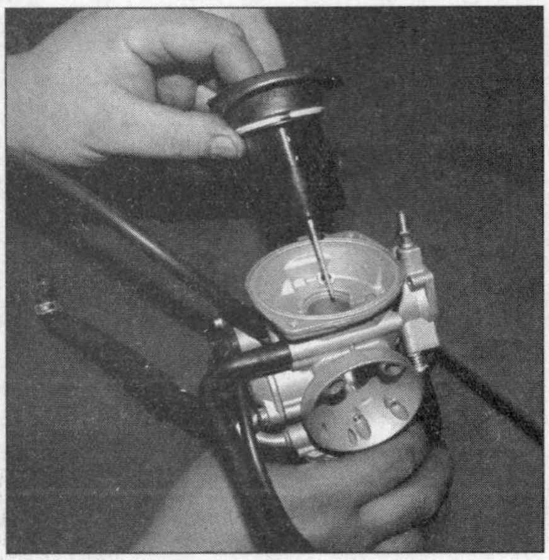

5.3c Pull out the diaphragm and piston, together with the jet needle

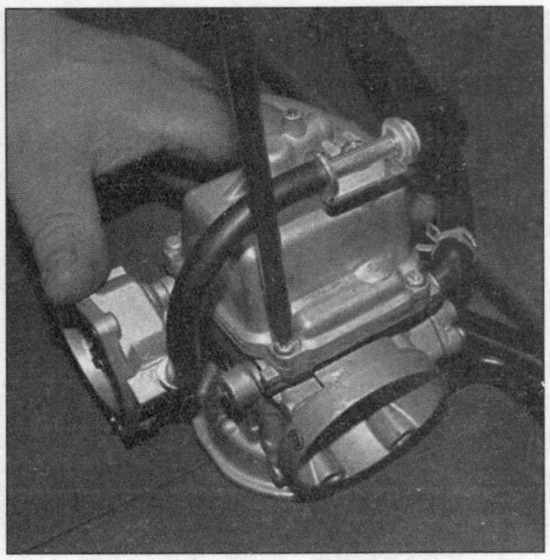

5.3d Remove the float chamber screws

5.3e Lift off the float chamber, together with its O-ring

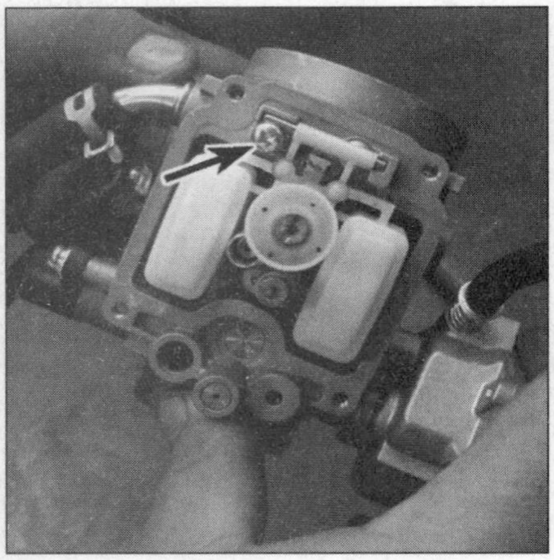

5.3f Remove the float screw

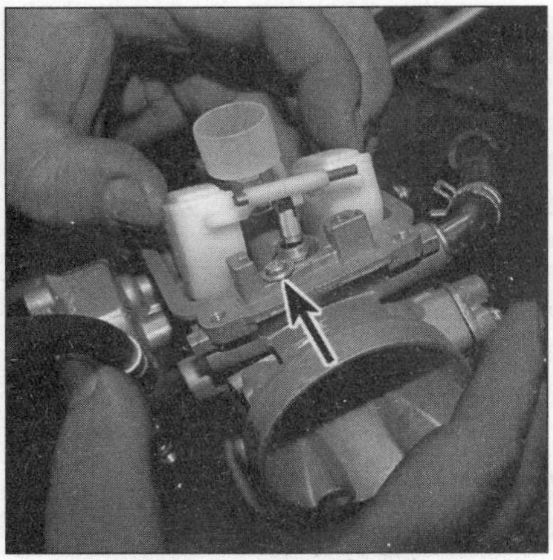

5.3g Lift out the float together with the needle valve and remove the screw that secures the needle valve seat

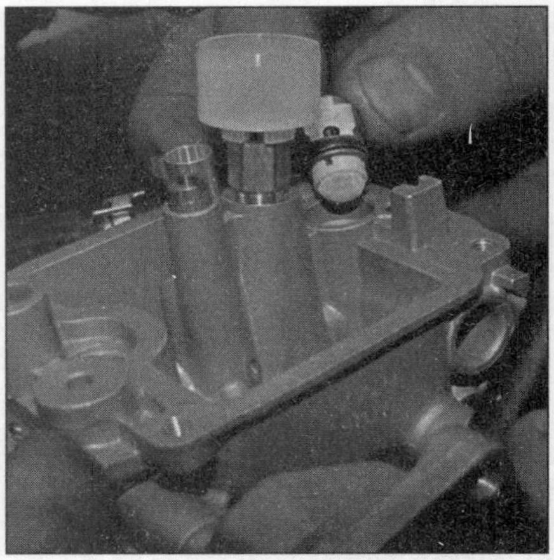

5.3h Remove the needle valve seat and fuel strainer

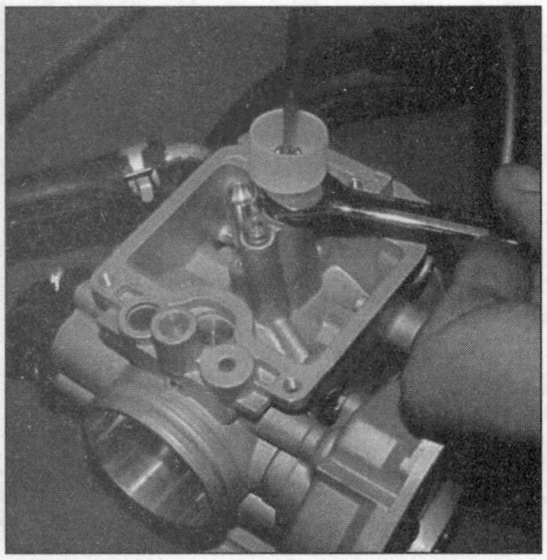

5.3i Hold the needle jet holder with a wrench on the hex and unscrew the main jet

5.3j Unscrew the needle jet holder and lift it out together with its O-ring

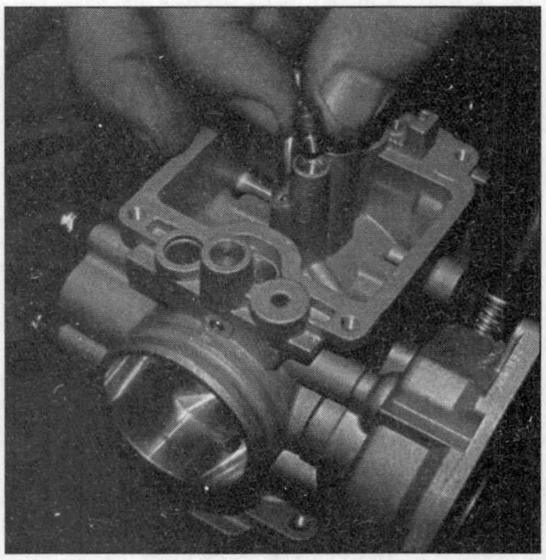

5.3k Unscrew the main jet

5.3l Unscrew the starter (choke) jet

5.3m Unscrew the pilot jet. On California models, drill and pry out the plug (arrow) for access to the idle mixture screw. On all models, turn the screw in until it bottoms lightly, counting the number of turns, then unscrew it all the way

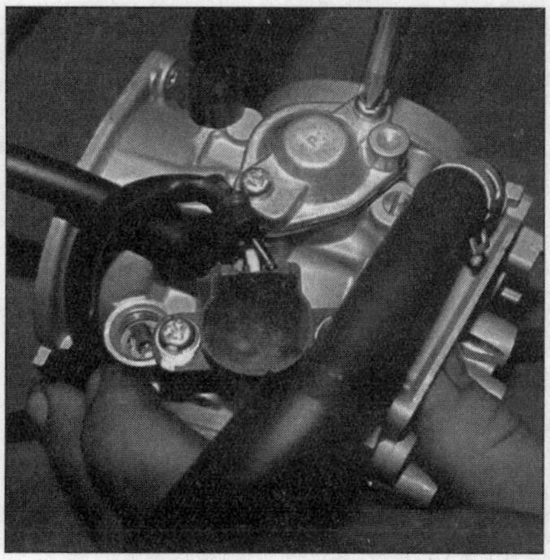

5.3n Remove the diaphragm cover screws

4 Submerge the metal components in the carburetor cleaner for approximately thirty minutes (or longer, if the directions recommend it).

5 After the carburetor has soaked long enough for the cleaner to loosen and dissolve most of the varnish and other deposits, use a brush to remove the stubborn deposits. Rinse it again, then dry it with compressed air. Blow out all of the fuel and air passages in the carburetor body.

Caution: Never clean the jets or passages with a piece of wire or a drill bit, as they will be enlarged, causing the fuel and air metering rates to be upset.

Inspection

6 Check the operation of the choke plunger. If it doesn't move smoothly, replace it. Check the plunger seat for wear or damage and replace it if problems are found. Inspect the hot start valve in the same manner.

7 Check the tapered portion of the pilot screw for wear or damage. Replace the screw if necessary.

8 Check the carburetor body, float chamber and carburetor top for cracks, distorted sealing surfaces and other damage. If any defects are found, replace the faulty component, although replacement of the entire carburetor will probably be necessary (check with your parts supplier for the availability of separate components).

9 Check the jet needle for straightness by rolling it on a flat surface (such as a piece of glass). Replace it if it's bent or if the tip is worn.

10 Check the tip of the fuel inlet valve needle. If it has grooves or scratches in it, it must be replaced. Push in on the rod in the other end of the needle, then release it - if it doesn't spring back, replace the valve needle.

11 Check the O-rings on the float chamber and the main jet access plug (in the float chamber). Replace them if they're damaged.

5.3o Remove the cover and spring

12 Check the floats for damage. This will usually be apparent by the presence of fuel inside one of the floats. If the floats are damaged, they must be replaced.

13 Check that the throttle valve moves up-and-down smoothly in the carburetor body. Check the surface of the throttle valve for wear and damage. If it's worn excessively or doesn't move smoothly in the bore, replace the carburetor.

6 Carburetor - reassembly and float height check

Reassembly

Caution: When installing the jets, be careful not to over-tighten them - they're made of soft material and can strip or shear easily.

5.3p Remove the diaphragm, noting how its rod engages the hole in the carburetor body

Note: *When reassembling the carburetor, be sure to use new O-rings.*

1 Install the clip on the jet needle if it was removed. Place it in the needle groove listed in this Chapter's Specifications. Install the needle and clip in the throttle valve.

2 Install the pilot screw along with its spring, washer and O-ring, turning it in until it seats lightly. Now, turn the screw out the number of turns written down during removal.

3 Reverse the disassembly steps to install the jets.

4 Invert the carburetor. Attach the fuel inlet valve needle to the float. Set the float into position in the carburetor, making sure the valve needle seats correctly. Install the float pivot pin.

5 Measure float height (see Step 7) before the float chamber is installed.

6 Install the float chamber gasket or O-ring. Place the float chamber on the carburetor and install the screws, tightening them securely. Install the main jet access plug in the bottom of the float chamber, using a new O-ring, and tighten it securely.

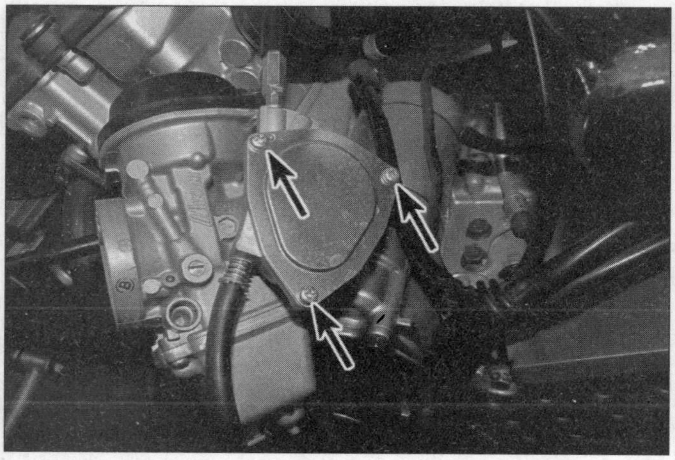

7.7a Remove the throttle housing cover screws

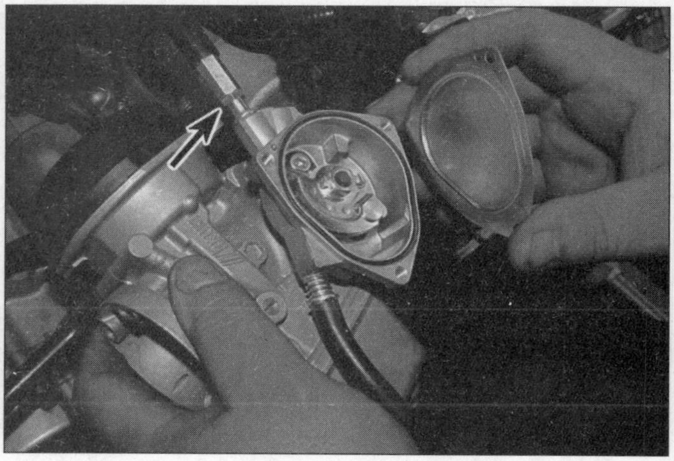

7.7b Remove the cover, then remove its O-ring and loosen the locknut

Float check

7 To check, hold the carburetor so the float hangs down, then tilt it back until the valve needle is just seated. Measure the distance from the float chamber gasket surface to the top of the float and compare your measurement to the float height listed in this Chapter's Specifications. Bend the float tang as necessary to change the adjustment.

7 Throttle and choke cables - removal and installation

Throttle cable

1 These vehicles are equipped with a single accelerator cable that operates the throttle plate in the carburetor.

2 Remove the fuel tank (see Section 2).

3 At the handlebar, loosen the throttle cable adjuster all the way (see Chapter 1).

4 Look for a punch mark on the handlebar next to the split in the throttle housing. If you don't see a mark, make one so the throttle housing can be installed in the correct position.

5 Remove three screws that secure the cover to the throttle housing.

6 Lift the cover off the housing and disconnect the throttle cable from the lever inside.

7 At the carburetor, remove the throttle pulley cover **(see illustrations)**.

8 Loosen the cable locknut to create slack in the cable **(see illustration 7.7b)**. Lift the cable out of the groove, turn it to align with the removal slot and slip the cable end plug out of the pulley **(see illustration)**.

9 Unscrew the adjusting nut all the way off of the throttle housing, then pull the cable out of the carburetor **(see illustration)**.

10 If necessary, remove the bolts that secure the throttle housing and its clamp to the handlebar and take them off.

11 Note how the cable is routed and remove it from the vehicle.

12 Route the cable into place. Make sure it doesn't interfere with any other components and isn't kinked or bent sharply.

13 Lubricate the carburetor end of the cable with multi-purpose grease. Reverse the disconnection steps to connect the throttle cable to the carburetor throttle pulley.

14 Reverse the disconnection steps to connect the cables to the throttle grip.

15 Operate the throttle and make sure it returns to the idle position by itself under spring pressure.

Warning: If the throttle doesn't return by itself, find and solve the problem before continuing with installation. A stuck throttle can lead to loss of control of the vehicle.

16 Refer to Chapter 1 for the cable adjustment procedure.

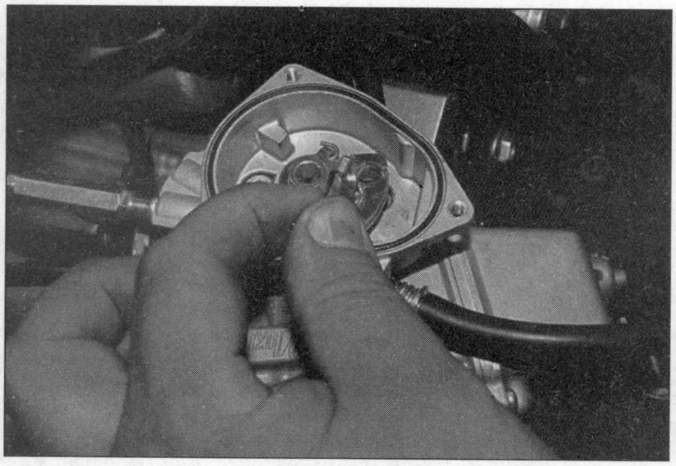

7.8 Lift the cable out of the pulley groove, turn it and lift the end plug out of the throttle pulley, then slide the end plug down the cable and slip it off

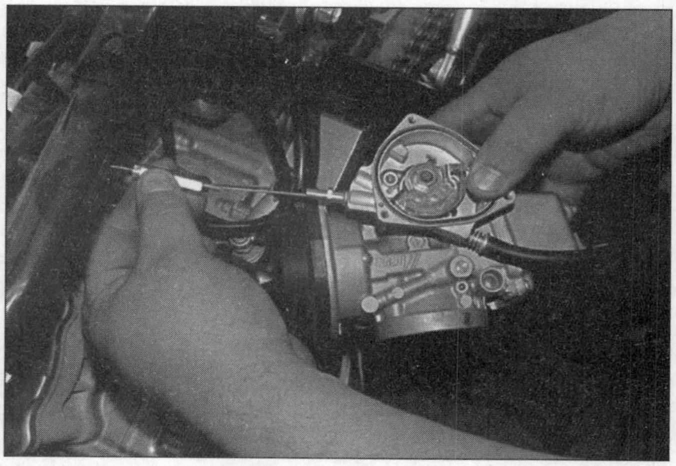

7.9 Unscrew the adjusting nut off the outer cable, then pull the cable out of the throttle cable housing

7.20 Unscrew the choke plunger nut from the carburetor and pull it out - compress the spring and slide the plunger sideways to remove it from the cable

8.2 If necessary, remove the heat shield bolts

8.3a Loosen the clamp bolt

8.3b Remove the muffler bolts and separate the muffler from the exhaust pipe

17 Turn the handlebars back and forth to make sure the cable does not cause the steering to bind.

18 Once you're sure the cable operates properly, install the fuel tank.

19 With the engine idling, turn the handlebars through their full travel (full left lock to full right lock) and note whether idle speed increases. If it does, the cable is routed incorrectly. Correct this dangerous condition before riding the vehicle.

Choke cable

20 Unscrew the choke nut from the carburetor and pull it out, together with the choke plunger **(see illustration)**. If necessary, compress the spring and slide the cable end plug out of the plunger.

21 Separate the halves of the left handlebar switch (see Chapter 5).

22 Disconnect the choke cable from the lever pulley at the left handlebar.

23 Note how the cable is routed and remove it from the vehicle.

24 Route the cable into place. Make sure it doesn't interfere with any other components and isn't kinked or bent sharply.

25 Installation is the reverse of the removal steps.

8 Exhaust system - removal and installation

1 Remove the right side cover (see Chapter 8).

2 If necessary, unbolt and remove the heat shield from the exhaust pipe **(see illustration)**.

3 Loosen the muffler clamp bolt and unscrew the mounting bolts **(see illustrations)**. Work the muffler free of the pipe and remove the gasket.

4 Detach the front pipe from the cylinder head and remove it from the machine **(see illustration)**.

5 To replace the muffler core, refer to Chapter 1.

6 Installation is the reverse of removal. Use a new gasket in the exhaust port and at the joint between the pipe and muffler.

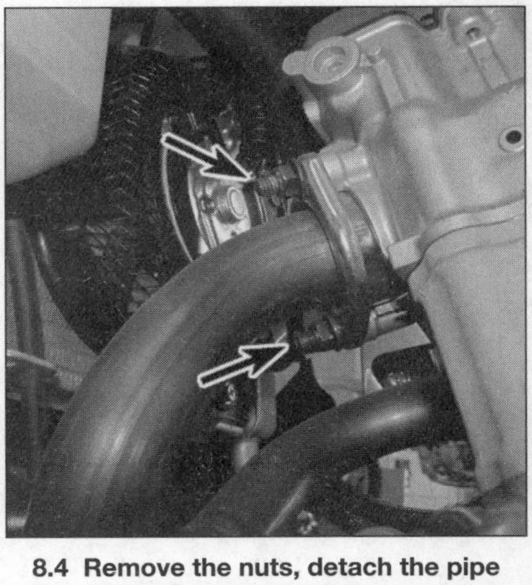

8.4 Remove the nuts, detach the pipe from the cylinder head and remove the gasket from the exhaust port

9.2 Loosen the screws to adjust the throttle position sensor - unscrew them all the way to remove the sensor

9 Throttle position sensor - check, removal and installation

Note: *This Section applies to 2005 and later models only.*

Check

1 Before checking the throttle position sensor, check and adjust engine idle speed and throttle cable freeplay (see Chapter 1).

2 Locate the sensor on the carburetor **(see illustration)**. Follow its wiring harness to the connector.

3 Connect an ohmmeter between the terminals of the black and blue wires.

4 Turn the ignition switch to On (but don't start the engine). The voltmeter should indicate 5 volts (this is the sensor input voltage). If it doesn't, check the wiring from the ECM to the throttle position sensor for breaks or bad connections.

5 Move the voltmeter positive terminal to the yellow wire's connector. Leave the voltmeter negative terminal connected to the black wire's terminal. The voltmeter should now indicate 0.58 to 0.87 volts. If the reading is incorrect, adjust the sensor as described below. Do not remove the sensor unless it needs to be replaced, or performance will be impaired.

Adjustment

6 This procedure requires a Torx bit.

7 Loosen the mounting screws **(see illustration 9.2)**. Carefully rotate the sensor back and forth to get the correct output voltage, then tighten the screw.

Replacement

8 Disconnect the electrical connector. Remove the mounting screw and take the sensor off.

9 Install the sensor, making sure its slot aligns with the tab in the carburetor. Tighten the mounting screw, leaving it loose enough so the sensor can be rotated.

10 Adjust the sensor output voltage as described above.

11 Once the correct reading is obtained, mark the sensor position on the carburetor with a felt pen.

12 Tighten the mounting screw, making sure that the felt pen marks stay aligned.

13 Remove the voltmeter and probes.

14 Reset the idle speed (see Chapter 1).

10 Air cleaner housing - removal and installation

1 Remove the seat (see Chapter 8) and fuel tank (see Section 2).

2 Loosen the clamping bands that secure the air intake and outlet tubes to the front of the air cleaner housing.

3 Remove the mounting bolt from each side of the air cleaner housing. Work the housing free of the intake and outlet tubes and lift it out of the frame.

4 Installation is the reverse of removal.

Chapter 4 Part B
Fuel, exhaust and emission control systems (fuel injected models)

Contents

Degrees of difficulty

Easy, suitable for novice with little experience	**Fairly easy,** suitable for beginner with some experience	**Fairly difficult,** suitable for competent DIY mechanic	**Difficult,** suitable for experienced DIY mechanic	**Very difficult,** suitable for expert DIY or professional

Specifications

Fuel injection system

System type	Single-point throttle body fuel injection
Throttle body	
Diameter	36 mm (1.42 inch)
ID number	33HO
Idle speed	1600 +/- 100 rpm
Fuel pressure	42 psi (294 kPa)
Intake air pressure sensor	
Input voltage	4.5 to 5.5 volts
Output voltage	
At idle (installed on engine)	Approximately 1.7 volts
At altitude/vacuum (in test rig)	
Zero to 610 meters (zero to 2000 feet/94 to 100 kPa)	3.1 to 3.6 volts
611 to 1524 meters (2001 to 5000 feet/85 to 94 kPa)	2.8 to 3.4 volts
1525 to 2438 meters (5001 to 8000 feet/76 to 85 kPa)	2.6 to 3.1 volts
2439 to 3048 meters (8001 to 10,000 feet/70 to 76 kPa)	2.4 to 2.9 volts

Fuel injection system (continued)

Intake air temperature sensor	
Input voltage	4.5 to 5.5 volts
Output voltage	0.2 to 4.9 volts
Resistance	Approximately 2.6 k-ohms at 20-degrees C (68-degrees F)
Throttle position sensor	
Input voltage	4.5 to 5.5 volts
Output voltage	
Throttle open	Approximately 3.8 volts
Throttle closed	Approximately 0.6 volts
Resistance	
Throttle open	Approximately 3.8 k-ohms
Throttle closed	Approximately 0.6 k-ohms
Engine coolant temperature sensor	
Input voltage	4.5 to 5.5 volts
Output voltage	0.2 to 4.9 volts
Resistance	
At 68-degrees F (20-degrees C)	Approximately 2.57 k-ohms
At 122-degrees F (50-degrees C)	Approximately 770 ohms
At 176-degrees F (80-degrees C)	Approximately 270 ohms
At 230-degrees F (110-degrees C)	Approximately 110 ohms
Crankshaft position sensor	
Resistance	400 to 600 ohms
Peak voltage during cranking	1.0 volt or more
Tip-over sensor	
Resistance	15.0 to 25.0 k-ohms
Voltage	
Level	0.4 to 1.4 volts
Tilted 65-degrees or more	3.7 to 4.4 volts
Gear position switch voltage	0.9 volts or more
Fuel injector resistance	9 to 17 ohms at 20-degrees C (68-degrees F)

Torque specifications

Fuel pump mounting bolts	10 Nm (84 inch-lbs)
Fuel valve mounting bolts	10 Nm (84 inch-lbs)
Intake air temperature sensor mounting screw	2.5 Nm (24 inch-lbs)
Throttle position sensor screws	3.5 Nm (30 inch-lbs)
Exhaust system nuts and bolts	23 Nm (16.5 ft-lbs)

1 Fuel injection system - general information

The fuel injection system is a single-point throttle body system. This means that there is one fuel injector, mounted on a throttle body that attaches to the engine much like a carburetor. The fuel injector injects fuel into the throttle body at the correct point in each engine cycle. The injector is turned on and off by the Engine Control Module (ECM). When the engine is running, the ECM constantly monitors engine operating conditions with an array of information sensors, calculates the correct amount of fuel, then varies the interval of time during which the injector is open. The fuel injection system provides much better control of the air/fuel mixture than a carburetor, and is therefore able to produce more power, better mileage and lower emissions.

The system uses the ECM and an array of information sensors to determine and deliver the correct air/fuel ratio under all operating conditions. The system consists of three sub-systems: input sensors, the ECM, and output actuators.

Input sensors

Throttle Position (TP) sensor

The Throttle Position (TP) sensor, mounted on the throttle body, is a potentiometer that monitors the opening angle of the throttle plate and sends a variable voltage signal to the ECM.

Intake Air Pressure (IAP) sensor

The Intake Air Pressure (IAP) sensor is located on the throttle body. The IAP sensor measures the pressure of incoming air and generates a variable voltage signal that's proportionate to the pressure. The ECM uses this data to calculate the load on the engine.

Intake Air Temperature (IAT) sensor

The IAT sensor, mounted on the air cleaner housing, relays a voltage signal to the ECM that varies in accordance with the temperature of the incoming air in the air cleaner housing. The ECM uses this information to calculate how rich or lean the air/fuel mixture should be.

Crankshaft Position (CKP) sensor

The crankshaft position sensor lets the ECM know where the crankshaft is in the induction cycle. The ECM uses this information to control timing of the fuel injector opening.

Engine Coolant Temperature (ECT) sensor

The ECT sensor monitors engine temperature and sends a voltage signal to the ECM. The ECM used this information to decide whether to enrich the fuel mixture for cold-engine operation.

Tip-over sensor

This is a safety device that signals the ECM to shut off the engine if the vehicle rolls over.

Gear position switch

This device, mounted on the engine above the shift pedal, signals transmission gear position to the ECM.

Engine control module

The Engine control module (ECM) is a microprocessor, mounted at the front of the vehicle behind the headlight. It receives signals from the input sensors, and uses this information to decide exactly when, and for exactly how long, to open the fuel injector. This controls injection timing as well as the amount of fuel injected.

The ECM also control other functions, such as ignition timing, cooling fan operation, and the warning lights.

Output actuators

The output actuators include an electric fuel pump located outside of the fuel tank behind the starter motor, the fuel rail and the fuel injector. The fuel injector delivers fuel into the intake air stream.

Fuel pump

The fuel pump is mounted externally and is connected to the fuel tank by hoses. Electrical power is supplied to the pump from the fuel pump relay, which is an integral part of the ECM.

Fuel valve

The fuel valve is mounted on the bottom of the fuel tank. It includes a filter screen and the fuel pressure regulator. The regulator maintains fuel pressure at a constant 42 psi (294 kPa).

Fuel rail and injector

The fuel rail is mounted on the throttle body, with a fuel injector between the throttle body and fuel rail. Fuel flows from the pump into the fuel rail, and as the injector opens, into the throttle body, then into the engine.

Throttle body

The throttle body controls the amount of air entering the engine. It's activated by a cable, which is controlled by the rider through a thumb lever on the right handlebar.

2 Fuel injection system - check

Note: *The following procedure is based on the assumption that the fuel pump is working and the fuel pressure is adequate (see Section 5).*

1 Check all electrical connectors that are related to the system. Check the ground wire connections for tightness. Loose connectors and poor grounds can cause many problems that resemble more serious malfunctions.

2 Verify that the battery is fully charged. The Engine Control Module (ECM), information sensors and output actuators (the fuel injector is an output actuator) depend on a stable voltage supply in order to meter fuel correctly.

3 Inspect the air filter element (see Chapter 1). A dirty or partially blocked filter will severely impede performance and economy.

4 Check the ignition fuse (see Chapter 5). If you find a blown fuse, replace it and see if it blows again. If it does, look for a wire shorted to ground in the circuit(s) protected by that fuse.

5 Check the air induction system between the throttle body and the intake manifold for air leaks, which will cause a lean air/fuel mixture ratio (when the mixture ratio becomes excessively lean, the engine will begin misfiring). Also inspect the condition of all vacuum hoses connected to the intake manifold and to the throttle body. A loose or broken vacuum hose will allow unmetered air into the intake manifold. Unmetered air, especially at idle and during other high-intake-manifold-vacuum conditions, will cause the engine to misfire.

6 Remove the air cleaner housing and check the throttle body for dirt, carbon, varnish, or other residue in the throttle body, particularly around the throttle plate. If it's dirty, clean it with a clean shop towel and a petroleum-based solvent. Do not use caustic carburetor cleaners.

7 With the engine running, place an automotive stethoscope against the injector and listen for a clicking sound that indicates operation. If you don't have a stethoscope, touch the tip of a long screwdriver against the injector and listen through the handle.

8 If you can hear the injector operating, but the engine is misfiring, the electrical circuits are functioning correctly, but the injector might be dirty or clogged. Try a commercial injector cleaning product (available at auto parts stores). If cleaning the injector doesn't help, the injector probably needs to be cleaned professionally, or replaced.

9 If the injector is not operating (it makes no sound), disconnect the injector electrical connector and measure the voltage between the injector wiring connector terminal and ground. The engine should be running (or cranking, if it won't run). The voltage reading should be the same reading you get by connecting the voltmeter between the terminals of the vehicle's battery. If it isn't, check the circuit for breaks or bad connections.

10 If the injector is not operating, but the voltage reading is correct, the ECM or the circuit between the ECM and the injector might be faulty.

11 As a further check on the injector, unplug its wiring connector (if not already done) and measure resistance between the injector terminals with an ohmeter. It should be within the range listed in this Chapter's Specifications.

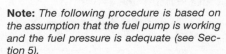

3 Self-diagnosis system and trouble codes

Self-diagnosis system general description

1 All models are equipped with an onboard self-diagnosis system. This system consists of an on-board computer known as the Engine Control Module (ECM), and information sensors, which monitor various functions of the engine and send data to the ECM. This system incorporates a series of diagnostic monitors that detect and identify fuel injection system faults and store the information in the computer memory. This system also tests sensors and output actuators, diagnoses drive cycles, freezes data and clears codes. In some cases of component failure, the ECM will substitute a fixed value for the variable voltage that the component would normally send to the ECM. This allows the engine to operate in fail-safe mode until the problem can be fixed.

2 This powerful diagnostic computer can be accessed using a simple on-off switch plugged into the diagnostic connector located near the battery. If you don't have the switch (Suzuki part no. 09930-82710) or an equivalent, a length of wire can be used instead. If a length of wire is used in place of the switch, connect one end of the wire to one of the wire terminals in the connector, but leave the other end free for the moment.

3 It isn't a good idea to attempt diagnosis or replacement of the ECM or emission control components at home while the vehicle is under warranty. Because any owner-induced damage to the ECM, sensors and/or control devices might void the warranty, take the vehicle to a dealer service department if the ECM or a system component malfunctions.

Diagnostic Trouble Codes (DTCs)

4 All fuel injected models are equipped with on-board diagnostics. When the ECM recognizes a malfunction in a monitored fuel injection system component or circuit, it turns on the FI light on the instrument cluster. The light normally illuminates briefly after the main key switch is turned On, and it also illuminates while the starter switch is operated. If a trouble code is set, the IF light will either flash, indicating that the engine can't be started, or glow steadily. A steady glow indicates that the engine will start but is running in fail-safe mode. The ECM will continue to display the IF light until the problem is fixed and the Diagnostic Trouble Code (DTC) is cleared from the ECM's memory.

Accessing the DTCs

5 If you have a scan tool, follow the manufacturer's instructions to access the DTCs. If you're using a Suzuki scan tool, plug into the diagnostic connector, then follow the instructions included with the tool to extract the DTCs.

6 If you don't have a scan tool, connect an on-off switch or a jumper wire to the diagnostic connector as described in Step 2.

7 After the problem has been found and repaired, clear the DTCs with the scan tool (if you have one), following the instructions provided by the tool's manufacturer. If you don't have a scan tool, disconnect the battery and reconnect it to clear the DTCs.

Diagnostic Trouble Codes

8 The accompanying table is a list of the Diagnostic Trouble Codes (DTCs). If the problem persists after you have checked the component and repaired the related connectors, wire harness and vacuum hoses (if applicable), have the vehicle checked by a dealer service department or other qualified repair shop.

Trouble codes

Code	Problem area	Causes	Symptom(s)
12	CKP sensor	Defective sensor, circuit problem	Engine will not start
14	Throttle position sensor	Defective sensor, circuit problem	Engine will run
15	Coolant temperature sensor	Defective sensor, circuit problem	Engine will run
17	Intake air pressure sensor	Defective sensor, circuit problem	Engine will run
21	Intake air temp sensor	Defective sensor, circuit problem	Engine will run
23	Tip-over sensor	Vehicle rollover, bad sensor, circuit problem	Engine will not start
24	Ignition coil	Coil or circuit problem, no power from battery	Engine will not run
31	Gear position switch	Switch, gearshift cam or circuit problem	Engine will run
32	Injector	Injector or circuit problem	Engine won't run
41	Fuel pump relay	ECM problem	Engine won't run
60	Cooling fan relay	Relay or circuit problem	Engine won't run

4 Fuel pressure relief procedure

***Warning:** Gasoline is extremely flammable, so take extra precautions when you work on any part of the fuel system. Don't smoke or allow open flames or bare light bulbs near the work area, and don't work in a garage where a gas-type appliance (such as a water heater or clothes dryer) is present. Since gasoline is carcinogenic, wear latex gloves when there's a possibility of being exposed to fuel, and, if you spill any fuel on your skin, rinse it off immediately with soap and water. Mop up any spills immediately and do not store fuel-soaked rags where they could ignite. The fuel system is under constant pressure, so, if any fuel lines are to be disconnected, the fuel pressure in the system must be relieved first. When you perform any kind of work on the fuel system, wear safety glasses and have a Class B type fire extinguisher on hand.*

***Warning:** Be sure to disconnect the battery (see Chapter 5) before disconnecting any fuel lines.*

The manufacturer does not specify a procedure for relieving residual fuel pressure when disconnecting fuel lines, only that you have shop rags handy to catch any spilled fuel. Observe the precautions described in the **Warnings** above. In addition, wear eye protection and catch any spilled fuel in an approved gasoline container.

5 Fuel pump/fuel pressure - check

***Warning:** Gasoline is extremely flammable, so take extra precautions when you work on any part of the fuel system. See the Warning in Section 4.*

General checks

1 Verify that there is fuel in the fuel tank.

2 Verify that the fuel pump actually runs. Turn the ignition switch to ON - you should hear a brief whirring noise for a few seconds as the pump comes on and pressurizes the system. **Note:** *If you can't hear the pump, open the fuel filler cap, then have an assistant turn the ignition switch to ON while you listen to the pump through the fuel filler neck.*

Fuel pump/fuel pressure test

3 To measure the fuel pressure, you'll need a fuel pressure gauge capable of reading pressures up to 50 psi (343 kPa). You will also need some fuel hose.

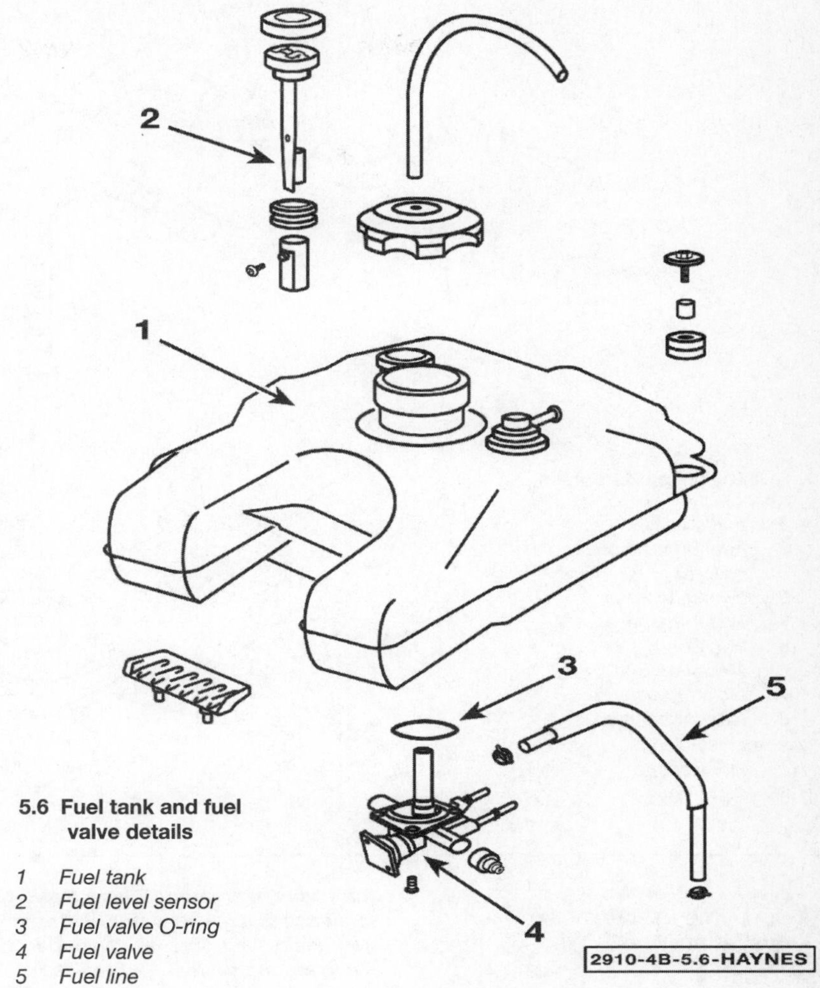

5.6 Fuel tank and fuel valve details

1 Fuel tank
2 Fuel level sensor
3 Fuel valve O-ring
4 Fuel valve
5 Fuel line

4 Before disconnecting any fuel line fittings, relieve the fuel system pressure (see Section 4).

5 Remove the fuel tank cover and front fender (see Chapter 8). Unbolt the fuel tank (see Section 7).

6 Disconnect the fuel line from the fuel valve on the underside of the tank **(see illustration)**. Connect the fuel pressure gauge between the tank fitting and the disconnected end of the hose, using a T-fitting.

7 Remove the ignition switch from the front fender and reconnect it to its wiring connector. Turn the switch to the On position and let the fuel pressure stabilize.

8 Note the indicated fuel pressure reading on the gauge and compare it with the value listed in this Chapter's Specifications.

9 If the indicated pressure is within the specified range, the system is operating correctly.

10 If the indicated pressure is lower than the specified range, the fuel filter screen might be clogged or the fuel pump or fuel pressure regulator might be defective. There are no individually replaceable parts on the pump, or on the fuel valve, installed in the fuel tank; if it won't supply the specified pressure, and the problem can't be solved by cleaning the pump intake, the pump must be replaced as an assembly.

11 After the test is complete, relieve the system fuel pressure (see Section 4).

12 Disconnect the cable from the negative battery terminal.

13 Remove your fuel pressure testing rig, then reconnect the fuel line to the tank fitting.

14 Reconnect the cable to the negative battery terminal (see Chapter 5). Start the engine and check for fuel leaks.

15 Bolt the fuel tank into position, then reinstall the front fender and fuel tank cover (see Chapter 8).

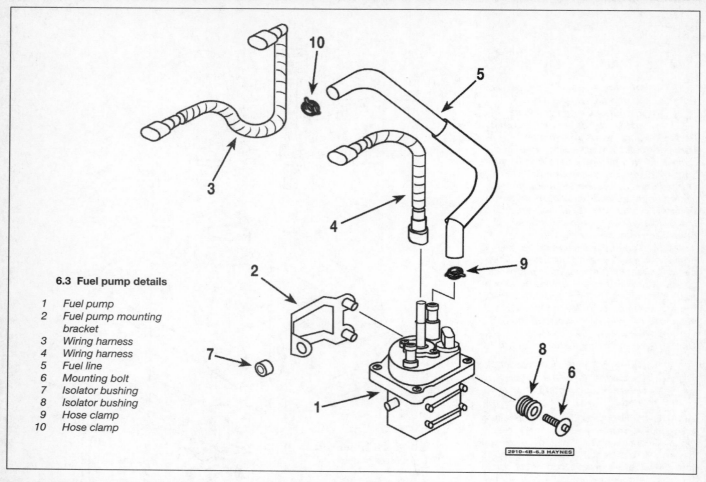

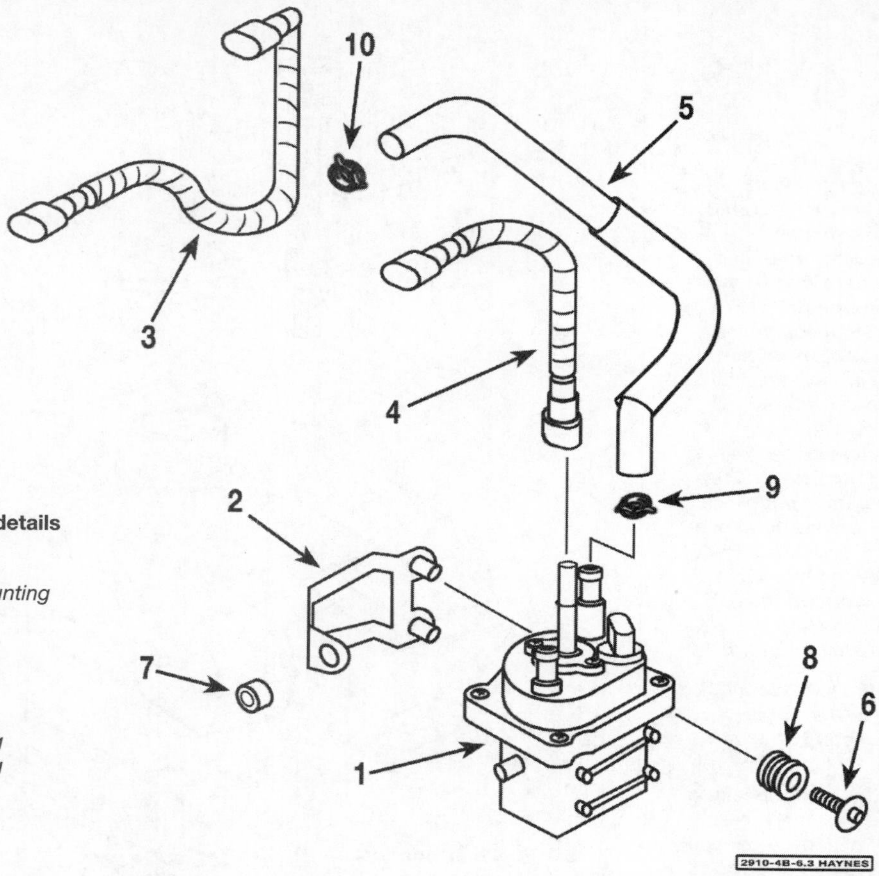

6.3 Fuel pump details

1 *Fuel pump*
2 *Fuel pump mounting bracket*
3 *Wiring harness*
4 *Wiring harness*
5 *Fuel line*
6 *Mounting bolt*
7 *Isolator bushing*
8 *Isolator bushing*
9 *Hose clamp*
10 *Hose clamp*

6 Fuel pump - removal and installation

1 Remove the seat and fuel tank cover (see Chapter 8).
2 Close the fuel valve on the tank.
3 Disconnect the wiring connector from the fuel pump **(see illustration)**.
4 Disconnect the fuel line from the tank fitting, referring to the precautions in Section 4 **(see illustration 5.6)**. Cap the fitting and plug the line.
5 Remove the fuel pump mounting bolts **(see illustration 6.3)** and remove the pump.
6 Installation is the reverse of removal.

7 Fuel tank - removal and installation

Warning: Gasoline is extremely flammable, so take extra precautions when you work on any part of the fuel system. Don't smoke or allow open flames or bare light bulbs near the work area, and don't work in a garage where a gas-type appliance (such as a water heater or clothes dryer) is present. Since gasoline is carcinogenic, wear fuel-resistant gloves when there's a possibility of being exposed to fuel, and, if you spill any fuel on your skin, rinse it off immediately with soap and water. Mop up any spills immediately and do not store fuel-soaked rags where they could ignite. When you perform any kind of work on the fuel system, wear safety glasses and have an extinguisher suitable for a class B type fire (flammable liquids) on hand.

Removal

1 Remove the seat, fuel tank cover and front fender (see Chapter 8). Remove the fuel filler cap.
2 On top of the tank, detach the vapor return hose and unplug the wiring connector for the fuel level sender **(see illustration 5.6)**.
3 Remove the cover from the air cleaner intake duct.
4 Remove the two mounting bolts at the rear of the tank.
5 Lift the tank enough to reach the fuel valve on the underside. Turn the fuel valve knob to Off and disconnect the fuel line. Disconnect the breather hose and fuel hose from the top of the fuel pump.
6 Pull the tank backward to clear the mounting bracket at the front and lift it off, together with the fuel valve.
7 If necessary, remove the heat shield that's mounted under the fuel tank.

Installation

8 Before installing the tank, check the condition of the rubber mounting isolator at the front, the bushings at the two rear bolt holes and the fuel and breather hoses - if they're hardened, cracked, or show any other signs of deterioration, replace them.
9 Installation is the reverse of removal. Make sure the tank does not pinch any wires. Tighten the tank mounting bolts securely, but don't overtighten them and strip the threads.

8 Fuel tank - cleaning and repair

1 All repairs to the fuel tank should be carried out by a professional who has experience in this critical and potentially dangerous work. Even after cleaning and flushing of the fuel system, explosive fumes can remain and ignite during repair of the tank.

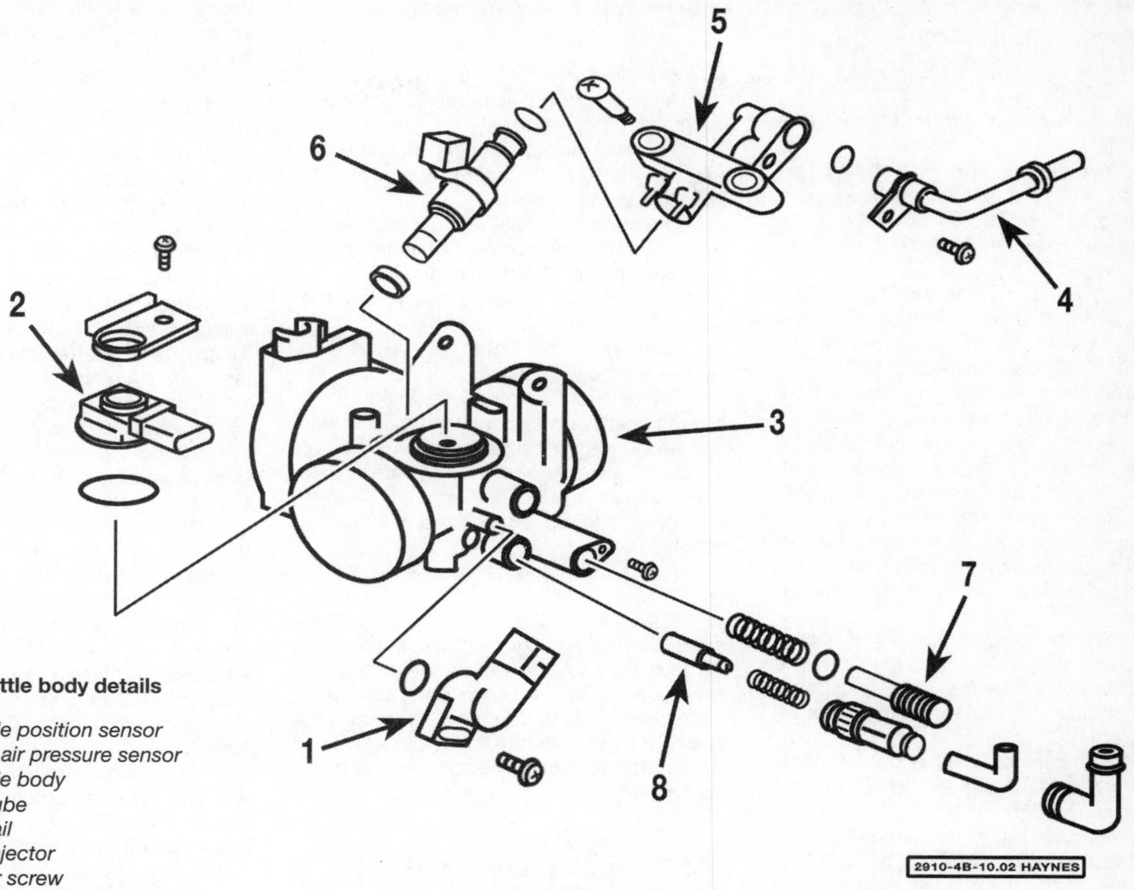

10.2 Throttle body details

1 *Throttle position sensor*
2 *Intake air pressure sensor*
3 *Throttle body*
4 *Fuel tube*
5 *Fuel rail*
6 *Fuel injector*
7 *Idle air screw*
8 *Starter (choke) valve*

2 If the fuel tank is removed from the vehicle, it should not be placed in an area where sparks or open flames could ignite the fumes coming out of the tank. Be especially careful inside garages where a gas-type appliance is located.

9 Air filter housing - removal and installation

1 Remove the air filter element cover and fuel tank cover (see Chapters 1 and 8).
2 Remove the air cleaner intake duct.
3 Disconnect the crankcase ventilation hose and the electrical connector for the IAT sensor from the air cleaner housing.
4 Loosen the clamp that connects the front of the air cleaner housing to the throttle body (see Section 11).
5 Remove the housing mounting bolts and collars.
6 Tilt the air cleaner housing and lift it out of the frame.
7 Installation is the reverse of removal.

10 Throttle position sensor - check, adjustment and replacement

Check

1 Check the engine idle speed and adjust it if necessary (see Chapter 1).
2 Locate the throttle position sensor (it's on the throttle body near the fuel pump) **(see illustration)**.
3 Connect the positive probe of a voltmeter (0 to 20 volt scale) to the yellow wire's terminal in the connector. Connect the voltmeter negative terminal to the brown/black wire's connector. **Note:** *The wiring connector must be connected during this check. If your voltmeter's terminals are too thick to fit into the connector terminals, insert short pieces of stiff wire into the connector to act as contacts for the voltmeter terminals.*
4 Turn the ignition switch to On (but don't start the engine). The voltmeter should indicate 0.6 to 3.8 volts (this is the sensor output voltage). If it doesn't, adjust the sensor as described below. Do not remove the sensor unless it needs to be replaced, or performance will be impaired.

Adjustment

5 Loosen the mounting screws **(see illustration 10.2)**. Carefully rotate the sensor back and forth to get the correct output voltage, then tighten the screw.

Replacement

6 Unbolt the fuel pump, leaving the hoses and wires connected, and move it out of the way (see Section 6).
7 Disconnect the sensor electrical connector. Remove the Torx mounting screws and remove the sensor.
8 Install the sensor and tighten the mounting screws, leaving them loose enough so the sensor can be rotated.
9 Adjust the sensor output voltage (see Step 5).
10 Once the correct reading is obtained, mark the sensor position on the throttle body with a felt pen.
11 Tighten the mounting screws, making sure that the felt pen marks stay aligned.
12 Remove the voltmeter and probes.

11 Throttle body - removal and installation

1 Remove the seat and front fender (see Chapter 8).
2 Remove the fuel tank and its heat shield (see Section 7).
3 Remove the oil tank (see Chapter 2).
4 Remove the exhaust system (see Section 20).
5 Disconnect the throttle and choke cables from the throttle body (see Section 13). Unless the cables need to be replaced, they can be left in the vehicle to ease installation.
6 Disconnect the wiring connectors for the throttle position sensor and intake air pressure sensor (see Sections 10 and 14).
7 Disconnect the wiring connector from the fuel injector **(see illustration 10.2)**. Disconnect the fuel hose from the fuel rail.
8 Loosen the clamps at the front and rear of the throttle body. Work the throttle body out of the intake manifold and air cleaner housing.
9 Lift the throttle body out and if necessary, remove the intake manifold. Cover the opening in the intake manifold or cylinder head with clean rags to keep out dirt, small parts, etc.
10 The fuel injector, throttle position sensor and air intake pressure sensor can be replaced separately.
11 If the throttle body needs to be cleaned, use a petroleum-based solvent only. Do not use caustic carburetor cleaning solutions.
12 Installation is the reverse of removal. Adjust throttle cable play (see Chapter 1).

12 Fuel rail and injector - removal and installation

1 Remove the throttle body (see Section 11).
2 Remove the screw that secures the fuel hose fitting to the fuel rail. Work the fitting free of the fuel rail and remove the O-ring.
3 Remove the fuel rail mounting screws **(see illustration 10.2)**. Take the fuel rail off the throttle body, together with the injector.
4 Pull the injector out of the fuel rail.
5 Clean all debris from the area around the injector with spray cleaner or compressed air.
6 Installation is the reverse of removal. Use new O-rings on the injector. Lubricate the O-rings with clean engine oil.

13 Throttle and choke cables - removal and installation

Throttle cable

1 This procedure is basically the same as for carbureted models, but the cable connects to the right side of the throttle body. Refer to Chapter 4A for the procedures.

Choke cable

2 Remove the front fender (see Chapter 8).
3 Separate the halves of the left handlebar switch housing (see Chapter 5) and detach the cable from the lever.
4 Unscrew the cable fitting from the left side of the throttle body and pull the cable out, together with the starter valve.
5 If necessary, compress the spring and slip the starter valve off the cable.
6 Note how the cable is routed and remove it from its retainers.
7 Route the cable into place. Make sure it doesn't interfere with any other components and isn't kinked or bent sharply.
8 Lubricate the ends of the cables with multi-purpose grease and connect them to the pulleys at the throttle body and at the left handlebar.
9 Reassemble the left handlebar switch housing (see Chapter 5).
10 Turn the handlebars back and forth to make sure the cable doesn't cause the steering to bind. With the engine idling, turn the handlebars back and forth and make sure idle speed doesn't change. If it does, find and fix the cause before riding the vehicle.
11 Install any components removed for access.

14 Intake Air Pressure (IAP) sensor - check and replacement

1 The IAP sensor is mounted on top of the throttle body **(see illustration 10.2)**.

Check

2 Remove the front fender (see Chapter 8).
3 Remove the fuel tank and the heat shield beneath it (see Section 1).
4 Disconnect the wiring harness from the sensor. Connect the positive probe of a voltmeter (0 to 20 volt scale) to the red wire's terminal in the connector. Connect the voltmeter negative terminal to the brown/black wire's connector.
5 Turn the ignition switch to On (but don't start the engine). The voltmeter should indicate 4.5 to 5.5 volts (this is the sensor input voltage). If it doesn't, check the wiring harness from the sensor to the ECM for breaks or bad connections.
6 Reconnect the wiring harness to the sensor.
7 Connect the voltmeter between the terminals for the green/black and brown/black wires. If the voltmeter probes are too large to connect to the terminals, insert short pieces of stiff wire into the terminals to serve as contacts for the voltmeter.
8 Start the engine and let it idle. The voltmeter should indicate approximately 1.7 volts (this is the sensor output voltage). If it doesn't, check the wiring harness from the sensor to the ECM for breaks or bad connections.
9 If the preceding checks haven't located the source of the problem, test the sensor separately. You'll need three 1.5-volt batteries and a hand-operated vacuum pump with a gauge. Remove the sensor from the throttle body as described below. Connect the batteries to each other in series, then check this setup with the voltmeter to be sure it produces between 4.5 and 5.5 volts. The battery setup duplicates the input voltage provided to the sensor by the ECM, and it must be within the specified range for the test to be accurate.
10 Connect the vacuum pump to the sensor's vacuum port. Connect the positive terminal of the battery setup to the sensor input terminal and the negative terminal of the battery setup to the sensor ground terminal.
11 Connect the voltmeter positive terminal to the sensor output terminal. Connect the voltmeter negative terminal to the negative terminal of the battery setup.
12 Operate the vacuum pump to gradually increase vacuum at the sensor port, and note the voltmeter readings. Compare the vacuum readings and voltmeter readings to the values listed in this Chapter's Specifications.
13 If the sensor doesn't produce the correct amount of output voltage at the specified settings, replace it with a new one. If it does perform as described, the problem is either in the circuit (wiring and connectors) or in the ECM itself. The only test for the ECM is to replace it with a known good one. Since this is an expensive component that can't be returned once purchased, this should be done by a dealer service department.

Replacement

14 Disconnect the electrical connector. Remove the mounting screw and remove the sensor from the throttle body.
15 Installation is the reverse of removal. Use a new O-ring.

15 Intake Air Temperature (IAT) sensor - check, removal and installation

Caution: The IAT sensor is delicate. Don't strike it with tools or drop it. If it's dropped, it should be replaced with a new one.

Check

1 Unplug the connector from the IAT sensor (it's on the left side of the air cleaner housing). Connect a voltmeter between the wire terminals in the sensor (positive to dark green, negative to black/brown).
2 Turn the ignition switch to On (but don't start the engine). The voltmeter should indi-

cate 4.5 to 5.5 volts. This is the input voltage from the ECM. If it isn't correct, check the circuit for breaks or bad connections.

3 If input voltage is OK, check the output voltage. With the sensor harness connected to the sensor and the ignition switch Off, connect the voltmeter positive terminal to the terminal for the dark green wire (insert a short piece of stiff wire into the connector if the voltmeter's probe won't fit). Connect the voltmeter negative terminal to ground (nearby bare metal on the engine).

4 Turn the ignition switch to On (but don't start the engine) and check the voltage reading. It should range between 0.2 and 4.9 volts.

5 If the voltmeter reading is incorrect, unplug the wiring connector from the sensor and measure resistance between the sensor terminals with an ohmmeter. At room temperature, sensor resistance should be at the value listed in this Chapter's Specifications. If you can't get a definite result by checking it on the vehicle, remove the sensor (see Step 8) and test it as described in Step 6.

6 Suspend the sensor in a pan of water, taking care not to get water on the electrical terminals. Cool the water to near freezing with ice. Measure the resistance with an ohmmeter and compare the reading to the value listed in this Chapter's Specifications. Slowly heat the water to the higher specified temperature and check resistance again.

7 If resistance is not within the specified range, replace the sensor with a new one.

Removal and installation

8 Remove the sensor screws and remove the sensor from the air cleaner housing.

9 Installation is the reverse of removal.

16 Crankshaft position sensor - check, removal and installation

1 The crankshaft position sensor is attached to the inside of the left crankcase cover.

Check

2 Follow the wiring harness from the left crankcase cover to the connector and disconnect it.

3 Connect an ohmmeter between the terminals of the green and blue wires in the sensor side of the connector (not the wiring harness side). Compare the measured resistance with the values listed in this Chapter's Specifications. If it's not within the specified range, replace it (see Steps 6 through 8).

4 If you have a voltmeter that can measure peak voltage, connect it to the same terminals that the ohmmeter was connected to. Place the transmission in Neutral, pull in the clutch, and crank the engine with the starter for a few seconds. Compare the peak voltage measurement to the value listed in this Chapter's Specifications. If it's not as specified, replace the sensor (see Steps 6 through 8).

5 If the sensor tests OK, check the wiring from the sensor to the ECM for breaks or bad connections.

Replacement

6 Remove the left crankcase cover (see Chapter 2).

7 Remove the sensor screws, remove the sensor and install a new one. Use non-permanent thread locking agent on the threads of the sensor screws.

8 Install the left crankcase cover (see Chapter 2).

17 Tip-over sensor - check and replacement

1 The tip-over sensor is located under the front fender, forward of the radiator.

2 Remove the left side cover (see Chapter 8).

3 Detach the tip-over sensor from its bracket, but leave the electrical connector connected to the sensor.

4 Connect the positive probe of a voltmeter (0 to 20 volt scale) to the yellow/green wire's terminal in the connector. Connect the voltmeter negative terminal to the black/blue wire's terminal. **Note:** *The wiring connector must be connected during this check. If your voltmeter's terminals are too thick to fit into the connector terminals, insert short pieces of stiff wire into the connector to act as contacts for the voltmeter terminals.*

5 Turn the main key switch to On, but don't start the engine.

6 Hold the sensor in its installed position and check the voltage reading; it should be within the range listed in this Chapter's Specifications. Tilt the sensor so its connector is downward. As it passes 65-degrees from its installed position, the voltage reading should increase to the higher range listed in this Chapter's Specifications.

7 If the sensor performs as specified, it's good. If not, disconnect its connector and replace it with a new one.

8 Installation is the reverse of removal.

18 Engine control module - removal and installation

1 The engine control module is located behind the headlight. It can be identified by its wire colors.

2 Disconnect the negative cable from the battery and remove the headlight housing (see Chapter 5).

3 Squeeze the connector latch and pull the connector out of the ECM.

4 Lift the ECM off its mounting bracket and remove it.

5 Installation is the reverse of removal.

19 Engine coolant temperature sensor - check, removal and installation

1 The engine coolant temperature sensor is screwed into the rear side of the cylinder head.

2 Make sure the engine is cool before starting this procedure.

3 Drain the cooling system below the level of the temperature sensor (see Chapter 1).

4 Disconnect the sensor wiring connector and unscrew the sensor from the cylinder head.

5 Suspend the temperature sensor in a pan of water, making sure water doesn't get into the electrical terminals.

Warning: Antifreeze is poisonous. Do not use a cooking pan.

6 Cool the water to near freezing with ice. Measure the resistance with an ohmmeter and compare the reading to the value listed in this Chapter's Specifications. Slowly heat the water to the higher specified temperature and check resistance again.

7 If resistance is not within the specified range, replace the sensor with a new one.

8 Installation is the reverse of removal. Use a new sealing washer on the sensor and fill the cooling system (see Chapter 1).

20 Exhaust system - removal and installation

This procedure is the same as for carbureted models (see Chapter 4A).

Notes

Chapter 5
Ignition and electrical systems

Contents

Degrees of difficulty

Easy, suitable for novice with little experience	**Fairly easy,** suitable for beginner with some experience	**Fairly difficult,** suitable for competent DIY mechanic	**Difficult,** suitable for experienced DIY mechanic	**Very difficult,** suitable for expert DIY or professional

Specifications

Battery

Type	Maintenance free
Capacity	12 volts, 8 amp-hours

Ignition system

Ignition coil resistance	
Primary	0.1 to 1.0 ohms
Secondary	12 to 20 k-ohms
Ignition coil primary peak voltage	
Carbureted models	130 volts or more
Fuel injected models	150 volts or more
Pick-up coil peak voltage (carbureted models)	2.0 volts or more
Signal coil peak voltage (carbureted models)	1.0 volt or more

Charging system

Alternator stator coil resistance

Carbureted models	
Charging coil	0.1 to 1.5 ohms (brown to brown)
Lighting coil	0.09 to 0.50 ohms (white to black)
Pick-up coil	350 to 670 ohms (green to blue)
Fuel injected models	0.1 to 1.5 ohms (brown to brown)

Alternator no-load voltage

Carbureted models	65 volts AC
Fuel injected models	55 volts AC

Regulator/rectifier regulated voltage

Carbureted models	14.0 to 15.5 volts at 5000 rpm
Fuel injected models	13.5 to 15.0 volts at 5000 rpm

Starter motor

Relay resistance	3 to 6 ohms

Fuse ratings

Carbureted models	
Main fuse	20 amps
Fan fuse (2004 and later)	15 amps
Fuel injected models	
Main fuse	20 amps
Ignition fuse	10 amps
Fan fuse	10 amps

Torque specifications

Alternator rotor nut	120 Nm (87 ft-lbs)
Starter clutch bolts	Not specified*
Starter mounting bolts	10 Nm (84 inch-lbs)
Starter clutch slip torque	30 to 55 Nm (21.5 to 40.0 ft-lbs)

**Use non-permanent thread locking agent on the bolt threads.*

1 General information

The electrical system on all models includes a battery and charging system, lighting system (including warning lights) and an electric starter.

The ignition system on carbureted models consists of an alternator that generates the current, a capacitive discharge ignition (CDI) unit that receives and stores it, and a pulse generator that triggers the CDI unit to discharge its current into the ignition coil, where it is stepped up to a voltage high enough to jump the spark plug gap. To aid in locating a problem in the ignition circuit, wiring diagrams are included at the end of this manual.

The CDI ignition system functions on the same principle as a breaker point ignition system with the pulse generator and CDI unit performing the tasks previously associated with the breaker points and mechanical advance system. As a result, adjustment and maintenance of breakerless ignition components is eliminated (with the exception of spark plug replacement).

The ignition system on fuel injected models is a transistor controlled ignition (TCI) type. This system is similar to the CDI system used on carbureted models, but ignition timing is controlled by the electronic control unit, which also controls the fuel injection system. Ignition system components that are also part of the fuel injection system (the ECM and crankshaft position sensor) are covered in Chapter 4B. **Note:** *Keep in mind that electrical parts, once purchased, can't be returned. To avoid unnecessary expense, make very sure the faulty component has been positively identified before buying a replacement part.*

2 Electrical troubleshooting

Electrical problems often stem from simple causes, such as loose or corroded connections. Prior to any electrical troubleshooting, always visually check the condition of the wires and connections in the circuit.

If testing instruments are going to be utilized, use the diagrams to plan where you will make the necessary connections in order to accurately pinpoint the trouble spot.

The basic tools needed for electrical troubleshooting include a test light or voltmeter, an ohmmeter or a continuity tester (which includes a bulb, battery and set of test leads) and a jumper wire, preferably with a circuit breaker incorporated, which can be used to bypass electrical components.

A continuity check is performed to see if a circuit, section of circuit or individual component is capable of passing electricity through it. Connect one lead of a self-powered test light or ohmmeter to one end of the circuit being tested and the other lead to the other end of the circuit. If the bulb lights (or the ohmmeter indicates little or no resistance), there is continuity, which means the circuit is passing electricity through it properly. The kill switch can be checked in the same way.

Remember that the electrical circuit on these vehicles is designed to conduct electricity through the wires, kill switch, etc. to the electrical component (CDI unit, etc.). From there it is directed to the frame (ground) where it is passed back to the alternator. Electrical problems are basically an interruption in the flow of electricity.

Because of their nature, the individual ignition system components can be checked but not repaired. If ignition system troubles occur, and the faulty component can be isolated, the only cure for the problem is to replace the part with a new one. Keep in mind that most electrical parts, once purchased, can't be returned. To avoid unnecessary expense, make very sure the faulty component has been positively identified before buying a replacement part.

Most battery damage is caused by heat, vibration, and/or low electrolyte levels, so keep the battery securely mounted, inspect it at regular intervals and make sure the charging system is functioning properly.

3 Battery - inspection and maintenance

1 The battery used is a maintenance free type.

2 Remove the seat (see Chapter 8). Check around the battery base (inside of the battery) for sediment, which is the result of sulfation caused by low electrolyte levels. These deposits will cause internal short circuits, which can quickly discharge the battery. Look for cracks in the case and replace the battery if either of these conditions is found.

Warning: Always disconnect the negative cable first and reconnect it last to prevent sparks that could cause the battery to explode.

3 Check the battery terminals and cable ends for tightness and corrosion. If corrosion is evident, remove the cables from the battery and clean the terminals and cable ends with a wire brush. If you need to remove the battery, remove the retainer and lift it out of the carrier **(see illustration)**. Reconnect the cables and apply a thin coat of petroleum jelly to the connections to slow further corrosion.

4 The battery case should be kept clean to prevent current leakage, which can discharge the battery over a period of time (especially when it sits unused). Wash the outside of the case with a solution of baking soda and water. Do not get any baking soda solution in the battery cells. Rinse the battery thoroughly, then dry it.

3.3 Unbolt and remove the battery retainer

5 If acid has been spilled on the frame or battery box, neutralize it with the baking soda and water solution, dry it thoroughly, then touch up any damaged paint.

6 If the vehicle sits unused for long periods of time, disconnect the cables from the battery terminals. Charge the battery approximately once every month (see Section 4).

4 Battery - charging

1 If the machine sits idle for extended periods or if the charging system malfunctions, the battery can be charged from an external source.

2 Be sure the battery charger you use is designed for maintenance-free batteries.

3 When charging the battery, always remove it from the machine. If the battery case is translucent, check the electrolyte level by looking through the case before hooking up the charger. If the electrolyte level is low, the battery must be discarded; never remove the sealing plug to add water.

4 Disconnect the battery cables (negative cable first), then connect a digital voltmeter between the battery terminals and measure the voltage (open circuit voltage).

5 If open circuit voltage is 12.8 volts or higher, the battery is fully charged. If it's lower, recharge the battery. On carbureted models, charge at 1.5 amps for 5 to 10 hours or 6 amps for 1 hour. On fuel injected models, charge at 0.9 amps for 5 to 10 hours or 4 amps for 1 hour.

6 A quick charge can be used in an emergency, provided the maximum charge rates and times are not exceeded (exceeding the maximum rate or time may ruin the battery). A quick charge should always be followed as

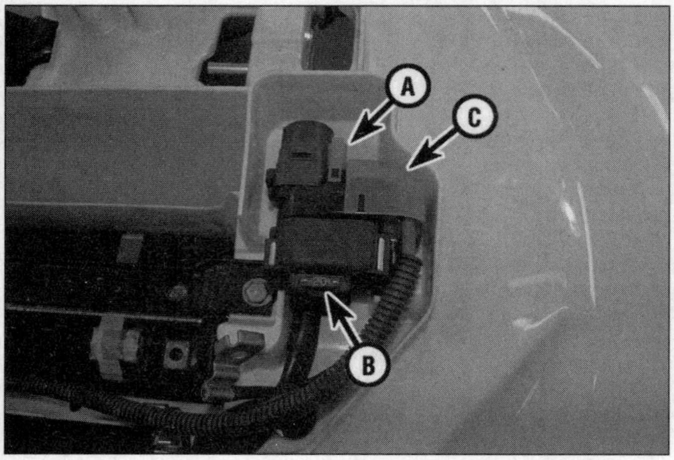

5.1a Location of the main fuse (A), spare fuse (B) and starter relay (C)

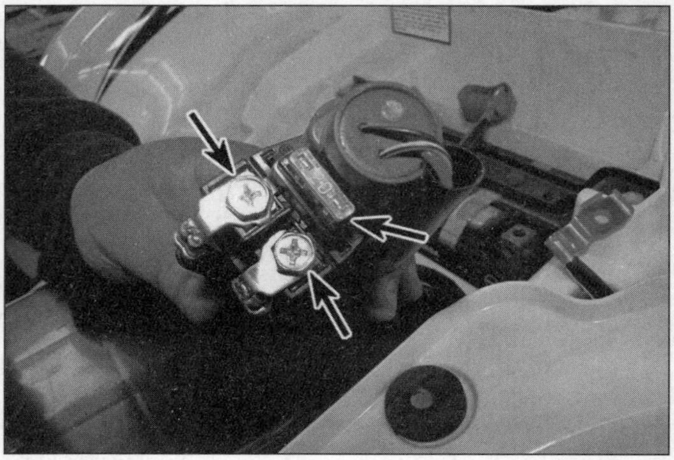

5.1b Pull the cover off to expose the fuse (right arrow) and the battery terminals (left arrows) on the starter relay

soon as possible by a charge at the standard rate and time.

7 Hook up the battery charger leads (positive lead to battery positive terminal and negative lead to battery negative terminal), then, and only then, plug in the battery charger.

Warning: The gas escaping from a charging battery is explosive, so keep open flames and sparks well away from the area. Also, the electrolyte is extremely corrosive and will damage anything it comes in contact with.

8 Allow the battery to charge for the specified time listed in Step 5. If the battery overheats or gases excessively, the charging rate is too high. Either disconnect the charger or lower the charging rate to prevent damage to the battery.

9 After the specified time, unplug the charger first, then disconnect the leads from the battery.

10 Wait 30 minutes, then measure voltage between the battery terminals. If it's 12.8 volts or higher, the battery is fully charged. If it's between 12.0 and 12.7 volts, charge the battery again (refer to Step 5 for charge rate and time).

5 Fuses - check and replacement

1 All models have a single main fuse of the bayonet type, located near the battery **(see illustrations)**. A spare fuse is located near the main fuse. 2004 and later models have a fan fuse, located in the fan fuse box on the rear side of the fan in the upper right corner. Fuel injected models have an ignition fuse, also located near the battery.

2 The fuse can be checked visually without removing it from its holder; look through the plastic to see if the metal element inside is broken. If so, pull the fuse out and push a new one in.

3 If the fuse blows, be sure to check the wiring harnesses very carefully for evidence of a short circuit. Look for bare wires and chafed, melted or burned insulation. If a fuse is replaced before the cause is located, the new fuse will blow immediately.

4 Never, under any circumstances, use a higher rated fuse or bridge the fuse terminals, as damage to the electrical system - or even a fire - could result.

5 Occasionally a fuse will blow or cause an open circuit for no obvious reason. Corrosion of the fuse ends and fuse holder terminals may occur and cause poor fuse contact. If this happens, remove the corrosion with a wire brush or emery paper, then spray the fuse end and terminals with electrical contact cleaner.

6 Ignition system - check

Warning: Because of the very high voltage generated by the ignition system, extreme care should be taken when these checks are performed.

1 If the ignition system is the suspected cause of poor engine performance or failure to start, a number of checks can be made to isolate the problem.

Engine will not start

2 Disconnect the spark plug wire (see Chapter 1). Connect the wire to a spare spark plug and lay the plug on the engine with the threads contacting the engine. If necessary, hold the spark plug with an insulated tool. Crank the engine over and make sure a well-defined, blue spark occurs between the spark plug electrodes.

Warning: Don't remove the spark plug from the engine to perform this check - atomized fuel being pumped out of the open spark plug hole could ignite, causing severe injury!

3 If no spark occurs, the following checks should be made:

4 Check the ignition coil primary resistance, secondary resistance and peak voltage (see Section 7).

5 On carbureted models, check the ignition pickup coil and signal coil (see Section 9).

6 On carbureted models, check the crankshaft position sensor (see Chapter 4B).

7 Make sure all electrical connectors are clean and tight. Check all wires for shorts, opens and correct installation.

8 If the preceding checks produce positive results but there is still no spark at the plug, check the CDI unit (carbureted models) (see Section 8) or the ECM (fuel injected models) (see Chapter 4B).

Engine starts but misfires

9 If the engine starts but misfires, make the following checks before deciding that the ignition system is at fault.

10 The ignition system must be able to produce a spark across an 8mm (5/16-inch) gap (minimum). A simple test fixture **(see illustration)** can be constructed to make sure the minimum spark gap can be jumped. Make sure the fixture electrodes are positioned 8mm (5/16-inch) apart.

11 Connect the spark plug wire to the protruding test fixture electrode, then attach the fixture's alligator clip to a good engine ground.

6.10 A simple spark gap testing fixture can be made from a block of wood, two nails, a large alligator clip, a screw and a piece of wire

7.7 Ignition coil primary terminals

12 Crank the engine over with the starter and see if well-defined, blue sparks occur between the test fixture electrodes. If the minimum spark gap test is positive, the ignition coil is functioning properly. If the spark will not jump the gap, or if it is weak (orange colored), refer to Steps 2 through and perform the component checks described.

7 Ignition coil - check, removal and installation

1 The primary and secondary coil resistances can be measured with an ohmmeter. If the coil is undamaged, and if the resistances are as specified, it is probably capable of proper operation. If you have a voltmeter that can measure peak voltage, you can make this additional test to confirm coil operation.

2 To inspect or remove the coil, remove the seat, front fender, fuel tank and fuel tank lower cover (see Chapters 8 and 4). If you're working on a fuel injected model, unbolt the fuel pump and move it aside for access to the coil (see Chapter 4B).

3 Check the coil visually for cracks and other damage.

Peak voltage check

4 Disconnect the spark plug wire from the plug (see Chapter 1 if necessary). Connect a new spark plug into the wire, then lay it on the engine so its electrode touches one of the small head bolts.

5 Connect the voltmeter to the coil primary wires (positive probe to black/white wire's terminal; negative probe to white/black wire's terminal).

6 Turn the ignition switch to the On position. Place the transmission in neutral, pull in the clutch lever and crank the engine with the starter for a few seconds. Check the peak voltage indicated by the voltmeter and compare it to the value listed in this Chapter's Specifications. If it's OK, perform the resistance checks in Steps 7 and 8. If peak voltage isn't as specified, replace the coil with a new one.

Resistance check

7 Connect an ohmmeter between the primary (small) terminals **(see illustration)**. Set the ohmmeter selector switch in the Rx1 position and compare the measured resistance to the primary resistance values listed in this Chapter's Specifications. If the resistance is not as specified, the coil is probably defective and should be replaced with a new one.

8 Connect the ohmmeter between the coil primary positive terminal and the spark plug cap **(see illustration 7.7)**. Place the ohmmeter selector switch in the Rx100 position and compare the measured resistance to the secondary resistance values listed in this Chapter's Specifications. If the resistance is not as specified, the coil is probably defective and should be replaced with a new one.

Removal and installation

9 If you haven't already done so, perform Step 2 for access to the coil.

10 Disconnect the spark plug wire, remove the coil mounting bolts and remove the coil.

11 Installation is the reverse of removal.

8 CDI unit (carbureted models) - check, removal and installation

Check

1 The CDI unit is tested by process of elimination (when all other possible causes of ignition problems have been checked and eliminated, the CDI unit is at fault).

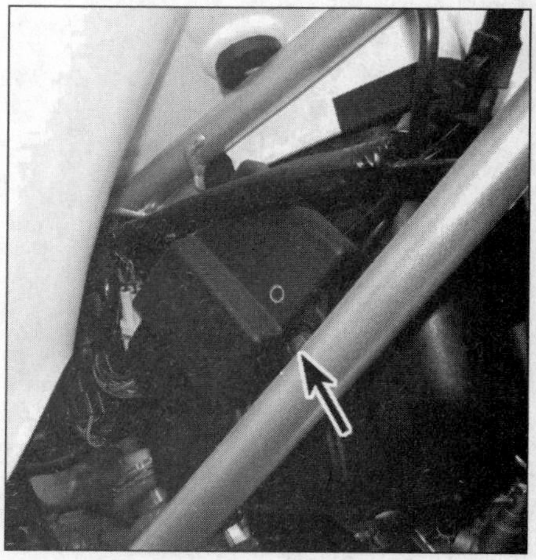

8.5 The CDI unit on carbureted models is located under the left rear fender

2 Check the ignition coil, pulse generator, signal coil and kill switch as described elsewhere in this Chapter.

3 Carefully check the wiring harnesses for breaks or bad connections.

4 If the harness and all other system components tested good, the CDI unit may be defective. Before buying a new one, it's a good idea to substitute a known good CDI unit.

Removal and installation

5 Locate the CDI unit under the left rear fender (it can be identified by its wire colors) **(see illustration)**. Unplug its connector and remove the mounting screws.

6 Installation is the reverse of removal.

9.1 Follow the alternator wiring harness to its connector and unplug it

9.8 Unscrew the rotor nut and remove the washer - you may need to pry it out

9.9a Thread the puller onto these threads on the rotor

9.9b Tighten the puller screw against the crankshaft, then hold the puller body with a wrench on the flats (arrows) and tighten the puller screw to push the rotor loose

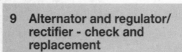

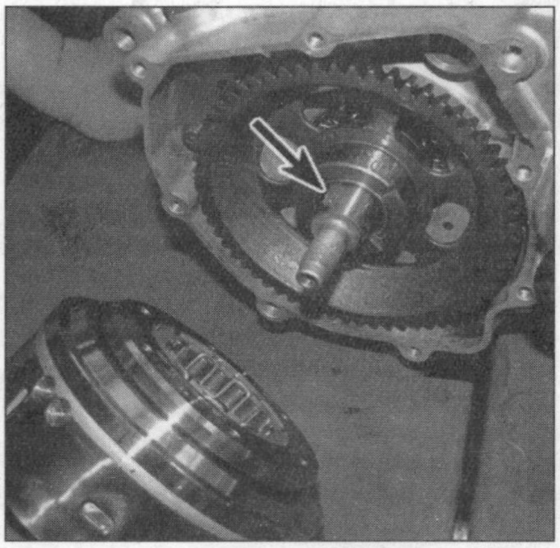

9.9c Pull the rotor off and locate the Woodruff key (arrow); be sure it's in its slot on installation

9 Alternator and regulator/rectifier - check and replacement

Note: *Fuel injected models use a crankshaft position sensor instead of a pickup coil. Refer to Chapter 4B for checking and replacement procedures.*

Alternator check

1 Locate the alternator wiring harnesses on the left side of the engine and follow them to their connectors **(see illustration)**.

Carbureted models

2 To check the ignition system pickup coil, disconnect the connector for the blue and green wires. Connect an ohmmeter to the wires in the alternator side of the connector (not the wiring harness side). If the readings are much outside the value listed in this Chapter's Specifications, replace the pickup coil (see Steps 17 through 20).

3 To check the signal coil, disconnect the connector for the black and white wires. Connect an ohmmeter to the wires in the alternator side of the connector (not the wiring harness side). If the readings are much outside the value listed in this Chapter's Specifications, replace the pickup coil (see Steps 17 through 20).

4 To check charging coil resistance, disconnect the connector for the three brown wires. Connect an ohmmeter between two wires at a time and measure the resistance between each pair. Compare the reading to the value listed in this Chapter's Specifications. If it's not within the specified range, replace the stator coil (see Steps 17 through 20).

5 To check for a shorted charging coil, connect the ohmmeter between each brown wire, one wire at a time, and ground. The ohmmeter should indicate no continuity (infinite resistance). If it doesn't, replace the stator coil (see Steps 17 through 20).

Fuel injected models

6 To check the stator coils, disconnect the coil connector (three black wires). Connect an ohmmeter between two wires at a time and measure the resistance between each pair. Compare the reading to the value listed in this Chapter's Specifications. If it's not within the specified range, replace the stator coil (see Steps 17 through 20).

Rotor replacement

Removal

Note: *To remove the alternator rotor, a special Suzuki puller or an aftermarket equivalent will be required. Don't try to remove the rotor without the proper puller, as it's almost sure to be damaged. Pullers are readily available from dealers and aftermarket tool suppliers.*

7 Remove the left crankcase cover (see Chapter 2).

8 Hold the alternator rotor with a universal holder. You can also use a strap wrench. If you don't have one of these tools and the engine is in the frame, the rotor can be locked by placing the transmission in gear and holding the rear brake on. Unscrew the rotor nut and remove the washer **(see illustration)**.

9 Thread an alternator puller into the center of the rotor and use it to remove the rotor **(see illustrations)**. If the rotor doesn't come

9.10 Be sure there aren't any small metal objects stuck to the rotor magnets; an inconspicuous item like this Woodruff key can ruin the rotor and stator if the engine is run

9.19 The regulator/rectifier is located on the left side of the frame

off easily, tap sharply on the end of the puller to release the rotor's grip on the tapered crankshaft end.

10 Pull the rotor off. Check the Woodruff key; if it's not secure in its slot, pull it out and set it aside for safekeeping. A convenient method is to stick the Woodruff key to the magnets inside the rotor **(see illustration)**, but don't forget it's there, as serious damage to the rotor and stator coils will occur if the engine is run with anything stuck to the magnets.

Installation

11 Take a look to make sure there isn't anything stuck to the inside of the rotor **(see illustration 9.10)**.

12 Degrease the center of the rotor and the end of the crankshaft.

13 Make sure the Woodruff key is positioned securely in its slot.

14 Align the rotor slot with the Woodruff key. Place the rotor on the crankshaft.

15 Install the rotor washer and nut. Hold the rotor from turning with one of the methods described in Step 8 and tighten the nut to the torque listed in this Chapter's Specifications.

16 The remainder of installation is the reverse of removal.

Stator coil and pickup coil replacement

17 The stator coil and the pickup coil used on carbureted models are replaced as a unit.

18 Remove the left engine cover and alternator rotor (see Steps 7 through 10).

19 Remove the Allen bolts that secure the stator coils (all models) and pickup coil (carbureted models) **(see illustration)**. Remove them from the inside of the left crankcase cover.

20 Installation is the reverse of removal. Tighten the Allen bolts to the torque listed in this Chapter's Specifications.

Regulator/rectifier

21 The regulator/rectifier is located on the left side of the vehicle, inside the rear fender **(see illustration)**.

Check

22 Testing of the voltage regulator/rectifier requires a special Suzuki tester. Ordinary ohmmeters will produce a wide variety of readings which may indicate that the regulator/rectifier is defective when it is actually good.

23 To check the charging system running voltage, connect a voltmeter between the battery terminals with the engine idling. Compare the reading to the output voltage listed in this Chapter's Specifications. If the charging system running voltage is too high or the output is too low, and no other cause (alternator or wiring problems) can be found, the regulator/rectifier may be defective.

24 If you suspect the regulator/rectifier, take it to a dealer service department or other repair shop for further checks, or substitute a known good unit and recheck the charging system output.

Replacement

25 Disconnect the electrical connector from the regulator/rectifier. Remove its mounting bolts and lift it off.

26 Installation is the reverse of removal.

10 Handlebar switches - check, removal and installation

1 The left handlebar switch housing includes the headlight high and low beam switch, the kill switch and the starter button.

Check

2 Follow the wires from the switch to their connectors and unplug them.

3 Connect an ohmmeter between the wire terminals in the switch side of the connectors (not the side that leads back to the wiring harness). Check switch continuity in all positions, referring to the wiring diagrams at the end of this manual.

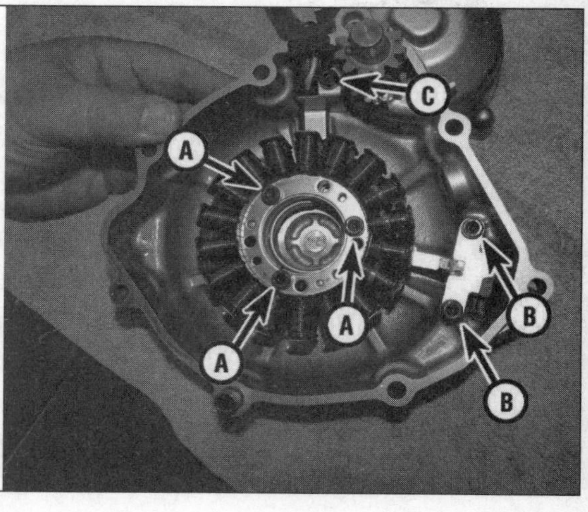

9.21 The stator coils and ignition pulse generator or crankshaft position sensor are secured by Allen bolts (carbureted model shown; fuel injected model similar)

A Stator coil bolts
B Pulse generator bolts
C Wiring harness retaining bolt

10.5 Remove the switch screws and separate the upper and lower halves of the switch housing

12.1 Locate the starter motor and disconnect its cable

4 If continuity isn't as shown in the wiring diagrams, replace the switch (see Steps 5 through 7).

Removal and installation

5 To remove the switch housing, remove its mounting screws **(see illustration)**, separate the upper and lower halves and take it off the handlebar. Remove the wiring harness retainers and unplug the switch electrical connectors.

6 If the switch problem appears to be caused by corrosion, you can try cleaning the switch contacts. If this doesn't help, the entire switch unit must be replaced. The switches aren't available separately.

7 Installation is the reverse of removal. Be sure the post molded into the top half of the switch housing fits into the hole in the top of the handlebar.

11 Starter circuit - component check and replacement

1 The electric starter circuit used on these models includes a clutch switch that prevents the starter from operating unless the clutch lever is pulled in.

2 Remove the seat (see Chapter 8) and locate the starter relay **(see illustrations 5.1a and 5.1b)**.

3 Disconnect the battery cables from the relay, negative cable first, then disconnect the wiring connector from the starter relay.

4 Connect an ohmmeter between the battery terminals on the relay **(see illustration 5.1b)**. The ohmmeter should indicate infinite resistance (no continuity).

5 Connect a fully charged battery (the vehicle's battery will work) to the relay terminals, using lengths of wire. The ohmmeter between the relay's battery terminals should now indicate continuity (little or no resistance).

6 If the relay doesn't perform as described, remove it from its mount and install a new one.

7 If the relay performs as it should, check the clutch switch (see Section 18).

12.5 Remove the mounting bolts (noting that one of them secures a ground cable), lift the starter and pull it out of the engine

12 Starter motor - check and replacement

Check

Warning: This check may cause sparks. Make sure there is no leaking gasoline or anything else flammable in the vicinity.

Warning: Make sure the transmission is in Neutral or the vehicle will jump forward during Step 2.

Caution: The jumper cable used for this procedure must be of a gauge at least as heavy as the battery cable or it may melt.

1 Locate the starter motor and disconnect its cable **(see illustration)**.

2 Connect a jumper cable from the battery positive terminal directly to the starter motor terminal. The starter should crank the engine.

3 If the starter doesn't crank at all, replace it. If it turns but doesn't crank the engine, remove and inspect the starter reduction gears and slipper clutch (see Sections 13 and 14).

Replacement

4 If you haven't already done so, disconnect the starter cable.

5 Remove the starter mounting bolts and remove the starter **(see illustration)**.

6 Installation is the reverse of removal. Use a new O-ring and tighten the bolts to the torque listed in this Chapter's Specifications.

13.2 Remove the slipper clutch cover bolts and the cover

13.3a Note how the slipper clutch fits in the recess . . .

13 Starter slipper clutch and reduction gears - removal, inspection and installation

1 These vehicles use two reduction gears, an idler gear and a starter clutch drive gear. The starter motor turns a slipper clutch (torque limiter), the slipper clutch turns the idler gear, the idler gear turns the starter clutch drive gear (large gear - which is mounted on the crankshaft behind the alternator rotor) and the starter clutch turns the crankshaft.

Removal

Slipper clutch

2 Remove the slipper clutch cover from the left side of the crankcase **(see illustration)**.

3 Pull the slipper clutch out of the engine **(see illustrations)**.

4 Remove the slipper clutch bushings from the cover and crankcase **(see illustrations)**.

Idler gear

5 Remove the left crankcase cover (see Chapter 2).

6 The idler gear may come out with the cover **(see illustration)** or stay in the crankcase. Pull the shaft out of the cover or crankcase, remove the snap-ring and slip the idler gear off its shaft. Remove the washers from the gear shaft.

Starter driven gear

7 Remove the left crankcase cover and alternator rotor (see Chapter 2 and Section 9). Remove the thrust washer behind the rotor.

13.3b . . . and pull it out

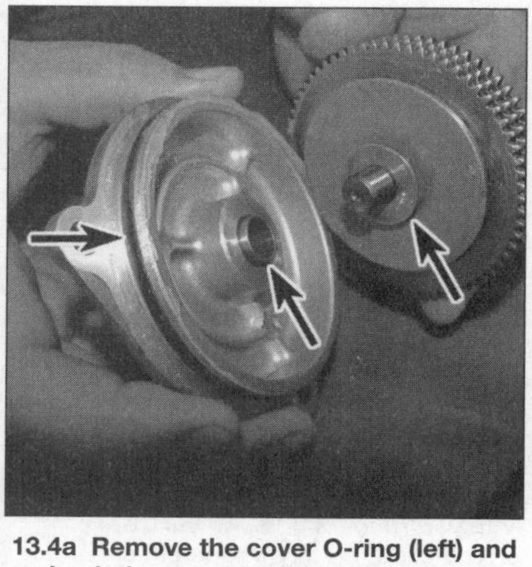

13.4a Remove the cover O-ring (left) and check the cover bushing (center) and washer (right)

13.4b Check the bushing in the crankcase cover (upper arrow) - spin the idler gear (lower arrow) to check the starter clutch

13.6 The idler gear may come off with the crankcase cover or remain in the engine - remove its snap-ring (arrow) to separate the idler gear from the shaft

13.8 Note which direction the starter clutch gear faces, then slip it off the crankshaft

13.11 Do not remove this snap-ring - it's not available separately, and the slipper clutch must be replaced as a unit

8 Slip the driven gear off the crankshaft, noting which direction it faces **(see illustration)**.

Inspection

9 Check the idler and driven gears for wear or damage such as chipped teeth. Check the shaft for scoring or heat damage that might indicate lack of lubrication. Replace the gears if problems are found. The idler gear can be disassembled by removing its snap-ring **(see illustration 13.6)**.

10 Check the slipper clutch bushings for wear or damage and replace them if problems are found.

11 Check the slipper clutch for visible damage, such as broken gear teeth. Replace it as a unit if problems are found. **Note:** *Do not remove the slipper clutch snap-ring* **(see illustration)**; *the slipper clutch can't be disassembled.* Place the slipper clutch in a vise, with the jaws padded with wood blocks, so the triple gears are gripped by the vise jaws and the single gear is upward. Rotate the single gear with a torque wrench. Attaching the torque wrench to the single gear requires Suzuki special tools - adapter 09930-73170 and socket 09930-73180.

12 Check the needle roller bearing on the inside of the driven gear. Since needle roller bearing wear is difficult to see, the driven gear bearing should be replaced if its condition is in doubt.

Installation

13 Installation is the reverse of removal.

14 Starter clutch - removal, inspection and installation

1 If the starter motor spins but doesn't crank the engine, perform a quick check of the starter clutch.

2 Remove the slipper clutch (see Section 13). Reach into the slipper clutch recess and spin the starter idler gear with a finger **(see illustration 13.4b)**. It should spin freely and smoothly in one direction and not at all in the other direction. If it spins both ways, the starter clutch is probably damaged. If the movement of the gear is rough or uneven, the starter clutch or one of the reduction gears may be damaged. Remove the starter clutch for further inspection (see Steps 3 and 4).

Removal

3 Remove the alternator rotor (see Section 9). The starter clutch is mounted in the back of the rotor **(see illustration 9.10)**.

4 Mark the starter clutch so you can reinstall it facing the correct direction. Remove the six Torx bolts that secure the starter clutch to the alternator rotor and remove the starter clutch.

Inspection

5 Check all parts for visible wear and damage and replace any parts that show problems.

6 Test the starter clutch. Place it in position on the back of the alternator rotor. Place the starter reduction gear in the starter clutch. Hold the rotor steady, with the reduction gear toward you, and try to twist the clutch. It should twist freely in a counterclockwise direction, but not at all in the clockwise direction.

7 If the gear will turn both ways or neither way, the starter clutch is bad. If the gear will turn freely clockwise, but not at all counterclockwise, the starter clutch rollers are installed upside down.

Installation

8 Installation is the reverse of removal. Tighten the starter clutch bolts to the torque listed in this Chapter's Specifications and use non-hardening Loctite on the bolt threads. Be sure to check the starter clutch function before completing final installation (see Steps 6 and 7).

15 Lighting circuit - check

1 If the headlight or taillight doesn't work, check the bulb. If it's good, check the socket for corrosion and the wiring for breaks or bad connections.

2 If neither light works, check the switch. Disconnect its wiring connector and connect an ohmmeter to the switch terminals. The ohmmeter should show little or no resistance when the switch is On, and infinite resistance when it's Off. If not, replace it.

3 If the brake light doesn't work, check it in the same manner as the headlight and taillight (see Steps 1 and 2). If none of the lights work and the switch is good, check the red wire between the starter relay and the ignition switch for breaks or bad connections.

16 Bulb replacement

Warning: If the bulb has just burned out, it will be hot enough to burn you. Let to cool before touching it.

Headlight

Caution: Don't touch the bulb glass with your fingers or it will burn out prematurely. If you do touch it, clean the glass with rubbing alcohol or soap and water.

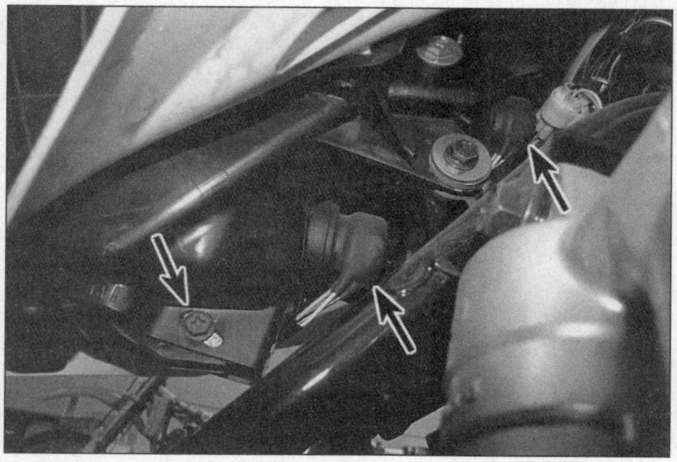

16.1a The headlight bulb(s) (upper arrows) are accessible from beneath the fender - loosen the bolt (lower arrow, typical) to adjust the headlight aim

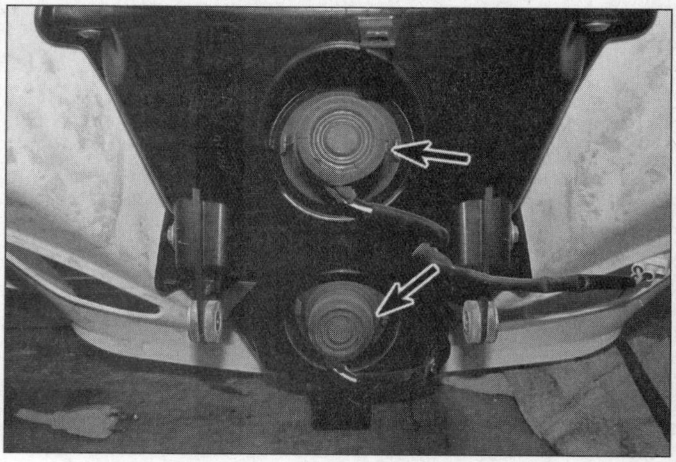

16.1b Pull the cover (arrows) off of the bulb

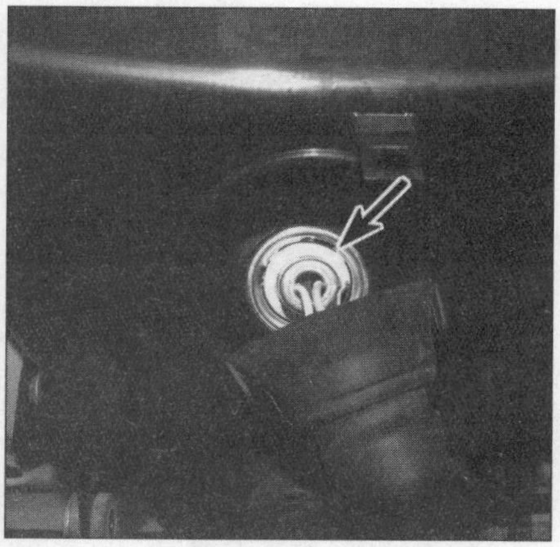

16.2 Twist the bulb socket and remove it from the housing

16.3a Pull the bulb out of the socket

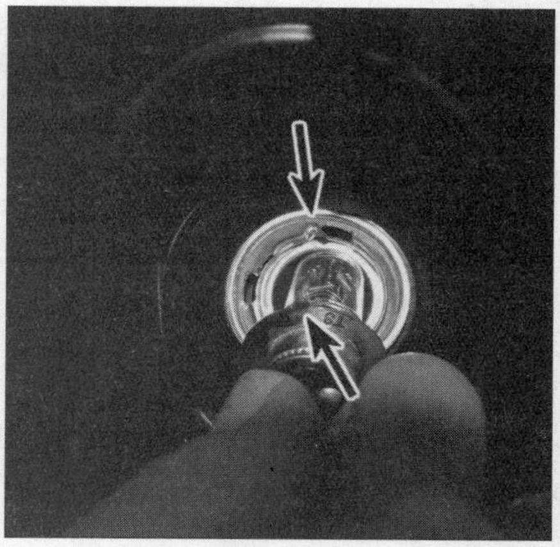

16.3b The tab fits into the groove in the housing

Carbureted models

1 Working beneath the fender, pull the rubber cap off of the headlight assembly **(see illustrations)**.

2 Remove the bulb socket from the headlight housing **(see illustration)**.

3 Press the bulb into its socket, turn it counterclockwise and pull it out **(see illustrations)**.

4 Installation is the reverse of removal. Align the notch in the metal bulb base with the groove in the socket **(see illustration 16.3b)**.

Fuel injected models

5 Working beneath the fender, remove the headlight adjusting bolt.

6 Lift the headlight housing for access to the bulb cover and remove the cover.

7 Unplug the wiring connector from the bulb.

8 Turn the bulb counterclockwise and remove it from the housing.

9 Installation is the reverse of removal.

Tail/brake light

10 Reach inside the rear fender, then turn the bulb socket counterclockwise and remove it from the housing **(see illustration)**.

11 Press the bulb into its socket and turn it counterclockwise to remove it.

12 Installation is the reverse of removal.

Warning lights

13 Detach the warning light housing from the handlebar and turn it over.

14 Remove the instrument light socket from the bracket, then pull the bulb out, push a new one in and reinstall the socket.

15 Installation is the reverse of removal.

17 Headlight adjustment

The headlight can only be adjusted vertically. Loosen the adjuster bolt located under the fender **(see illustration 16.1a)**. Move the headlight housing up or down to the desired position, then tighten the bolt.

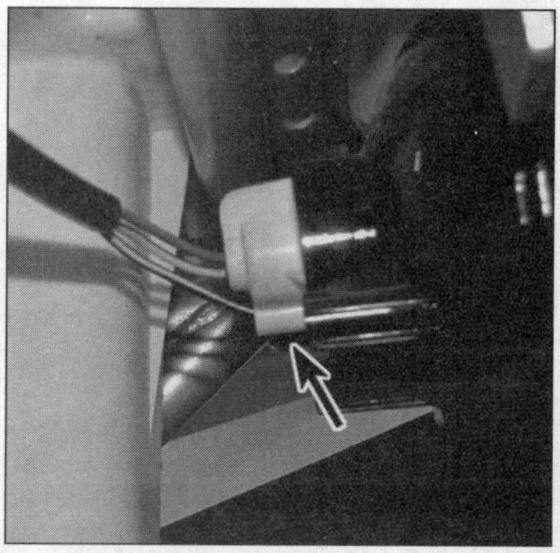

16.10 Pull the cover (arrow) off the bulb, press the bulb into its socket and turn it counterclockwise to remove it

18.1 The clutch switch is located in the lever bracket - compress the prong (arrow) and pull on the switch to remove it

19.1 The gear position switch is located on the left side of the engine, inside the drive sprocket cover

18 Clutch switch - check and replacement

1 The clutch switch is mounted in the clutch lever pivot **(see illustration)**.

2 Follow the wiring harness from the switch to its connector and disconnect it.

3 Connect an ohmmeter between the terminals in the switch side of the connector. With the clutch lever pulled in, there should be no resistance (zero ohms). With the lever released, there should be infinite resistance.

4 If the switch doesn't perform as described, slide back the lever pivot cover, press the switch retainer prong and pull the switch out of the clutch lever pivot. Push a new switch in until the retainer prong engages, then connect the wiring harness and reposition the cover.

19 Gear position switch - check and replacement

1 Disconnect the electrical connector from the switch **(see illustration)**.

2 Connect one lead of an ohmmeter to the black wire's terminal in the switch connector (the switch side, not the wiring harness side). Connect the other lead to the blue wire's terminal. There should be no resistance between the switch and ground when the transmission is in Neutral. In any other gear, there should be infinite resistance.

3 Connect one lead of an ohmmeter to the black wire's terminal in the switch connector (the switch side, not the wiring harness side). Connect the other lead to the white wire's terminal. There should be no resistance between the switch and ground when the forward-reverse shifter is in forward. In any other position, there should be infinite resistance.

4 Connect one lead of an ohmmeter to the black wire's terminal in the switch connector (the switch side, not the wiring harness side). Connect the other lead to the red wire's terminal. There should be no resistance between the switch and ground when the forward-reverse shifter is in forward. In any other position, there should be infinite resistance.

5 If the switch doesn't perform as described, unscrew it and screw in a new one, using a new gasket.

20 Brake light switches - check, replacement and adjustment

1 Locate the switch **(see illustrations)**. Follow the wiring harness from the switch to

20.1a Remove the screw to detach the front brake light switch from the lever bracket

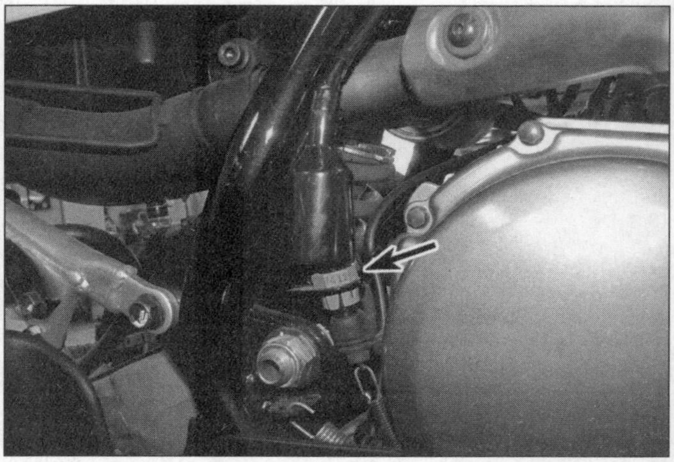

20.1b Unhook the spring and rotate the nut, not the switch body, to separate the rear brake light switch from the bracket

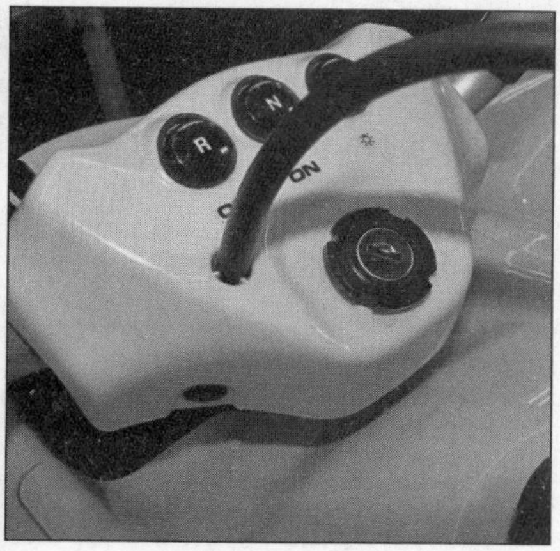

21.1 Unscrew the ring nut and remove the ignition switch from the handlebar cover or fender

its connector and disconnect it.

2 Connect an ohmmeter between the terminals in the switch side of the connector. Operate the brake lever or pedal. With the lever pulled in or the pedal pressed, there should be no resistance (zero ohms). With the lever or pedal released, there should be infinite resistance.

3 If the front brake light switch doesn't perform as described, replace it; the switch is not adjustable. To replace it, press the switch retainer prong and pull the switch out of the brake lever pivot. Push a new switch in until the retainer prong engages, then connect the wiring harness.

4 The rear brake light switch can be adjusted. Hold the switch body so it won't turn and turn the adjusting nut to raise or lower the switch in the bracket **(see illustration 20.1b)**.

5 If adjustment of the rear brake light switch doesn't help, replace the switch with a new one. Unhook the switch from the brake pedal, unscrew the nut off the switch body and take it out of the bracket. Reverse the removal procedure to install the new switch, then adjust it (see Step 4).

21 Ignition switch - check and replacement

1 The ignition switch (main key switch) is located in the warning light cluster on top of the handlebar (carbureted models) **(see illustration)** or in the left side of the front fender (fuel injected models).

Check

2 To check the switch, follow its wiring harness to the connector and disconnect it. The following tests will be made with an ohmmeter connected to the switch side of the connector (not the wiring harness side).

Carbureted models

3 Place the switch in the Off position. Connect an ohmmeter to the orange and green wires. The ohmmeter should indicate continuity (zero ohms). If it doesn't, replace the switch.

4 Place the switch in the On position. Connect an ohmmeter to the orange and red wires. The ohmmeter should indicate continuity (zero ohms). If it doesn't, replace the switch.

5 Place the switch in the Light position. Connect an ohmmeter between all three wires (red, orange and green), two wires at a time. The ohmmeter should indicate continuity (zero ohms) in all cases. If it doesn't, replace the switch.

Fuel injected models

6 Place the switch in the Off position. Connect an ohmmeter between all three wires (black/red, black/orange and brown), two wires at a time. The ohmmeter should indicate no continuity (infinite resistance) in all cases. If it doesn't, replace the switch.

7 Place the switch in the On position. Connect an ohmmeter to the black/orange and black/red wires. The ohmmeter should indicate continuity (zero ohms). If it doesn't, replace the switch.

8 Place the switch in the Light position. Connect an ohmmeter between all three wires (black/red, black/orange and brown), two wires at a time. The ohmmeter should indicate continuity (zero ohms) in all cases. If it doesn't, replace the switch.

Replacement

9 Locate and disconnect the switch wiring connector (see Steps 1 and 2).

10 Unscrew the switch nut and lift the switch out of the fender.

11 Installation is the reverse of removal.

Notes

Chapter 6
Steering, suspension and final drive

Contents

Degrees of difficulty

Easy, suitable for novice with little experience	**Fairly easy,** suitable for beginner with some experience	**Fairly difficult,** suitable for competent DIY mechanic	**Difficult,** suitable for experienced DIY mechanic	**Very difficult,** suitable for expert DIY or professional

Specifications

Front spring preload	
2003 and 2004 (notch position, standard setting)	3 (center notch)
2005 and later (installed length)	
Standard	287.7 mm (11.32 inches)
Minimum (hardest setting)	280.7 mm (11.05 inches)
Maximum (softest setting)	294.7 mm (11.60 inches)
Front shock absorber compression damping (standard setting, clicks out from fully turned in)	
2003 and 2004	Not applicable
2005 and later	1-3/4
Front shock absorber rebound damping (standard setting, clicks out from fully turned in)	
2003 and 2004	Not applicable
2005 and later	1-1/2
Rear spring preload (installed length)	
Standard	233 mm (9.17 inches)
Minimum (hardest setting)	228.5 mm (9.00 inches)
Maximum (softest setting)	238 mm (9.37 inches)
Rear spring compression damping (standard setting, clicks out from fully turned in)	2
Rear spring rebound damping (standard setting, clicks out from fully turned in)	
2003 and 2004	16
2005 and later	1-1/2
Rear axle runout limit	6.0 mm (0.24 inch)

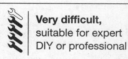

Torque specifications

Steering

Handlebar bracket bolts	26 Nm (19 ft-lbs)
Handlebar bracket nuts (2005 and later carbureted models)	60 Nm (43.5 ft-lbs)
Steering shaft nut	49 Nm (35.5 ft-lbs)
Steering shaft (upper) bearing bolts	23 Nm (16.5 ft-lbs)
Tie-rod nuts	
2003 and 2004	60 Nm (43.5 ft-lbs)
2005 and later	29 Nm (21 ft-lbs)
Tie-rod locknuts	29 Nm (21 ft-lbs)

Front suspension

Front shock absorber bolts and nuts	60 Nm (43.5 ft-lbs)
Balljoint castle nuts	
2003 and 2004	43 Nm (31 ft-lbs)
2005 and later	29 Nm (21 ft-lbs)
Front suspension arm pivot bolts and nuts	65 Nm (47 ft-lbs)

Rear suspension

Rear shock absorber bolts and nuts	
2003 and 2004	
Upper	60 Nm (43.5 ft-lbs)
Lower	55 Nm (40 ft-lbs)
2005 and later (upper and lower)	60 Nm (43.5 ft-lbs)
Rear suspension linkage nuts and bolts	78 Nm (56.5 ft-lbs)
Swingarm pivot bolt and nut	95 Nm (69 ft-lbs)

Final drive

Front sprocket bolts	10 Nm (84 inch-lbs) (1)
Rear sprocket bolts	
2003	54 Nm (39 ft-lbs)
2004	55 Nm (40 ft-lbs)
2005 and later	60 Nm (43.5 ft-lbs)
Rear axle locknuts	
2003 and 2004 (inner and outer nuts)	130 Nm (180 ft-lbs)
2005 and later	
Inner nut	20 Nm (168 in-lbs)
Outer nut	173.5 Nm (240 ft-lbs)
Rear axle housing bolts (2)	
2003	
M10 bolts (small)	73 Nm (53 ft-lbs)
M12 bolts (large)	100 Nm (72 ft-lbs)
2004 and later	100 Nm (72 ft-lbs)

1. *Apply non-permanent thread locking agent to the bolt threads.*
2. *Apply high-strength thread locking agent to the nut threads.*

2.3 Look for a punch mark next to the bracket parting line (arrow); make your own mark if you don't see one

2.4 Mark the front side of each bracket, then remove the bracket bolts (arrows) and lift off the bracket and handlebar

1 General information

The front suspension consists of upper and lower control arms on each side of the vehicle, supported by a shock absorber with a concentric coil spring.

The steering system consists of knuckles mounted at the outer ends of the front suspension and connected to a steering shaft by tie-rods. The steering shaft is turned by a one-piece handlebar.

The rear suspension on all models consists of a single shock absorber with concentric coil spring, progressive linkage and a swingarm. Final drive is by a chain and sprockets.

2 Handlebar - removal and installation

Removing the handlebar to service other components

1 If you're removing the handlebar simply to gain access to the steering shaft, it's not necessary to remove the clutch lever bracket, the left switch housing, the throttle cable housing or the front brake master cylinder.

2 Pull the fuel tank breather hose out of the hole in the handlebar cover (carbureted models) **(see illustration 2.1 in Chapter 4A)**, or steering shaft (fuel injected models). Remove the trim clips (if equipped) and pull the handlebar cover off (see Chapter 8).

3 Look for a punch mark on the front of each handlebar bracket. Also look for a punch mark in the handlebar that indicates its position relative to the handlebar brackets **(see illustration)**. If you can't find the factory punch marks, make your own marks to ensure that the brackets are correctly oriented when they're reinstalled.

4 Remove the handlebar bracket bolts **(see illustration)**, remove the upper bracket halves, then lift the handlebar off the lower bracket halves.

5 If you're working on a carbureted model, remove the nuts and take the lower bracket halves off the steering shaft **(see illustration)**.

Caution: Support the handlebar assembly with a piece of wire or rope; allowing it to hang free will damage the cables, hoses and wiring.

6 If you're working on a fuel injected model, remove the nuts from the underside of the lower bracket and lift the bracket off of the steering shaft.

7 Installation is the reverse of removal. If you're working on a fuel injected model, make sure the raised boss on top of the lower bracket is toward the front of the vehicle. Make sure that the factory punch marks (or the ones you made prior to disassembly) face to the front. Tighten the handlebar bracket bolts to the torque listed in this Chapter's Specifications.

Caution: Tighten the front bracket bolts first, then the rear bracket bolts. This will leave a gap between the upper and lower bracket halves at the rear of each bracket* (see illustration)*. Don't try to close the gap by overtightening or you'll break the brackets.

Replacing the handlebar

8 If you're replacing the handlebar, remove all cable ties, then remove the clutch lever bracket, the left switch housing, the throttle cable housing (see Chapter 4), and the front brake master cylinder (see Chapter 7).

9 Follow Steps 2 through 4. If you need to remove the lower brackets, follow Step 5 (carbureted models) or Step 6 (fuel injected models).

2.5 Remove the lower bracket nuts (carbureted models)

2.7 Tighten the front bolts first, then the rear bolts, leaving a gap at the rear of each bracket

3.6 To detach the lower end of the steering shaft from the frame, remove this cotter pin and nut

3.7 Note how the brake line and wiring harnesses are routed, then bend back the lockwasher tabs and remove the upper bracket bolts (arrows)

10 Installation is the reverse of removal. Tighten the handlebar bracket bolts to the torque listed in this Chapter's Specifications, observing the Caution in Step 7.

3 Steering shaft - removal, inspection and installation

Removal

1 Remove the handlebar and brackets (see Section 2).
2 Remove the front fender and fuel tank cover (see Chapter 8).
3 Remove the oil tank and radiator (see Chapters 2 and 3).
4 Straighten the lockwasher tabs and remove the two nuts, the lockwasher, the washer and the steering shaft bearing halves.
5 Disconnect the inner ends of the tie-rods from the steering shaft (see Section 5).
6 Remove the cotter pin and nut from the bottom of the steering shaft **(see illustration)**. Remove the washer and O-ring.
7 Remove the steering shaft and bushings from the vehicle **(see illustration)**.
8 Pry out the seals from the steering shaft's lower pivot in the frame, unscrew the retainer with a hex bit and remove the lower bearing from the frame.

Inspection

9 Clean all the parts with solvent and dry them thoroughly, using compressed air, if available.
10 Inspect the steering shaft bearings and seals for wear, deterioration or damage. Replace them if there's any doubt about their condition. If you need to replace the lower bushings, remove and install it with a drawbolt as described in *Tools and Workshop Tips* at the end of this manual.
11 Inspect the steering shaft and its integral steering arm for bending or other signs of damage. Do not attempt to repair any steering components. Replace them with new parts if defects are found.

Installation

12 Installation is the reverse of removal, with the following additions:

a) *Lubricate the steering shaft upper bearing and seals with grease.*
b) *Use new locknuts, lockwasher and cotter pins and tighten all fasteners to the torque values listed in this Chapter's Specifications.*

4 Shock absorbers - removal, installation and adjustment

Removal and installation

Warning: Do not attempt to disassemble these shock absorbers. They are nitrogen-charged under high pressure. Replace the shocks and springs as a unit.

Front shock absorbers

Note: *This procedure applies to either front shock absorber.*

1 Support the front of the vehicle securely on jackstands and remove the front wheels.
2 Support the outer ends of the front lower arms with jackstands so they won't drop when the shock absorbers are removed.
3 Remove the nuts and bolts that attach the upper end of the shock to the frame bracket and the lower end to the bracket on the lower control arm bracket **(see illustrations)**. Separate the shock from the frame bracket and from the control arm bracket and lift it out.
4 Inspect the shock absorber for signs of wear or damage such as oil leaks, bending, a weak spring and worn bushings. Replace

4.3a Unbolt the lower end of the shock from the suspension arm

4.3b Unbolt the upper end from the frame (upper arrow) - the upper end of the shock has adjusters for compression damping (center arrow) and spring pre-load (lower arrow)

4.8 Remove the mounting bolt and nut from the upper end of the shock . . .

4.9 . . . and from the lower end (lower arrow) - the rebound damping adjuster (upper arrow) is in the lower end of the shock

4.18 2005 and later models have a compression damping adjuster at the top of the rear shock (arrow)

both shock absorbers as a pair if any problems are found.

5 Installation is the reverse of removal. Tighten the nuts and bolts to the torque listed in this Chapter's Specifications.

Rear shock absorber

6 Jack up the rear end of the vehicle and support it securely on jackstands. Slip a rag beneath the shock so the swingarm and shock body won't be scratched.

7 Remove the cushion rod and lever (the rear portion of the shock linkage) (see Section 11).

8 Remove the mounting bolt and nut at the top of the shock **(see illustration)**.

9 Remove the mounting bolt and nut at the lower end of the shock **(see illustration)**. Raise the swingarm and lower the shock out of the vehicle.

10 Installation is the reverse of removal, with the following additions: Use non-permanent thread locking agent on the threads of the shock bolts. Tighten the nuts and bolts to the torques listed in this Chapter's Specifications.

Adjustment

Front shock absorbers

11 On 2004 and earlier models, front shock absorber spring preload is adjusted by turning the adjuster ring at the bottom of the shock with a spanner wrench. (The spanner should be in your machine's toolkit; if not, you can obtain one at a dealer parts department.) Refer to this Chapter's Specifications for suspension settings.

12 On 2005 and later models, front shock absorber spring preload is adjusted by changing the spring length. Remove the shock absorber from the vehicle. Loosen the locknut (the lower nut), turn the adjuster ring to obtain the desired preload, then tighten the locknut **(see illustration 4.3b)**. Settings are listed in this Chapter's Specifications.

13 Front shock absorber rebound damping (if equipped) is adjusted by turning the screw on the bottom of the shock absorber. Turning the adjuster clockwise increases the rebound damping force (slower rebound); turning the adjuster counterclockwise decreases the rebound damping force (faster rebound). To set the rebound damping adjuster to its standard position, turn it all the way in, then back it out the number of clicks listed in this Chapter's Specifications.

Caution: Do NOT attempt to turn the rebound adjuster beyond the maximum or minimum setting.

14 Front shock absorber compression damping on models so equipped is adjusted by turning the screw on the shock reservoir **(see illustration 4.3b)**. Turning the adjuster clockwise increases the compression damping force (slower rebound); turning the adjuster counterclockwise decreases the compression damping force (faster rebound). To set the adjuster to its standard position, turn it all the way in, then back it out the number of clicks listed in this Chapter's Specifications.

Caution: Do NOT attempt to turn the compression damping adjuster beyond the maximum or minimum setting.

Rear shock absorber

15 The rear shock absorber is fully adjustable for spring preload, compression damping and rebound damping.

16 Spring preload is adjusted by changing the length of the spring. Loosen the preload adjuster locknut at the top of the shock, then turn the adjuster nut with a spanner wrench **(see illustration 4.8)**. The spanner should be in your machine's tool kit; if not, you can obtain one at a dealer. Turn the adjuster clockwise to reduce spring length or counterclockwise to increase spring length. Measure the spring length and compare your measurement to the values listed in this Chapter's Specifications.

Caution: Do NOT attempt to turn the spring preload adjuster beyond the maximum or minimum setting.

Tighten the locknut when you're done.

17 Rebound damping force is adjusted by turning the adjuster at the bottom of the shock **(see illustration 4.9)**. Turning the adjuster clockwise increases the rebound damping force (slower rebound); turning the adjuster counterclockwise decreases the rebound damping force (faster rebound). To set the rebound damping adjuster to its standard position, turn it all the way in, then back it out the number of clicks listed in this Chapter's Specifications.

Caution: Do NOT attempt to turn the rebound adjuster beyond the maximum or minimum setting.

18 Rear shock absorber compression damping on 2005 and later models is adjusted by turning the screw on the shock reservoir **(see illustration)**. Turning the adjuster clockwise increases the compression damping force (slower rebound); turning the adjuster counterclockwise decreases the compression damping force (faster rebound). To set the adjuster to its standard position, turn it all the way in, then back it out the number of clicks listed in this Chapter's Specifications.

Caution: Do NOT attempt to turn the compression damping adjuster beyond the maximum or minimum setting.

5 Tie-rods - removal, inspection and installation

Removal

1 Place the steering in the straight-ahead position.

2 If both of the tie-rods are to be removed, mark them "Left" and "Right" so they're not accidentally switched during reassembly.

5.3 Remove the cotter pin and nut from the outer end of the tie-rod . . .

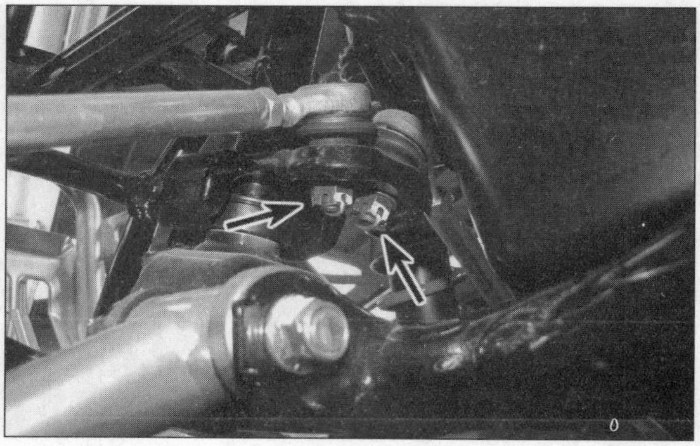

5.4 . . . and from the inner end

6.5 Remove the balljoint nuts and cotter pins

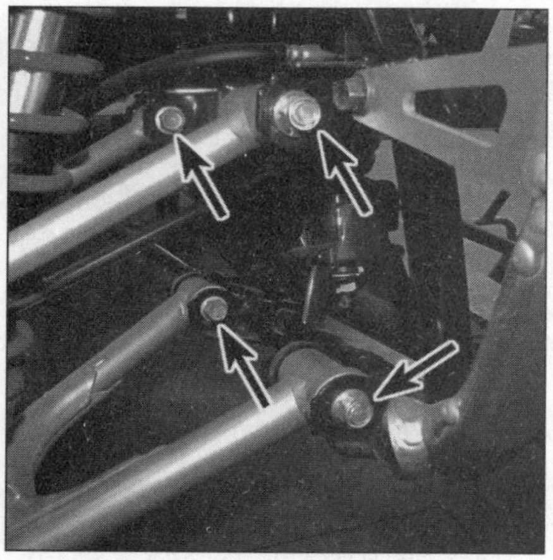

7.4 Remove the pivot nuts and bolts - the bolt heads face toward each other

3 Remove the cotter pin from the nut at the outer end of the tie-rod and undo the nut **(see illustration)**.

4 Separate the tie-rod stud from the knuckle with a tie rod puller or pickle fork balljoint separator **(see illustration)**.

Caution: It's very easy to damage the rubber boot on the tie-rod with a pickle fork separator. If you're going to use the tie-rod again, it's best to use another type of tool.

5 Repeat the procedure to disconnect the inner end of the tie rod from the steering shaft.

Inspection

6 Check the tie-rod shaft for bending or other damage and replace it if any problems are found. Don't try to straighten the shaft.

7 Check the tie-rod balljoint boots for cracks or deterioration. Twist and rotate the threaded studs. They should move easily, without roughness or looseness. If a boot or stud show any problems, unscrew the tie-rod end from the tie-rod and install a new one.

Installation

8 Thread the tie-rod ends onto the tie-rods. The length of exposed threads on each end of the tie-rod must be even. The flat on the tie-rod that's used to adjust toe-in goes at the outer end of the tie-rod.

9 The remainder of Installation is the reverse of removal, with the following additions:

a) Use new cotter pins and bend them to hold the nuts securely.

b) Check front wheel toe-in and adjust as necessary (see Chapter 1).

6 Steering knuckles - removal, inspection, and installation

Removal

1 Jack up the front end of the vehicle and support it securely on jackstands. Remove the front wheels.

2 Disconnect the outer end of the tie-rod from the steering knuckle (see Section 5).

3 Remove the outer disc cover, the front brake caliper, the wheel hub and the inner disc cover (see Chapter 7).

4 Remove the front shock absorber (see Section 4).

5 Remove the cotter pin and nut from the upper and lower balljoint studs **(see illustration)**.

6 Separating the balljoints from the steering knuckle requires a separator tool. Automotive tie-rod separator tools are suitable (try it for fit before you buy it, if possible) and can be rented from tool yards or purchased inexpensively.

7 If balljoint separation proves difficult, the knuckle and suspension arms can be removed as a single assembly, then taken to a dealer for balljoint removal.

Inspection

8 Inspect the knuckle carefully for cracks, bending or other damage. Replace it if any problems are found. If the vehicle has been in a collision or has been bottomed hard, it's a good idea to have the knuckle magnafluxed by a machine shop to check for hidden cracks.

Installation

9 Installation is the reverse of removal. Use new cotter pins and tighten the nuts to the torque listed in this Chapter's Specifications.

7 Suspension arms and balljoints - removal, inspection and installation

Suspension arms

Removal

1 Securely block both rear wheels so the vehicle won't roll. Loosen the front wheel nuts with the tires still on the ground, then jack up the front end, support it securely on jackstands and remove the front wheels.

2 Remove the steering knuckle (see Section 6). If you're removing an upper arm, detach the brake hose from the arm (see Chapter 7).

3 Unbolt the shock absorber from the lower suspension arm (see Section 4).

4 Remove the pivot bolts and nuts and remove the suspension arm **(see illustration)**.

Inspection

5 Inspect the suspension arm(s) for bending, cracks or corrosion. Replace damaged parts. Don't attempt to straighten them.

7.10 Remove the snap-ring to separate the balljoint from the suspension arm

8.2a This is the special tool you'll need to remove the axle nuts - it will also fit the nut on the right side of the axle shaft, as shown here, but there's normally no need to remove this nut

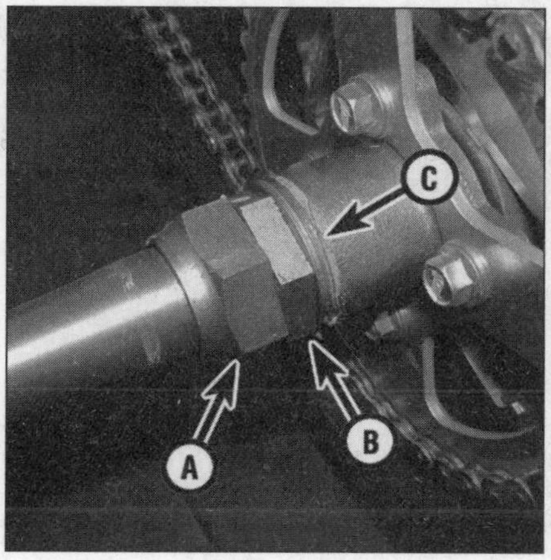

8.2b Unscrew the outer nut (A), inner nut (B) and two conical washers (C) - the concave sides of the washers face each other on installation

6 Inspect all rubber bushings for cracks or deterioration. Check the inner collars on the lower suspension arms for damage or corrosion. Inspect the pivot bolts for wear as well. Replace the bushings and pivot bolts if they're worn or deteriorated.

7 Check the balljoint boot for cracks or deterioration. Twist and rotate the threaded stud. It should move easily, without roughness or looseness. The lower balljoints can't be replaced separately from the suspension arms. If the boot or stud show any problems, replace the suspension arm together with the balljoint. To replace an upper balljoint, see Step 10.

Installation

8 Installation is the reverse of removal, but don't torque the suspension fasteners while the vehicle is off the ground. Tighten the nuts and bolts *slightly* while the vehicle is jacked up, then tighten them to the torque listed in this Chapter's Specifications after the vehicle is resting on its wheels.

Balljoints

9 On lower suspension arms, the balljoints are an integral part of the suspension arms; they cannot be separated. If the balljoint or the suspension arm is damaged or worn, they must be replaced as a single assembly.

10 On upper suspension arms, the balljoints can be removed from the suspension arms and replaced separately. With the suspension arm disconnected from the knuckle, remove the snap-ring **(see illustration)** and press the balljoint out of the suspension arm. If you don't have a press, have the balljoint pressed out by a dealer service department or other qualified shop.

8 Rear axle shaft - removal, inspection and installation

Warning: The axle nuts are secured with high-strength thread locking agent and tightened to a very high torque. It's best to loosen them with the rear tires still on the ground, then jack up the rear end so you can remove the wheels and axle shaft. If you must tighten or loosen them with the vehicle jacked up, be sure the vehicle is securely positioned on jackstands so it can't fall.

Removal

1 Block the front wheels so the vehicle won't roll.

2 Set the parking brake and place the transmission in gear to keep the axle from turning. If this isn't possible (for example, because the rear caliper or drive chain has been removed), insert a rod through the sprocket flange into the rear axle housing. Unscrew the axle locknut and axle nut with a 36 mm wrench (Suzuki part no. 09940-92540 or equivalent, available from aftermarket suppliers) **(see illustration)**. Once the nuts are loose, slip them off the axle shaft, then remove the two concave washers and the sprocket flange **(see illustrations)**.

3 Jack up the rear end of the vehicle and support it securely, positioning the jackstands so they won't obstruct removal of the axle. The supports must be secure enough so the vehicle won't be knocked off of them while the axle is removed. Remove the rear wheels.

4 Loosen the drive chain and remove the rear wheel hubs (see Chapters 1 and 7).

5 Disengage the chain from the rear

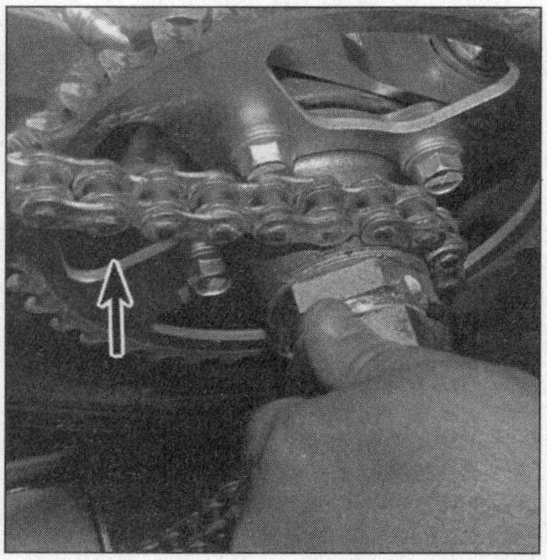

8.2c If the parking brake and drive chain won't hold the axle from turning, insert a bar through the sprocket into the axle housing (arrow)

8.2d The nuts are secured with high-strength thread locking agent

8.7 Remove the axle to the right side of the vehicle

8.8a If the sprocket flange is damaged, replace the axle shaft as a unit

8.8b Check the splines and threads for damage

sprocket, then remove the sprocket and hub from the axle (see Section 15).

6 Release the parking brake so the rear brake caliper can be removed. Remove the caliper (see Chapter 7). The brake hose and cable can be left connected. Secure the caliper out of the way.

7 Thread the nut back on to the left-hand end of the axle to protect the threads. Tape a socket over the nut, then tap on the nut to free the axle from the hub. Once the axle is free, remove the nut and remove the axle from the right side of the vehicle **(see illustration)**.

Inspection

8 Check the axle for obvious damage, such as step wear of the splines or bending, and replace it as necessary **(see illustration)**.

9 Inspect the brake disc and replace it if necessary (see Chapter 7).

10 Place the axle in V-blocks and set up a dial indicator to contact each of the outer ends in turn (see *Tools and Workshop Tips* at the end of this manual for information on dial indicators). Rotate the axle and compare runout to the value listed in this Chapter's Specifications. If runout is excessive, replace the axle.

11 Inspect the hub seals and bearings (see Chapter 7).

12 Inspect the sprockets (see Section 15) and drive chain (see Section 14).

Installation

13 Apply high-strength thread locking agent (red Loctite no. 271 or equivalent) to the nut threads on the axle. Tighten the axle nut with a torque wrench adapter (Suzuki tool 09940-92460 or an equivalent crow's foot wrench) as described in the following steps.

14 Before tightening the axle nuts, calculate the amount of torque to apply. Because the tool increases the applied torque by lengthening the torque wrench, you'll need to apply slightly less indicated torque to get the correct actual torque. With a typical 16-inch torque wrench, the indicated torque should be as follows:

117 ft-lbs (162 Nm) for 2003 and 2004 models

156 ft-lbs (216 Nm) for 2005 and later models

15 If your torque wrench is longer than 16 inches, the indicated torque will be lower. Calculate the torque as described in Step 16.

16 To calculate the torque, take two measurements:

The length of the torque wrench, from the center of the handle to the center of the head

The combined length of the torque wrench with the special tool attached, from the handle to the center of the tool

Multiply the length of the torque wrench by the specified torque listed in this Chapter's Specifications. Divide the result by the combined length of the torque wrench and tool. The result is the torque that should be indicated on the torque wrench scale.

17 The remainder of installation is the reverse of removal.

18 Check and adjust the drive chain (see Chapter 1).

9 Rear axle housing - removal, inspection and installation

Removal

1 Block the front wheels so the vehicle won't roll.

2 Jack up the rear end of the vehicle and support it securely, positioning the jackstands so they won't obstruct removal of the axle. The supports must be secure enough so the vehicle won't be knocked off of them while the axle is removed. Remove the rear wheels.

3 Remove the drive sprocket (see Section 15).

4 Remove the rear axle shaft (see Section 8).

5 Remove the bolts from the top of the axle housing **(see illustration)**.

6 Pull the axle housing out of the swingarm toward the right side of the vehicle. If it's stuck, tap it gently with a soft-faced mallet.

7 If necessary, unscrew the chain adjuster nut(s), remove the adjuster plate and take the rubber boot off the adjuster shaft **(see illustration)**.

Inspection

8 If the bolt threads in the bottom of the axle housing are corroded or damaged, try to clean them up with a tap.

9 Check the axle shaft seals for wear or deterioration **(see illustration)**. Spin the bearings with a finger and check them for roughness, looseness or noise. If there's any problem with the bearings or seals, replace them. The procedure is basically the same as for front wheel bearings (see Chapter 7).

Installation

10 Installation is the reverse of removal, with the following additions:

a) *If you removed the chain adjuster boot, install it with its small diameter end toward the axle housing.*

b) *Install the shorter two of the four axle housing bolts in the holes closest to the front of the vehicle.*

c) *Tighten all fasteners to the torque listed in this Chapter's Specifications.*

10 Swingarm bearings - check

1 Remove the rear wheels (see Chapter 7), then remove the rear shock absorber (see Section 4).

2 Grasp the rear of the swingarm with one hand and place your other hand at the junction of the swingarm and the frame. Try to move the rear of the swingarm from side-to-side. If the bearings are worn, they will allow some freeplay, which produces movement between the swingarm and the frame at the front (the swingarm will move forward and

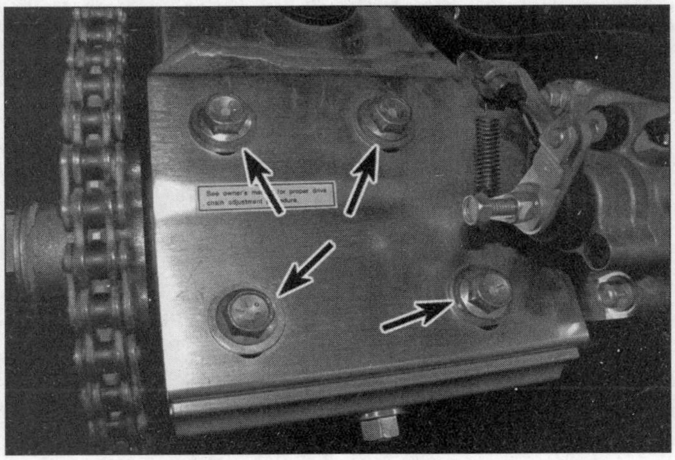

9.5 Remove the bolts from the top of the axle housing

9.7 Unscrew the nuts and remove the chain adjuster(s) (right arrow), then remove the adjuster plate (left arrow)

backward at the front, not from side-to-side). If any play is noted, the bearings should be replaced with new ones (see Section 13).

3 Next, move the swingarm up and down through its full travel. It should move freely, without any binding or rough spots. If it does not move freely, remove the swingarm (see Section 12) and inspect (and replace, if necessary) the bearings (see Section 13).

11 Shock linkage - removal, inspection and installation

Removal

1 Raise the rear end of the vehicle and support it securely on jackstands.

2 Unbolt the skid plates from the underside of the linkage and swingarm.

3 Remove the nuts and bolts that secure the cushion rod to the cushion lever and shock absorber **(see illustration)**, and remove the cushion rod.

4 Remove the shock absorber lower mounting bolt (see Section 4). Remove the nut and bolt that secure the cushion lever to the frame **(see illustration)**, and remove the cushion lever.

Inspection

5 Pry the collars off the bearings and push out the spacers.

6 Inspect the dust seals (they're installed next to the needle roller bearings). Replace them if they're worn or if grease has been leaking past them.

7 Check the needle roller bearings in the cushion lever and cushion rod for wear, damage, corrosion or the bluish tint that indicates overheating. If any of these problems are found, replace the bearings. They can be removed and installed with a drawbolt of the type described in *Tools and Workshop Tips* at the end of this manual. On installation, pull the bearings in to the depths listed in this Chapter's Specifications.

8 Lubricate the bearings with water-resistant multipurpose grease.

Installation

9 Installation is the reverse of removal. Tighten the pivot bolt and locknut to the torque listed in this Chapter's Specifications.

12 Swingarm - removal and installation

1 If the swingarm is only being removed for bearing replacement, the brake assembly, rear hub and rear axle need not be removed from the swingarm.

Removal

2 Raise the rear end of the vehicle and support it securely on jackstands.

3 Remove the rear wheels, the rear wheel hubs, the brake caliper and the brake disc (see Chapter 7).

4 Unbolt the skid plate from the underside of the linkage. Take the drive chain off the sprockets (see Section 14).

9.9 Check the axle housing seals and bearings

11.3 Remove the nuts and bolts and detach the cushion rod from the swingarm and cushion lever

11.4 Remove the nut and bolt to detach the cushion lever from the frame

12.8a Remove the pivot bolt nut

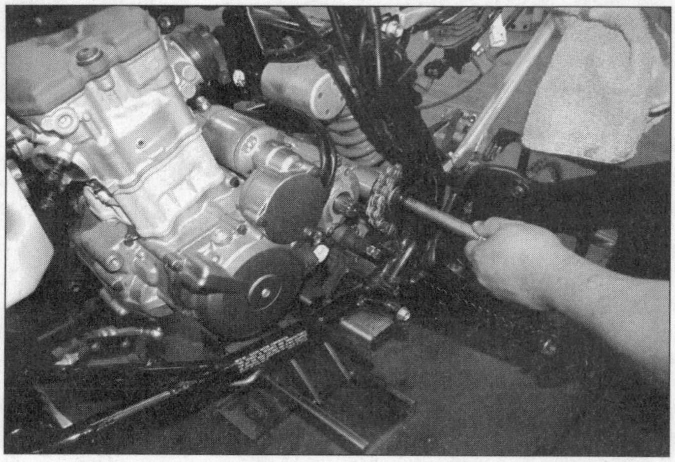

12.8b Pull the pivot bolt out of the engine and swingarm

5 If you're replacing the swingarm, remove the rear axle (see Section 8).
6 Support the swingarm so it won't drop, then detach the lower end of the shock absorber from the relay arm (see Section 4).
7 Remove the cushion rod and cushion lever (see Section 11).
8 Unscrew the locknut, then pull the pivot bolt out of the swingarm **(see illustrations)**.
9 Pull the swingarm back and away from the vehicle.
10 Inspect the pivot bearings in the swingarm for dryness or deterioration (see Section 10).

Installation

11 Lift the swingarm into position in the frame. Install the pivot bolt and locknut to hold the swingarm in the frame, but don't tighten them yet.
12 Raise and lower the swingarm several times, moving it through its full travel to seat the bearings and pivot bolt.
13 Tighten the pivot bolt and locknut to the torque listed in this Chapter's Specifications.
14 The remainder of installation is the reverse of removal.

13 Swingarm bearings - replacement

1 The swingarm pivot bolt rides on two needle roller bearings.
2 Remove the swingarm (see Section 12).
3 Remove the collar and pry the seal from each side of the swingarm.
4 Inspect the swingarm pivot bearing in each end of the swingarm. If either bearing is rough or loose, or has excessive play, replace the bearings as a set.
5 Remove the bearings with a drawbolt of the type described in *Tools and Workshop Tips* at the end of this manual.
6 While the bearings are removed, remove the collar, clean it thoroughly, inspect it for burrs, scoring and other damage. If the collar is damaged or worn, replace it. Lubricate the collar with grease and insert it back into the swingarm (make sure that the pivot bore is clean).
7 Install the new collars and bearings with the same tool used for removal.
8 Pack the bearings with waterproof lithium-based wheel bearing grease.
9 Tap new seals into position with a seal driver or a socket just slightly smaller than the outside diameter of the seal.

14 Drive chain - removal, cleaning, inspection and installation

Removal

1 To remove the drive chain, you'll need to remove the swingarm (see Section 12) or use a chain breaker tool as described in *Tools and Workshop Tips* at the end of this manual, following the manufacturer's instructions.

Warning: Do not use a chain that has a clip-on master link on these vehicles, as it may separate during operation and cause personal injury and damage to the vehicle. Use an endless chain only.

2 Remove the front sprocket cover from the engine **(see illustrations)**.

14.2a Remove the cover bolts . . .

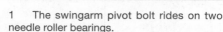

14.2b . . . and remove the cover, together with the spacer

15.4a Remove the sprocket bolts

15.4b Rotate the washer to align with the splines in the transmission shaft and take it off, then remove the sprocket

3 Loosen the chain adjusters as needed to create slack so you can disengage the chain from the rear sprocket (see Chapter 1).

4 Lift the chain off the sprockets and remove it from the vehicle.

5 Check the chain guide and rollers on the swingarm and frame for wear or damage and replace them as necessary (see Chapter 1).

Cleaning and inspection

6 The drive chain has small rubber O-rings between the chain plates. Soak the chain in kerosene and use a brush to work the solvent into the spaces between the links and plates.

Caution: Do NOT use steam, high-pressure washes or solvents, all of which can damage the O-rings, to clean the chain. Use only kerosene.

7 Wipe the chain dry, then inspect it carefully for worn or damaged links. Replace the chain if wear or damage is found at any point.

8 If the chain is worn or damaged, inspect the sprockets. If the sprockets are worn or damaged, replace them.

Caution: Do NOT install a new chain on worn sprockets; it will wear out quickly.

9 Lubricate the chain (the manufacturer recommends heavy engine oil).

Installation

10 Installation is the reverse of removal. Adjust the chain (see Chapter 1).

15 Sprockets - check and replacement

1 Whenever the sprockets are inspected, also inspect the chain. Replace the chain if it's worn; installing a worn chain on new sprockets will cause them to wear quickly.

2 Check the teeth on the engine sprocket and rear sprocket for wear. The engine sprocket is visible through the cover slots.

3 If the sprockets are worn, remove the chain (see Section 14) and the left rear wheel and hub (see Chapter 7).

4 To remove the engine sprocket, remove the sprocket cover (see Section 14). Remove the two bolts that secure the sprocket retaining washer, then remove the washer and pull the sprocket off the transmission shaft **(see illustrations)**.

5 Inspect the seal behind the engine sprocket. If it has been leaking, remove the seal retainer, pry the seal out (take care not to scratch the seal bore) and tap in a new seal with a socket the same diameter as the seal **(see illustration)**.

6 To remove the rear sprocket, hold the Allen bolts with a wrench and unscrew the nuts **(see illustration)**. Slip the sprocket over the end of the axle.

7 Installation is the reverse of removal, with the following additions:

15.5 If the transmission shaft seal has been leaking, remove the retainer screws (arrows) and take off the seal retainer so the seal can be pried out

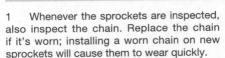

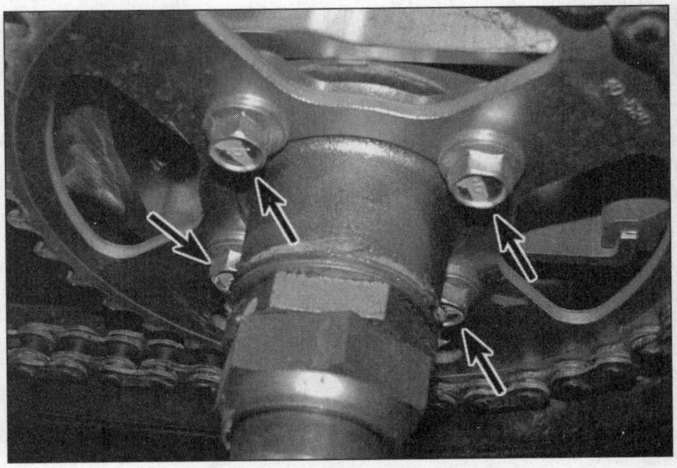

15.6 Remove the rear sprocket nuts

15.7 Install the sprocket flange with its shoulder toward the axle housing

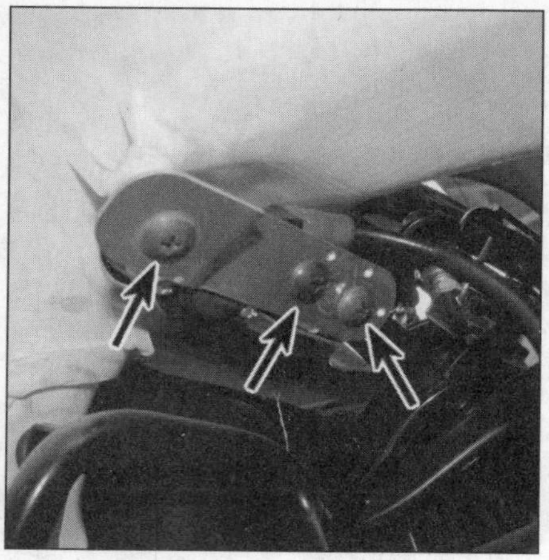

16.1 Reverse knob bracket screw (outer arrows) and bracket-to-knob screw (center arrow) locations

16.6a Remove the bolt that secures the cable housing to the support

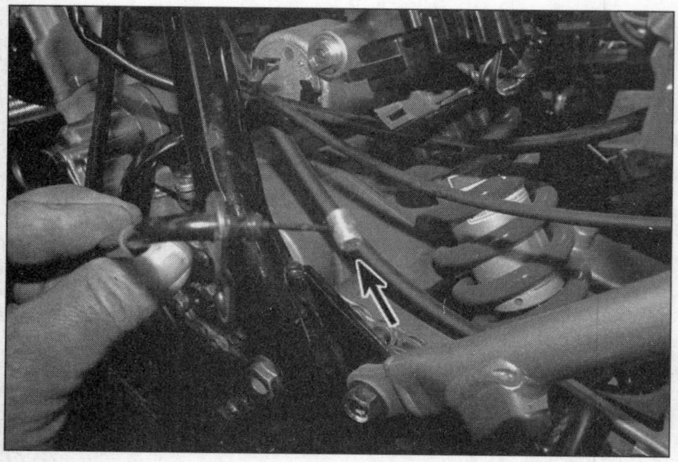

16.6b Slip the cable out of the bracket, turn the cable to align it with the slot in the reverse shaft and lift the cable end plug (arrow) out of the reverse shaft

16.7 Note how the reverse cable is routed

a) *Install the engine sprocket with the letter "A" marked on it facing away from the engine.*
b) *Install the sprocket washer with its OUTSIDE mark facing away from the engine.*
c) *Install the rear sprocket with its shoulder toward the rear axle housing* **(see illustration)**.
d) *Tighten the drive sprocket bolts and driven sprocket nuts and bolts to the torque listed in this Chapter's Specifications.*
e) *Install the chain (see Section 14) and adjust it (see Chapter 1).*

16 Reverse lock cable - removal and installation

1 Working beneath the front fender, detach the reverse knob bracket **(see illustration)**.

2 Slip the bracket through the fender hole, then remove the screw and detach the bracket from the knob.

3 Remove the screws and remove the cable cover from the knob.

4 Remove the screw and washer that secure the cable pulley to the knob. Take the pulley out of the knob and detach the cable from it.

5 Remove the drive sprocket cover from the engine (see Section 15).

6 Unbolt the cable and detach it from the engine **(see illustrations)**.

7 Note how the cable is routed **(see illustrations)** and remove it from the vehicle.

8 Installation is the reverse of removal. When installing the spring in the knob, make sure its inner end hooks into the notch inside the housing and its outer end hooks into the pulley.

Chapter 7
Brakes, wheels and tires

Contents

Degrees of difficulty

Easy, suitable for novice with little experience	**Fairly easy,** suitable for beginner with some experience	**Fairly difficult,** suitable for competent DIY mechanic	**Difficult,** suitable for experienced DIY mechanic	**Very difficult,** suitable for expert DIY or professional

Specifications

Brakes

Brake pedal height	See Chapter 1
Brake pad thickness (limit)	To wear indicator, or 0.030 inch (1.0 mm)
Brake disc	
Front	
Maximum runout	0.30 mm (0.012 inch)
Minimum allowable thickness	Refer to the marks stamped in the disc
Rear	
Maximum runout	0.30 mm (0.012 inch)
Minimum allowable thickness	Refer to the marks stamped in the disc

Wheels and tires

Tire pressures	See *Daily (pre-ride) checks* at the beginning of this manual
Tire tread depth	See *Daily (pre-ride) checks* at the beginning of this manual

Torque specifications

Wheel lug nuts	50 Nm (36 ft-lbs)
Front hub nuts	65 Nm (47 ft-lbs)
Rear hub nuts	100 Nm (72 ft-lbs) (1)
Front brake	
Caliper mounting bolts	26 Nm (19 ft-lbs)
Brake pad retaining bolts	18 Nm (156 in-lbs) (3)
Brake hose-to-caliper banjo bolts	23 Nm (16.5 ft-lbs) (2)
Brake disc retaining bolts	23 Nm (16.5 ft-lbs) (3)
Rear brake	
Caliper-to-bracket bolts	26 Nm (19 ft-lbs)
Brake pad retaining bolts	18 Nm (156 in-lbs) (3)
Brake hose-to-caliper banjo bolt	23 Nm (16.5 ft-lbs) (2)
Brake disc retaining bolts	22 Nm (16.5 ft-lbs) (3)
Parking brake case/bracket bolts	28 Nm (20.5 ft-lbs) (3)
Parking brake adjusting bolt locknut	18 Nm (13 ft-lbs)
Front master cylinder	
Brake hose banjo bolt	23 Nm (16.5 ft-lbs) (2)
Handlebar clamp bolts	7 Nm (61 inch-lbs)
Rear master cylinder	
Brake hose banjo bolt	23 Nm (16.5 ft-lbs) (2)

1 If the cotter pin holes don't line up, tighten the nut just enough to align them. Don't loosen the nut to align the cotter pin holes.

2 Use new sealing washers.

3 Apply non-permanent thread locking agent to the threads.

4.2 Remove the outer disc shield from the hub

4.3 Bend back the cotter pin and pull it out

4.4 Have an assistant firmly apply the front brakes while you crack the hub nut loose

1 General information

The vehicles covered by this manual are equipped with three hydraulically-operated disc brakes: a disc at each front wheel and a single disc on the rear axle. The front brakes are operated by a lever-actuated master cylinder on the right end of the handlebar; the rear brake is operated by a pedal-actuated master cylinder on the right side of the vehicle, behind the right footrest. The rear brake caliper is equipped with a parking brake system, which is actuated by a lever on the left end of the handlebar.

The front calipers have dual pistons. The rear caliper has a single piston.

All models are equipped with wheels which require very little maintenance and allow tubeless tires to be used.

Caution: Brake components rarely require disassembly. Do not disassemble components unless absolutely necessary.

2 Wheels - inspection, removal and installation

Inspection

1 Clean the wheels thoroughly to remove mud and dirt that may interfere with the inspection procedure or mask defects. Make a general check of the wheels and tires as described in Chapter 1.

2 The wheels should be visually inspected for cracks, flat spots on the rim and other damage. Since tubeless tires are involved, look very closely for dents in the area where the tire bead contacts the rim. Dents in this area may prevent complete sealing of the tire against the rim, which leads to deflation of the tire over a period of time.

3 If damage is evident, the wheel will have to be replaced with a new one. Never attempt to repair a damaged wheel.

Removal

4 Securely block the wheels at the opposite end of the vehicle from the wheel being removed, so it can't roll.

5 Loosen the lug nuts on the wheel being removed. Jack up one end of the vehicle and support it securely on jackstands.

6 Remove the lug nuts and pull the wheel off.

Installation

7 Position the wheel on the studs. Make sure the directional arrow on the tire points in the forward rotating direction of the wheel.

8 Install the wheel nuts with their tapered sides toward the wheel. This is necessary to locate the wheel accurately on the hub.

9 Snug the wheel nuts evenly in a criss-cross pattern.

10 Remove the jackstands, lower the vehicle and tighten the wheel nuts, again in a criss-cross pattern, to the torque listed in this Chapter's Specifications.

3 Tires - general information

1 Tubeless tires are used as standard equipment on this vehicle. Unlike motorcycle tires, they run at very low air pressures and are completely unsuited for use on pavement. Inflating ATV tires to excessive pressures will rupture them, making replacement of the tire necessary.

2 The force required to break the seal between the rim and the bead of the tire is substantial, much more than required for motorcycle tires, and is beyond the capabilities of an individual working with normal tire irons or even a normal bead breaker. A special bead breaker is required for ATV tires; it produces a great deal of force and concentrates it in a relatively small area.

3 Repair of the punctured tire and replacement on the wheel rim requires special tools, skills and experience that the average do-it-yourselfer lacks.

4 For these reasons, if a puncture or flat occurs with an ATV tire, the wheel should be removed from the vehicle and taken to a dealer service department or a repair shop for repair or replacement of the tire. The accompanying illustrations can be used as a guide to tire replacement in an emergency, provided the necessary bead breaker is available.

4 Front wheel hub and bearing - removal and installation

Removal

Note: *This procedure applies to either front hub.*

1 Remove the front wheel (see Section 2).

2 Slip the hub plate off the hub **(see illustration)**.

3 Bend back the cotter pin and pull it out of the hub nut **(see illustration)**.

4 Have an assistant apply the front brake while you loosen the hub nut **(see illustration)**. Remove the hub nut and the washer.

5 Remove the front brake caliper (see Section 6).

6 Pull the hub off the spindle. If the hub is

4.6 You may need a slide hammer and adapter to pull the hub off the spindle

5.2 Pull the caliper body in the direction shown to press the piston in and provide removal clearance for the pads

stuck, remove it with a puller **(see illustration)**. Remove the bearing spacer from the outside of the hub and the collar from the inside.

7 If necessary, unbolt the disc shield from the steering knuckle and remove the shield.

Bearing inspection and replacement

8 Wipe off the spindle and hub.

Caution: Do NOT immerse the hub in any kind of cleaning solvent. The sealed hub bearings, which cannot be disassembled and repacked, could be damaged if any solvent enters them.

9 Insert your fingers into each hub bearing and turn the bearing. If the bearing feels rough, loose or noisy, replace it.

10 Pry out the old seals and discard them.

11 To drive each bearing from the hub, lay the hub on a workbench, with the outer side of the hub facing down, then insert a soft metal (brass) drift into the hub from the inner side of the hub, push the floating spacer to the side and tap gently against the inner face of the outer bearing. Then flip over the hub, inner side facing down, insert the drift from the outer side of the hub, and drive out the inner bearing the same way.

12 Pack the new bearings with multipurpose grease.

13 To install the new bearings, place them in the hub with the sealed side facing outward. Drive them into place with an old socket or a bearing driver. The socket must have an outside diameter that's the same, or slightly smaller than, the outer diameter of the bearings.

Caution: Do NOT strike the center race or the ball bearings.

14 Tap new inner and outer seals into place with a block of wood. Do NOT use the old seals.

Installation

15 Installation is the reverse of removal. Lubricate the spindle with multipurpose grease. Tighten the hub nut to the torque listed in this Chapter's Specifications. If necessary, tighten it an additional amount to align the cotter pin slots. Don't loosen the nut to align the slots. Install a new cotter pin and bend it to secure the nut.

5 Front brake pads - replacement

Note: *Always replace both pairs of brake pads at the same time.*

1 Remove the front wheel (see Section 2). Remove the hub plate.

2 Slide the caliper to compress the pistons into the bore, providing removal clearance for the pads **(see illustration)**.

3 Loosen the brake pad retaining bolts **(see illustration)**. The pad retaining bolts are easier to loosen while the caliper is still bolted to the steering knuckle.

4 If you're removing the caliper to overhaul it, remove the brake hose-to-caliper banjo bolt **(see illustration)** and disconnect

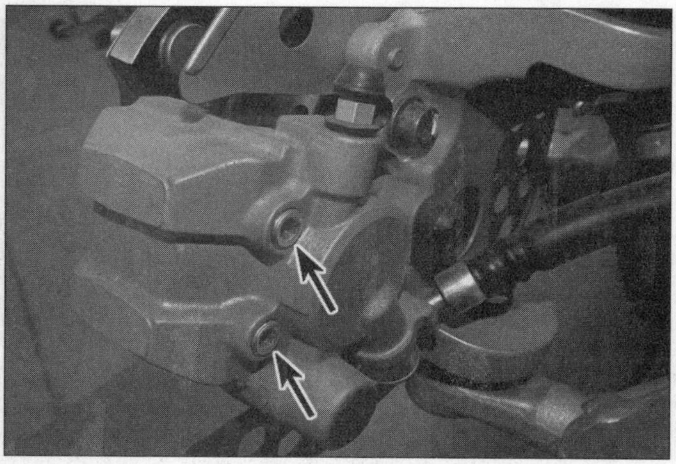

5.3 Loosen - but don't remove - the brake pad retaining bolts while the caliper is still bolted to the steering knuckle

5.4 If you need to disconnect the brake hose, note how its neck fits inside the retainer prong (arrow) and unscrew the banjo bolt

5.5 **Remove the caliper mounting bolts and remove the caliper**

5.7 **Remove the pad retaining bolts**

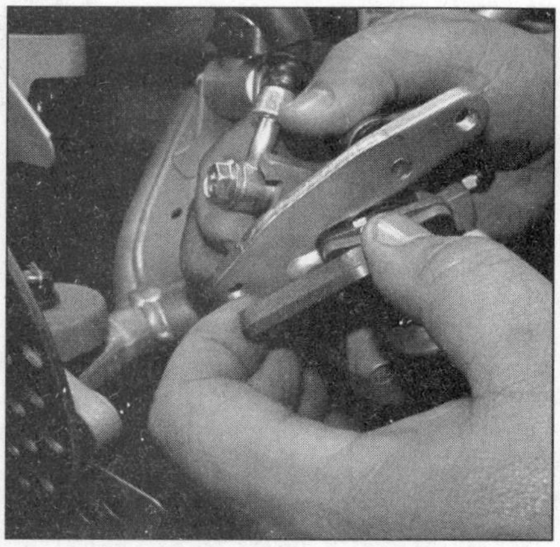

5.8a **Remove the outer brake pad . . .**

5.8b **. . . and the inner pad**

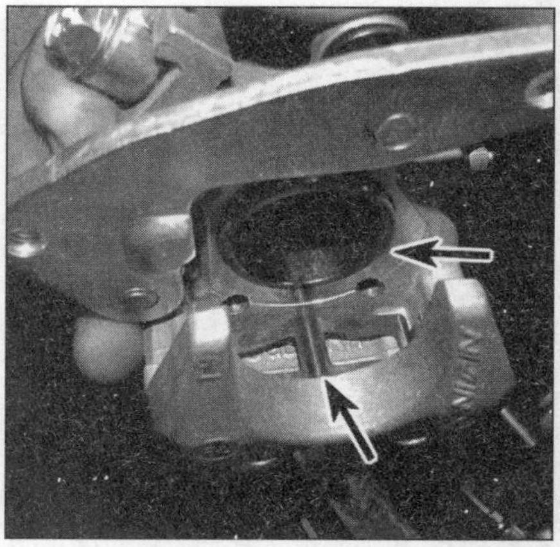

5.9 **Inspect the pad spring (lower arrow) and check for leakage past the piston seal (upper arrow)**

the brake hose from the caliper now. If you're only removing the caliper to replace the brake pads, or to remove the steering knuckle, do NOT disconnect the brake hose from the caliper.

5 Unbolt the caliper from the steering knuckle **(see illustration)**.

6 Remove the caliper. If you're only removing the caliper to replace the brake pads, hang the caliper from the suspension with a coat hanger.

Caution: Do NOT allow the caliper to hang from its brake hose.

7 Remove the brake pad retaining bolts **(see illustration)**.

8 Remove the brake pads **(see illustrations)**.

9 Inspect the pad spring **(see illustration)**. If it's damaged or distorted, replace it.

10 If the inner brake pad has a shim, remove it and install it on the new inner pad.

11 Check the area around the pistons for fluid leakage **(see illustration 5.9)**. If fluid has been leaking past the pistons, overhaul the caliper as described in Section 6.

12 Installation is the reverse of removal. Using a C-clamp, depress the pistons back into the caliper bores to provide enough room for the new pads to clear the disc. Be sure to tighten the caliper bolts to the torque listed in this Chapter's Specifications. Apply non-permanent thread locking agent to the threads of the brake pad bolts and tighten them to the torque listed in this Chapter's Specifications.

13 Replace the brake pads on the other front caliper as described above.

6 Front brake caliper - removal, overhaul and installation

Warning: The dust created by the brake system is harmful to your health. Never blow it out with compressed air and don't inhale any of it. An approved filtering mask should be worn when working on the brakes. Do not, under any circumstances, use petroleum-based solvents to clean brake parts. Use brake cleaner only!

Note: *This procedure applies to both front calipers.*

Removal

1 Disconnect the brake hose from the caliper and remove the caliper from the steering knuckle.

2 Remove the brake pads, shim (if equipped) and pad spring (see Section 5).

Overhaul

3 Clean the exterior of the caliper with denatured alcohol or brake system cleaner.

4 Place a few rags between the piston and the caliper frame to act as a cushion, lay the caliper on the work bench so that the piston is facing down, toward the work bench surface, then use compressed air, directed into the fluid inlet, to remove the piston(s). Use only small quick blasts of air to ease the piston out of the bore. If a piston is blown out with too much force, it might be damaged.

6.7 Use a wood or plastic tool to remove the old piston seal from its groove in the bore (if you use a metal tool, don't scratch the bore)

8.1 Loosen the locknut and back off the parking brake adjusting bolt. Slide the caliper to compress the piston into the bore to provide removal clearance for the pads

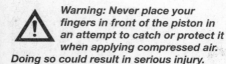

8.2 Before removing the rear caliper, bend back the lockwasher tabs and loosen both of the brake pad retaining bolts

Warning: Never place your fingers in front of the piston in an attempt to catch or protect it when applying compressed air. Doing so could result in serious injury.

5 If compressed air isn't available, reconnect the caliper to the brake hose and pump the brake lever until the piston is free. You'll have to put brake fluid in the master cylinder reservoir and get most of the air out of the hose to use this method.

6 Once the piston is protruding from the caliper, remove it and the old dust seal.

7 Using a wood or plastic tool, remove the piston seal **(see illustration)**.

8 Clean the piston and piston bore with denatured alcohol, fresh brake fluid or brake system cleaner and dry them off with filtered, unlubricated compressed air. Inspect the surfaces of the piston and the piston bores for rust, corrosion, nicks, burrs and loss of plating. If you find defects on the surface of either piston or piston bore, replace the piston and caliper assembly (the piston is matched to the caliper). If the caliper is in bad shape, also inspect the master cylinder.

9 Lubricate the new piston seal with clean brake fluid and install it in its groove in the caliper bore. Make sure it's not twisted and is fully and correctly seated.

10 Lubricate the piston with clean brake fluid and install it into its bore in the caliper. Using your thumbs, push the piston all the way in, making sure it doesn't become cocked in the bore.

11 Install the new dust seal. Make sure that the inner lip of the seal is seated in its groove in the piston and the outer circumference of the seal is seated in its groove in the caliper bore.

Installation

12 Install the caliper and brake pads (see Section 5).

13 Install the brake hose-to-caliper banjo bolt **(see illustration 5.4)**. Be sure to use new sealing washers. Tighten the banjo bolt to the torque listed in this Chapter's Specifications.

14 Remove and overhaul the other front brake caliper.

15 Bleed the front brake system (see Section 15).

7 Front brake disc - inspection, removal and installation

Note: *This procedure applies to both front discs.*

1 Remove the front wheels (see Section 2).

Inspection

2 Visually inspect the surface of the disc for score marks and other damage. Light scratches are normal after use and won't affect brake operation, but deep grooves and heavy score marks will reduce braking efficiency and accelerate pad wear. If the disc is badly grooved, it must be machined or replaced.

3 To check disc runout, mount a dial indicator with the plunger on the indicator touching the surface of the disc about 1/2-inch from the outer edge (if necessary, refer to the dial indicator section in *Tools and Workshop Tips* at the end of this manual). Slowly turn the wheel hub and watch the indicator needle, comparing your reading with the disc runout limit listed in this Chapter's Specifications. If the runout is greater than allowed, replace the disc.

4 The disc must not be machined or allowed to wear to a thickness less than the minimum stamped in the center or on the edge of the disc. The thickness of the disc can be checked with a micrometer. If the thickness of the disc is less than the minimum specified, it must be replaced.

Removal and installation

5 Remove the front wheel hub (see Section 4).

6 To detach the brake disc from the hub, remove the four disc retaining bolts.

7 Installation is the reverse of removal. Tighten the disc retaining bolts to the torque listed in this Chapter's Specifications.

8 Rear brake pads - replacement

Warning: The dust created by the brake system is harmful to your health. Never blow it out with compressed air and don't inhale any of it. An approved filtering mask should be worn when working on the brakes. Do not, under any circumstances, use petroleum-based solvents to clean brake parts. Use brake cleaner only!

1 Loosen the parking brake adjusting locknut and back off the bolt, then pull the caliper body toward the bracket to press the piston in slightly **(see illustration)**. This will free the pads so they will be easier to remove.

2 Bend back the lockwasher tabs and loosen the brake pad retaining bolts **(see illustration)** (they will be easier to loosen while the caliper is still bolted onto the caliper bracket)

3 If you're planning to overhaul the caliper, remove the brake hose-to-caliper banjo bolt. Disconnect the brake hose from the caliper

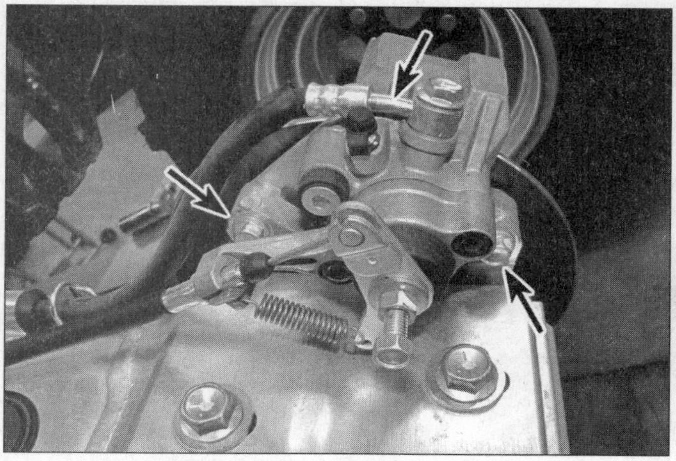

8.4a Remove the caliper mounting bolts (lower arrows); be sure the lower neck of the banjo fitting (upper arrow) is against the stop on the caliper when the hose is installed

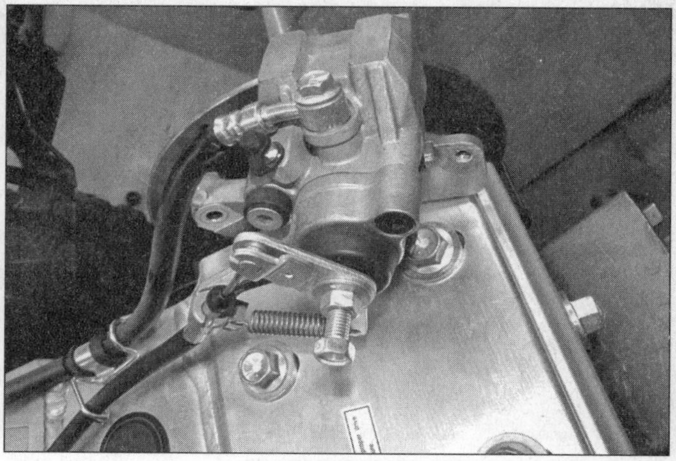

8.4b Lift the caliper off

and discard the old sealing washers. If you're simply replacing the brake pads, or if you're only removing the caliper to remove other components, such as the axle, do NOT disconnect the brake hose.

4 Remove the brake caliper bolts **(see illustration)** and remove the caliper **(see illustration)**. While the caliper is off the disc, tie it up out of the way.

5 Remove the brake pad retaining bolts and lockplate, then remove the brake pads **(see illustration 8.2 and the accompanying illustrations)**.

6 Inspect the pad spring **(see illustration)**. Check the area around the pistons for brake fluid leakage. If fluid has been leaking, overhaul the caliper (see Section 9).

7 Installation is the reverse of removal. If you disconnected the brake fluid hose from the caliper, reinstall it with its neck inside the notch in the caliper body **(see illustration 8.1)**. Use new sealing washers on the banjo fitting and tighten the bolt to the torque listed in this Chapter's Specifications. Be sure to tighten the caliper retaining bolts and the pad retaining bolts to the torque listed in this Chapter's Specifications.

9 Rear brake caliper - removal, overhaul and installation

Warning: The dust created by the brake system is harmful to your health. Never blow it out with compressed air and don't inhale any of it. An approved filtering mask should be worn when working on the brakes. Do not, under any circumstances, use petroleum-based solvents to clean brake parts. Use brake cleaner only!

Removal

1 Disconnect the parking brake cable (see Section 18).

8.5a Remove the pad retaining bolts, then remove the outer brake pad . . .

2 Disconnect the brake hose from the caliper, remove the caliper and remove the brake pads (see Section 8).

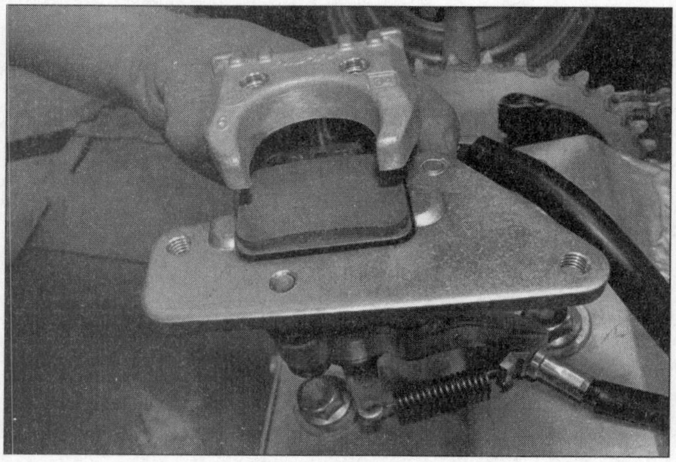

8.5b . . . and the inner pad

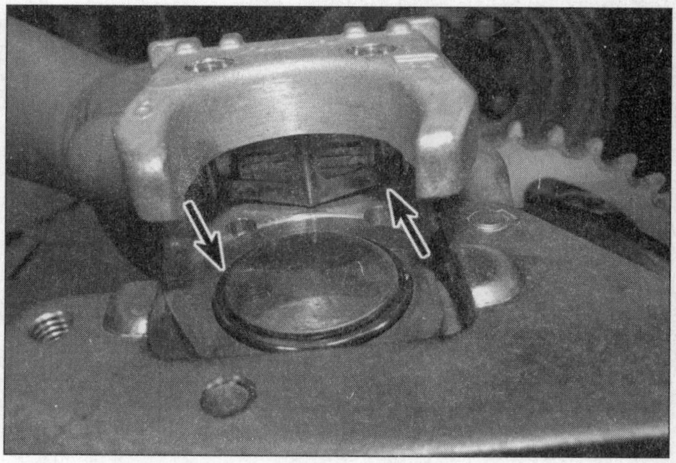

8.6 Inspect the pad spring and check for leakage past the piston seal

9.5 The parking brake case is secured by two Allen bolts

10.2 Remove the cotter pin (arrow) and unscrew the nut

10.4 Remove the washer and hub

Overhaul

3 Clean the exterior of the caliper with denatured alcohol or brake system cleaner.

4 Loosen the parking brake adjuster locknut and unscrew the bolt **(see illustration 8.1)**. Remove the parking brake lever and return spring.

5 Remove the parking brake case Allen bolts, detach the case/bracket assembly from the caliper body and remove the gasket **(see illustration)**. Set the parking brake case aside for now.

6 Separate the caliper bracket from the caliper.

7 Place a few rags between the piston and the caliper frame to act as a cushion and lay the caliper on the work bench so that the piston is facing down (toward the work bench surface). Use compressed air, directed into the fluid inlet, to remove the piston. Use only small quick blasts of air to ease the piston out of the bore. If a piston is blown out with too much force, it might be damaged.

Warning: Never place your fingers in front of the piston in an attempt to catch or protect it when applying compressed air. Doing so could result in serious injury.

8 If compressed air isn't available, reconnect the caliper to the brake hose and pump the brake lever until the piston is free. You'll have to put brake fluid in the master cylinder reservoir and get most of the air out of the hose to use this method.

9 Once the piston is protruding from the caliper, remove it and remove the old dust seal.

10 Using a wood or plastic tool, remove the piston seal.

11 Clean the piston and piston bore with denatured alcohol, fresh brake fluid or brake system cleaner and dry them off with filtered, unlubricated compressed air. Inspect the surfaces of the piston and the piston bores for rust, corrosion, nicks, burrs and loss of plating. If you find defects on the surface of either piston or piston bore, replace the piston and caliper assembly (the piston is matched to the caliper). If the caliper is in bad shape, inspect the master cylinder too. Check the pin boot for damage or deterioration and replace it if problems are found.

12 Lubricate the new piston seal with clean brake fluid and install it in its groove in the caliper bore. Make sure it's not twisted and is fully and correctly seated.

13 Lubricate the piston with clean brake fluid and install it into its bore in the caliper. Using your thumbs, push the piston all the way in, making sure it doesn't become cocked in the bore.

14 Install the new dust seal. Make sure that the inner lip of the seal is seated in its groove in the piston and the outer circumference of the seal is seated in its groove in the caliper bore.

15 Remove the case cover from the case **(see illustration 9.5)**. Unscrew the parking brake shaft from the parking brake case.

16 Lubricate the parking brake shaft with grease and install it in the case. The notch in the hex end of the parking brake shaft is installed between the two notches on the case next to the shaft bore.

17 When installing the parking brake lever, make sure it's positioned as shown in the parking brake adjustment procedure in Chapter 1.

Installation

18 Install the caliper and brake pads (see Sections 8 and 9).

19 Connect the brake hose-to-caliper banjo bolt, making sure its stop is against the boss on the caliper. Be sure to use new sealing washers. Tighten the banjo bolt to the torque listed in this Chapter's Specifications.

20 Bleed the front brake system (see Section 15).

21 Adjust the parking brake (see Chapter 1).

10 Rear wheel hubs - removal and installation

1 Remove the rear wheels (see Section 2).

2 Bend back the cotter pin and pull it out of the hub nut **(see illustration)**.

3 Apply the parking brake to lock the rear axle. Unscrew the hub nut and remove the washer.

4 Pull the hub off the axle shaft **(see illustration)**. Clean the hub and the axle splines.

5 Installation is the reverse of removal.

11 Rear brake disc - inspection, removal and installation

Inspection

1 Visually inspect the surface of the disc for score marks and other damage. Light scratches are normal after use and won't affect brake operation, but deep grooves and heavy score marks will reduce braking efficiency and accelerate pad wear. If the disc is badly grooved it must be machined or replaced.

2 To check disc runout, mount a dial indicator with the plunger on the indicator touching the surface of the disc about 1/2-inch from the outer edge (if necessary, refer to the dial indicator section in *Tools and Workshop Tips* at the end of this manual). Slowly turn the wheel hub and watch the indicator needle, comparing your reading with the disc runout limit listed in this Chapter's Specifications. If the runout is greater than allowed, replace the disc.

3 The disc must not be machined or allowed to wear to a thickness less than the minimum stamped in the center or on the edge of the disc. The thickness of the disc can be checked with a micrometer. If the thickness of the disc is less than the minimum, it must be replaced.

11.6 The brake disc bolts are accessible after the axle is removed

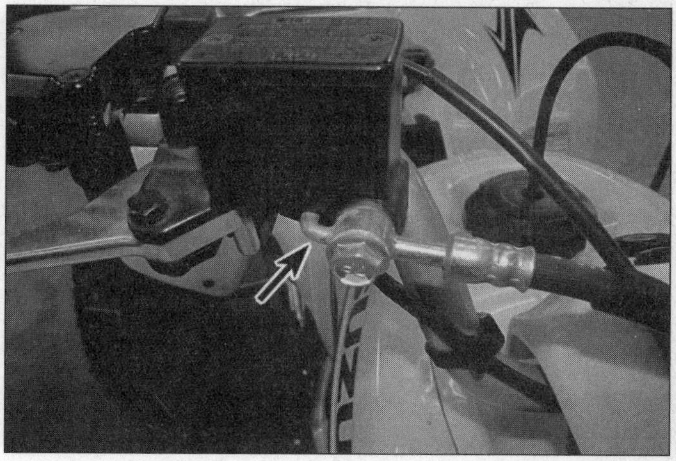

12.4 The front master cylinder hose has a stop that goes under the master cylinder body (arrow)

Removal and installation

4 Remove the rear brake caliper (see Section 9).

5 Remove the driven sprocket and rear axle shaft (see Chapter 6).

6 Remove the disc retaining bolts **(see illustration)** and remove the disc.

7 Installation is the reverse of removal. Be sure to tighten the disc retaining bolts to the torque listed in this Chapter's Specifications.

12 Front brake master cylinder - removal, overhaul and installation

1 If the front brake master cylinder is leaking fluid, or if the lever does not produce a firm feel when the brake lever is applied, and bleeding the brakes does not help, master cylinder overhaul is recommended.

2 Before disassembling the master cylinder, read through the entire procedure and make sure that you have the correct rebuild kit. Also, you will need some new, clean brake fluid of the recommended type, some clean rags and internal snap-ring pliers. **Note:** *To prevent damage to the paint from spilled brake fluid, always cover the top cover or upper fuel tank when working on the master cylinder.*

Caution: Disassembly, overhaul and reassembly of the brake master cylinder must be done in a spotlessly clean work area to avoid contamination and possible failure of the brake hydraulic system components.

Removal

3 Remove the reservoir cover retaining screw. Remove the reservoir and the rubber diaphragm. Siphon as much brake fluid from the reservoir as you can to avoid spilling it.

4 Pull back the rubber dust boot (if equipped), loosen the brake hose banjo bolt **(see illustration)** and separate the brake hose from the master cylinder. Wrap the end of the hose in a clean rag and suspend the hose in an upright position or bend it down carefully and place the open end in a clean container. The objective is to prevent excessive loss of brake fluid, fluid spills and system contamination.

5 Remove the master cylinder mounting bolts **(see illustration)** and separate the master cylinder from the handlebar.

Caution: Do not tip the master cylinder upside down or any brake fluid still in the reservoir will run out.

12.5 Remove the master cylinder mounting bolts

Overhaul

6 Remove the brake lever pivot bolt nut, remove the pivot bolt and remove the lever.

7 Carefully remove the rubber dust boot from the end of the piston **(see illustration)**. Using snap-ring pliers, remove the snap-ring and slide out the piston assembly and the spring **(see illustration)**.

8 Lay the parts out in the order in which they're removed to prevent confusion during reassembly.

12.7a Remove the snap-ring . . .

12.7b . . . and take the piston and spring out of the master cylinder

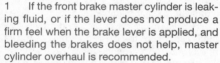

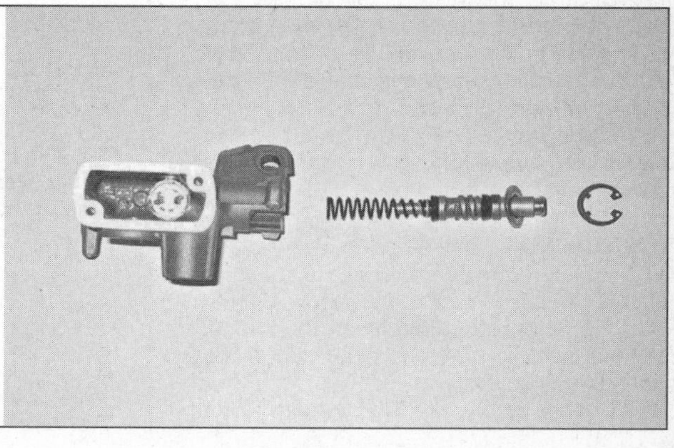

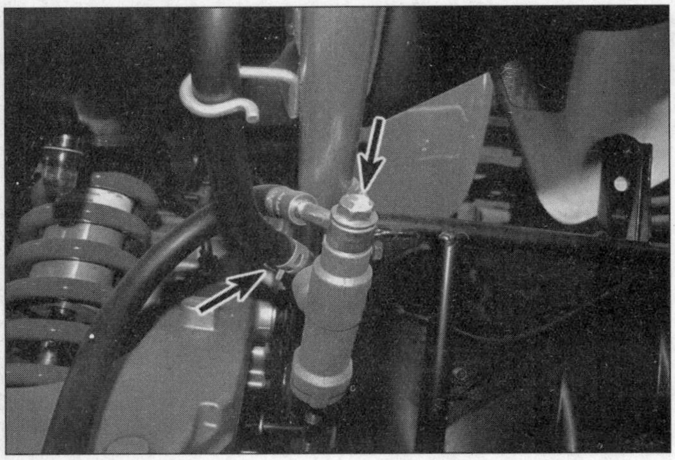

13.4 Rear master cylinder banjo bolt (right) and reservoir hose clamp (left)

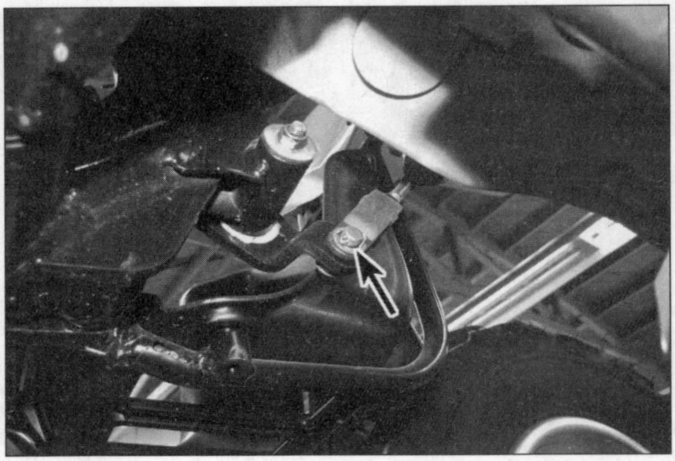

13.5 Remove the cotter pin (arrow), washer and clevis pin to detach the master cylinder from the brake pedal

9 Clean all of the parts with brake system cleaner (available at motorcycle dealerships and auto parts stores), isopropyl alcohol or clean brake fluid. Make sure the delivery port at the bottom of the master cylinder reservoir is clear.

Caution: Do not, under any circumstances, use a petroleum-based solvent to clean brake parts. If compressed air is available, use it to dry the parts thoroughly (make sure it's filtered and unlubricated). Check the master cylinder bore for corrosion, scratches, nicks and score marks. If damage is evident, the master cylinder must be replaced with a new one. If the master cylinder is in poor condition, then the calipers should be checked as well.

10 The dust seal, piston assembly and spring are included in the rebuild kit. Use all of the new parts, regardless of the apparent condition of the old ones.

11 Before reassembling the master cylinder, soak the piston and the rubber cup seals in clean brake fluid for ten or fifteen minutes. Lubricate the master cylinder bore with clean brake fluid, then carefully insert the piston and related parts in the reverse order of disassembly. Make sure the lips on the cup seals do not turn inside out when they are slipped into the bore.

12 Depress the piston, then install the snap-ring (make sure the snap-ring is properly seated in the groove). Install the rubber dust boot (make sure the lip is seated properly in the piston groove).

13 Lubricate the brake lever pivot bolt and the friction surface on the lever that pushes against the piston assembly.

Installation

14 Attach the master cylinder to the handlebar. Make sure that the arrow on the clamp is pointing up **(see illustration 12.5)**. Tighten the bolts to the torque listed in this Chapter's Specifications.

15 Connect the brake hose to the master cylinder, using new sealing washers. Tighten the banjo bolt to the torque listed in this Chapter's Specifications.

16 Fill the master cylinder with the recommended brake fluid (see Chapter 1), then bleed the front brake system (see Section 15).

13 Rear brake master cylinder - removal, overhaul and installation

1 If the rear brake master cylinder is leaking fluid, or if the lever does not produce a firm feel when the brake pedal is applied, and bleeding the brakes does not help, master cylinder overhaul is recommended.

2 Before disassembling the master cylinder, read through the entire procedure and make sure that you have the correct rebuild kit. Also, you will need some new, clean brake fluid of the recommended type, some clean rags and internal snap-ring pliers. **Note:** *To prevent damage to the paint from spilled brake fluid, always cover the top cover or upper fuel tank when working on the master cylinder.*

Caution: Disassembly, overhaul and reassembly of the brake master cylinder must be done in a spotlessly clean work area to avoid contamination and possible failure of the brake hydraulic system components.

Removal

3 Unscrew the reservoir cover and siphon as much brake fluid from the reservoir as you can to avoid spilling it. Refer to *Daily (pre-ride) Checks* at the front of this manual if necessary.

4 Squeeze the reservoir hose clamp **(see illustration)** and slide it down the hose. Detach the reservoir hose from the master cylinder reservoir. Plug or pinch off the end of the hose and suspend the hose in an upright position or bend it down carefully and place the open end in a clean container. Try to prevent excessive loss of brake fluid, fluid spills and system contamination.

5 Remove the cotter pin and clevis pin, then disconnect the pushrod clevis from the rear brake pedal **(see illustration)**.

6 Remove the banjo bolt to disconnect the brake hose (to the rear caliper) from the master. Discard the old sealing washers.

7 Remove the master cylinder mounting bolts and detach the master cylinder from the frame. If necessary, unbolt the brake fluid reservoir from the frame and lift it out **(see illustration)**.

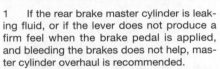

13.7 The reservoir is secured by a mounting bolt

14.2a The front brake line is bolted to the frame where it branches off to the wheels

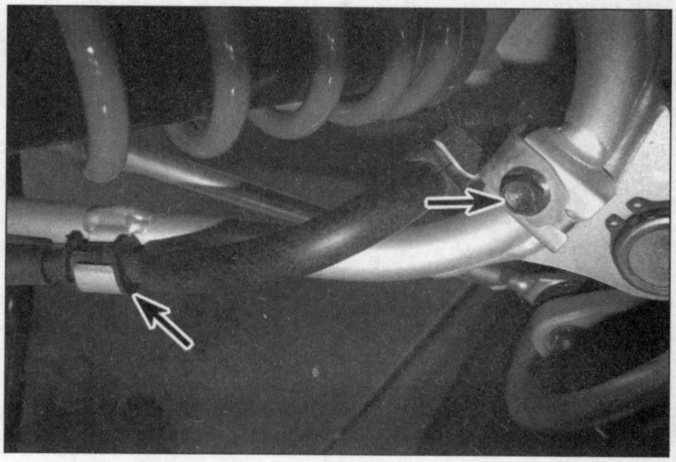

14.2b Each front brake hose is secured to its suspension arm by a clip and a bolted retainer

Overhaul

8 Back off the pushrod clevis locknut, mark the position of the clevis by marking the threads with a large felt pen or some other suitable marking agent, then unscrew the clevis from the pushrod. Unscrew and remove the locknut from the pushrod. Carefully remove the rubber dust boot from the pushrod. Using snap-ring pliers, remove the snap-ring and slide out the piston assembly and the spring.

9 Lay the parts out in the order they were removed to prevent confusion during reassembly.

10 Clean all of the parts with brake system cleaner (available at motorcycle dealerships and auto parts stores), isopropyl alcohol or clean brake fluid.

Caution: Do not, under any circumstances, use a petroleum-based solvent to clean brake parts. If compressed air is available, use it to dry the parts thoroughly (make sure it's filtered and unlubricated). Check the master cylinder bore for corrosion, scratches, nicks and score marks. If damage is evident, the master cylinder must be replaced with a new one. If the master cylinder is in poor condition, then the calipers should be checked as well.

11 The dust seal, piston assembly and spring are included in the rebuild kit. Use all of the new parts, regardless of the apparent condition of the old ones.

12 Before reassembling the master cylinder, soak the piston and the rubber cup seals in clean brake fluid for ten or fifteen minutes. Lubricate the master cylinder bore with clean brake fluid, then carefully insert the piston and related parts in the reverse order of disassembly. Make sure the lips on the cup seals do not turn inside out when they are slipped into the bore.

13 Depress the piston, then install the snap-ring (make sure the snap-ring is properly seated in the groove).

14.2c The rear brake hose (lower arrow) and parking brake cable (upper arrow) are attached to the top of the swingarm

14 Install the rubber dust boot onto the pushrod, push it all the way on and make sure the lip is seated correctly over the ridge on the end of the master cylinder. Install the locknut on the pushrod. Screw it on beyond the mark you made for the clevis prior to disassembly. Screw the clevis onto the pushrod. Make sure that it's aligned with the mark you made before disassembly. Tighten the locknut securely.

Installation

15 Connect the rear caliper brake hose to the master cylinder, using new sealing washers. Tighten the banjo bolt to the torque listed in this Chapter's Specifications.

16 Install the master cylinder on the frame and install - but don't tighten - the master cylinder retaining bolts.

17 Reattach the pushrod clevis to the rear brake pedal.

18 Tighten the rear brake master cylinder retaining bolts to the torque listed in this Chapter's Specifications.

19 Reattach the reservoir hose to the master cylinder. Use a new hose clamp.

20 Fill the master cylinder with the recommended brake fluid (see Chapter 1), then bleed the front brake system (see Section 15).

14 Brake hoses and lines - inspection and replacement

Inspection

1 Once a week (or, if the vehicle is used less frequently, before every ride), check the condition of the brake hoses.

2 Twist and flex the rubber hoses while looking for cracks, bulges and seeping fluid **(see illustrations)**. Check extra carefully around the areas where the hoses connect with the metal fittings, as these are common areas for hose failure.

3 Inspect the metal banjo fittings connected to the brake hoses. If the fittings are rusted, scratched or cracked, replace them.

Replacement

4 Cover the surrounding area with plenty of rags, then disconnect the ends of the hose. If you're replacing a brake hose, remove the banjo bolt from the caliper and disconnect

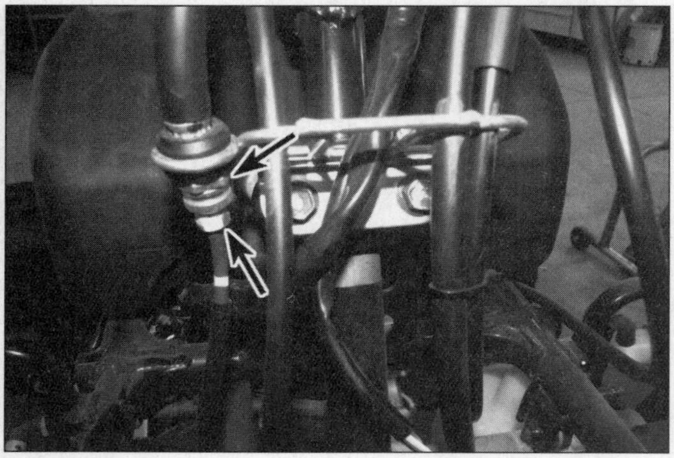

14.5 To disconnect a metal line from a hose, hold the hose fitting (upper arrow) and unscrew the nut (lower arrow) with a flare nut wrench

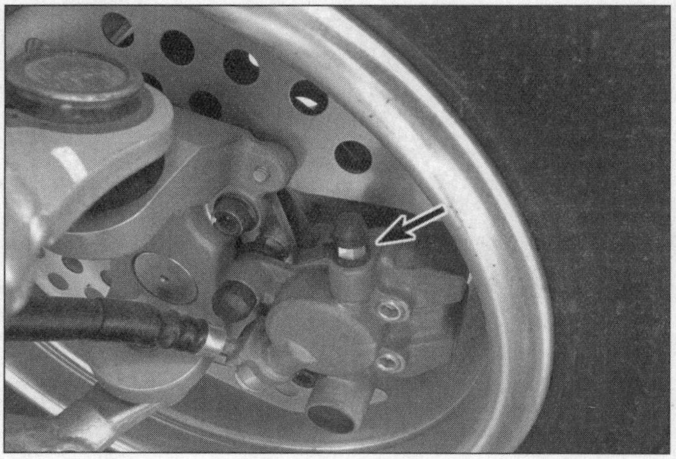

15.5a Front caliper bleed valve (left side shown; right side mirror image)

the hose. Discard the old sealing washers.

5 To disconnect a front brake hose from a metal line, hold the hex on the end of the rubber hose with a wrench and unscrew the metal line fitting with a flare nut wrench **(see illustration)**.

6 All rear brake hoses are attached to the rear master cylinder and to the rear caliper by banjo bolts.

7 Position the new hose, making sure it isn't twisted or otherwise strained, between the two components. Where a hose is attached by a banjo bolt, use new sealing washers on both sides of the fitting, and tighten banjo bolts to the torque listed in this Chapter's Specifications. On non-banjo fittings, tighten the fitting securely.

8 Flush the old brake fluid from the system, refill the system with the recommended fluid (see Chapter 1) and bleed the air from the system (see Section 15). Check the operation of the brakes carefully before riding the motorcycle.

15 Brake system - bleeding

1 Bleeding the brake system removes all the air bubbles from the brake fluid reservoirs, the lines and the brake calipers. Bleeding is necessary whenever a brake system hydraulic connection is loosened, when a component or hose is replaced, or when the master cylinder or caliper is overhauled. Leaks in the system may also allow air to enter, but leaking brake fluid will reveal their presence and warn you of the need for repair.

2 To bleed the brakes, you will need some new, clean brake fluid of the recommended type (see Chapter 1), a length of clear vinyl or plastic tubing, a small container partially filled with clean brake fluid, some rags and a wrench to fit the brake caliper bleeder valves.

3 Cover the fuel tank and any other painted surfaces near the reservoir to prevent damage in the event that brake fluid is spilled.

4 Remove the front reservoir cover screws and remove the cover and diaphragm (or, on rear brakes, simply unscrew the reservoir cover). Slowly pump the brake lever (or brake pedal) a few times, until no air bubbles can be seen floating up from the holes at the bottom of the reservoir. Doing this bleeds the air from the master cylinder end of the line. Top up the reservoir with new fluid, then install the reservoir diaphragm and cover, but don't tighten the screws (or cover); you may have to remove the cover and diaphragm several times during the procedure.

5 Remove the rubber dust cover from the bleeder valve on the caliper **(see illustrations)** and slip a box wrench over the bleeder. Attach one end of the clear vinyl or plastic tubing to the bleed valve and submerge the other end in the brake fluid in the container.

6 Carefully pump the brake lever or brake pedal three or four times and hold it while opening the caliper bleeder valve. When the valve is opened, brake fluid will flow out of the caliper into the clear tubing and the lever will move toward the handlebar (or the pedal will move down). Retighten the bleeder valve, then release the brake lever or pedal.

7 Repeat this procedure until no air bubbles are visible in the brake fluid leaving the caliper, and the lever or pedal is firm when applied. **Note:** *Remember to add fluid to the reservoir as the level drops. Use only new, clean brake fluid of the recommended type. Never re-use the fluid lost during bleeding.*

8 Keep an eye on the fluid level in the reservoir, especially if there's a lot of air in the system. Every time you crack open the bleeder valve, the fluid level in the reservoir drops a little. Do not allow the fluid level to drop below the lower mark during the bleeding process. If the level looks low, remove the reservoir cover and add some fluid.

15.5b Rear caliper bleed valve

9 Inspect the fluid level in the reservoir one more time, adding some fluid if necessary. Install the diaphragm and reservoir cover and tighten the screws securely. Wipe up any spilled brake fluid and check the entire system for leaks. **Note:** *If bleeding is difficult, it may be necessary to let the brake fluid in the system stabilize for a few hours (it may be aerated). Repeat the bleeding procedure when the tiny bubbles in the system have settled out.*

16 Brake pedal - removal and installation

1 Remove the cotter pin and clevis pin to disconnect the master cylinder pushrod from the pedal **(see illustration 13.5)**.

2 Unhook the brake switch spring and pedal return spring from the pedal.

17.3 Tap the spacer downward to expose the edge of the inner bearing race so it can be driven out

3 Unscrew the nut and remove the washer from the pedal pivot shaft. Slide the pivot shaft out of the frame.
4 Installation is the reverse of the removal steps.

17 Rear axle bearings - removal and installation

1 Remove the rear axle shaft (see Chapter 6).
2 Pry the seals out of the axle housing.
3 Use a hammer and punch to push the bearing spacer sideways **(see illustration)**. This will expose the inner edge of the wheel bearing. Insert the punch from the opposite side of the axle housing and drive the bearing out, working around it in a circle.
4 Pull the spacer out of the axle housing.
5 Insert the punch in the axle housing from the side opposite the remaining bearing. Drive the bearing out.
6 Pack the new bearings with multipurpose lithium grease. Drive one bearing into position using a bearing driver or a socket the same diameter as the bearing outer care. The sealed side of the bearing faces outward.
7 Install the spacer, then install the remaining bearing in the other side of the axle housing.
8 Install the seals with their closed sides outward, using the same tools used to install the bearings.

18 Parking brake cable - removal and installation

1 At the left handlebar, loosen the parking brake cable adjuster (see Chapter 1). Rotate the parking brake cable out of the lever slot, then lower its end plug out of the lever.
2 At the rear caliper, loosen the parking brake cable adjuster locknut and back off the bolt **(see illustration 8.1)**. Disconnect the return spring from the lever.
3 Pull the cable housing out of the lever bracket, then slip the cable sideways through the slot in the bracket.
4 Free the cable from its retainers on the swingarm **(see illustration 14.2c)**.
5 Follow the cable from the swingarm up to the lever, freeing it from its remaining retainers. Noting how the cable is routed, remove it from the vehicle.
6 Installation is the reverse of removal.

Notes

Chapter 8
Bodywork and frame

Contents

Degrees of difficulty

Easy, suitable for novice with little experience	**Fairly easy,** suitable for beginner with some experience	**Fairly difficult,** suitable for competent DIY mechanic	**Difficult,** suitable for experienced DIY mechanic	**Very difficult,** suitable for expert DIY or professional

1 General information

This Chapter covers the procedures necessary to remove and install the body panels and other body parts. Since many service and repair operations on these vehicles require removal of the panels and/or other body parts, the procedures are grouped here and referred to from other Chapters.

In the case of damage to the panels or other body parts, it is usually necessary to remove the broken component and replace it with a new (or used) one. The material that the plastic body parts is composed of doesn't lend itself to conventional repair techniques. There are, however, some shops that specialize in plastic welding, so it would be a good idea to check around first before throwing the damaged part away.

Note: *When attempting to remove any body panel, first study the panel closely, noting any fasteners and associated fittings, to be sure of returning everything to its correct place on installation. In some cases, the aid of an assistant will be required when removing panels, to avoid damaging the surface. Once the visible fasteners have been removed, try to lift off the panel as described but DO NOT FORCE the panel - if it will not release, check that all fasteners have been removed and try again. Where a panel engages another by means of tabs and slots, be careful not to break the tabs or to damage the bodywork. Remember that a few moments of patience at this stage will save you a lot of money in replacing broken panels!*

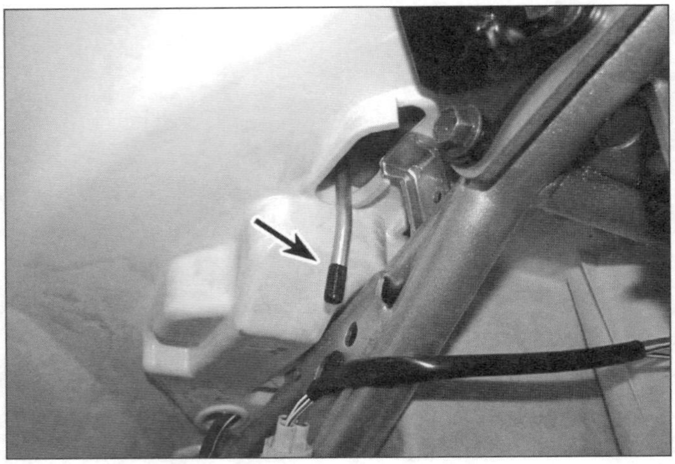

2.1 To release the seat, pull on this latch

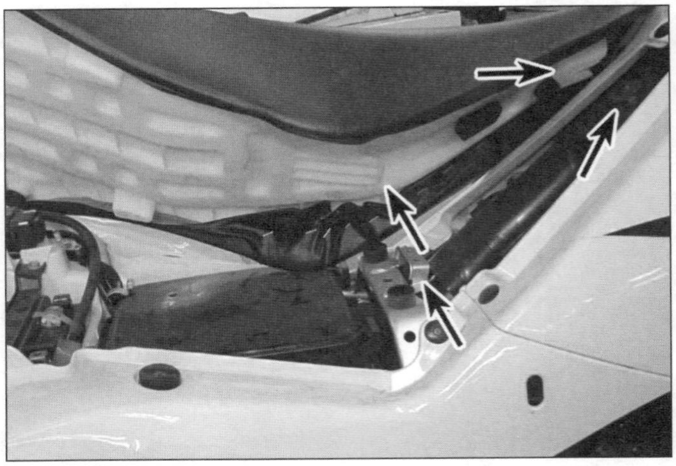

2.3 Make sure the hooks on the seat engage the catches on the frame

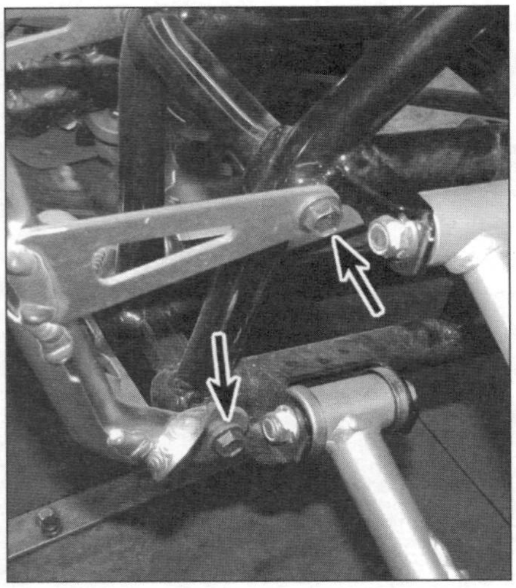

3.1 Left side front bumper mounting bolt locations - right side is a mirror image

2 Seat - removal and installation

1 Lift the latch at the rear of the seat **(see illustration)** and lift the back end of the seat.
2 Pull the seat rearward to disengage the catches at the front and center of the seat from their corresponding fittings in the frame. Lift the seat from the vehicle.
3 Installation is the reverse of removal. Engage the catches at the front and center of the seat with their fittings in the frame **(see illustrations)**.

3 Bumpers - removal and installation

1 Remove the front bumper mounting bolts **(see illustration)** and separate the bumper from the vehicle.
2 Remove the rear bumper mounting bolts **(see illustration)** and separate the bumper from the vehicle.
3 Installation is the reverse of removal. Tighten the bumper bolts securely. Use non-permanent thread locking agent on the bolts that secure the rear bumpers to the fender.

4 Fuel tank cover - removal and installation

1 Pull the fuel tank overflow hose out of the steering shaft and remove the fuel tank filler cap **(see illustration)**.
2 Remove the trim clips at the rear corners of the cover **(see illustration)**. Disengage the tabs along the edges of the cover and lift the cover off the fuel tank.
3 Installation is the reverse of removal.

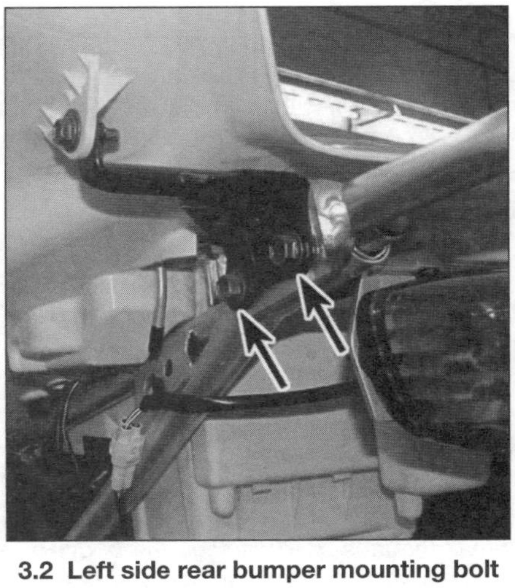

3.2 Left side rear bumper mounting bolt locations - right side is a mirror image

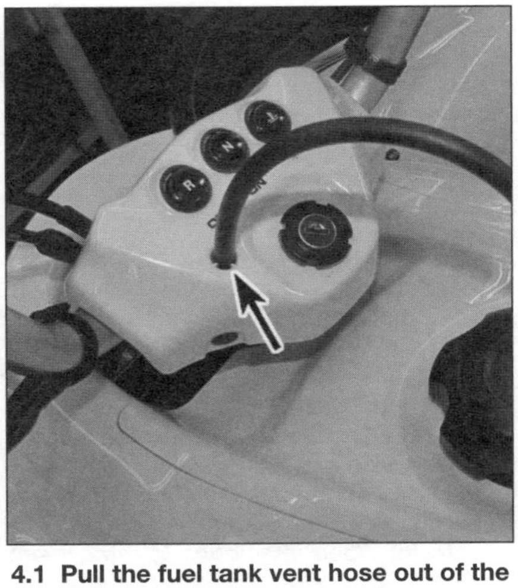

4.1 Pull the fuel tank vent hose out of the handlebar cover (carbureted models) and remove the fuel filler cap (all models)

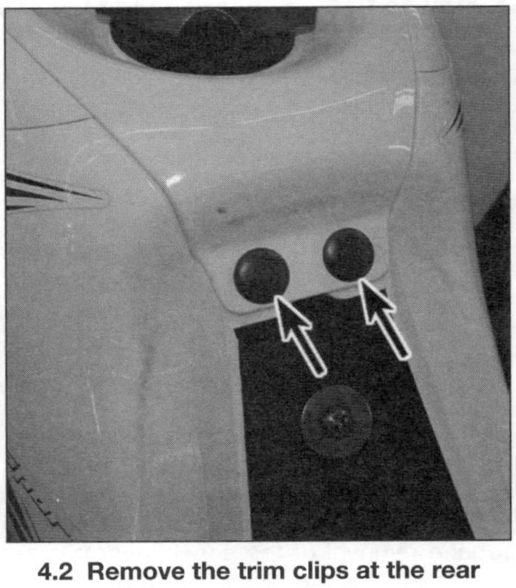

4.2 Remove the trim clips at the rear edge of the cover

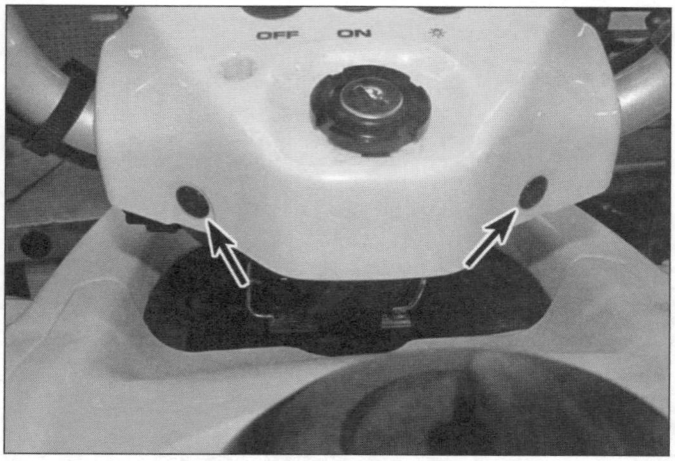

5.1a On carbureted models, remove the trim clips from the handlebar cover

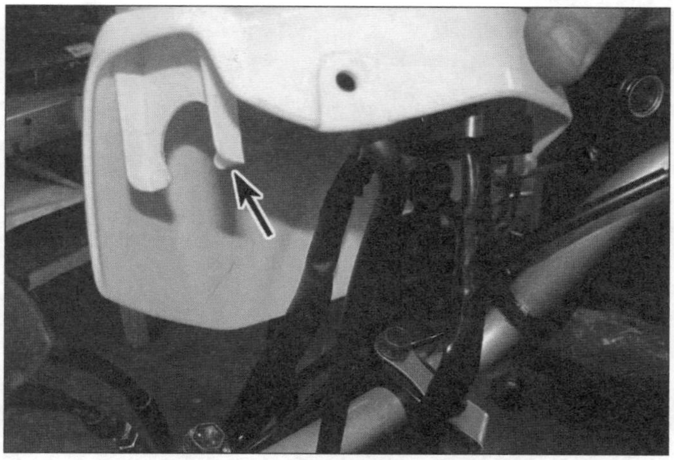

5.1b Pull off the cover, disengaging its molded retainers from the handlebar

5 Handlebar cover - removal and installation

1 On carbureted models, remove the trim clips on the sides of the cover **(see illustration)**. Disengage the cover from the handlebar and lift it off **(see illustration)**.
2 On fuel injected models, free the cover from the handlebar and lift it off.
3 Installation is the reverse of removal.

6 Side covers (Suzuki and Kawasaki) - removal and installation

1 Remove the seat (see Section 2). On fuel injected models, remove the fuel tank cover (see Section 4).
2 On carbureted models, remove the trim clips at the lower rear corner and lower front corner **(see illustrations)**. Remove another trim clip at the upper center, then disengage the tabs and remove the cover **(see illustrations)**.
3 On fuel injected models, remove two screws and one trim clip and remove the cover.
4 Installation is the reverse of removal.

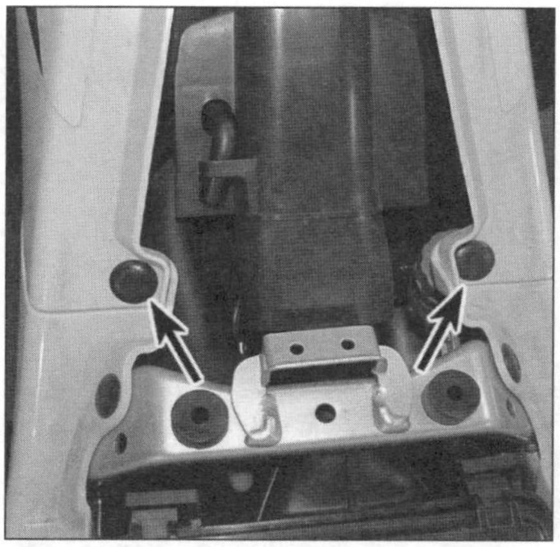

6.2a Remove the trim clip at the rear corner of the side cover . . .

6.2b . . . at the lower front . . .

6.2c . . . and at the upper front (arrow) - disengage the slots at the top from the front fender tabs . . .

6.2d . . . and disengage the tabs at the rear from the rear fender tabs

7.5a Remove the fender mounting bolts at the right front . . .

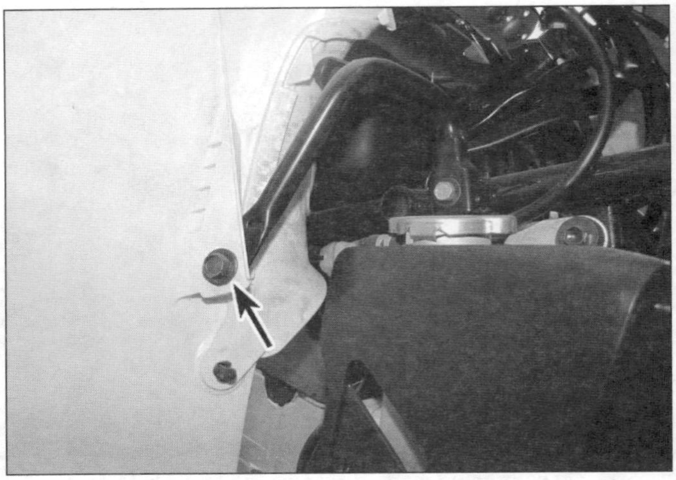
7.5b . . . right rear . . .

7.5c . . . left front . . .

7 Front fender - removal and installation

Suzuki and Kawasaki

1 Remove the seat (see Section 2), side covers (see Section 6) and fuel tank cover (see Section 4).
2 On fuel injected models, locate and disconnect the wiring connector for the ignition switch (it's under the front fender).
3 Remove the screws that secure the reverse selector knob and detach the knob from the fender (see Chapter 6 if necessary).
4 Follow the wiring harness from the headlight housing to the connectors and disconnect them.
5 Remove the mounting bolts from each side of the fender **(see illustrations)**.
6 Lift the fender off, together with the headlight housing **(see illustration)**. If necessary, remove the screws that secure the headlight housing to the fender and remove the housing.
7 Installation is the reverse of removal.

Arctic Cat

8 Arctic Cat models have a small front fender attached to the main body panel on each side of the vehicle. Remove the mounting screws and remove the fender.
9 Installation is the reverse of removal.

8 Rear fender - removal and installation

Suzuki and Kawasaki

1 Remove the seat (see Section 2).
2 Remove the battery, starter relay and fuse box (see Chapter 5).

7.5d . . . and at the left rear

7.6 Remove the fender and headlight housing as an assembly

3 Remove the rear fender trim clips and retaining screws **(see illustrations)** and lift the fender off.

4 Installation is the reverse of removal.

Arctic Cat

5 This procedure is the same as for the front fender (see Section 7).

9 Main body panel (Arctic Cat) - removal and installation

1 These models have a single main body panel that includes the side covers and supports the front and rear fenders.

2 Remove the seat and fuel tank cover (see Sections 2 and 4).

3 Remove the screws or trim clips that support the body panel at the seat bracket **(see illustration 8.3a)**.

4 At the front of the vehicle, remove the screw that attaches the body panel bracket to the frame (one is on the left side, forward of the coolant reserve tank filler cap; the other is opposite on the left side).

5 Below the front tip of the body panel, remove the bolt that secures the panel to the headlight housing.

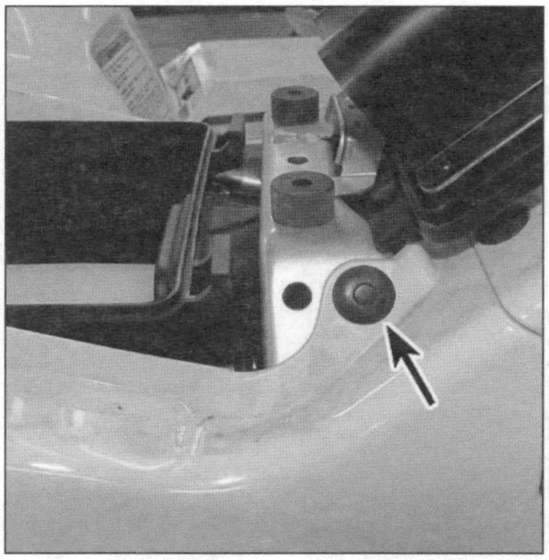

8.3a Remove the trim clip at each front corner of the rear fender (right side shown)

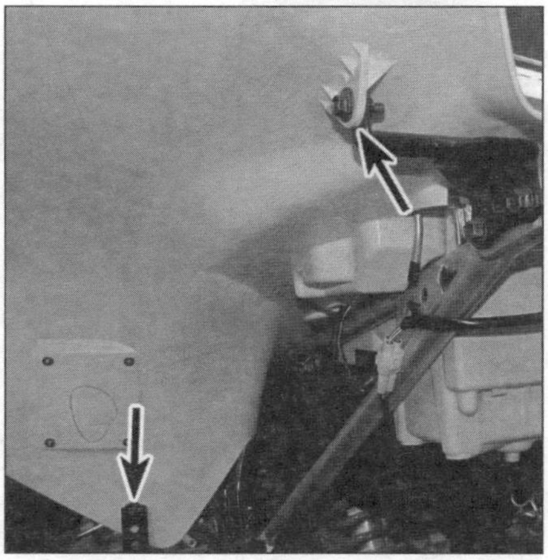

8.3b Detach the fender from the upper and lower brackets (left side shown)

6 At the end of each front support bracket, remove the nut from the plastic stud built into the body panel (there's one on each side of the vehicle).

7 Make sure all fasteners have been removed. Lift the panel, rotate it clockwise (viewed from the top) so its opening aligns with the handlebars, then lift it off.

8 Installation is the reverse of removal.

10.1 Mudguard mounting screw locations

10 Footrests - removal and installation

1 Remove the screws and detach the mudguard from the footrest **(see illustration)**.

2 Unbolt the reinforcing bracket and remove it.

3 Remove the two bolts that attach the footrest to the frame.

4 Installation is the reverse of removal.

11 Skid plates - removal and installation

1 To remove the skid plates from the swingarm and suspension linkage, remove the bolts and remove the skid plate **(see illustrations)**.

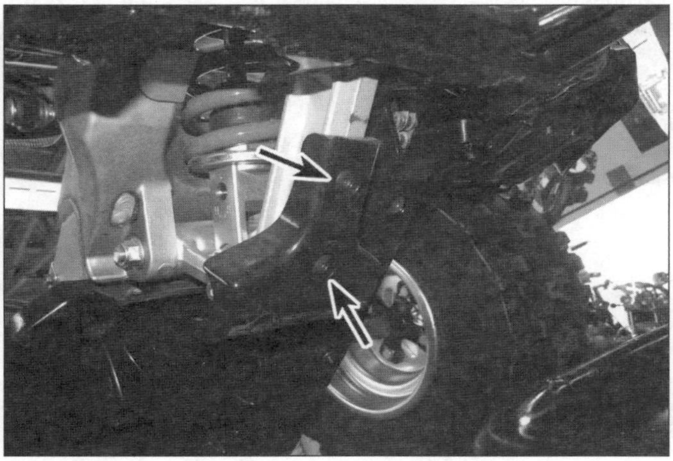

11.1a Suspension linkage skid plate bolt locations

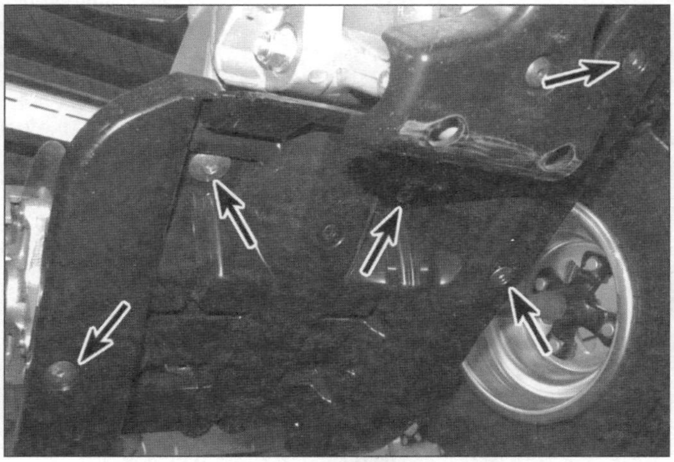

11.1b Swingarm skidplate bolt locations

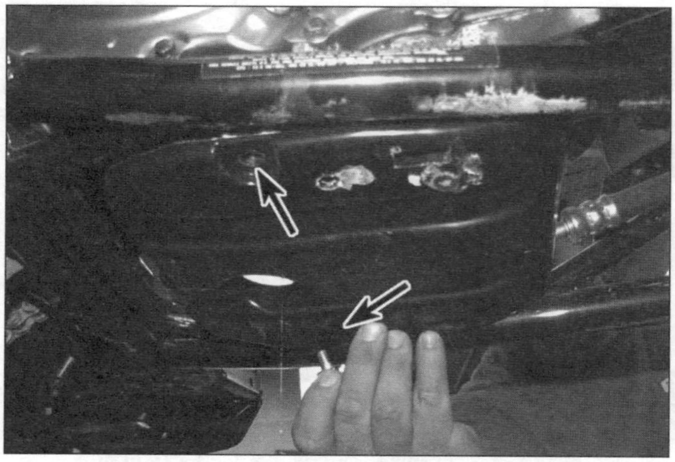

11.2a Oil pan skid plate mounting bolt locations

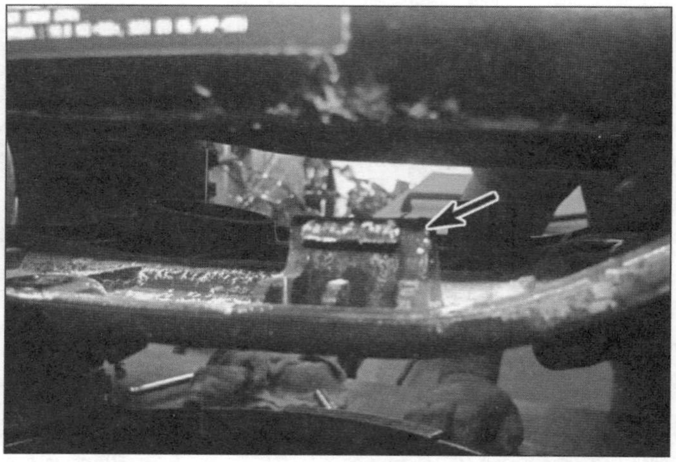

11.2b Disengage the molded skid plate retainers

2 To remove the oil pan skid plate, remove its mounting bolts **(see illustration)**. Disengage the molded retainers from the frame and take the skid plate out **(see illustration)**.

3 Installation is the reverse of removal.

12 Sub-frame - removal and installation

1 Remove the seat (see Section 2) and remove rear fender or main body panel (see Section 8 or 9). Remove the rear bumper (see Section 3).

2 Remove the exhaust system and air cleaner housing (see Chapter 4).

3 Unbolt the footrest from the sub-frame (see Section 10).

4 Free the rear master cylinder reservoir hose from its retainer (see Chapter 7 if necessary).

5 Remove the sub-frame mounting bolts and remove the subframe **(see illustration)**.

6 Installation is the reverse of removal.

12.5 Remove the sub-frame mounting bolts

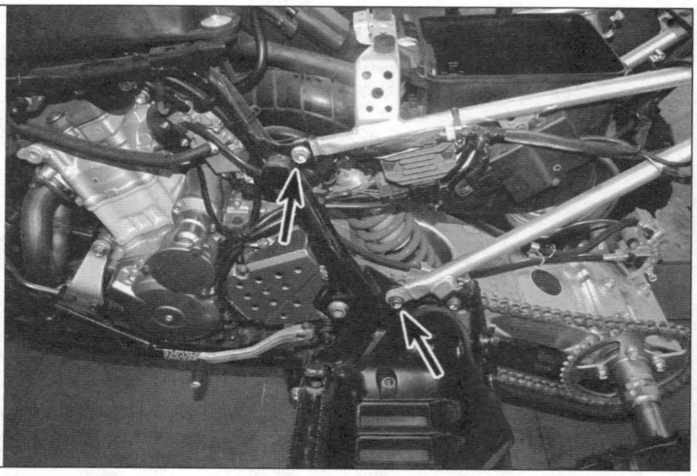

13 Frame - general information, inspection and repair

1 All models use a double-cradle frame, with a detachable rear extension made of aluminum tubing.

2 The frame shouldn't require attention unless accident damage has occurred. In most cases, frame replacement is the only satisfactory remedy for such damage. A few frame specialists have the jigs and other equipment necessary for straightening the frame to the required standard of accuracy, but even then there is no simple way of assessing to what extent the frame may have been over-stressed.

3 After the machine has accumulated a lot of miles, the frame should be examined closely for signs of cracking or splitting at the welded joints. Corrosion can also cause weakness at these joints. Loose engine mount bolts can cause elongation of the bolt holes and can fracture the engine mounting points. Minor damage can often be repaired by welding, depending on the nature and extent of the damage.

4 Remember that a frame that is out of alignment will cause handling problems. If misalignment is suspected as the result of an accident, it will be necessary to strip the machine completely so the frame can be thoroughly checked.

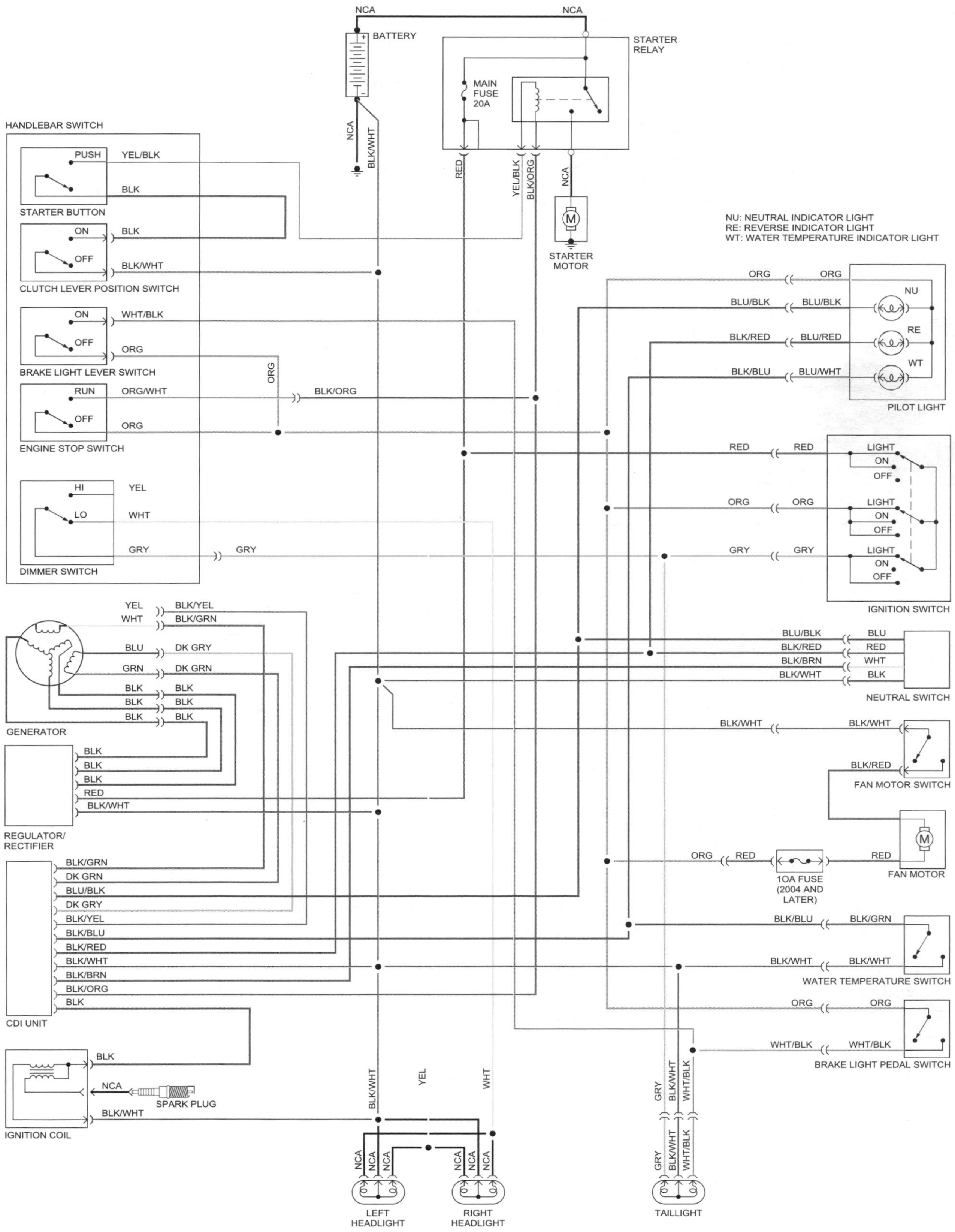

Wiring diagram (2003 through 2008 models)

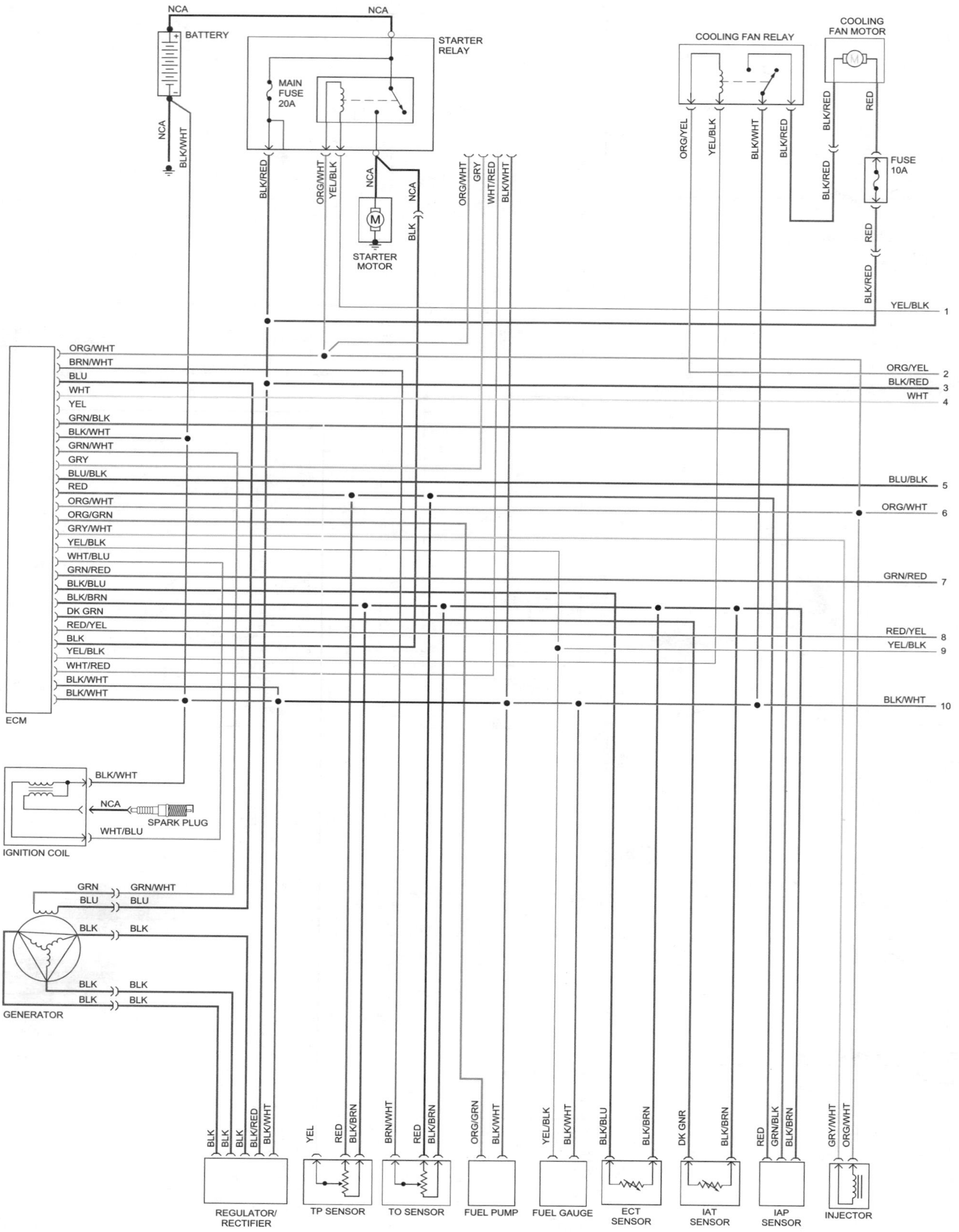

Wiring diagram (2009 and later models) - page 1 of 2

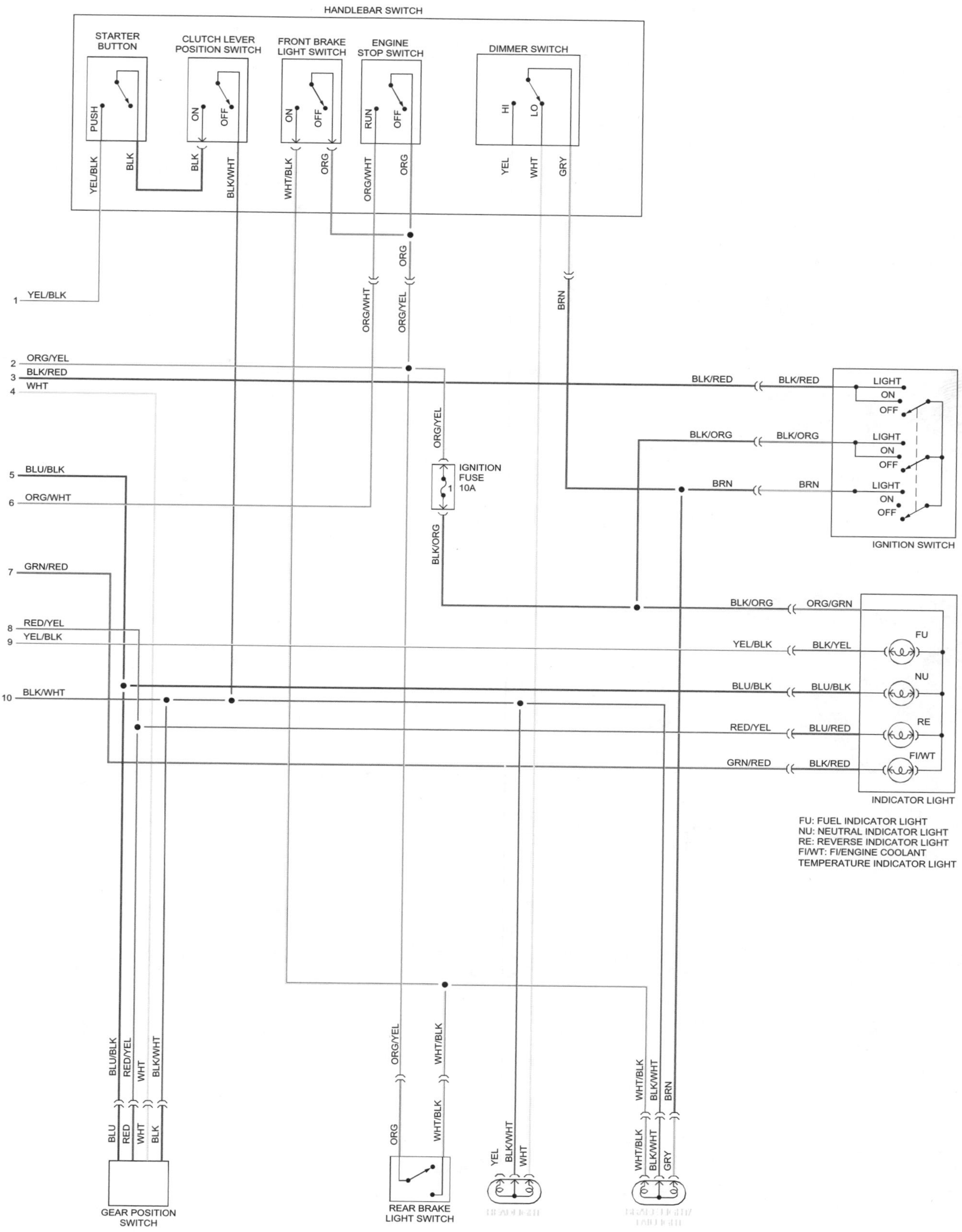

Wiring diagram (2009 and later models) - page 2 of 2

Notes

Dimensions and weights

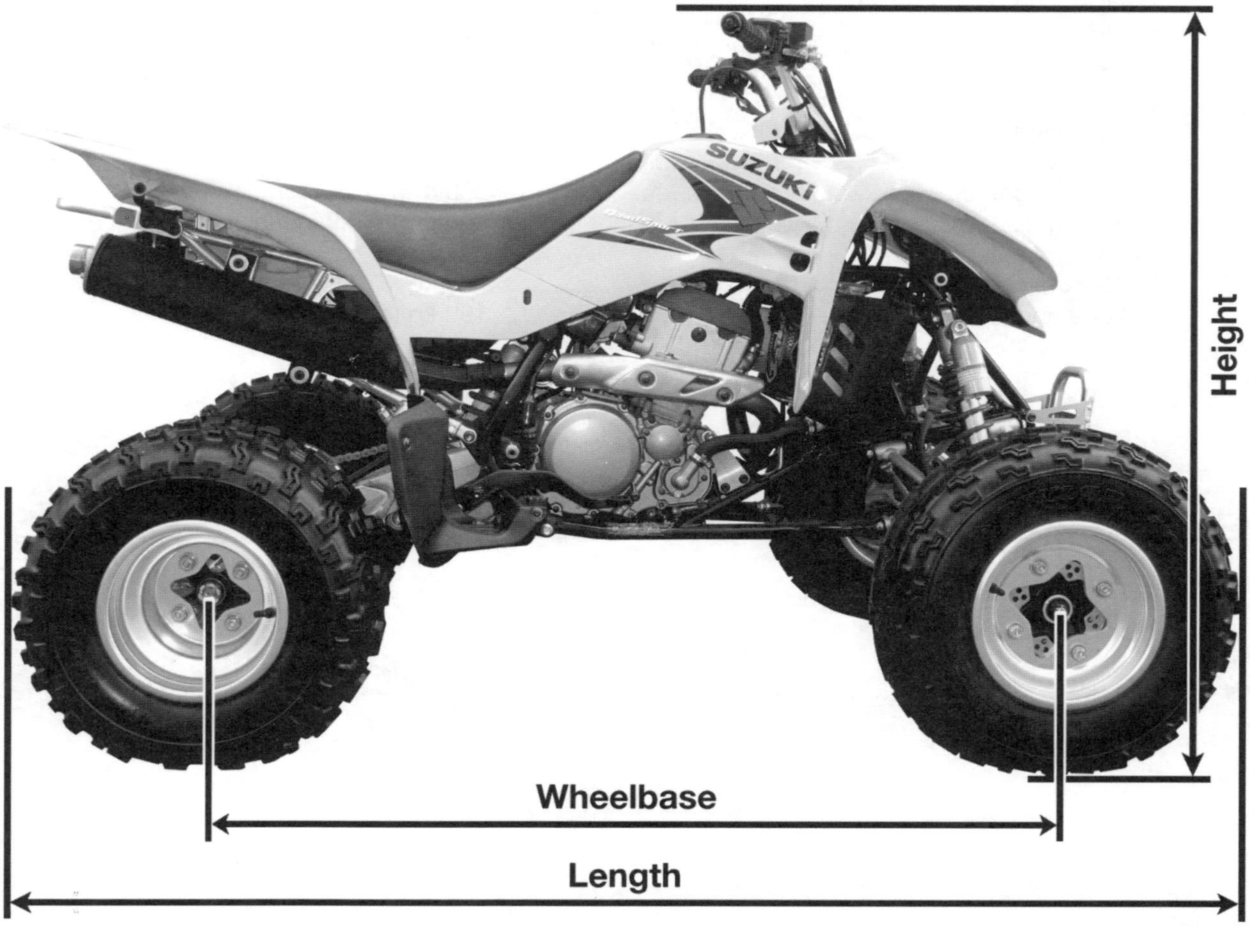

General Specifications

Wheelbase	1245 mm (49.0 inches)
Width	
All except 2009 and later Suzuki	1165 mm (45.9 inches)
2009 and later Suzuki	1190 mm (46.9 inches)
Length	1830 mm (72.0 inches)
Overall height	
All except 2009 and later Suzuki	1160 mm (45.7 inches)
2009 and later Suzuki	1145 mm (45.1 inches)
Ground clearance	265 mm (10.4 inches)
Seat height	810 mm (31.9 inches)
Dry weight	
All except 2009 and later Suzuki	169 kg (373 lbs)
2009 and later Suzuki	193 kg (425 lbs)

Notes

Buying tools

A good set of tools is a fundamental requirement for servicing and repairing a motorcycle. Although there will be an initial expense in building up enough tools for servicing, this will soon be offset by the savings made by doing the job yourself. As experience and confidence grow, additional tools can be added to enable the repair and overhaul of the motorcycle. Many of the special tools are expensive and not often used so it may be preferable to rent them, or for a group of friends or motorcycle club to join in the purchase.

As a rule, it is better to buy more expensive, good quality tools. Cheaper tools are likely to wear out faster and need to be replaced more often, nullifying the original savings.

Warning: To avoid the risk of a poor quality tool breaking in use, causing injury or damage to the component being worked on, always aim to purchase tools which meet the relevant national safety standards.

The following lists of tools do not represent the manufacturer's service tools, but serve as a guide to help the owner decide which tools are needed for this level of work. In addition, items such as an electric drill, hacksaw, files, soldering iron and a workbench equipped with a vise, may be needed. Although not classed as tools, a selection of bolts, screws, nuts, washers and pieces of tubing always come in useful.

For more information about tools, refer to the Haynes *Motorcycle Workshop Practice Techbook* (Bk. No. 3470).

Manufacturer's service tools

Inevitably certain tasks require the use of a service tool. Where possible an alternative tool or method of approach is recommended, but sometimes there is no option if personal injury or damage to the component is to be avoided. Where required, service tools are referred to in the relevant procedure.

Service tools can usually only be purchased from a motorcycle dealer and are identified by a part number. Some of the commonly-used tools, such as rotor pullers, are available in aftermarket form from mail-order motorcycle tool and accessory suppliers.

Maintenance and minor repair tools

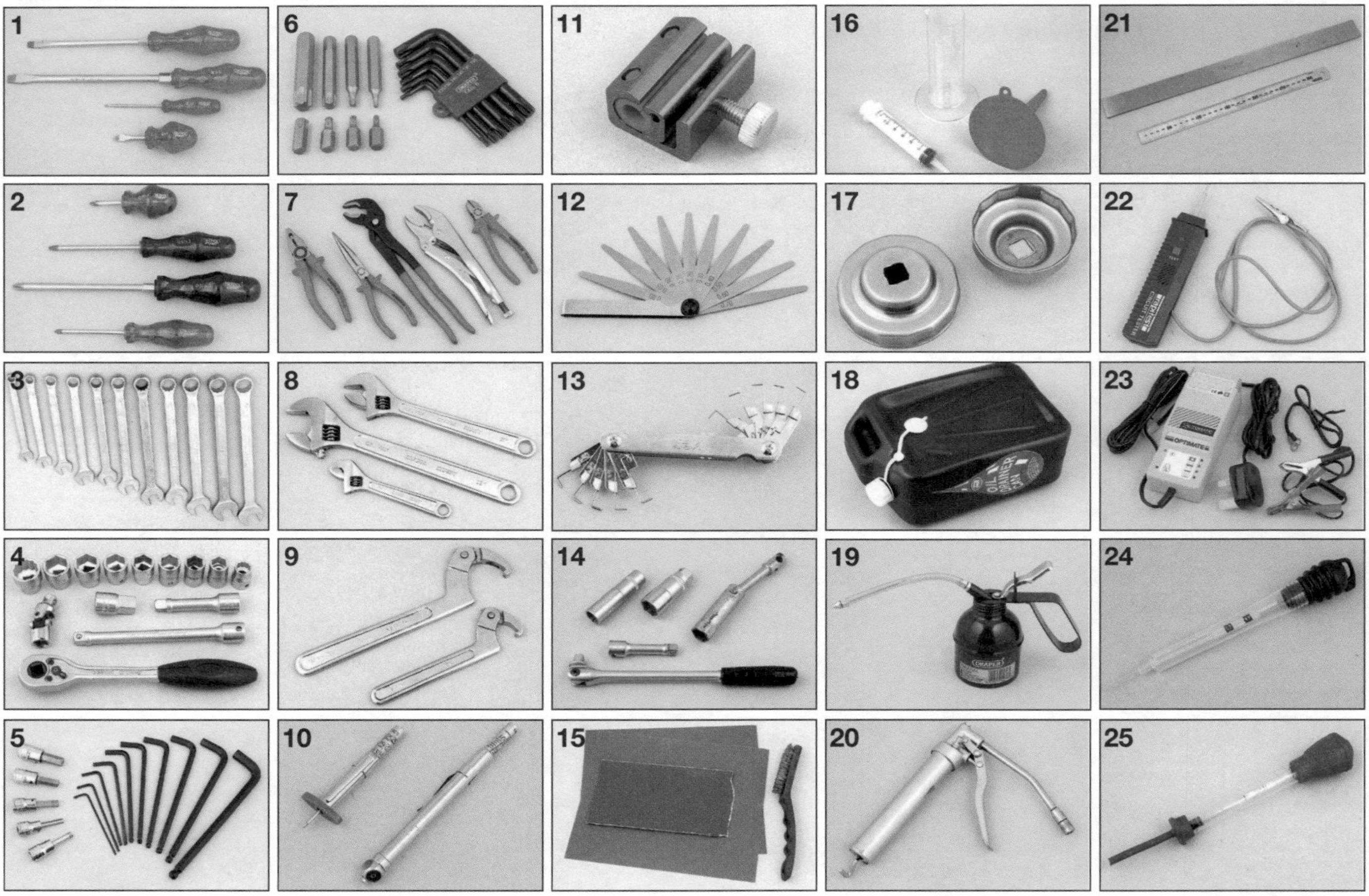

1 *Set of flat-bladed screwdrivers*
2 *Set of Phillips head screwdrivers*
3 *Combination open-end and box wrenches*
4 *Socket set (3/8 inch or 1/2 inch drive)*
5 *Set of Allen keys or bits*
6 *Set of Torx keys or bits*
7 *Pliers, cutters and self-locking grips (vise grips)*
8 *Adjustable wrenches*
9 *C-spanners*
10 *Tread depth gauge and tire pressure gauge*
11 *Cable oiler clamp*
12 *Feeler gauges*
13 *Spark plug gap measuring tool*
14 *Spark plug wrench or deep plug sockets*
15 *Wire brush and emery paper*
16 *Calibrated syringe, measuring cup and funnel*
17 *Oil filter adapters*
18 *Oil drainer can or tray*
19 *Pump type oil can*
20 *Grease gun*
21 *Straight-edge and steel rule*
22 *Continuity tester*
23 *Battery charger*
24 *Hydrometer (for battery specific gravity check)*
25 *Antifreeze tester (for liquid-cooled engines)*

Repair and overhaul tools

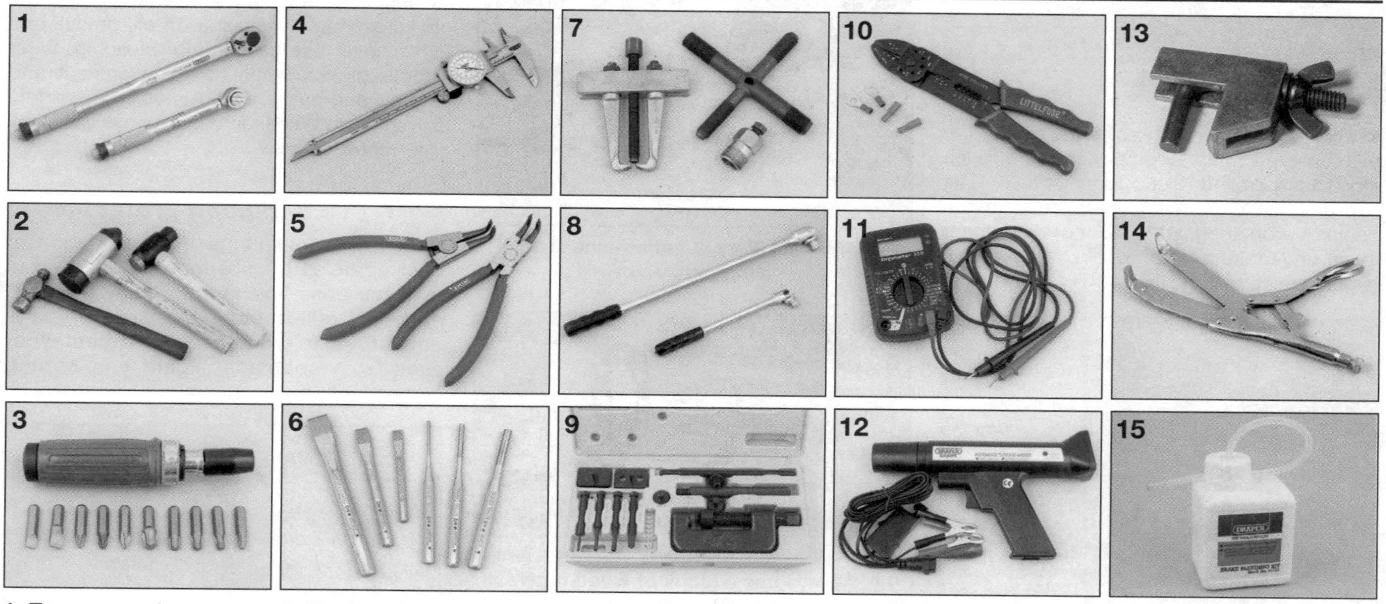

1 Torque wrench (small and mid-ranges)
2 Conventional, plastic or soft-faced hammers
3 Impact driver set
4 Vernier caliper
5 Snap-ring pliers (internal and external, or combination)
6 Set of cold chisels and punches
7 Selection of pullers
8 Breaker bars
9 Chain breaking/ riveting tool set
10 Wire stripper and crimper tool
11 Multimeter (measures amps, volts and ohms)
12 Stroboscope (for dynamic timing checks)
13 Hose clamp (wingnut type shown)
14 Clutch holding tool
15 One-man brake/clutch bleeder kit

Special tools

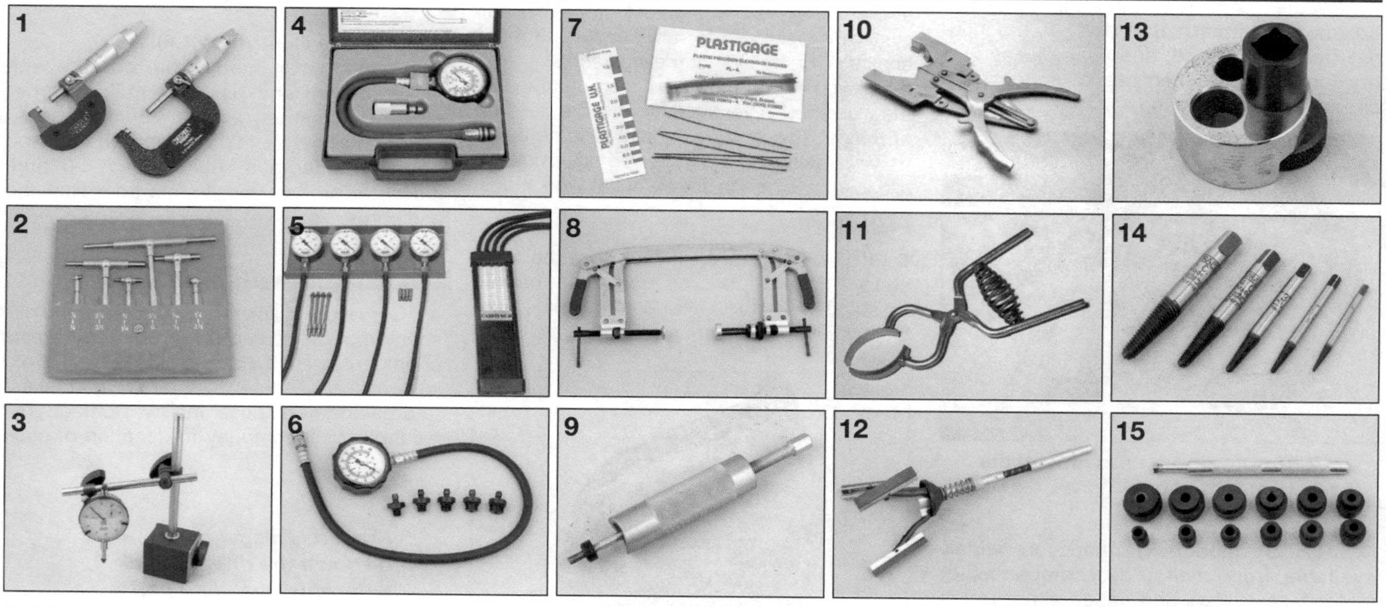

1 Micrometers (external type)
2 Telescoping gauges
3 Dial gauge
4 Cylinder compression gauge
5 Vacuum gauges (left) or manometer (right)
6 Oil pressure gauge
7 Plastigage kit
8 Valve spring compressor (4-stroke engines)
9 Piston pin drawbolt tool
10 Piston ring removal and installation tool
11 Piston ring clamp
12 Cylinder bore hone (stone type shown)
13 Stud extractor
14 Screw extractor set
15 Bearing driver set

1 Workshop equipment and facilities

The workbench

● Work is made much easier by raising the bike up on a ramp - components are much more accessible if raised to waist level. The hydraulic or pneumatic types seen in the dealer's workshop are a sound investment if you undertake a lot of repairs or overhauls **(see illustration 1.1)**.

1.1 Hydraulic motorcycle ramp

● If raised off ground level, the bike must be supported on the ramp to avoid it falling. Most ramps incorporate a front wheel locating clamp which can be adjusted to suit different diameter wheels. When tightening the clamp, take care not to mark the wheel rim or damage the tire - use wood blocks on each side to prevent this.

● Secure the bike to the ramp using tie-downs **(see illustration 1.2)**. If the bike has only a sidestand, and hence leans at a dangerous angle when raised, support the bike on an auxiliary stand.

1.2 Tie-downs are used around the passenger footrests to secure the bike

● Auxiliary (paddock) stands are widely available from mail order companies or motorcycle dealers and attach either to the wheel axle or swingarm pivot **(see illustration 1.3)**. If the motorcycle has a centerstand, you can support it under the crankcase to prevent it toppling while either wheel is removed **(see illustration 1.4)**.

1.3 This auxiliary stand attaches to the swingarm pivot

1.4 Always use a block of wood between the engine and jack head when supporting the engine in this way

Fumes and fire

● Refer to the Safety first! page at the beginning of the manual for full details. Make sure your workshop is equipped with a fire extinguisher suitable for fuel-related fires (Class B fire - flammable liquids) - it is not sufficient to have a water-filled extinguisher.

● Always ensure adequate ventilation is available. Unless an exhaust gas extraction system is available for use, ensure that the engine is run outside of the workshop.

● If working on the fuel system, make sure the workshop is ventilated to avoid a build-up of fumes. This applies equally to fume build-up when charging a battery. Do not smoke or allow anyone else to smoke in the workshop.

Fluids

● If you need to drain fuel from the tank, store it in an approved container marked as suitable for the storage of gasoline **(see illustration 1.5)**. Do not store fuel in glass jars or bottles.

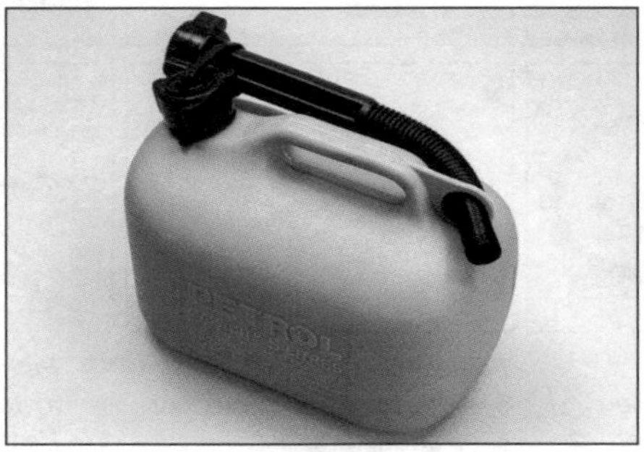

1.5 Use an approved can only for storing gasoline

● Use proprietary engine degreasers or solvents which have a high flash-point, such as kerosene, for cleaning off oil, grease and dirt - never use gasoline for cleaning. Wear rubber gloves when handling solvent and engine degreaser. The fumes from certain solvents can be dangerous - always work in a well-ventilated area.

Dust, eye and hand protection

● Protect your lungs from inhalation of dust particles by wearing a filtering mask over the nose and mouth. Many frictional materials still contain asbestos which is dangerous to your health. Protect your eyes from spouts of liquid and sprung components by wearing a pair of protective goggles **(see illustration 1.6)**.

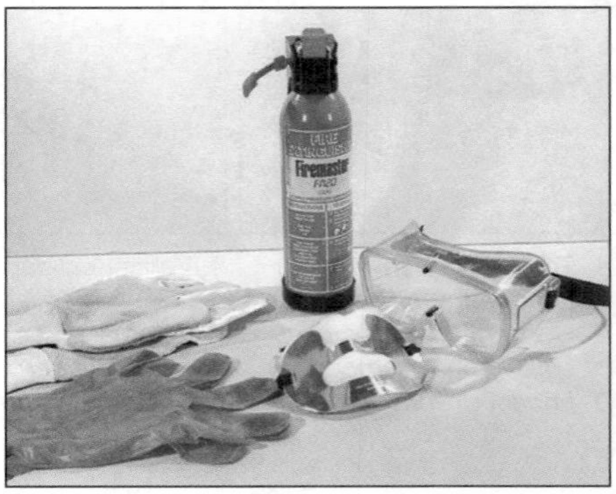

1.6 A fire extinguisher, goggles, mask and protective gloves should be at hand in the workshop

● Protect your hands from contact with solvents, fuel and oils by wearing rubber gloves. Alternatively apply a barrier cream to your hands before starting work. If handling hot components or fluids, wear suitable gloves to protect your hands from scalding and burns.

What to do with old fluids

● Old cleaning solvent, fuel, coolant and oils should not be poured down domestic drains or onto the ground. Package the fluid up in old oil containers, label it accordingly, and take it to a garage or disposal facility. Contact your local disposal company for location of such sites.

Note: It is illegal to dump oil down the drain. Check with your local auto parts store, disposal facility or environmental agency to see if they accept the oil for recycling.

2 Fasteners - screws, bolts and nuts

Fastener types and applications

Bolts and screws

● Fastener head types are either of hexagonal, Torx or splined design, with internal and external versions of each type **(see illustrations 2.1 and 2.2);** splined head fasteners are not in common use on motorcycles. The conventional slotted or Phillips head design is used for certain screws. Bolt or screw length is always measured from the underside of the head to the end of the item **(see illustration 2.11)**.

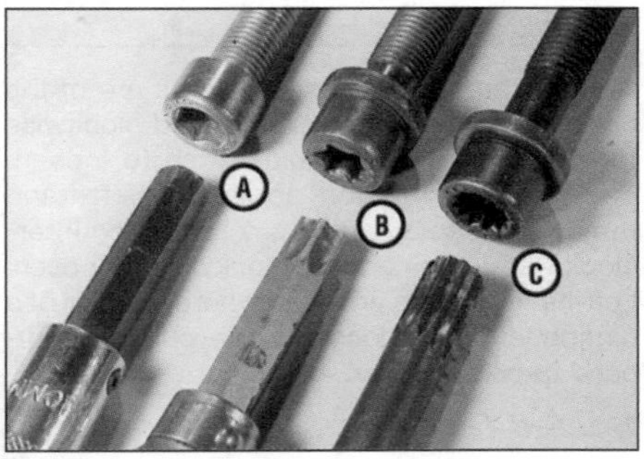

2.1 Internal hexagon/Allen (A), Torx (B) and splined (C) fasteners, with corresponding bits

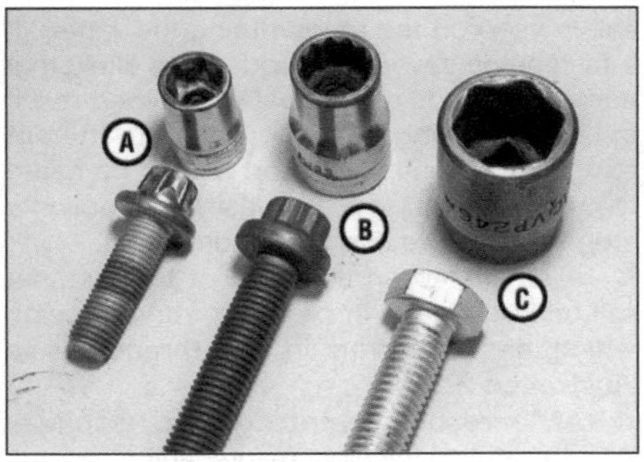

2.2 External Torx (A), splined (B) and hexagon (C) fasteners, with corresponding sockets

● Certain fasteners on the motorcycle have a tensile marking on their heads, the higher the marking the stronger the fastener. High tensile fasteners generally carry a 10 or higher marking. Never replace a high tensile fastener with one of a lower tensile strength.

Washers **(see illustration 2.3)**

● Plain washers are used between a fastener head and a component to prevent damage to the component or to spread the load when torque is applied. Plain washers can also be used as spacers or shims in certain assemblies. Copper or aluminum plain washers are often used as sealing washers on drain plugs.

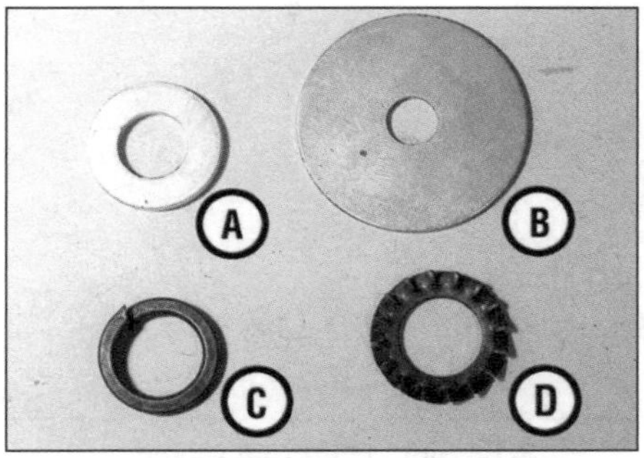

2.3 Plain washer (A), penny washer (B), spring washer (C) and serrated washer (D)

● The split-ring spring washer works by applying axial tension between the fastener head and component. If flattened, it is fatigued and must be replaced. If a plain (flat) washer is used on the fastener, position the spring washer between the fastener and the plain washer.

● Serrated star type washers dig into the fastener and component faces, preventing loosening. They are often used on electrical ground connections to the frame.

● Cone type washers (sometimes called Belleville) are conical and when tightened apply axial tension between the fastener head and component. They must be installed with the dished side against the component and often carry an OUTSIDE marking on their outer face. If flattened, they are fatigued and must be replaced.

● Tab washers are used to lock plain nuts or bolts on a shaft. A portion of the tab washer is bent up hard against one flat of the nut or bolt to prevent it loosening. Due to the tab washer being deformed in use, a new tab washer should be used every time it is removed.

● Wave washers are used to take up endfloat on a shaft. They provide light springing and prevent excessive side-to-side play of a component. Can be found on rocker arm shafts.

Nuts and cotter pins

● Conventional plain nuts are usually six-sided **(see illustration 2.4)**. They are sized by thread diameter and pitch. High tensile nuts carry a number on one end to denote their tensile strength.

2.4 Plain nut (A), shouldered locknut (B), nylon insert nut (C) and castellated nut (D)

● Self-locking nuts either have a nylon insert, or two spring metal tabs, or a shoulder which is staked into a groove in the shaft - their advantage over conventional plain nuts is a resistance to loosening due to vibration. The nylon insert type can be used a number of times, but must be replaced when the friction of the nylon insert is reduced, i.e. when the nut spins freely on the shaft. The spring tab type can be reused unless the tabs are damaged. The shouldered type must be replaced every time it is removed.

● Cotter pins are used to lock a castellated nut to a shaft or to prevent loosening of a plain nut. Common applications are wheel axles and brake torque arms. Because the cotter pin arms are deformed to lock around the nut a new cotter pin must always be used on installation - always use the correct size cotter pin which will fit snugly in the shaft hole. Make sure the cotter pin arms are correctly located around the nut **(see illustrations 2.5 and 2.6)**.

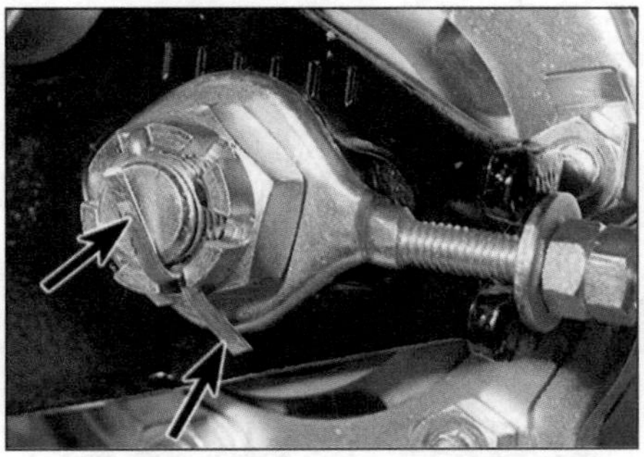

2.5 Bend cotter pin arms as shown (arrows) to secure a castellated nut

2.6 Bend cotter pin arms as shown to secure a plain nut

Caution: If the castellated nut slots do not align with the shaft hole after tightening to the torque setting, tighten the nut until the next slot aligns with the hole - never loosen the nut to align its slot.

● R-pins (shaped like the letter R), or slip pins as they are sometimes called, are sprung and can be reused if they are otherwise in good condition. Always install R-pins with their closed end facing forwards **(see illustration 2.7)**.

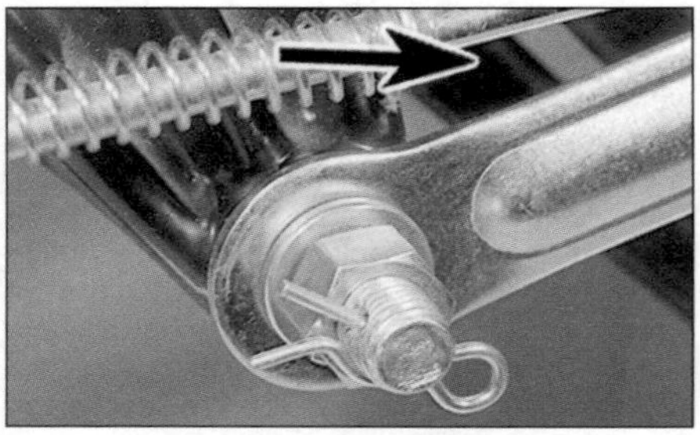

2.7 Correct fitting of R-pin. Arrow indicates forward direction

Snap-rings (see illustration 2.8)

● Snap-rings (sometimes called circlips) are used to retain components on a shaft or in a housing and have corresponding external or internal ears to permit removal. Parallel-sided (machined) snap-rings can be installed either way round in their groove, whereas stamped snap-rings (which have a chamfered edge on one face) must be installed with the chamfer facing the thrust load **(see illustration 2.9)**.

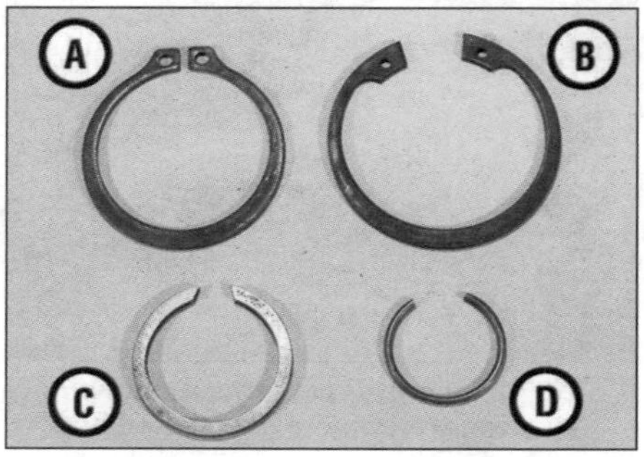

2.8 External stamped snap-ring (A), internal stamped snap-ring (B), machined snap-ring (C) and wire snap-ring (D)

● Always use snap-ring pliers to remove and install snap-rings; expand or compress them just enough to remove them. After installation, rotate the snap-ring in its groove to ensure it is securely seated. If installing a snap-ring on a splined shaft, always align its opening with a shaft channel to ensure the snap-ring ends are well supported and unlikely to catch **(see illustration 2.10)**.

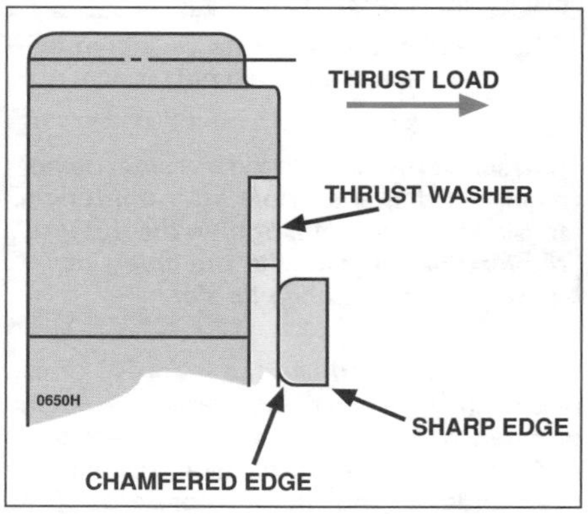

2.9 Correct fitting of a stamped snap-ring

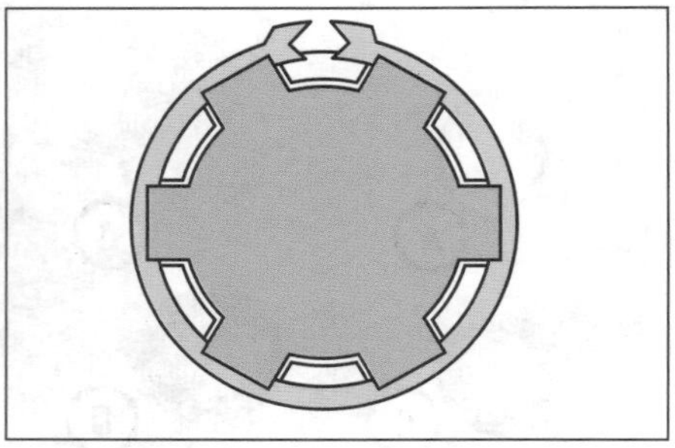

2.10 Align snap-ring opening with shaft channel

● Snap-rings can wear due to the thrust of components and become loose in their grooves, with the subsequent danger of becoming dislodged in operation. For this reason, replacement is advised every time a snap-ring is disturbed.

● Wire snap-rings are commonly used as piston pin retaining clips. If a removal tang is provided, long-nosed pliers can be used to dislodge them, otherwise careful use of a small flat-bladed screwdriver is necessary. Wire snap-rings should be replaced every time they are disturbed.

Thread diameter and pitch

● Diameter of a male thread (screw, bolt or stud) is the outside diameter of the threaded portion **(see illustration 2.11)**. Most motorcycle manufacturers use the ISO (International Standards Organization) metric system expressed in millimeters. For example, M6 refers to a 6 mm diameter thread. Sizing is the same for nuts, except that the thread diameter is measured across the valleys of the nut.

● Pitch is the distance between the peaks of the thread **(see illustration 2.11)**. It is expressed in millimeters, thus a common bolt size may be expressed as 6.0 x 1.0 mm (6 mm thread diameter and 1 mm pitch). Generally pitch increases in proportion to thread diameter, although there are always exceptions.

● Thread diameter and pitch are related for conventional fastener applications and the accompanying table can be used as a guide. Additionally, the AF (Across Flats), wrench or socket size dimension of the bolt or nut **(see illustration 2.11)** is linked to thread and pitch specification. Thread pitch can be measured with a thread gauge **(see illustration 2.12)**.

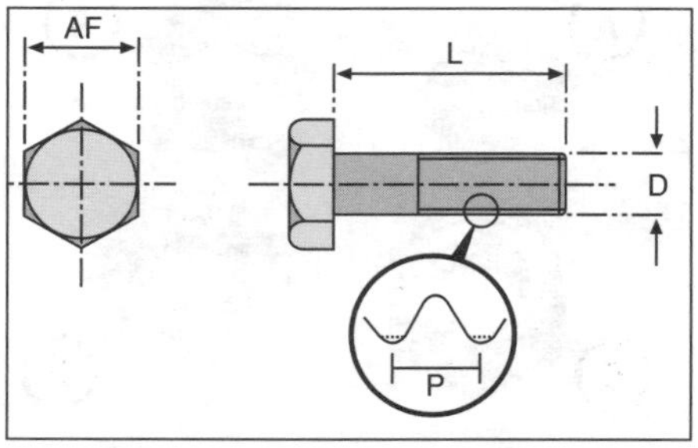

2.11 Fastener length (L), thread diameter (D), thread pitch (P) and head size (AF)

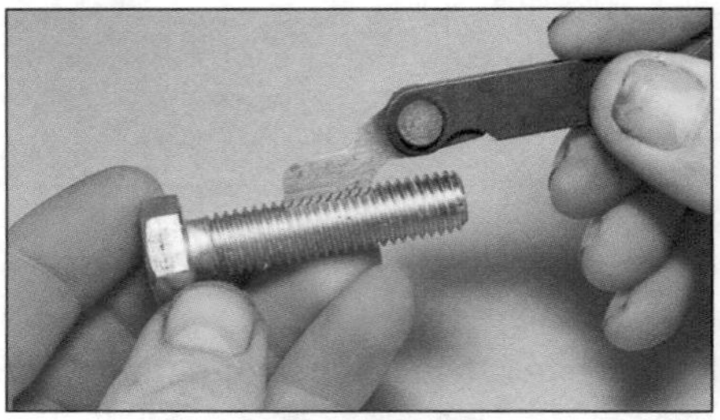

2.12 Using a thread gauge to measure pitch

AF size	Thread diameter x pitch (mm)
8 mm	M5 x 0.8
8 mm	M6 x 1.0
10 mm	M6 x 1.0
12 mm	M8 x 1.25
14 mm	M10 x 1.25
17 mm	M12 x 1.25

● The threads of most fasteners are of the right-hand type, ie they are turned clockwise to tighten and counterclockwise to loosen. The reverse situation applies to left-hand thread fasteners, which are turned counterclockwise to tighten and clockwise to loosen. Left-hand threads are used where rotation of a component might loosen a conventional right-hand thread fastener.

Seized fasteners

● Corrosion of external fasteners due to water or reaction between two dissimilar metals can occur over a period of time. It will build up sooner in wet conditions or in countries where salt is used on the roads during the winter. If a fastener is severely corroded it is likely that normal methods of removal will fail and result in its head being ruined. When you attempt removal, the fastener thread should be heard to crack free and unscrew easily - if it doesn't, stop there before damaging something.

● A smart tap on the head of the fastener will often succeed in breaking free corrosion which has occurred in the threads **(see illustration 2.13)**.

● An aerosol penetrating fluid (such as WD-40) applied the night beforehand may work its way down into the thread and ease removal. Depending on the location, you may be able to make up a modeling-clay well around the fastener head and fill it with penetrating fluid.

2.13 A sharp tap on the head of a fastener will often break free a corroded thread

● If you are working on an engine internal component, corrosion will most likely not be a problem due to the well lubricated environment. However, components can be very tight and an impact driver is a useful tool in freeing them **(see illustration 2.14)**.

2.14 Using an impact driver to free a fastener

● Where corrosion has occurred between dissimilar metals (e.g. steel and aluminum alloy), the application of heat to the fastener head will create a disproportionate expansion rate between the two metals and break the seizure caused by the corrosion. Whether heat can be applied depends on the location of the fastener - any surrounding components likely to be damaged must first be removed **(see illustration 2.15)**. Heat can be applied using a paint stripper heat gun or clothes iron, or by immersing the component in boiling water - wear protective gloves to prevent scalding or burns to the hands.

2.15 Using heat to free a seized fastener

● As a last resort, it is possible to use a hammer and cold chisel to work the fastener head unscrewed **(see illustration 2.16)**. This will damage the fastener, but more importantly extreme care must be taken not to damage the surrounding component.

Caution: Remember that the component being secured is generally of more value than the bolt, nut or screw - when the fastener is freed, do not unscrew it with force, instead work the fastener back and forth when resistance is felt to prevent thread damage.

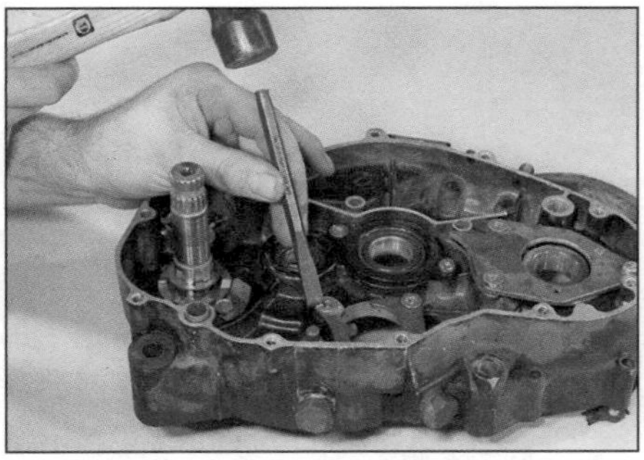

2.16 Using a hammer and chisel to free a seized fastener

Broken fasteners and damaged heads

● If the shank of a broken bolt or screw is accessible you can grip it with self-locking grips. The knurled wheel type stud extractor tool or self-gripping stud puller tool is particularly useful for removing the long studs which screw into the cylinder mouth surface of the crankcase or bolts and screws from which the head has broken off **(see illustration 2.17)**. Studs can also be removed by locking two nuts together on the threaded end of the stud and using a wrench on the lower nut **(see illustration 2.18)**.

2.17 Using a stud extractor tool to remove a broken crankcase stud

2.18 Two nuts can be locked together to unscrew a stud from a component

● A bolt or screw which has broken off below or level with the casing must be extracted using a screw extractor set. Centerpunch the fastener to centralize the drill bit, then drill a hole in the fastener **(see illustration 2.19)**. Select a drill bit which is approximately half to three-quarters the diameter of the fastener

2.19 When using a screw extractor, first drill a hole in the fastener . . .

and drill to a depth which will accommodate the extractor. Use the largest size extractor possible, but avoid leaving too small a wall thickness otherwise the extractor will merely force the fastener walls outwards wedging it in the casing thread.

● If a spiral type extractor is used, thread it counterclockwise into the fastener. As it is screwed in, it will grip the fastener and unscrew it from the casing **(see illustration 2.20)**.

2.20 . . . then thread the extractor counterclockwise into the fastener

● If a taper type extractor is used, tap it into the fastener so that it is firmly wedged in place. Unscrew the extractor (counter-clockwise) to draw the fastener out.

● Alternatively, the broken bolt/screw can be drilled out and the hole retapped for an oversize bolt/screw or a diamond-section thread insert. It is essential that the drilling is carried out squarely and to the correct depth, otherwise the casing may be ruined - if in doubt, entrust the work to a machine shop.

Warning: Stud extractors are very hard and may break off in the fastener if care is not taken - ask a machine shop about spark erosion if this happens.

● Bolts and nuts with rounded corners cause the correct size wrench or socket to slip when force is applied. Of the types of wrench/socket available always use a six-point type rather than an eight or twelve-point type - better grip

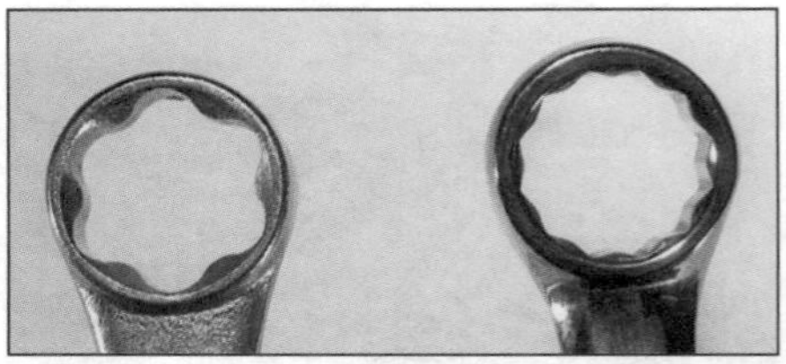

2.21 Comparison of surface drive box wrench (left) with 12-point type (right)

is obtained. Surface drive wrenches grip the middle of the hex flats, rather than the corners, and are thus good in cases of damaged heads **(see illustration 2.21)**.

- Slotted-head or Phillips-head screws are often damaged by the use of the wrong size screwdriver. Allen-head and Torx-head screws are much less likely to sustain damage. If enough of the screw head is exposed you can use a hacksaw to cut a slot in its head and then use a conventional flat-bladed screwdriver to remove it. Alternatively use a hammer and cold chisel to tap the head of the fastener around to loosen it. Always replace damaged fasteners with new ones, preferably Torx or Allen-head type.

A dab of valve grinding compound between the screw head and screw-driver tip will often give a good grip.

Thread repair

- Threads (particularly those in aluminum alloy components) can be damaged by overtightening, being assembled with dirt in the threads, or from a component working loose and vibrating. Eventually the thread will fail completely, and it will be impossible to tighten the fastener.
- If a thread is damaged or clogged with old locking compound it can be renovated with a thread repair tool (thread chaser) **(see illustrations 2.22 and 2.23);** special thread chasers are available for spark plug hole threads. The tool will not cut a new thread, but clean and true the original thread. Make sure that you use the correct diameter and pitch tool. Similarly, external threads can be cleaned up with a die or a thread restorer file **(see illustration 2.24)**.

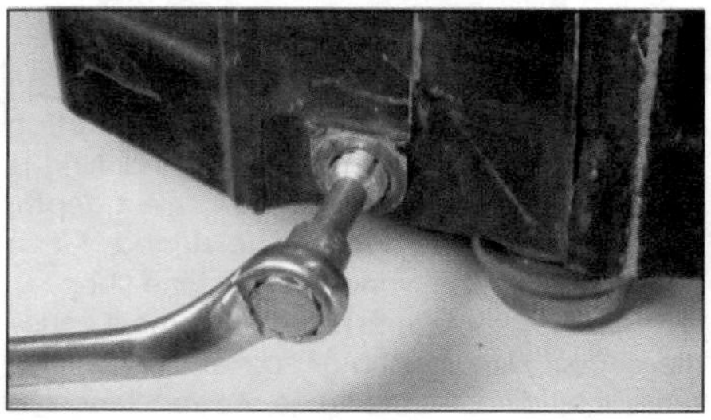

2.22 A thread repair tool being used to correct an internal thread

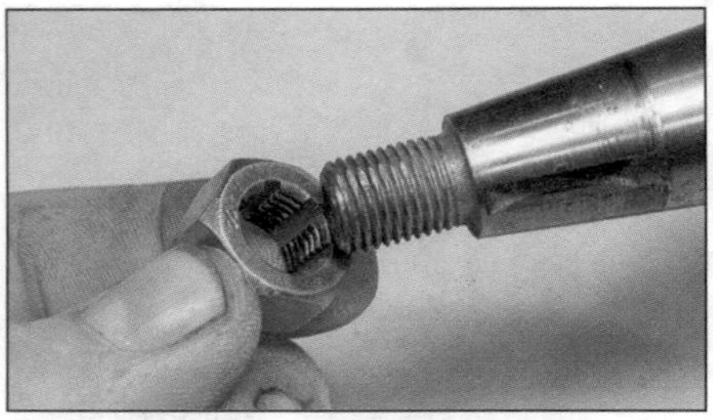

2.23 A thread repair tool being used to correct an external thread

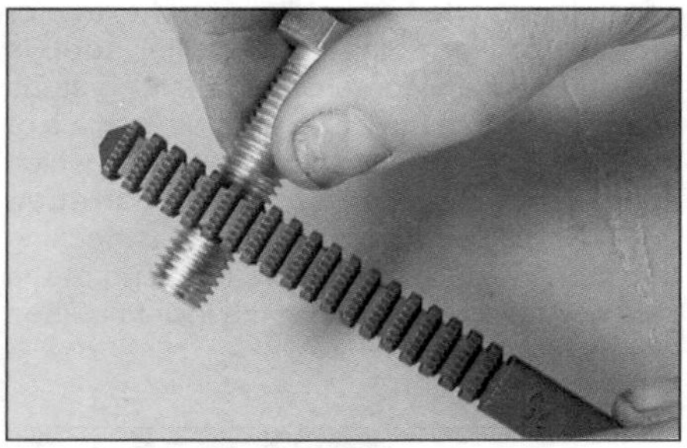

2.24 Using a thread restorer file

- It is possible to drill out the old thread and retap the component to the next thread size. This will work where there is enough surrounding material and a new bolt or screw can be obtained. Sometimes, however, this is not possible - such as where the bolt/screw passes through another component which must also be suitably modified, also in cases where a spark plug or oil drain plug cannot be obtained in a larger diameter thread size.
- The diamond-section thread insert (often known by its popular trade name of Heli-Coil) is a simple and effective method of replacing the thread and retaining the original size. A kit can be purchased which contains the tap, insert and installing tool **(see illustration 2.25)**. Drill out the damaged thread with the size drill specified **(see illustration 2.26)**. Carefully retap the thread **(see illustration 2.27)**. Install the insert on the installing tool and thread it slowly into place using a light downward pressure **(see illustrations 2.28 and 2.29)**. When positioned between a 1/4 and 1/2 turn below the surface withdraw the installing tool and use the break-off tool to press down on the tang, breaking it off **(see illustration 2.30)**.
- There are epoxy thread repair kits on the market which can rebuild stripped internal threads, although this repair should not be used on high load-bearing components.

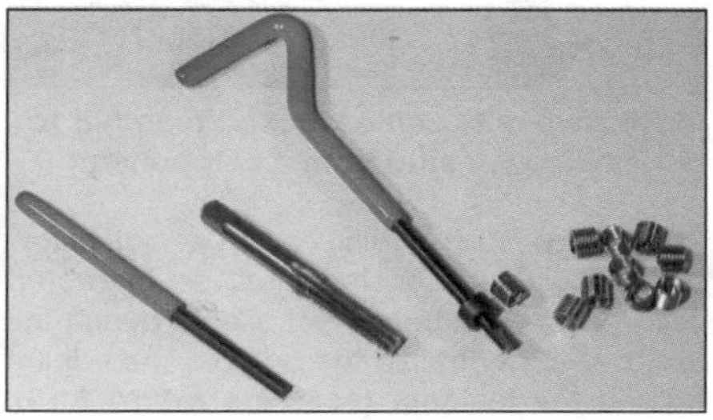

2.25 Obtain a thread insert kit to suit the thread diameter and pitch required

2.26 To install a thread insert, first drill out the original thread . . .

2.27 . . . tap a new thread . . .

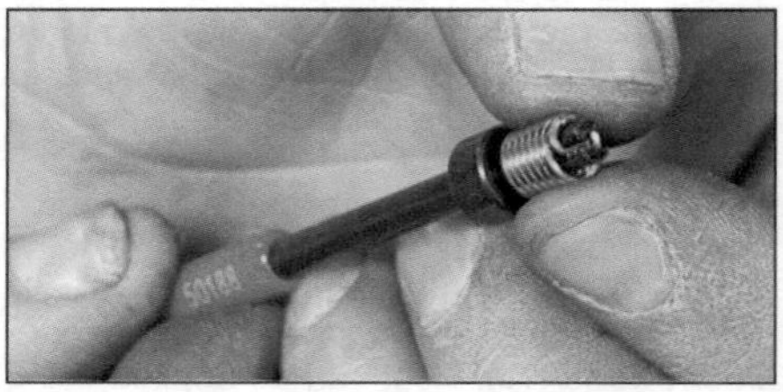

2.28 . . . fit insert on the installing tool . . .

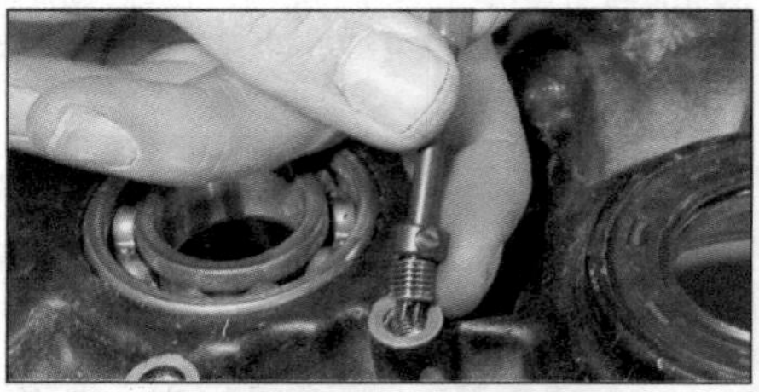

2.29 . . . and thread into the component . . .

2.30 . . . break off the tang when complete

Thread locking and sealing compounds

● Locking compounds are used in locations where the fastener is prone to loosening due to vibration or on important safety-related items which might cause loss of control of the motorcycle if they fail. It is also used where important fasteners cannot be secured by other means such as lockwashers or cotter pins.

● Before applying locking compound, make sure that the threads (internal and external) are clean and dry with all old compound removed. Select a compound to suit the component being secured - a non-permanent general locking and sealing type is suitable for most applications, but a high strength type is needed for permanent fixing of studs in castings. Apply a drop or two of the compound to the first few threads of the fastener, then thread it into place and tighten to the specified torque. Do not apply excessive thread locking compound otherwise the thread may be damaged on subsequent removal.

● Certain fasteners are impregnated with a dry film type coating of locking compound on their threads. Always replace this type of fastener if disturbed.

● Anti-seize compounds, such as copper-based greases, can be applied to protect threads from seizure due to extreme heat and corrosion. A common instance is spark plug threads and exhaust system fasteners.

3 Measuring tools and gauges

Feeler gauges

● Feeler gauges (or blades) are used for measuring small gaps and clearances **(see illustration 3.1)**. They can also be used to measure endfloat (sideplay) of a component on a shaft where access is not possible with a dial gauge.

● Feeler gauge sets should be treated with care and not bent or damaged. They are etched with their size on one face. Keep them clean and very lightly oiled to prevent corrosion build-up.

3.1 Feeler gauges are used for measuring small gaps and clearances - thickness is marked on one face of gauge

● When measuring a clearance, select a gauge which is a light sliding fit between the two components. You may need to use two gauges together to measure the clearance accurately.

Micrometers

● A micrometer is a precision tool capable of measuring to 0.01 or 0.001 of a millimeter. It should always be stored in its case and not in the general toolbox. It must be kept clean and never dropped, otherwise its frame or measuring anvils could be distorted resulting in inaccurate readings.

● External micrometers are used for measuring outside diameters of components and have many more applications than internal micrometers. Micrometers are available in different size ranges, typically 0 to 25 mm, 25 to 50 mm, and upwards in 25 mm steps; some large micrometers have interchangeable anvils to allow a range of measurements to be taken. Generally the largest precision measurement you are likely to take on a motorcycle is the piston diameter.

● Internal micrometers (or bore micrometers) are used for measuring inside diameters, such as valve guides and cylinder bores. Telescoping gauges and small hole gauges are used in conjunction with an external micrometer, whereas the more expensive internal micrometers have their own measuring device.

External micrometer

Note: *The conventional analogue type instrument is described. Although much easier to read, digital micrometers are considerably more expensive.*

● Always check the calibration of the micrometer before use. With the anvils closed (0 to 25 mm type) or set over a test gauge (for the larger types) the scale should read zero **(see illustration 3.2)**; make sure that the anvils (and test piece) are clean first. Any discrepancy can be adjusted by referring to the instructions supplied with the tool. Remember that the micrometer is a precision measuring tool - don't force the anvils closed, use the ratchet (4) on the end of the micrometer to close it. In this way, a measured force is always applied.

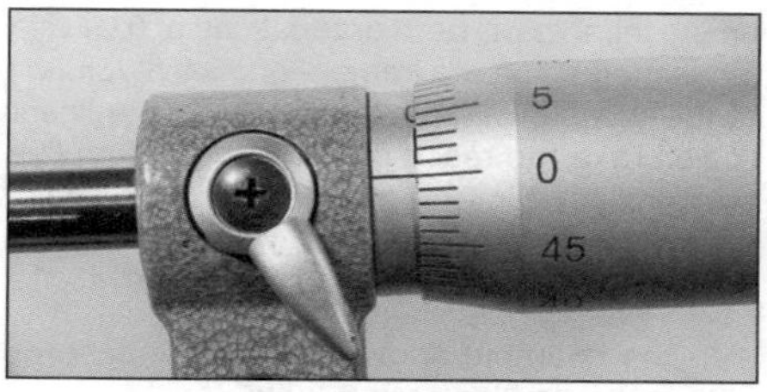

3.2 Check micrometer calibration before use

● To use, first make sure that the item being measured is clean. Place the anvil of the micrometer (1) against the item and use the thimble (2) to bring the spindle (3) lightly into contact with the other side of the item **(see illustration 3.3)**. Don't tighten the thimble down because this will damage the micrometer - instead use the ratchet (4) on the end of the micrometer. The ratchet mechanism applies a measured force preventing damage to the instrument.

● The micrometer is read by referring to the linear scale on the sleeve and the annular scale on the thimble. Read off the sleeve first to obtain the base measurement, then add the fine measurement from the thimble to obtain the overall reading. The linear scale on the sleeve represents the measuring range of the micrometer (eg 0 to 25 mm). The annular scale

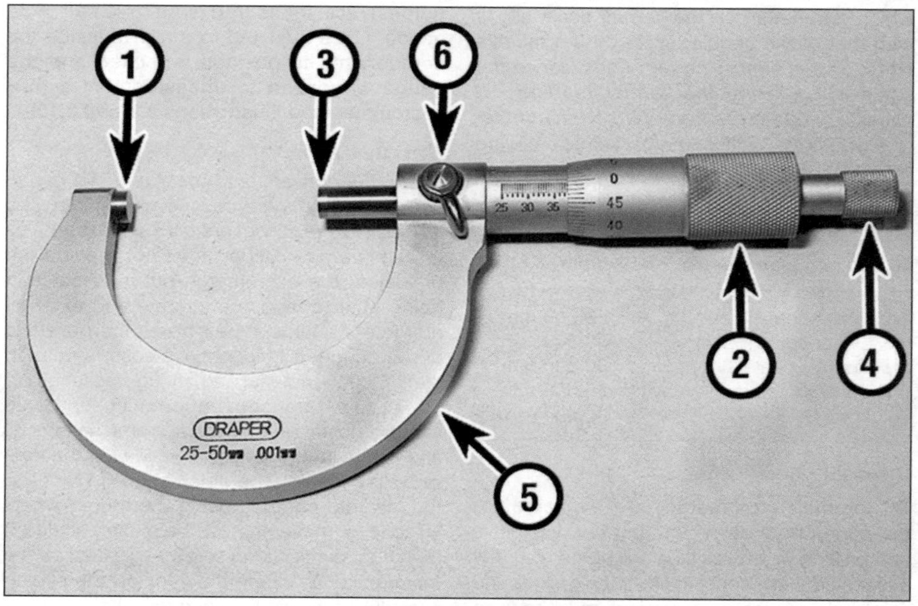

3.3 Micrometer component parts

1 Anvil
2 Thimble
3 Spindle
4 Ratchet
5 Frame
6 Locking lever

on the thimble will be in graduations of 0.01 mm (or as marked on the frame) - one full revolution of the thimble will move 0.5 mm on the linear scale. Take the reading where the datum line on the sleeve intersects the thimble's scale. Always position the eye directly above the scale otherwise an inaccurate reading will result.

In the example shown the item measures 2.95 mm **(see illustration 3.4)**:

Linear scale	2.00 mm
Linear scale	0.50 mm
Annular scale	0.45 mm
Total figure	**2.95 mm**

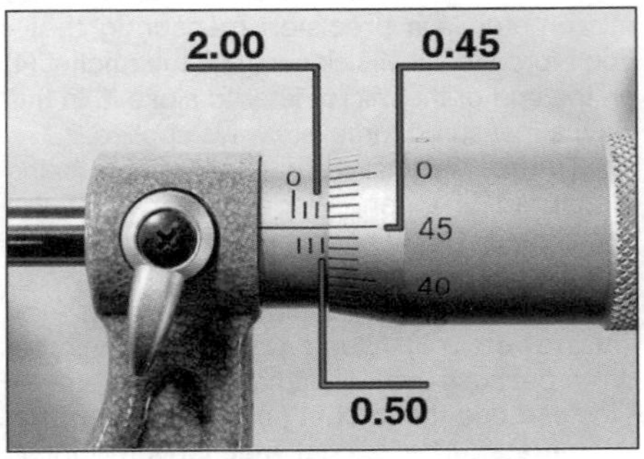

3.4 Micrometer reading of 2.95 mm

Most micrometers have a locking lever (6) on the frame to hold the setting in place, allowing the item to be removed from the micrometer.

- Some micrometers have a vernier scale on their sleeve, providing an even finer measurement to be taken, in 0.001 increments of a millimeter. Take the sleeve and thimble measurement as described above, then check which graduation on the vernier scale aligns with that of the annular scale on the thimble **Note:** *The eye must be perpendicular to the scale when taking the vernier reading - if necessary rotate the body of the micrometer to ensure this.* Multiply the vernier scale figure by 0.001 and add it to the base and fine measurement figures.

In the example shown the item measures 46.994 mm **(see illustrations 3.5 and 3.6)**:

Linear scale (base)	46.000 mm
Linear scale (base)	00.500 mm
Annular scale (fine)	00.490 mm
Vernier scale	00.004 mm
Total figure	**46.994 mm**

Internal micrometer

- Internal micrometers are available for measuring bore diameters, but are expensive and unlikely to be available for home use. It is suggested that a set of telescoping gauges and small hole gauges, both of which must be used with an external micrometer, will suffice for taking internal measurements on a motorcycle.
- Telescoping gauges can be used to measure internal diameters of components. Select a gauge with the correct size range, make sure its ends are clean and insert it into the bore. Expand the gauge, then lock its position and withdraw it from the bore **(see illustration 3.7)**. Measure across the gauge ends with a micrometer **(see illustration 3.8)**.
- Very small diameter bores (such as valve guides) are measured with a small hole gauge. Once adjusted to a slip-fit inside the component, its position is locked and the gauge withdrawn for measurement with a micrometer **(see illustrations 3.9 and 3.10)**.

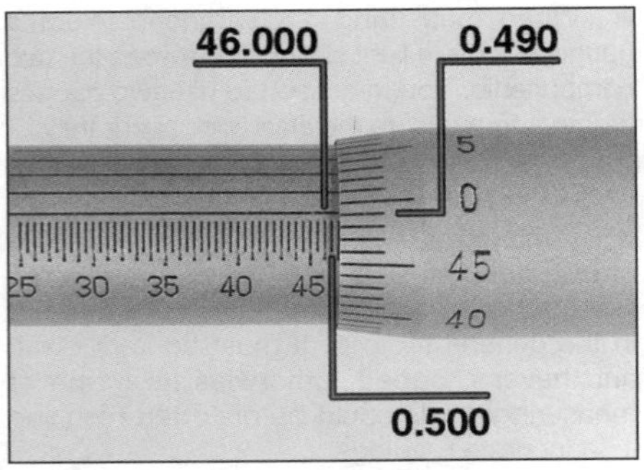

3.5 Micrometer reading of 46.99 mm on linear and annular scales . . .

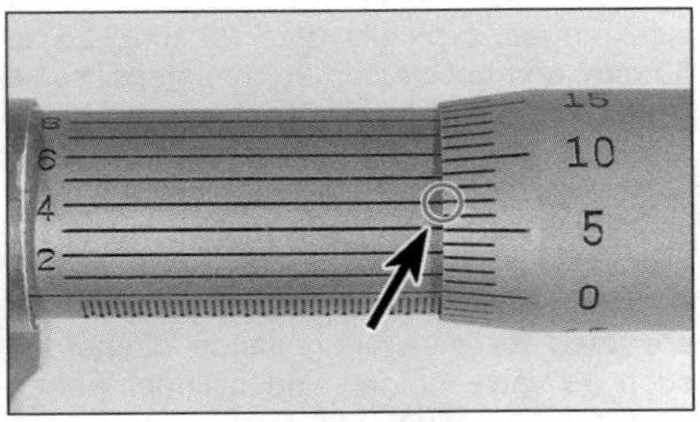

3.6 . . . and 0.004 mm on vernier scale

Vernier caliper

Note: *The conventional linear and dial gauge type instruments are described. Digital types are easier to read, but are far more expensive.*

- The vernier caliper does not provide the precision of a micrometer, but is versatile in being able to measure internal and external diameters. Some types also incorporate a depth gauge. It is ideal for measuring clutch plate friction material and spring free lengths.
- To use the conventional linear scale vernier, loosen off the vernier clamp screws (1) and set its jaws over (2), or inside (3), the item to be measured **(see illustration 3.11)**. Slide the jaw into contact, using the thumb-wheel (4) for fine movement of the sliding scale (5) then tighten the clamp screws (1). Read off the main scale (6) where the zero on the sliding scale (5) intersects it, taking the whole number to the left of the zero; this provides the base measurement. View along the sliding scale and select the division which lines up exactly with any of the divisions on the main scale, noting that the divisions usually represents 0.02 of a millimeter. Add this fine measurement to the base measurement to obtain the total reading.

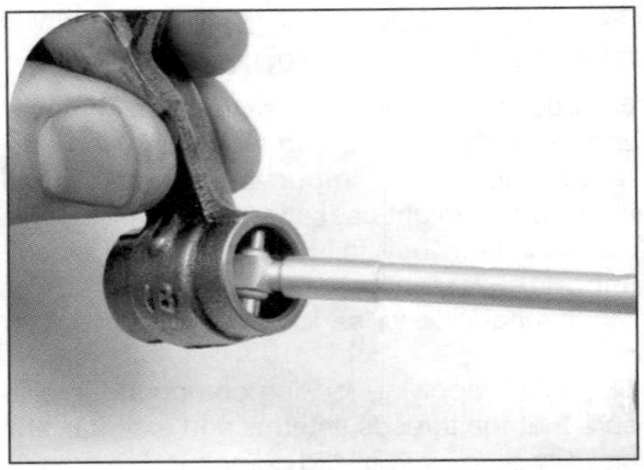

3.7 Expand the telescoping gauge in the bore, lock its position . . .

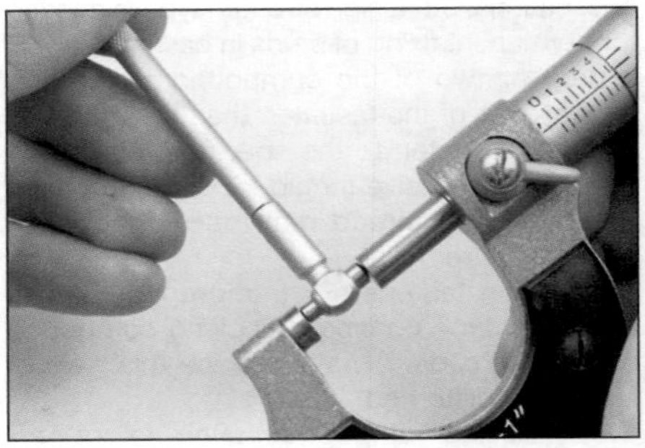

3.8 . . . then measure the gauge with a micrometer

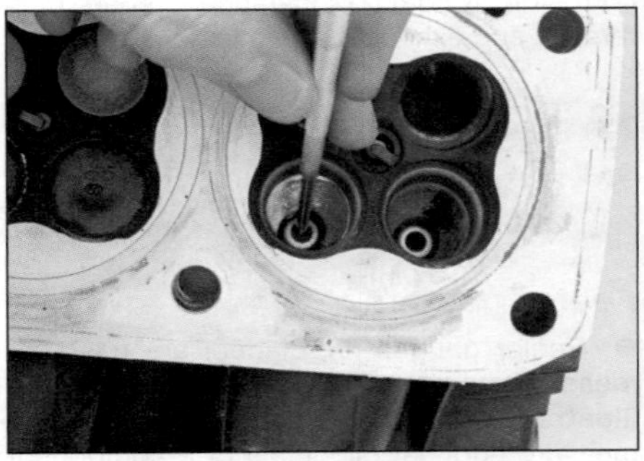

3.9 Expand the small hole gauge in the bore, lock its position . . .

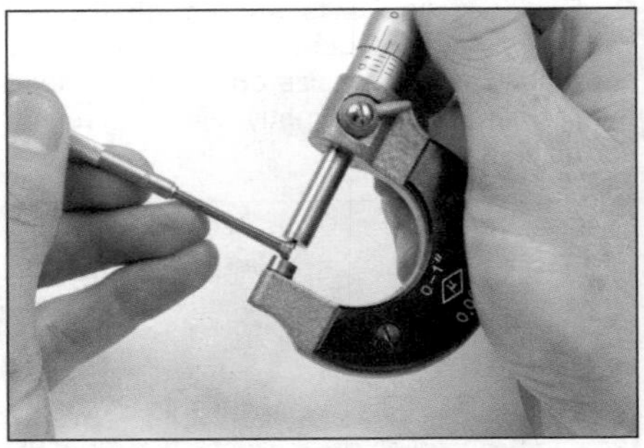

3.10 . . . then measure the gauge with a micrometer

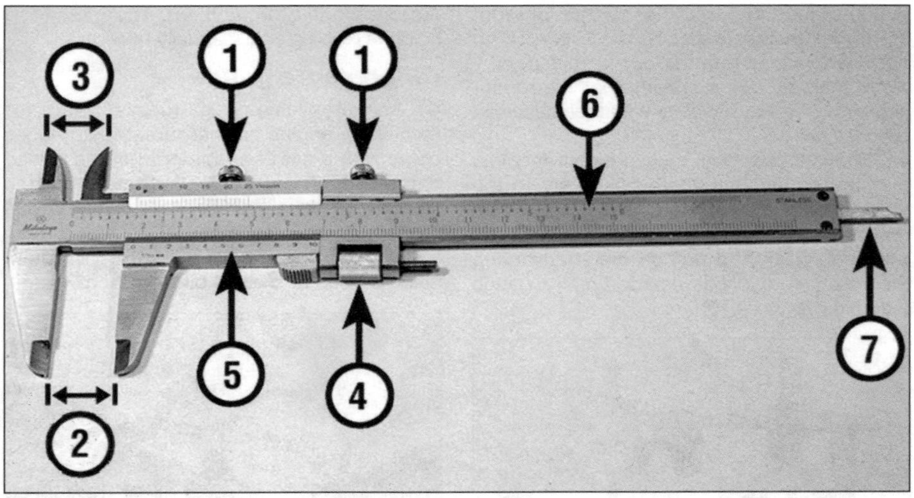

3.11 Vernier component parts (linear gauge)

1 Clamp screws
2 External jaws
3 Internal jaws
4 Thumbwheel
5 Sliding scale
6 Main scale
7 Depth gauge

In the example shown the item measures 55.92 mm **(see illustration 3.12)**:

Base measurement	55.00 mm
Fine measurement	00.92 mm
Total figure	**55.92 mm**

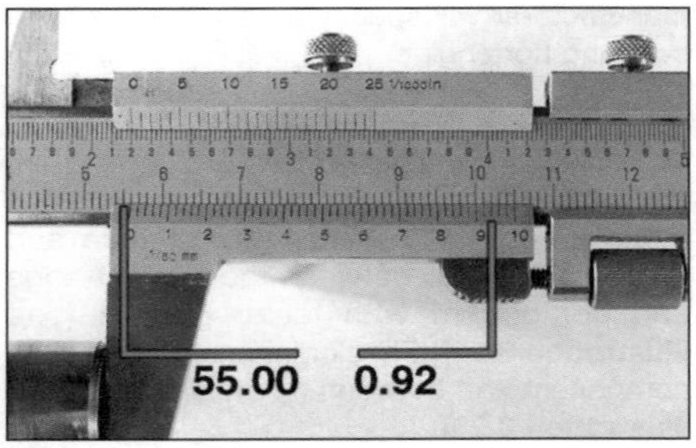

3.12 Vernier gauge reading of 55.92 mm

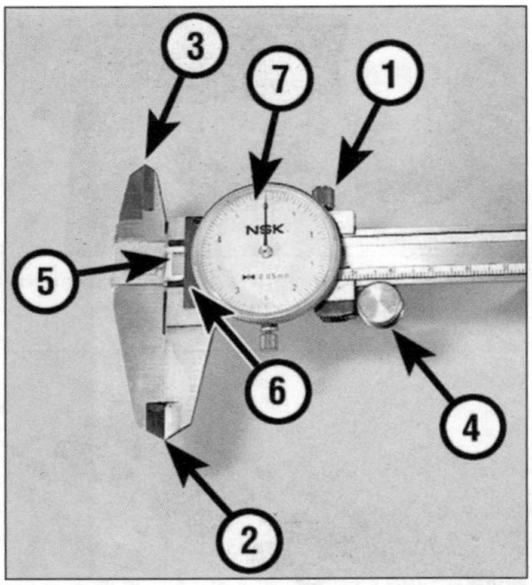

3.13 Vernier component parts (dial gauge)

1 Clamp screw
2 External jaws
3 Internal jaws
4 Thumbwheel
5 Main scale
6 Sliding scale
7 Dial gauge

● Some vernier calipers are equipped with a dial gauge for fine measurement. Before use, check that the jaws are clean, then close them fully and check that the dial gauge reads zero. If necessary adjust the gauge ring accordingly. Slacken the vernier clamp screw (1) and set its jaws over (2), or inside (3), the item to be measured **(see illustration 3.13)**. Slide the jaws into contact, using the thumbwheel (4) for fine movement. Read off the main scale (5) where the edge of the sliding scale (6) intersects it, taking the whole number to the left of the zero; this provides the base measurement. Read off the needle position on the dial gauge (7) scale to provide the fine measurement; each division represents 0.05 of a millimeter. Add this fine measurement to the base measurement to obtain the total reading.

In the example shown the item measures 55.95 mm **(see illustration 3.14)**:

Base measurement	55.00 mm
Fine measurement	00.95 mm
Total figure	**55.95 mm**

3.14 Vernier gauge reading of 55.95 mm

Plastigage

● Plastigage is a plastic material which can be compressed between two surfaces to measure the oil clearance between them. The width of the compressed Plastigage is measured against a calibrated scale to determine the clearance.

● Common uses of Plastigage are for measuring the clearance between crankshaft journal and main bearing inserts, between crankshaft journal and big-end bearing inserts, and between camshaft and bearing surfaces. The following example describes big-end oil clearance measurement.

● Handle the Plastigage material carefully to prevent distortion. Using a sharp knife, cut a length which corresponds with the width of the bearing being measured and place it carefully across the journal so that it is parallel with the shaft **(see illustration 3.15)**. Carefully install both bearing shells and the connecting rod. Without rotating the rod on the journal tighten its bolts or nuts (as applicable) to the specified torque. The connecting rod and bearings are then disassembled and the crushed Plastigage examined.

3.15 Plastigage placed across shaft journal

● Using the scale provided in the Plastigage kit, measure the width of the material to determine the oil clearance **(see illustration 3.16)**. Always remove all traces of Plastigage after use using your fingernails.

Caution: Arriving at the correct clearance demands that the assembly is torqued correctly, according to the settings and sequence (where applicable) provided by the motorcycle manufacturer.

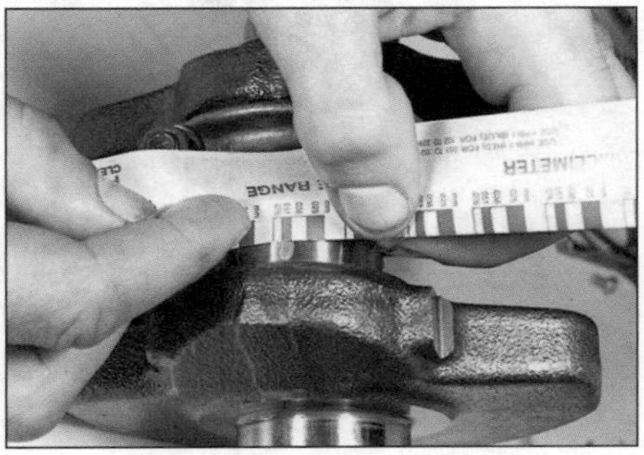

3.16 Measuring the width of the crushed Plastigage

Dial gauge or DTI (Dial Test Indicator)

● A dial gauge can be used to accurately measure small amounts of movement. Typical uses are measuring shaft runout or shaft endfloat (sideplay) and setting piston position for ignition timing on two-strokes. A dial gauge set usually comes with a range of different probes and adapters and mounting equipment.

● The gauge needle must point to zero when at rest. Rotate the ring around its periphery to zero the gauge.

● Check that the gauge is capable of reading the extent of movement in the work. Most gauges have a small dial set in the face which records whole millimeters of movement as well as the fine scale around the face periphery which is calibrated in 0.01 mm divisions. Read off the small dial first to obtain the base measurement, then add the measurement from the fine scale to obtain the total reading.

Base measurement	1.00 mm
Fine measurement	0.48 mm
Total figure	**1.48 mm**

3.17 Dial gauge reading of 1.48 mm

In the example shown the gauge reads 1.48 mm **(see illustration 3.17)**:

● If measuring shaft runout, the shaft must be supported in vee-blocks and the gauge mounted on a stand perpendicular to the shaft. Rest the tip of the gauge against the center of the shaft and rotate the shaft slowly while watching the gauge reading **(see illustration 3.18)**. Take several measurements along the length of the shaft and record the maximum gauge reading as the amount of runout in the shaft. **Note:** *The reading obtained will be total runout at that point - some manufacturers specify that the runout figure is halved to compare with their specified runout limit.*

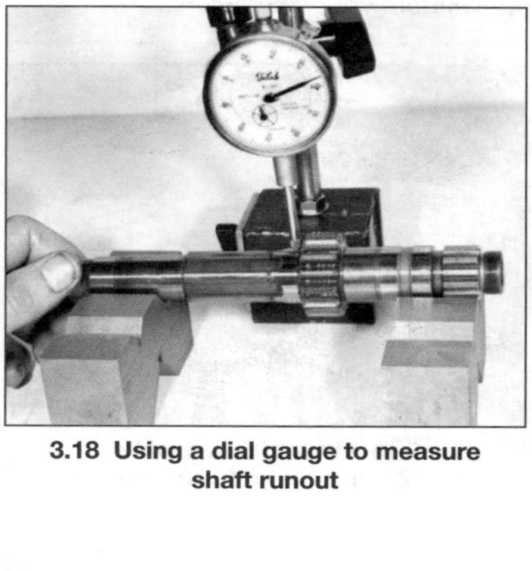

3.18 Using a dial gauge to measure shaft runout

● Endfloat (sideplay) measurement requires that the gauge is mounted securely to the surrounding component with its probe touching the end of the shaft. Using hand pressure, push and pull on the shaft noting the maximum endfloat recorded on the gauge **(see illustration 3.19)**.

3.19 Using a dial gauge to measure shaft endfloat

● A dial gauge with suitable adapters can be used to determine piston position BTDC on two-stroke engines for the purposes of ignition timing. The gauge, adapter and suitable length probe are installed in the place of the spark plug and the gauge zeroed at TDC. If the piston position is specified as 1.14 mm BTDC, rotate the engine back to 2.00 mm BTDC, then slowly forwards to 1.14 mm BTDC.

Cylinder compression gauges

● A compression gauge is used for measuring cylinder compression. Either the rubber-cone type or the threaded adapter type can be used. The latter is preferred to ensure a perfect seal against the cylinder head. A 0 to 300 psi (0 to 20 Bar) type gauge (for gasoline engines) will be suitable for motorcycles.

● The spark plug is removed and the gauge either held hard against the cylinder head (cone type) or the gauge adapter screwed into the cylinder head (threaded type) **(see illustration 3.20)**. Cylinder compression is measured with the engine turning over, but not running - carry out the compression test as described in *Troubleshooting Equipment*. The gauge will hold the reading until manually released.

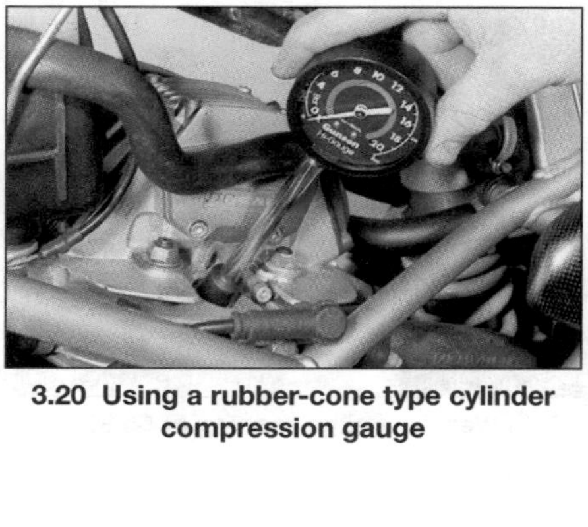

3.20 Using a rubber-cone type cylinder compression gauge

Oil pressure gauge

● An oil pressure gauge is used for measuring engine oil pressure. Most gauges come with a set of adapters to fit the thread of the take-off point **(see illustration 3.21)**. If the take-off point specified by the motorcycle manufacturer is an external oil pipe union, make sure that the specified replacement union is used to prevent oil starvation.

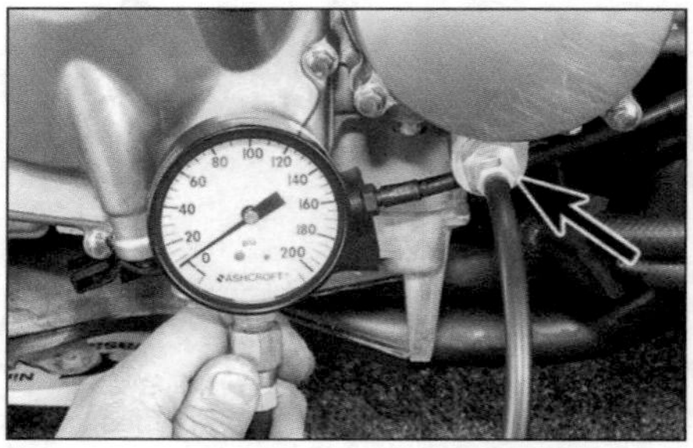

3.21 Oil pressure gauge and take-off point adapter (arrow)

● Oil pressure is measured with the engine running (at a specific rpm) and often the manufacturer will specify pressure limits for a cold and hot engine.

Straight-edge and surface plate

● If checking the gasket face of a component for warpage, place a steel rule or precision straight-edge across the gasket face and measure any gap between the straight-edge and component with feeler gauges **(see illustration 3.22)**. Check diagonally across the component and between mounting holes **(see illustration 3.23)**.

3.22 Use a straight-edge and feeler gauges to check for warpage

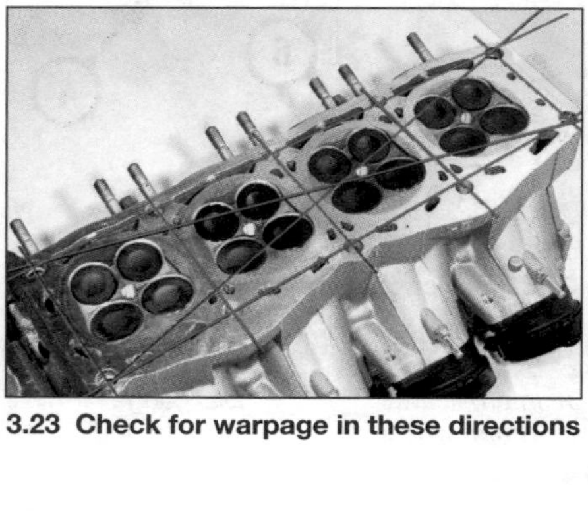

3.23 Check for warpage in these directions

● Checking individual components for warpage, such as clutch plain (metal) plates, requires a perfectly flat plate or piece of plate glass and feeler gauges.

4 Torque and leverage

What is torque?

● Torque describes the twisting force around a shaft. The amount of torque applied is determined by the distance from the center of the shaft to the end of the lever and the amount of force being applied to the end of the lever; distance multiplied by force equals torque.

● The manufacturer applies a measured torque to a bolt or nut to ensure that it will not loosen in use and to hold two components securely together without movement in the joint. The actual torque setting depends on the thread size, bolt or nut material and the composition of the components being held.

● Too little torque may cause the fastener to loosen due to vibration, whereas too much torque will distort the joint faces of the component or cause the fastener to shear off. Always stick to the specified torque setting.

Using a torque wrench

● Check the calibration of the torque wrench and make sure it has a suitable range for the job. Torque wrenches are available in Nm (Newton-meters), kgf m (kilograms-force meter), lbf ft (pounds-feet), lbf in (inch-pounds). Do not confuse lbf ft with lbf in.

● Adjust the tool to the desired torque on the scale **(see illustration 4.1)**. If your torque wrench is not calibrated in the units specified, carefully convert the figure (see *Conversion Factors*). A manufacturer sometimes gives a torque setting as a range (8 to 10 Nm) rather than a single figure - in this case set the tool midway between the two settings. The same torque may be expressed as 9 Nm ± 1 Nm. Some torque wrenches have a method of locking the setting so that it isn't inadvertently altered during use.

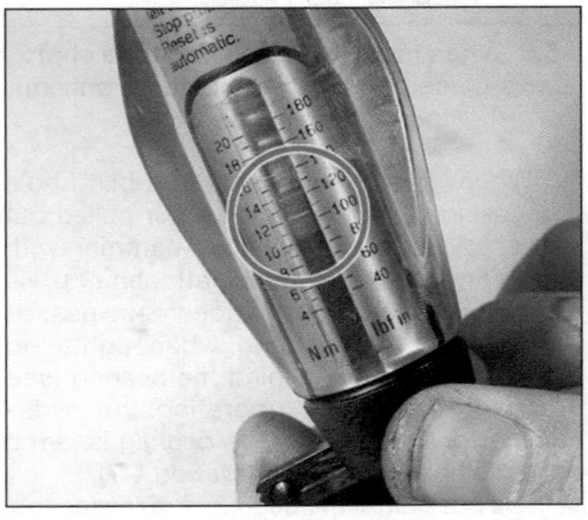

4.1 Set the torque wrench index mark to the setting required, in this case 12 Nm

● Install the bolts/nuts in their correct location and secure them lightly. Their threads must be clean and free of any old locking compound. Unless specified the threads and flange should be dry - oiled threads are necessary in certain circumstances and the manufacturer will take this into account in the specified torque figure. Similarly, the manufacturer may also specify the application of thread-locking compound.

● Tighten the fasteners in the specified sequence until the torque wrench clicks, indicating that the torque setting has been reached. Apply the torque again to double-check the setting. Where different thread diameter fasteners secure the component, as a rule tighten the larger diameter ones first.

● When the torque wrench has been finished with, release the lock (where applicable) and fully back off its setting to zero - do not leave the torque wrench tensioned. Also, do not use a torque wrench for loosening a fastener.

Angle-tightening

● Manufacturers often specify a figure in degrees for final tightening of a fastener. This usually follows tightening to a specific torque setting.

● A degree disc can be set and attached to the socket **(see illustration 4.2)** or a protractor can be used to mark the angle of movement on the bolt/nut head and the surrounding casting **(see illustration 4.3)**.

4.2 Angle tightening can be accomplished with a torque-angle gauge . . .

4.3 . . . or by marking the angle on the surrounding component

Loosening sequences

● Where more than one bolt/nut secures a component, loosen each fastener evenly a little at a time. In this way, not all the stress of the joint is held by one fastener and the components are not likely to distort.

● If a tightening sequence is provided, work in the REVERSE of this, but if not, work from the outside in, in a criss-cross sequence **(see illustration 4.4)**.

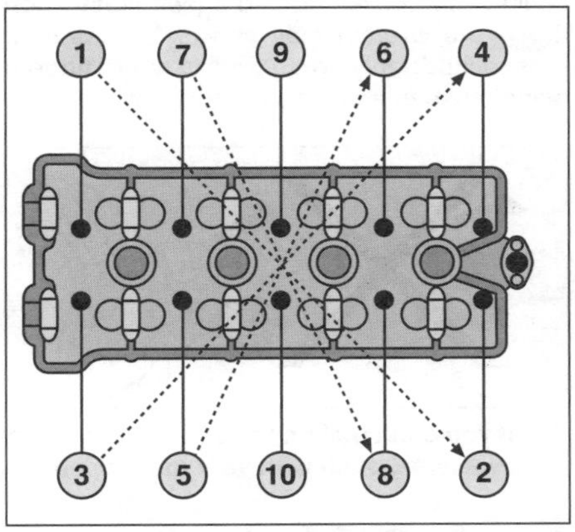

4.4 When loosening, work from the outside inwards

Tightening sequences

● If a component is held by more than one fastener it is important that the retaining bolts/nuts are tightened evenly to prevent uneven stress build-up and distortion of sealing faces. This is especially important on high-compression joints such as the cylinder head.

● A sequence is usually provided by the manufacturer, either in a diagram or actually marked in the casting. If not, always start in the center and work outwards in a criss-cross pattern **(see illustration 4.5)**. Start off by securing all bolts/nuts finger-tight, then set the torque wrench and tighten each fastener by a small amount in sequence until the final torque is reached. By following this practice,

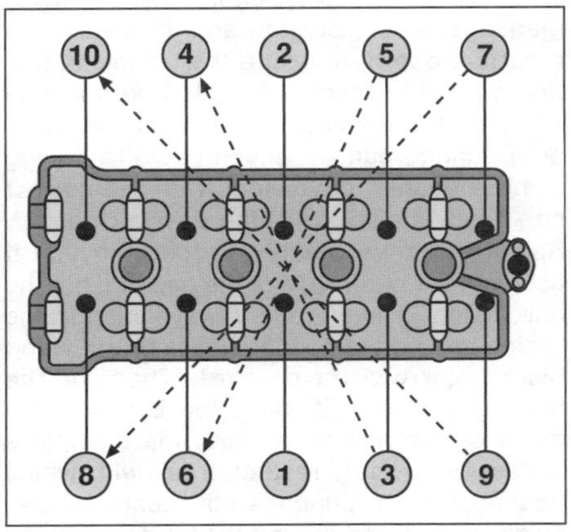

4.5 When tightening, work from the inside outwards

the joint will be held evenly and will not be distorted. Important joints, such as the cylinder head and big-end fasteners often have two- or three-stage torque settings.

Applying leverage

- Use tools at the correct angle. Position a socket or wrench on the bolt/nut so that you pull it towards you when loosening. If this can't be done, push the wrench without curling your fingers around it **(see illustration 4.6)** - the wrench may slip or the fastener loosen suddenly, resulting in your fingers being crushed against a component.

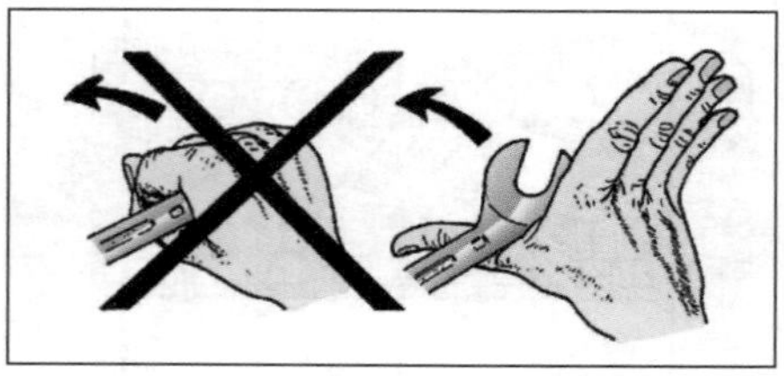

4.6 If you can't pull on the wrench to loosen a fastener, push with your hand open

- Additional leverage is gained by extending the length of the lever. The best way to do this is to use a breaker bar instead of the regular length tool, or to slip a length of tubing over the end of the wrench or socket.
- If additional leverage will not work, the fastener head is either damaged or firmly corroded in place (see *Fasteners*).

5 Bearings

Bearing removal and installation

Drivers and sockets

- Before removing a bearing, always inspect the casing to see which way it must be driven out - some casings will have retaining plates or a cast step. Also check for any identifying markings on the bearing and, if installed to a certain depth, measure this at this stage. Some roller bearings are sealed on one side - take note of the original installed position.
- Bearings can be driven out of a casing using a bearing driver tool (with the correct size head) or a socket of the correct diameter. Select the driver head or socket so that it contacts the outer race of the bearing, not the balls/rollers or inner race. Always support the casing around the bearing housing with wood blocks, otherwise there is a risk of fracture. The bearing is driven out with a few blows on the driver or socket from a heavy mallet. Unless access is severely restricted (as with wheel bearings), a pin-punch is not recommended unless it is moved around the bearing to keep it square in its housing.
- The same equipment can be used to install bearings. Make sure the bearing housing is supported on wood blocks and line up the bearing in its housing. Install the bearing as noted on removal - generally they are installed with their marked side facing outwards. Tap the bearing squarely into its housing using a driver or socket which bears only on the bearing's outer race - contact with the bearing balls/rollers or inner race will destroy it **(see illustrations 5.1 and 5.2)**.
- Check that the bearing inner race and balls/rollers rotate freely.

5.1 Using a bearing driver against the bearing's outer race

5.2 Using a large socket against the bearing's outer race

Pullers and slide-hammers

- Where a bearing is pressed on a shaft a puller will be required to extract it **(see illustration 5.3).** Make sure that the puller clamp or legs fit securely behind the bearing and are unlikely to slip out. If pulling a bearing off a gear shaft for example, you may have to locate the puller behind a gear pinion if there is no access to the race and draw the gear pinion off the shaft as well **(see illustration 5.4)**.

5.3 This bearing puller clamps behind the bearing and pressure is applied to the shaft end to draw the bearing off

Caution: Ensure that the puller's center bolt locates securely against the end of the shaft and will not slip when pressure is applied. Also ensure that puller does not damage the shaft end.

5.4 Where no access is available to the rear of the bearing, it is sometimes possible to draw off the adjacent component

- Operate the puller so that its center bolt exerts pressure on the shaft end and draws the bearing off the shaft.
- When installing the bearing on the shaft, tap only on the bearing's inner race - contact with the balls/rollers or outer race will destroy the bearing. Use a socket or length of tubing as a drift which fits over the shaft end **(see illustration 5.5)**.

5.5 When installing a bearing on a shaft use a piece of tubing which bears only on the bearing's inner race

- Where a bearing locates in a blind hole in a casing, it cannot be driven or pulled out as described above. A slide-hammer with knife-edged bearing puller attachment will be required. The puller attachment passes through the bearing and when tightened expands to fit firmly behind the bearing **(see illustration 5.6)**. By operating the slide-hammer part of the tool the bearing is jarred out of its housing **(see illustration 5.7)**.
- It is possible, if the bearing is of reasonable weight, for it to drop out of its housing if the casing is heated as described opposite. If

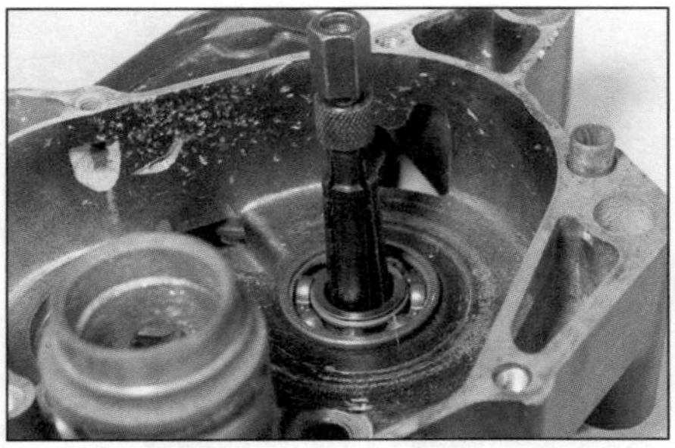

5.6 Expand the bearing puller so that it locks behind the bearing . . .

5.7 . . . attach the slide hammer to the bearing puller

this method is attempted, first prepare a work surface which will enable the casing to be tapped face down to help dislodge the bearing - a wood surface is ideal since it will not damage the casing's gasket surface. Wearing protective gloves, tap the heated casing several times against the work surface to dislodge the bearing under its own weight **(see illustration 5.8)**.

5.8 Tapping a casing face down on wood blocks can often dislodge a bearing

● Bearings can be installed in blind holes using the driver or socket method described above.

Drawbolts

● Where a bearing or bushing is set in the eye of a component, such as a suspension linkage arm or connecting rod small-end, removal by drift may damage the component. Furthermore, a rubber bushing in a shock absorber eye cannot successfully be driven out of position. If access is available to a hydraulic press, the task is straightforward. If not, a drawbolt can be fabricated to extract the bearing or bushing.

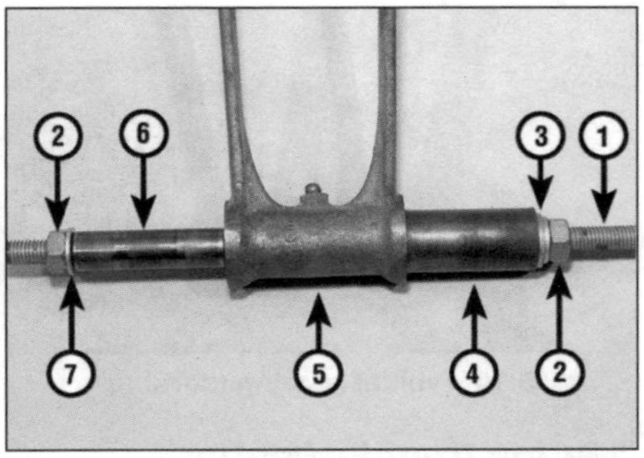

5.9 Drawbolt component parts assembled on a suspension arm

1 *Bolt or length of threaded bar*
2 *Nuts*
3 *Washer (external diameter greater than tubing internal diameter)*
4 *Tubing (internal diameter sufficient to accommodate bearing)*
5 *Suspension arm with bearing*
6 *Tubing (external diameter slightly smaller than bearing)*
7 *Washer (external diameter slightly smaller than bearing)*

5.10 Drawing the bearing out of the suspension arm

● To extract the bearing/bushing you will need a long bolt with nut (or piece of threaded bar with two nuts), a piece of tubing which has an internal diameter larger than the bearing/bushing, another piece of tubing which has an external diameter slightly smaller than the bearing/bushing, and a selection of washers **(see illustrations 5.9 and 5.10)**. Note that the pieces of tubing must be of the same length, or longer, than the bearing/bushing.

● The same kit (without the pieces of tubing) can be used to draw the new bearing/bushing back into place **(see illustration 5.11)**.

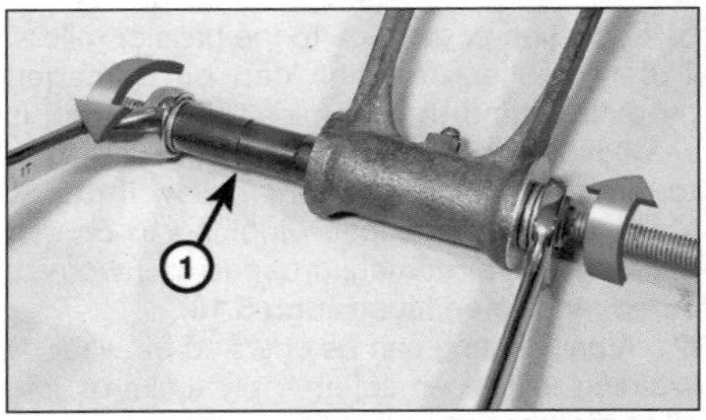

5.11 Installing a new bearing (1) in the suspension arm

Temperature change

● If the bearing's outer race is a tight fit in the casing, the aluminum casing can be heated to release its grip on the bearing. Aluminum will expand at a greater rate than the steel bearing outer race. There are several ways to do this, but avoid any localized extreme heat (such as a blow torch) - aluminum alloy has a low melting point.

● Approved methods of heating a casing are using a domestic oven (heated to 100°C/200°F) or immersing the casing in boiling water **(see illustration 5.12)**. Low temperature range localized heat sources such as a paint stripper heat gun or clothes iron can also be used **(see illustration 5.13)**. Alternatively, soak a rag in boiling water, wring it out and wrap it around the bearing housing.

Warning: All of these methods require care in use to prevent scalding and burns to the hands. Wear protective gloves when handling hot components.

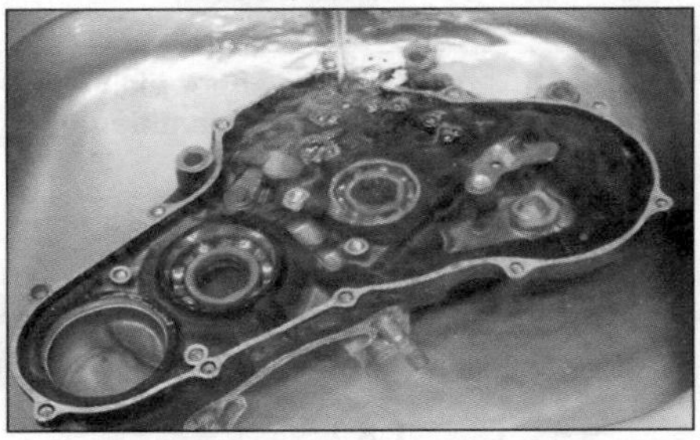

5.12 A casing can be immersed in a sink of boiling water to aid bearing removal

5.13 Using a localized heat source to aid bearing removal

● If heating the whole casing note that plastic components, such as the neutral switch, may suffer - remove them beforehand.

● After heating, remove the bearing as described above. You may find that the expansion is sufficient for the bearing to fall out of the casing under its own weight or with a light tap on the driver or socket.

● If necessary, the casing can be heated to aid bearing installation, and this is sometimes the recommended procedure if the motorcycle manufacturer has designed the housing and bearing fit with this intention.

● Installation of bearings can be eased by placing them in a freezer the night before installation. The steel bearing will contract slightly, allowing easy insertion in its housing. This is often useful when installing steering head outer races in the frame.

Bearing types and markings

● Plain shell bearings, ball bearings, needle roller bearings and tapered roller bearings will all be found on motorcycles **(see illustrations 5.14 and 5.15)**. The ball and roller types are usually caged between an inner and outer race, but uncaged variations may be found.

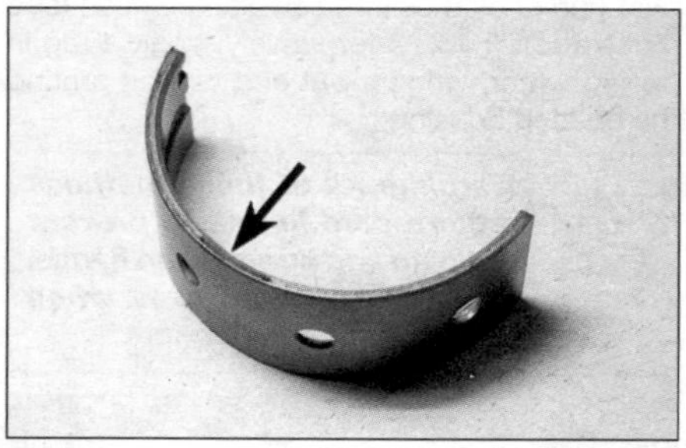

5.14 Shell bearings are either plain or grooved. They are usually identified by color code (arrow)

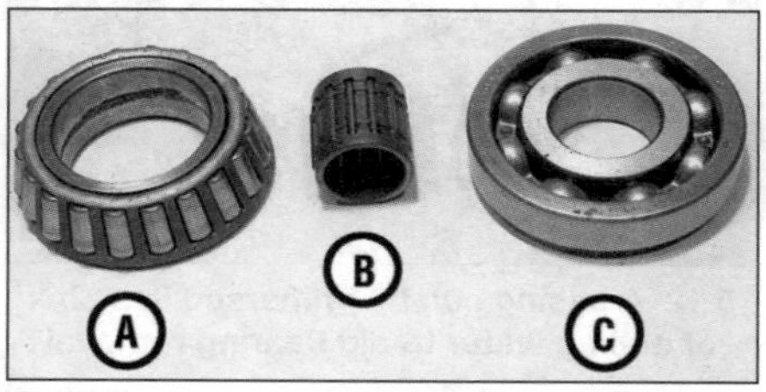

5.15 Tapered roller bearing (A), needle roller bearing (B) and ball journal bearing (C)

● Shell bearings (often called inserts) are usually found at the crankshaft main and connecting rod big-end where they are good at coping with high loads. They are made of a phosphor-bronze material and are impregnated with self-lubricating properties.

● Ball bearings and needle roller bearings consist of a steel inner and outer race with the balls or rollers between the races. They require constant lubrication by oil or grease and are good at coping with axial loads. Taper roller bearings consist of rollers set in a tapered cage set on the inner race; the outer race is separate. They are good at coping with axial loads and prevent movement along the shaft - a typical application is in the steering head.

● Bearing manufacturers produce bearings to ISO size standards and stamp one face of the bearing to indicate its internal and external diameter, load capacity and type **(see illustration 5.16)**.

● Metal bushings are usually of phosphor-bronze material. Rubber bushings are used in suspension mounting eyes. Fiber bushings have also been used in suspension pivots.

5.16 Typical bearing marking

Bearing troubleshooting

● If a bearing outer race has spun in its housing, the housing material will be damaged. You can use a bearing locking compound to bond the outer race in place if damage is not too severe.

● Shell bearings will fail due to damage of their working surface, as a result of lack of lubrication, corrosion or abrasive particles in the oil **(see illustration 5.17)**. Small particles of dirt in the oil may embed in the bearing material whereas larger particles will score the bearing and shaft journal. If a number of short journeys are made, insufficient heat will be generated to drive off condensation which has built up on the bearings.

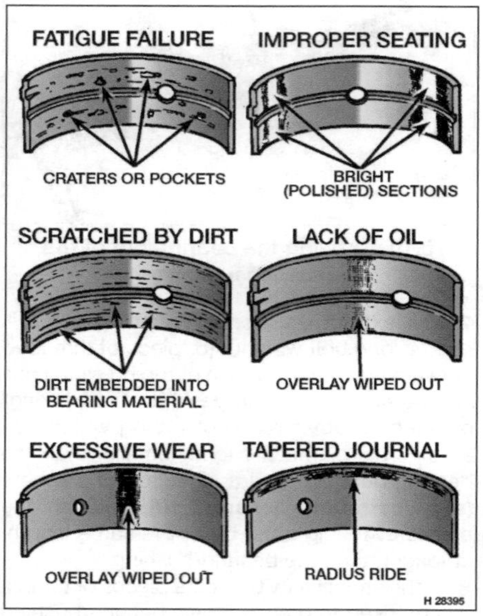

5.17 Typical bearing failures

● Ball and roller bearings will fail due to lack of lubrication or damage to the balls or rollers. Tapered-roller bearings can be damaged by overloading them. Unless the bearing is sealed on both sides, wash it in kerosene to remove all old grease then allow it to dry. Make a visual inspection looking to dented balls or rollers, damaged cages and worn or pitted races **(see illustration 5.18)**.

● A ball bearing can be checked for wear by listening to it when spun. Apply a film of light oil to the bearing and hold it close to the ear - hold the outer race with one hand and spin the inner race with the other hand **(see illustration 5.19)**. The bearing should be almost silent when spun; if it grates or rattles it is worn.

5.18 Example of ball journal bearing with damaged balls and cages

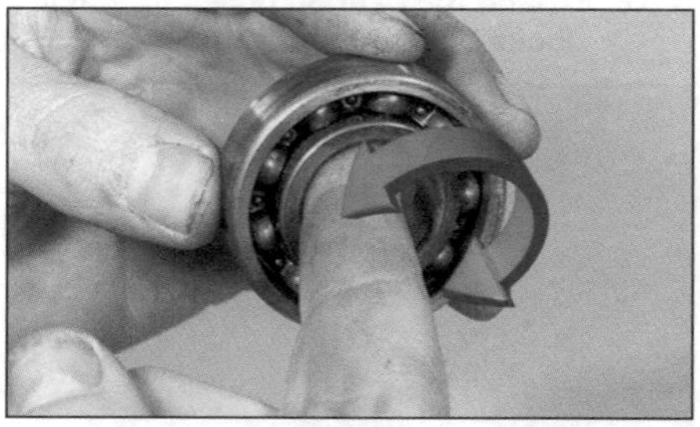

5.19 Hold outer race and listen to inner race when spun

6 Oil seals

Oil seal removal and installation

● Oil seals should be replaced every time a component is dismantled. This is because the seal lips will become set to the sealing surface and will not necessarily reseal.

● Oil seals can be pried out of position using a large flat-bladed screwdriver **(see illustration 6.1)**. In the case of crankcase seals, check first that the seal is not lipped on the inside, preventing its removal with the crankcases joined.

6.1 Pry out oil seals with a large flat-bladed screwdriver

● New seals are usually installed with their marked face (containing the seal reference code) outwards and the spring side towards the fluid being retained. In certain cases, such as a two-stroke engine crankshaft seal, a double lipped seal may be used due to there being fluid or gas on each side of the joint.

● Use a bearing driver or socket which bears only on the outer hard edge of the seal to install it in the casing - tapping on the inner edge will damage the sealing lip.

Oil seal types and markings

● Oil seals are usually of the single-lipped type. Double-lipped seals are found where a liquid or gas is on both sides of the joint.

● Oil seals can harden and lose their sealing ability if the motorcycle has been in storage for a long period - replacement is the only solution.

● Oil seal manufacturers also conform to the ISO markings for seal size - these are molded into the outer face of the seal **(see illustration 6.2)**.

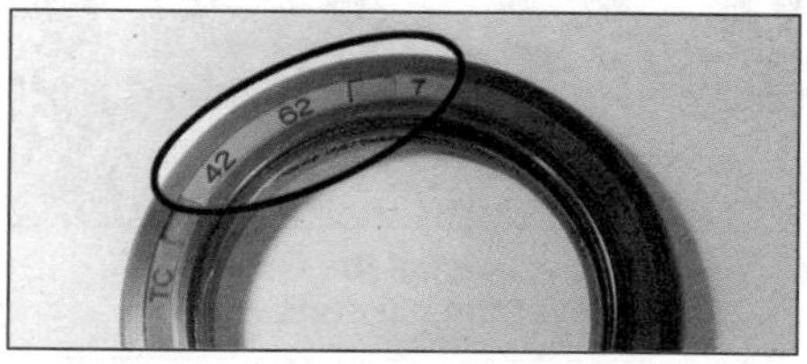

6.2 These oil seal markings indicate inside diameter, outside diameter and seal thickness

7 Gaskets and sealants

Types of gasket and sealant

● Gaskets are used to seal the mating surfaces between components and keep lubricants, fluids, vacuum or pressure contained within the assembly. Aluminum gaskets are sometimes found at the cylinder joints, but most gaskets are paper-based. If the mating surfaces of the components being joined are undamaged the gasket can be installed dry, although a dab of sealant or grease will be useful to hold it in place during assembly.

● RTV (Room Temperature Vulcanizing) silicone rubber sealants cure when exposed to moisture in the atmosphere. These sealants are good at filling pits or irregular gasket faces, but will tend to be forced out of the joint under very high torque. They can be used to replace a paper gasket, but first make sure that the width of the paper gasket is not essential to the shimming of internal components. RTV sealants should not be used on components containing gasoline.

● Non-hardening, semi-hardening and hard setting liquid gasket compounds can be used with a gasket or between a metal-to-metal joint. Select the sealant to suit the application: universal non-hardening sealant can be used on virtually all joints; semi-hardening on joint faces which are rough or damaged; hard setting sealant on joints which require a permanent bond and are subjected to high temperature and pressure. **Note:** *Check first if the paper gasket has a bead of sealant impregnated in its surface before applying additional sealant.*

● When choosing a sealant, make sure it is suitable for the application, particularly if being applied in a high-temperature area or in the vicinity of fuel. Certain manufacturers produce sealants in either clear, silver or black colors to match the finish of the engine. This has a particular application on motorcycles where much of the engine is exposed.

● Do not over-apply sealant. That which is squeezed out on the outside of the joint can be wiped off, whereas an excess of sealant on the inside can break off and clog oilways.

Breaking a sealed joint

● Age, heat, pressure and the use of hard setting sealant can cause two components to stick together so tightly that they are difficult to separate using finger pressure alone. Do not resort to using levers unless there is a pry point provided for this purpose **(see illustration 7.1)** or else the gasket surfaces will be damaged.

● Use a soft-faced hammer **(see illustration 7.2)** or a wood block and conventional hammer to strike the component near the mating surface. Avoid hammering against cast extremities since they may break off. If this method fails, try using a wood wedge between the two components.

Caution: If the joint will not separate, double-check that you have removed all the fasteners.

7.1 If a pry point is provided, apply gentle pressure with a flat-bladed screwdriver

7.2 Tap around the joint with a soft-faced mallet if necessary - don't strike cooling fins

Removal of old gasket and sealant

● Paper gaskets will most likely come away complete, leaving only a few traces stuck on the sealing faces of the components. It is imperative that all traces are removed to ensure correct sealing of the new gasket.

● Very carefully scrape all traces of gasket away making sure that the sealing surfaces are not gouged or scored by the scraper **(see illustrations 7.3, 7.4 and 7.5)**. Stubborn deposits can be removed by spraying with an aerosol gasket remover. Final preparation of

Most components have one or two hollow locating dowels between the two gasket faces. If a dowel cannot be removed, do not resort to gripping it with pliers - it will almost certainly be distorted. Install a close-fitting socket or Phillips screwdriver into the dowel and then grip the outer edge of the dowel to free it.

7.3 Paper gaskets can be scraped off with a gasket scraper tool . . .

7.4 . . . a knife blade . . .

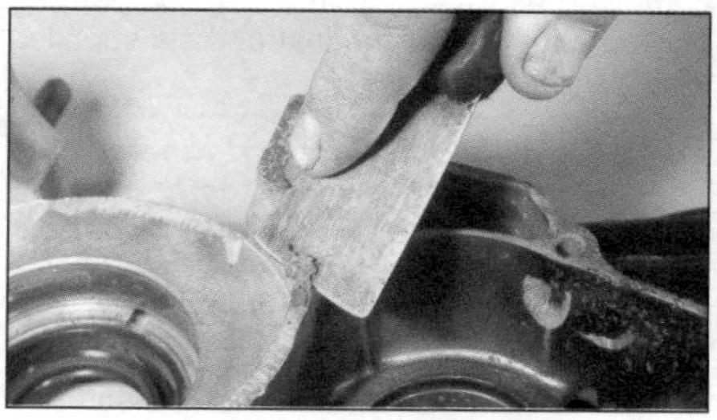

7.5 . . . or a household scraper

7.6 Fine abrasive paper is wrapped around a flat file to clean up the gasket face

7.7 A kitchen scourer can be used on stubborn deposits

the gasket surface can be made with very fine abrasive paper or a plastic kitchen scourer **(see illustrations 7.6 and 7.7)**.

● Old sealant can be scraped or peeled off components, depending on the type originally used. Note that gasket removal compounds are available to avoid scraping the components clean; make sure the gasket remover suits the type of sealant used.

8 Chains

Breaking and joining final drive chains

● Drive chains for all but small bikes are continuous and do not have a clip-type connecting link. The chain must be broken using a chain breaker tool and the new chain securely riveted together using a new soft rivet-type link. Never use a clip-type connecting link instead of a rivet-type link, except in an emergency. Various chain breaking and riveting tools are available, either as separate tools or combined as illustrated in the accompanying photographs - read the instructions supplied with the tool carefully.

Warning: The need to rivet the new link pins correctly cannot be overstressed - loss of control of the motorcycle is very likely to result if the chain breaks in use.

● Rotate the chain and look for the soft link. The soft link pins look like they have been deeply center-punched instead of peened over like all the other pins **(see illustration 8.9)** and its sideplate may be a different color. Position the soft link midway between the sprockets and assemble the chain breaker tool over one of the soft link pins **(see illustration 8.1)**. Operate the tool to push the pin out through the chain **(see illustration 8.2)**. On an O-ring chain, remove the O-rings **(see illustration 8.3)**. Carry out the same procedure on the other soft link pin.

8.1 Tighten the chain breaker to push the pin out of the link . . .

8.2 . . . withdraw the pin, remove the tool . . .

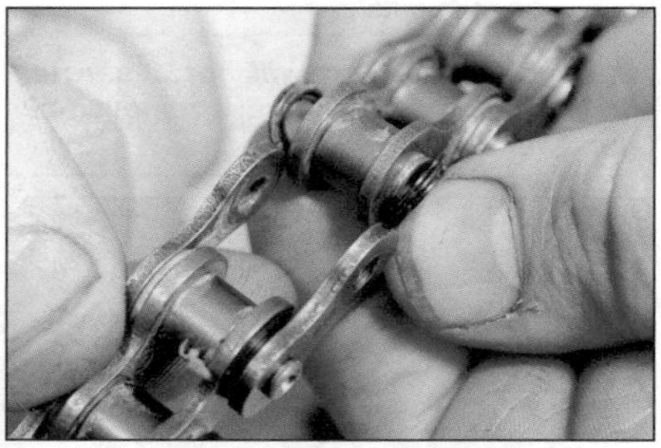

8.3 . . . and separate the chain link

Caution: Certain soft link pins (particularly on the larger chains) may require their ends to be filed or ground off before they can be pressed out using the tool.

● Check that you have the correct size and strength (standard or heavy duty) new soft link - do not reuse the old link. Look for the size marking on the chain sideplates **(see illustration 8.10)**.

● Position the chain ends so that they are engaged over the rear sprocket. On an O-ring chain, install a new O-ring over each pin of the link and insert the link through the two chain ends **(see illustration 8.4)**. Install a new O-ring over the end of each pin, followed by the sideplate (with the chain manufacturer's marking facing outwards) **(see illustrations 8.5 and 8.6)**. On an unsealed chain, insert the link through the two chain ends, then install the sideplate with the chain manufacturer's marking facing outwards.

● Note that it may not be possible to install the sideplate using finger pressure alone. If using a joining tool, assemble it so that the plates of the tool clamp the link and press the sideplate over the pins **(see illustration 8.7)**. Otherwise, use two small sockets placed over

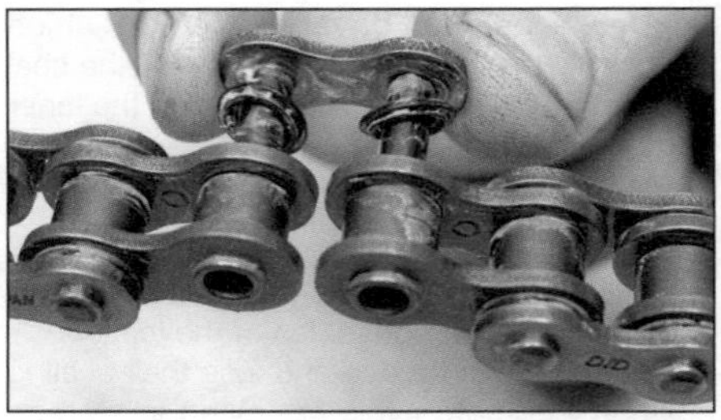

8.4 Insert the new soft link, with O-rings, through the chain ends . . .

8.5 . . . install the O-rings over the pin ends . . .

8.6 . . . followed by the sideplate

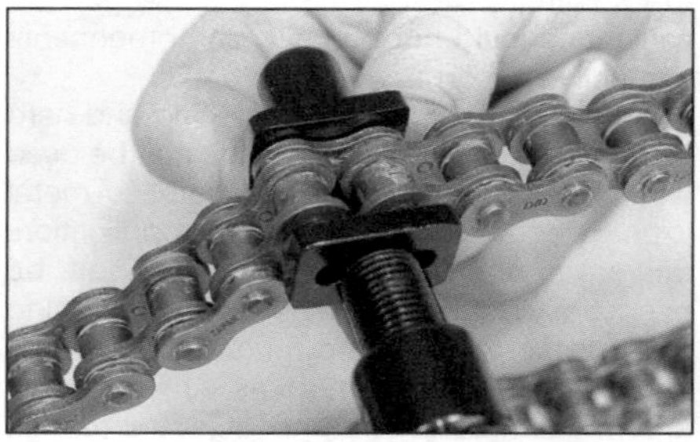

8.7 Push the sideplate into position using a clamp

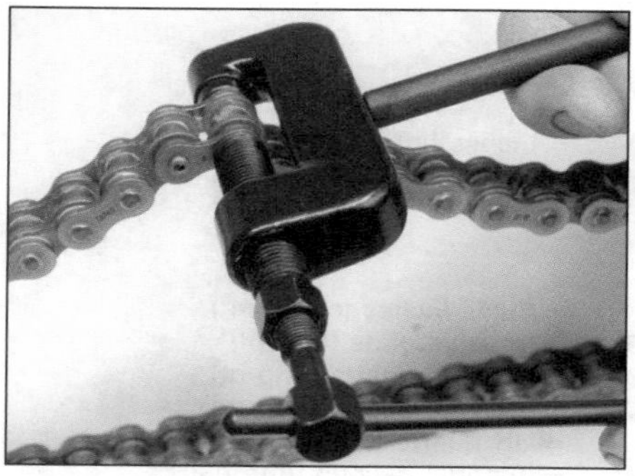

8.8 Assemble the chain riveting tool over one pin at a time and tighten it fully

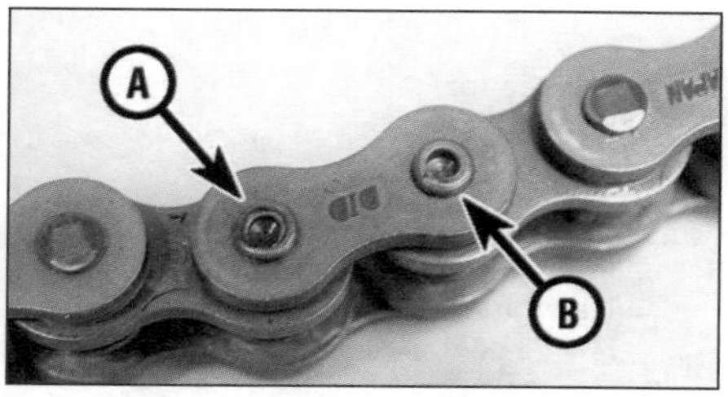

8.9 Pin end correctly riveted (A), pin end unriveted (B)

the rivet ends and two pieces of the wood between a C-clamp. Operate the clamp to press the sideplate over the pins.

● Assemble the joining tool over one pin (following the manufacturer's instructions) and tighten the tool down to spread the pin end securely **(see illustrations 8.8 and 8.9)**. Do the same on the other pin.

> ***Warning: Check that the pin ends are secure and that there is no danger of the sideplate coming loose. If the pin ends are cracked the soft link must be replaced.***

Final drive chain sizing

● Chains are sized using a three digit number, followed by a suffix to denote the chain type **(see illustration 8.10)**. Chain type is either standard or heavy duty (thicker sideplates), and also unsealed or O-ring/X-ring type.

● The first digit of the number relates to the pitch of the chain, ie the distance from the center of one pin to the center of the next pin **(see illustration 8.11)**. Pitch is expressed in eighths of an inch, as follows:

8.10 Typical chain size and type marking

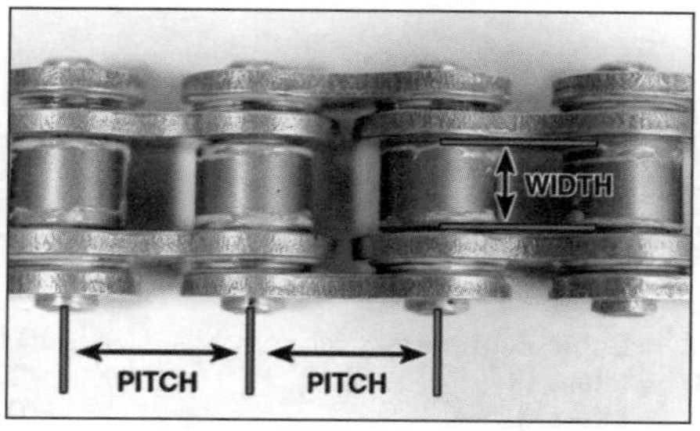

8.11 Chain dimensions

> Sizes commencing with a 4 (for example 428) have a pitch of 1/2 inch (12.7 mm)
>
> Sizes commencing with a 5 (for example 520) have a pitch of 5/8 inch (15.9 mm)
>
> Sizes commencing with a 6 (for example 630) have a pitch of 3/4 inch (19.1 mm)

● The second and third digits of the chain size relate to the width of the rollers, for example the 525 shown has 5/16 inch (7.94 mm) rollers **(see illustration 8.11)**.

9 Hoses

Clamping to prevent flow

● Small-bore flexible hoses can be clamped to prevent fluid flow while a component is worked on. Whichever method is used, ensure that the hose material is not permanently distorted or damaged by the clamp.

a) A brake hose clamp available from auto parts stores **(see illustration 9.1)**.

b) A wingnut type hose clamp **(see illustration 9.2)**.

c) Two sockets placed on each side of the hose and held with straight-jawed self-locking pliers **(see illustration 9.3)**.

d) Thick card stock on each side of the hose held between straight-jawed self-locking pliers **(see illustration 9.4)**.

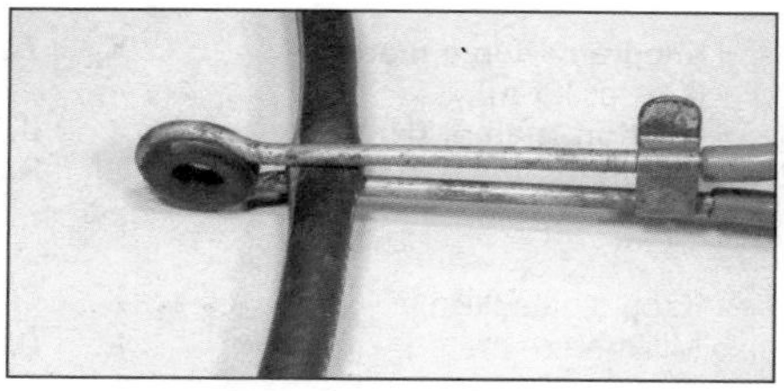

9.1 Hoses can be clamped with an automotive brake hose clamp . . .

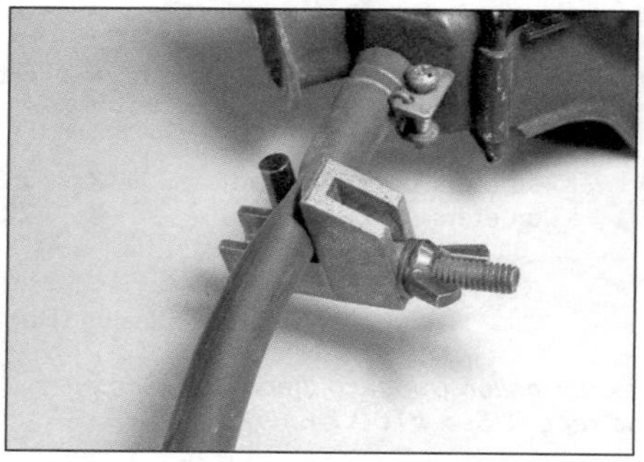

9.2 . . . a wingnut type hose clamp . . .

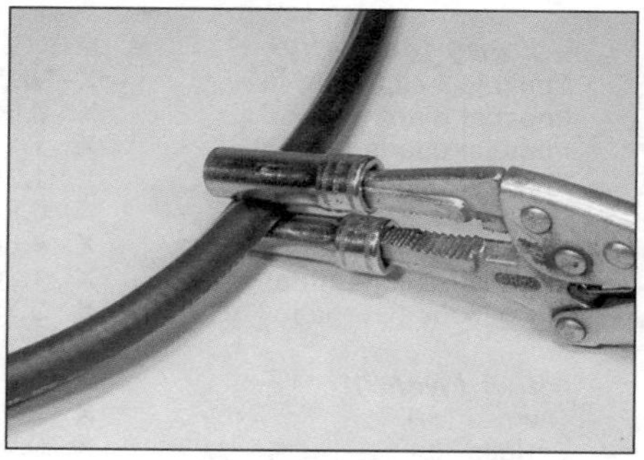

9.3 . . . two sockets and a pair of self-locking grips . . .

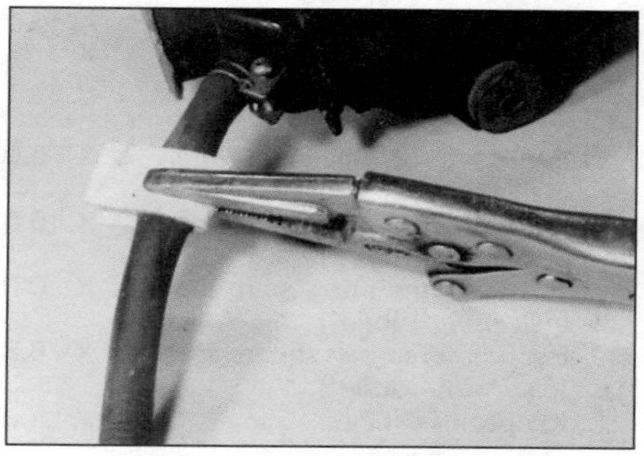

9.4 . . . or thick card and self-locking grips

Freeing and fitting hoses

● Always make sure the hose clamp is moved well clear of the hose end. Grip the hose with your hand and rotate it while pulling it off the union. If the hose has hardened due to age and will not move, slit it with a sharp knife and peel its ends off the union **(see illustration 9.5)**.

● Resist the temptation to use grease or soap on the unions to aid installation; although it helps the hose slip over the union it will equally aid the escape of fluid from the joint. It is preferable to soften the hose ends in hot water and wet the inside surface of the hose with water or a fluid which will evaporate.

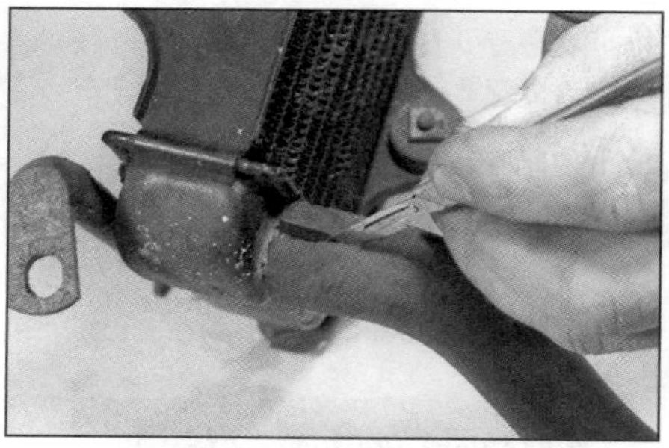

9.5 Cutting a coolant hose free with a sharp knife

Conversion Factors

Length (distance)

Inches (in)	X 25.4	= Millimeters (mm)	X 0.0394	= Inches (in)
Feet (ft)	X 0.305	= Meters (m)	X 3.281	= Feet (ft)
Miles	X 1.609	= Kilometers (km)	X 0.621	= Miles

Volume (capacity)

Cubic inches (cu in; in^3)	X 16.387	= Cubic centimeters (cc; cm^3)	X 0.061	= Cubic inches (cu in; in^3)
Imperial pints (Imp pt)	X 0.568	= Liters (l)	X 1.76	= Imperial pints (Imp pt)
Imperial quarts (Imp qt)	X 1.137	= Liters (l)	X 0.88	= Imperial quarts (Imp qt)
Imperial quarts (Imp qt)	X 1.201	= US quarts (US qt)	X 0.833	= Imperial quarts (Imp qt)
US quarts (US qt)	X 0.946	= Liters (l)	X 1.057	= US quarts (US qt)
Imperial gallons (Imp gal)	X 4.546	= Liters (l)	X 0.22	= Imperial gallons (Imp gal)
Imperial gallons (Imp gal)	X 1.201	= US gallons (US gal)	X 0.833	= Imperial gallons (Imp gal)
US gallons (US gal)	X 3.785	= Liters (l)	X 0.264	= US gallons (US gal)

Mass (weight)

Ounces (oz)	X 28.35	= Grams (g)	X 0.035	= Ounces (oz)
Pounds (lb)	X 0.454	= Kilograms (kg)	X 2.205	= Pounds (lb)

Force

Ounces-force (ozf; oz)	X 0.278	= Newtons (N)	X 3.6	= Ounces-force (ozf; oz)
Pounds-force (lbf; lb)	X 4.448	= Newtons (N)	X 0.225	= Pounds-force (lbf; lb)
Newtons (N)	X 0.1	= Kilograms-force (kgf; kg)	X 9.81	= Newtons (N)

Pressure

Pounds-force per square inch (psi; lbf/in^2; lb/in^2)	X 0.070	= Kilograms-force per square centimeter (kgf/cm^2; kg/cm^2)	X 14.223	= Pounds-force per square inch (psi; lbf/in^2; lb/in^2)
Pounds-force per square inch (psi; lbf/in^2; lb/in^2)	X 0.068	= Atmospheres (atm)	X 14.696	= Pounds-force per square inch (psi; lbf/in^2; lb/in^2)
Pounds-force per square inch (psi; lbf/in^2; lb/in^2)	X 0.069	= Bars	X 14.5	= Pounds-force per square inch (psi; lbf/in^2; lb/in^2)
Pounds-force per square inch (psi; lbf/in^2; lb/in^2)	X 6.895	= Kilopascals (kPa)	X 0.145	= Pounds-force per square inch (psi; lbf/in^2; lb/in^2)
Kilopascals (kPa)	X 0.01	= Kilograms-force per square centimeter (kgf/cm^2; kg/cm^2)	X 98.1	= Kilopascals (kPa)

Torque (moment of force)

Pounds-force inches (lbf in; lb in)	X 1.152	= Kilograms-force centimeter (kgf cm; kg cm)	X 0.868	= Pounds-force inches (lbf in; lb in)
Pounds-force inches (lbf in; lb in)	X 0.113	= Newton meters (Nm)	X 8.85	= Pounds-force inches (lbf in; lb in)
Pounds-force inches (lbf in; lb in)	X 0.083	= Pounds-force feet (lbf ft; lb ft)	X 12	= Pounds-force inches (lbf in; lb in)
Pounds-force feet (lbf ft; lb ft)	X 0.138	= Kilograms-force meters (kgf m; kg m)	X 7.233	= Pounds-force feet (lbf ft; lb ft)
Pounds-force feet (lbf ft; lb ft)	X 1.356	= Newton meters (Nm)	X 0.738	= Pounds-force feet (lbf ft; lb ft)
Newton meters (Nm)	X 0.102	= Kilograms-force meters (kgf m; kg m)	X 9.804	= Newton meters (Nm)

Vacuum

Inches mercury (in. Hg)	X 3.377	= Kilopascals (kPa)	X 0.2961	= Inches mercury
Inches mercury (in. Hg)	X 25.4	= Millimeters mercury (mm Hg)	X 0.0394	= Inches mercury

Power

Horsepower (hp)	X 745.7	= Watts (W)	X 0.0013	= Horsepower (hp)

Velocity (speed)

Miles per hour (miles/hr; mph)	X 1.609	= Kilometers per hour (km/hr; kph)	X 0.621	= Miles per hour (miles/hr; mph)

*Fuel consumption**

Miles per gallon, Imperial (mpg)	X 0.354	= Kilometers per liter (km/l)	X 2.825	= Miles per gallon, Imperial (mpg)
Miles per gallon, US (mpg)	X 0.425	= Kilometers per liter (km/l)	X 2.352	= Miles per gallon, US (mpg)

Temperature

Degrees Fahrenheit = (°C x 1.8) + 32

Degrees Celsius (Degrees Centigrade; °C) = (°F - 32) x 0.56

**It is common practice to convert from miles per gallon (mpg) to liters/100 kilometers (l/100km), where mpg (Imperial) x l/100 km = 282 and mpg (US) x l/100 km = 235*

DECIMALS to MILLIMETERS

Decimal	mm	Decimal	mm
0.001	0.0254	0.500	12.7000
0.002	0.0508	0.510	12.9540
0.003	0.0762	0.520	13.2080
0.004	0.1016	0.530	13.4620
0.005	0.1270	0.540	13.7160
0.006	0.1524	0.550	13.9700
0.007	0.1778	0.560	14.2240
0.008	0.2032	0.570	14.4780
0.009	0.2286	0.580	14.7320
0.010	0.2540	0.590	14.9860
0.020	0.5080	0.600	15.2400
0.030	0.7620	0.610	15.4940
0.040	1.0160	0.620	15.7480
0.050	1.2700	0.630	16.0020
0.060	1.5240	0.640	16.2560
0.070	1.7780	0.650	16.5100
0.080	2.0320	0.660	16.7640
0.090	2.2860	0.670	17.0180
0.100	2.5400	0.680	17.2720
0.110	2.7940	0.690	17.5260
0.120	3.0480	0.700	17.7800
0.130	3.3020	0.710	18.0340
0.140	3.5560	0.720	18.2880
0.150	3.8100	0.730	18.5420
0.160	4.0640	0.740	18.7960
0.170	4.3180	0.750	19.0500
0.180	4.5720	0.760	19.3040
0.190	4.8260	0.770	19.5580
0.200	5.0800	0.780	19.8120
0.210	5.3340	0.790	20.0660
0.220	5.5880	0.800	20.3200
0.230	5.8420	0.810	20.5740
0.240	6.0960	0.820	21.8280
0.250	6.3500	0.830	21.0820
0.260	6.6040	0.840	21.3360
0.270	6.8580	0.850	21.5900
0.280	7.1120	0.860	21.8440
0.290	7.3660	0.870	22.0980
0.300	7.6200	0.880	22.3520
0.310	7.8740	0.890	22.6060
0.320	8.1280	0.900	22.8600
0.330	8.3820	0.910	23.1140
0.340	8.6360	0.920	23.3680
0.350	8.8900	0.930	23.6220
0.360	9.1440	0.940	23.8760
0.370	9.3980	0.950	24.1300
0.380	9.6520	0.960	24.3840
0.390	9.9060	0.970	24.6380
0.400	10.1600	0.980	24.8920
0.410	10.4140	0.990	25.1460
0.420	10.6680	1.000	25.4000
0.430	10.9220		
0.440	11.1760		
0.450	11.4300		
0.460	11.6840		
0.470	11.9380		
0.480	12.1920		
0.490	12.4460		

FRACTIONS to DECIMALS to MILLIMETERS

Fraction	Decimal	mm	Fraction	Decimal	mm
1/64	0.0156	0.3969	33/64	0.5156	13.0969
1/32	0.0312	0.7938	17/32	0.5312	13.4938
3/64	0.0469	1.1906	35/64	0.5469	13.8906
1/16	0.0625	1.5875	9/16	0.5625	14.2875
5/64	0.0781	1.9844	37/64	0.5781	14.6844
3/32	0.0938	2.3812	19/32	0.5938	15.0812
7/64	0.1094	2.7781	39/64	0.6094	15.4781
1/8	0.1250	3.1750	5/8	0.6250	15.8750
9/64	0.1406	3.5719	41/64	0.6406	16.2719
5/32	0.1562	3.9688	21/32	0.6562	16.6688
11/64	0.1719	4.3656	43/64	0.6719	17.0656
3/16	0.1875	4.7625	11/16	0.6875	17.4625
13/64	0.2031	5.1594	45/64	0.7031	17.8594
7/32	0.2188	5.5562	23/32	0.7188	18.2562
15/64	0.2344	5.9531	47/64	0.7344	18.6531
1/4	0.2500	6.3500	3/4	0.7500	19.0500
17/64	0.2656	6.7469	49/64	0.7656	19.4469
9/32	0.2812	7.1438	25/32	0.7812	19.8438
19/64	0.2969	7.5406	51/64	0.7969	20.2406
5/16	0.3125	7.9375	13/16	0.8125	20.6375
21/64	0.3281	8.3344	53/64	0.8281	21.0344
11/32	0.3438	8.7312	27/32	0.8438	21.4312
23/64	0.3594	9.1281	55/64	0.8594	21.8281
3/8	0.3750	9.5250	7/8	0.8750	22.2250
25/64	0.3906	9.9219	57/64	0.8906	22.6219
13/32	0.4062	10.3188	29/32	0.9062	23.0188
27/64	0.4219	10.7156	59/64	0.9219	23.4156
7/16	0.4375	11.1125	15/16	0.9375	23.8125
29/64	0.4531	11.5094	61/64	0.9531	24.2094
15/32	0.4688	11.9062	31/32	0.9688	24.6062
31/64	0.4844	12.3031	63/64	0.9844	25.0031
1/2	0.5000	12.7000	1	1.0000	25.4000

Preparing for storage

Before you start

If repairs or an overhaul is needed, see that this is carried out now rather than left until you want to ride the vehicle again.

Give the vehicle a good wash and scrub all dirt from its underside. Make sure the vehicle dries completely before preparing for storage.

Engine

● Remove the spark plug and lubricate the cylinder bore with approximately a teaspoon of motor oil using a spout-type oil can **(see illustration 1)**. Reinstall the spark plug. Crank the engine over a couple of times to coat the piston rings and bores with oil. If the machine has a recoil starter, use this to turn the engine over. If not, flick the kill switch to the OFF position and crank the engine over on the starter **(see illustration 2)**. If the nature of the ignition system prevents the starter operating with the kill switch in the OFF position, remove the spark plug and fit it back in its cap; ensure that the plug is grounded against the cylinder head when the starter is operated **(see illustration 3)**.

> ***Warning: It is important that the plug is grounded away from the spark plug hole otherwise there is a risk of atomized fuel from the cylinder igniting.***

> **HAYNES HiNT** ***On a single cylinder four-stroke engine, you can seal the combustion chamber completely by positioning the piston at TDC on the compression stroke.***

● Drain the carburetor otherwise there is a risk of jets becoming blocked by gum deposits from the fuel **(see illustration 4)**.

● If the machine is going into long-term storage, consider adding a fuel stabilizer to the fuel in the tank. If the tank is drained completely, and it's a metal tank, corrosion of its internal surfaces may occur if left unprotected for a long period. The tank can be treated with a rust preventative especially for this purpose. Alternatively, remove the tank and pour half a liter of motor oil into it, install the filler cap and shake the tank to coat its internals with oil before draining off the excess. The same effect can also be achieved by spraying WD40 or a similar water-dispersant around the inside of the tank via its flexible nozzle.

● Make sure the cooling system contains the correct mix of antifreeze. Antifreeze also contains important corrosion inhibitors.

● The air intakes and exhaust can be sealed off by covering or plugging the openings. Ensure that you do not seal in any condensation; run the engine until it is

1
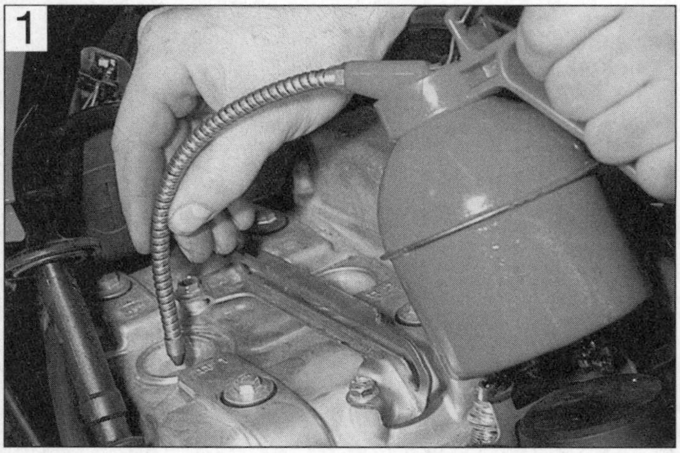

Squirt a drop of motor oil into each cylinder

2
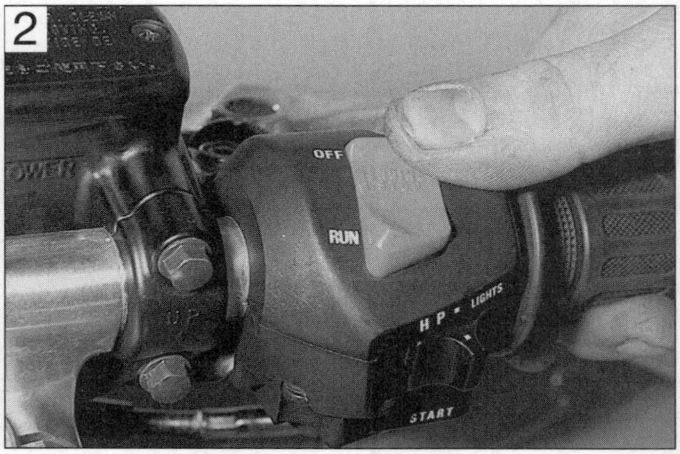

Flick the kill switch to OFF . . .

3
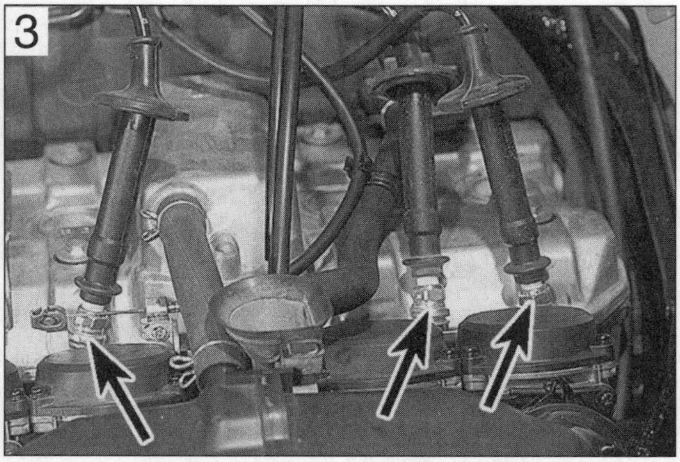

. . . and ensure that the metal bodies of the plugs (arrows) are grounded against the cylinder head

4
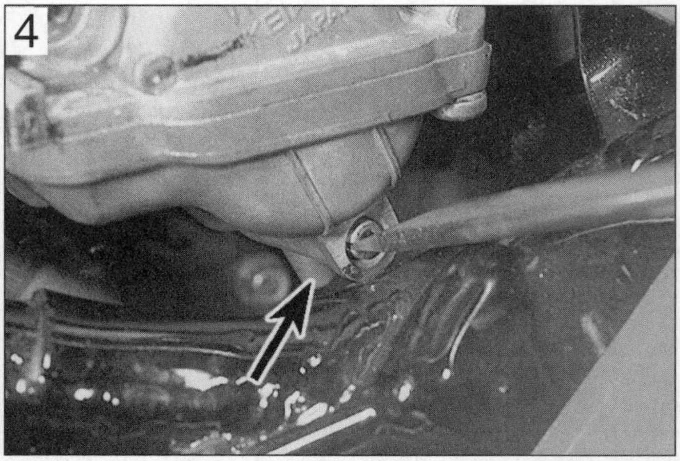

Connect a hose to the carburetor float chamber drain stub (arrow) and unscrew the drain screw

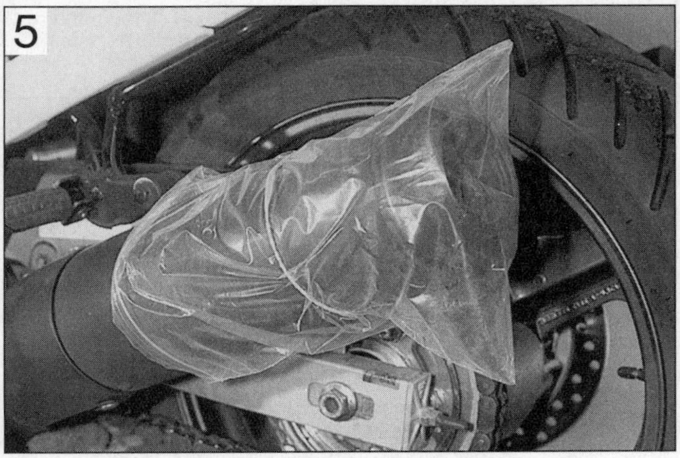

Exhausts can be sealed off with a plastic bag

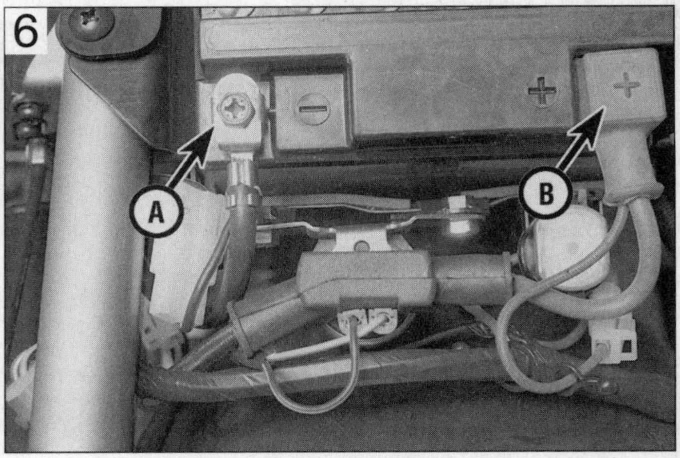

Disconnect the negative lead (A) first, followed by the positive lead (B)

hot, then switch off and allow to cool. Tape a piece of thick plastic over the silencer end **(see illustration 5)**. Note that some advocate pouring a tablespoon of motor oil into the silencer before sealing them off.

Battery

● Remove it from the machine - in extreme cases of cold the battery may freeze and crack its case **(see illustration 6)**.
● Check the electrolyte level and top up if necessary (conventional refillable batteries). Clean the terminals.
● Store the battery off the vehicle and away from any sources of fire. Position a wooden block under the battery if it is to sit on the ground.
● Give the battery a trickle charge for a few hours every month or keep it on a maintenance charger **(see illustration 7)**.

Tires

● Place the machine on jackstands; not only will this protect the tires, but will also ensure that no load is placed on the suspension bushings or wheel bearings.

Pivots and controls

● Lubricate all lever, pedal, stand and footrest pivot points. If grease nipples are fitted to the suspension components, apply lubricant to the pivots.
● Lubricate all control cables.

Other components

● Apply a wax protectant to all painted and plastic components. Wipe off any excess, but don't polish to a shine. Where fitted, clean the screen with soap and water.
● Coat metal parts with Vaseline (petroleum jelly).
● Apply a vinyl cleaner to the seat.

Storage conditions

● Aim to store the machine in a shed or garage which does not leak and is free from damp.

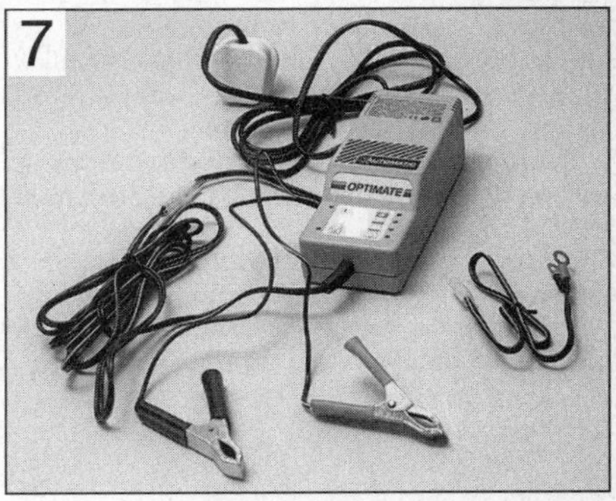

Use a suitable battery charger - this kit also assesses battery condition

● Drape an old blanket or bedspread over the vehicle to protect it from dust and direct contact with sunlight (which will fade paint).

Getting back on the road

Engine and transmission

● Change the oil and replace the oil filter. If this was done prior to storage, check that the oil hasn't emulsified - a thick whitish substance which occurs through condensation.
● Remove the spark plug. Using a spout-type oil can, squirt a few drops of oil into the cylinder. This will provide initial lubrication as the piston rings and bore come back into contact. Service the spark plug, or buy a new one, and install it in the engine.
● Check that the clutch isn't stuck on. The plates can stick together if left standing for some time, preventing clutch operation. Engage a gear and try rocking the machine back and forth with the clutch lever held against the handlebar. If this doesn't work on cable-operated clutches, hold the clutch lever back against the handlebar with a strong rubber band or cable tie for a couple of hours **(see illustration 8)**.
● If the air intakes or silencer end(s) were blocked off, remove the plug or cover used.

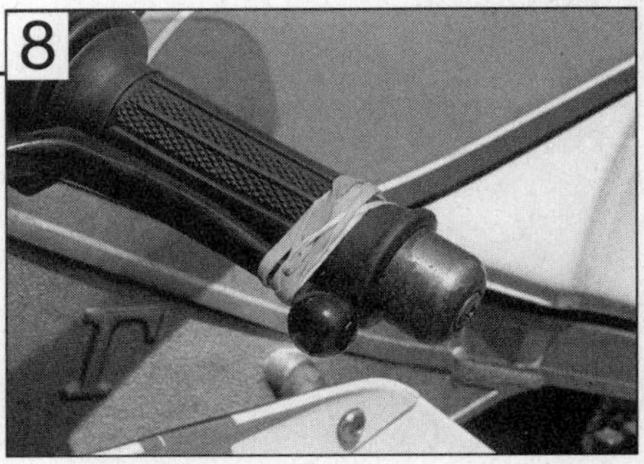

Hold the clutch lever back against the handlebar with rubber bands or a cable tie

● If the fuel tank was coated with a rust preventative, oil or a stabilizer added to the fuel, drain and flush the tank and dispose of the fuel sensibly. If no action was taken with the fuel tank prior to storage, it is advised that the old fuel is disposed of since it will go bad over a period of time. Refill the fuel tank with fresh fuel.

Frame and running gear

● Oil all pivot points and cables.
● Check the tire pressures.
● Lubricate the final drive chain (where applicable).
● Check that the brakes operate correctly. Apply each brake hard and check that it's not possible to move the vehicle forwards, then check that the brake frees off again once released. Brake caliper pistons can stick due to corrosion around the piston head, or on the sliding caliper types, due to corrosion of the slider pins. If the brake doesn't free after repeated operation, take the caliper off for examination. Similarly drum brakes can stick due to a seized operating cam, cable or rod linkage.
● If the vehicle has been in long-term storage, replace the brake fluid and clutch fluid (where applicable).
● Depending on where the vehicle has been stored, the wiring, cables and hoses may have been nibbled by rodents. Make a visual check and investigate disturbed wiring loom tape.

Battery

● If the battery has been previously removed and given top up charges it can simply be reconnected. Remember to connect the positive cable first and the negative cable last.
● On conventional refillable batteries, if the battery has not received any attention, remove it from the vehicle and check its electrolyte level. Top up if necessary then charge the battery. If the battery fails to hold a charge and a visual check show heavy white sulfation of the plates, the battery is probably defective and must be replaced. This is particularly likely if the battery is old. Confirm battery condition with a specific gravity check.
● On sealed (MF) batteries, if the battery has not received any attention, remove it from the machine and charge it according to the information on the battery case - if the battery fails to hold a charge it must be replaced.

Starting procedure

● If a recoil starter is fitted, turn the engine over a couple of times with the ignition OFF to distribute oil around the engine. If no recoil starter is fitted, flick the engine kill switch OFF and the ignition ON and crank the engine over a couple of times to work oil around the upper cylinder components. If the nature of the ignition system is such that the starter won't work with the kill switch OFF, remove the spark plug, fit it back into its cap and ground its body on the cylinder head. Reinstall the spark plug afterwards.

Warning: It is important that the plug is grounded away from the spark plug hole otherwise there is a risk of atomized fuel from the cylinder igniting.

● Switch the kill switch to RUN, operate the choke and start the engine. If the engine won't start don't continue cranking the engine - not only will this flatten the battery, but the starter motor will overheat. Switch the ignition off and try again later. If the engine refuses to start, go through the troubleshooting procedures in this manual. **Note:** *If the machine has been in storage for a long time, old fuel or a carburetor blockage may be the problem. Gum deposits in carburetors can block jets - if a carburetor cleaner doesn't prove successful the carburetors must be dismantled for cleaning.*

● Once the engine has started, check that the lights and horn work properly.

● Treat the machine gently for the first ride and check all fluid levels on completion. Settle the machine back into the maintenance schedule.

This Section provides an easy reference-guide to the more common faults that are likely to afflict your machine. Obviously, the opportunities are almost limitless for faults to occur as a result of obscure failures, and to try and cover all eventualities would require a book. Indeed, a number have been written on the subject.

Successful troubleshooting is not a mysterious art but the application of a bit of knowledge combined with a systematic and logical approach to the problem. Approach any troubleshooting by first accurately identifying the symptom and then checking through the list of possible causes, starting with the simplest or most obvious and progressing in stages to the most complex. Take nothing for granted, but above all apply liberal quantities of common sense.

The main symptom of a fault is given in the text as a major heading below which are listed the various systems or areas which may contain the fault. Details of each possible cause for a fault and the remedial action to be taken are given. Further information should be sought in the relevant Chapter.

1 Engine doesn't start or is difficult to start

Starter motor does not rotate

- ☐ Engine kill switch Off.
- ☐ Fuse blown. Check fuse (Chapter 5).
- ☐ Battery voltage low. Check and recharge battery (Chapter 5).
- ☐ Starter motor defective. Make sure the wiring to the starter is secure. Test starter relay (Chapter 5). If the relay is good, then the fault is in the wiring or motor.
- ☐ Starter relay faulty. Check it according to the procedure in Chapter 5.
- ☐ Starter switch not contacting. The contacts could be wet, corroded or dirty. Disassemble and clean the switch (Chapter 5).
- ☐ Wiring open or shorted. Check all wiring connections and harnesses to make sure that they are dry, tight and not corroded. Also check for broken or frayed wires that can cause a short to ground (see Wiring Diagrams at the end of this manual).
- ☐ Ignition (main) switch defective. Check the switch according to the procedure in Chapter 5. Replace the switch with a new one if it is defective.
- ☐ Engine kill switch defective. Check for wet, dirty or corroded contacts. Clean or replace the switch as necessary (Chapter 5).
- ☐ Starting circuit cut-off relay, neutral relay, neutral switch, reverse switch or front brake switch defective. Check the switches according to the procedure in Chapter 5. Replace the switch with a new one if it is defective.

Starter motor rotates but engine does not turn over

- ☐ Starter motor clutch defective. Inspect and repair or replace (Chapter 5).
- ☐ Damaged starter idle or wheel gears. Inspect and replace the damaged parts (Chapter 5).

Starter works but engine won't turn over (seized)

- ☐ Seized engine caused by one or more internally damaged components. Failure due to wear, abuse or lack of lubrication. Damage can include seized valves, valve lifters, camshaft, piston, crankshaft, connecting rod bearings, or transmission gears or bearings. Refer to Chapter 2 for engine disassembly.

No fuel flow

- ☐ No fuel in tank.
- ☐ Tank cap air vent or breather hose obstructed. Usually caused by dirt or water. Remove it and clean the cap vent hole.
- ☐ Clogged strainer in fuel tap (carbureted models). Remove and clean the strainer (Chapter 1).
- ☐ Fuel line clogged. Disconnect the fuel line and carefully blow through it.
- ☐ Inlet needle valve clogged (carbureted models). A very bad batch of fuel with an unusual additive may have been used, or some other foreign material has entered the tank. Many times after a machine has been stored for many months without running, the fuel turns to a varnish-like liquid and forms deposits on the inlet needle valve and jets. The carburetor should be removed and overhauled if draining the float chamber doesn't solve the problem.
- ☐ Fuel pump or pressure regulator defective or fuel filter clogged (fuel injected models). See Chapter 4B.

Engine flooded

- ☐ Float level too high (carbureted models). Check as described in Chapter 4A and replace the float if necessary.
- ☐ Inlet needle valve worn or stuck open (carbureted models). A piece of dirt, rust or other debris can cause the inlet needle to seat improperly, causing excess fuel to be admitted to the float bowl. In this case, the float chamber should be cleaned and the needle and seat inspected. If the needle and seat are worn, then the leaking will persist and the parts should be replaced with new ones (Chapter 4A).
- ☐ Starting technique incorrect (carbureted models). Under normal circumstances (if all the carburetor functions are sound) the machine should start with little or no throttle. When the engine is cold, the choke should be operated and the engine started without opening the throttle. When the engine is at operating temperature, only a very slight amount of throttle should be necessary. If the engine is flooded, turn the fuel tap off and hold the throttle open while cranking the engine. This will allow additional air to reach the cylinder. Remember to turn the fuel tap back on after the engine starts.
- ☐ Injector needle valve worn or stuck open (fuel injected models). A piece of dirt, rust or other debris can cause the needle to seat improperly, causing excess fuel to be admitted to the throttle body. If the engine is hard to start after sitting overnight, the injector may be slowly leaking fuel into the engine. The injector should be cleaned and the needle and seat inspected (see Chapter 4B). If the needle and seat are worn, the injector should be replaced.
- ☐ Starting technique incorrect (fuel injected models). Under normal circumstances (if all the components of the fuel injection system are good), the engine should start with the throttle closed.

1 Engine doesn't start or is difficult to start (continued)

No spark or weak spark

- ☐ Ignition switch Off.
- ☐ Engine kill switch turned to the Off position.
- ☐ Battery voltage low. Check and recharge battery as necessary (Chapter 5).
- ☐ Spark plug dirty, defective or worn out. Locate reason for fouled plug using spark plug condition chart and follow the plug maintenance procedures in Chapter 1.
- ☐ Spark plug cap or plug wire faulty. Check condition. Replace either or both components if cracks or deterioration are evident (see Chapter 5).
- ☐ Spark plug cap not making good contact. Make sure the cap is securely attached to the plug wire and fits securely over the top of the spark plug.
- ☐ CDI pulse generator (carbureted models) or crankshaft position sensor (fuel injected models) defective. Check the unit, referring to Chapter 5 (carbureted models) or Chapter 4B (fuel injected models).
- ☐ CDI unit (carbureted models) or ECU (fuel injected models) defective. Check the unit, referring to Chapter 5 (carbureted models) or Chapter 4B (fuel injected models).
- ☐ Ignition coil defective. Check the coil, referring to Chapter 5.
- ☐ Main key switch or kill switch shorted. This is usually caused by water, corrosion, damage or excessive wear. The kill switch can be disassembled and cleaned with electric contact cleaner. If cleaning doesn't help, replace the switches (see Chapter 5).
- ☐ Wiring shorted or broken between:
  - *a) Main key switch or engine kill switch*
  - *b) CDI unit (carbureted models) or ECU (fuel injected models) and engine kill switch*
  - *c) CDI unit (carbureted models) or ECU (fuel injected models) and ignition coil*
  - *d) Ignition coil and spark plug*
  - *e) CDI unit and pulse generator (carbureted models) or crankshaft position sensor and ECU (fuel injected models)*

Compression low

- ☐ Spark plug loose. Remove the plug and inspect the threads. Reinstall and tighten to the specified torque (Chapter 1).
- ☐ Cylinder head not sufficiently tightened down. If the cylinder head is suspected of being loose, then there's a chance that the gasket or head is damaged if the problem has persisted for any length of time. The head nuts and bolts should be tightened to the proper torque in the correct sequence (Chapter 2).
- ☐ Improper valve clearance. This means that the valve is not closing completely and compression pressure is leaking past the valve. Check and adjust the valve clearances (Chapter 1).
- ☐ Cylinder and/or piston worn. Excessive wear will cause compression pressure to leak past the rings. This is usually accompanied by worn rings as well. A top end overhaul is necessary (Chapter 2).
- ☐ Piston rings worn, weak, broken, or sticking. Broken or sticking piston rings usually indicate a lubrication or carburetion problem that causes excess carbon deposits or seizures to form on the pistons and rings. Top end overhaul is necessary (Chapter 2).
- ☐ Piston ring-to-groove clearance excessive. This is caused by excessive wear of the piston ring lands. Piston replacement is necessary (Chapter 2).
- ☐ Cylinder head gasket damaged. If the head is allowed to become loose, or if excessive carbon build-up on a piston crown and combustion chamber causes extremely high compression, the head gasket may leak. Retorquing the head is not always sufficient to restore the seal, so gasket replacement is necessary (Chapter 2).
- ☐ Cylinder head warped. This is caused by overheating or improperly tightened head nuts and bolts. Machine shop resurfacing or head replacement is necessary (Chapter 2).
- ☐ Valve spring broken or weak. Caused by component failure or wear; the spring(s) must be replaced (Chapter 2).
- ☐ Valve not seating properly. This is caused by a bent valve (from over-revving or improper valve adjustment), burned valve or seat (improper carburetion) or an accumulation of carbon deposits on the seat (from carburetion or lubrication problems). The valves must be cleaned and/or replaced and the seats serviced if possible (Chapter 2).

Stalls after starting

- ☐ Improper choke action. Make sure the choke knob or lever is getting a full stroke and staying in the out position.
- ☐ Ignition malfunction. See Chapter 5.
- ☐ Carburetor malfunction (carbureted models). See Chapter 4A.
- ☐ Fuel contaminated. The fuel can be contaminated with either dirt or water, or can change chemically if the machine is allowed to sit for several months or more. Drain the tank and float bowl and refill with fresh fuel (Chapter 4).
- ☐ Intake air leak. Check for a loose joint between the carburetor or throttle body and intake manifold. On a carbureted model, check for a loose carburetor top. On a fuel injected model, check the intake air pressure sensor hose for cracks or a loose fit.
- ☐ Engine idle speed incorrect. On carbureted models, refer to Chapter 1 and adjust the idle speed. On fuel injected models, refer to Chapter 4B and check the idle speed control valve.

Rough idle

- ☐ Ignition malfunction. See Chapter 5.
- ☐ Idle speed incorrect. See Chapter 1.
- ☐ Carburetor or fuel injection system malfunction. See Chapter 4.
- ☐ Idle fuel/air mixture incorrect. See Chapter 4.
- ☐ Fuel contaminated. The fuel can be contaminated with either dirt or water, or can change chemically if the machine is allowed to sit for several months or more. Drain the tank and fuel system (Chapter 4).
- ☐ Intake air leak. Check for a loose joint between the carburetor or throttle body and intake manifold. On a carbureted model, check for a loose carburetor top. On a fuel injected model, check the intake air pressure sensor hose for cracks or a loose fit.
- ☐ Air cleaner clogged. Service or replace the air cleaner element (Chapter 1).

2 Poor running at low speed

Spark weak

- ☐ Battery voltage low. Check and recharge battery (Chapter 5).
- ☐ Spark plug fouled, defective or worn out. Refer to Chapter 1 for spark plug maintenance.
- ☐ Spark plug cap or secondary (HT) wiring defective. Refer to Chapters 1 and 5 for details on the ignition system.
- ☐ Spark plug cap not making contact.
- ☐ Incorrect spark plug. Wrong type, heat range or cap configuration. Check and install correct plug listed in Chapter 1. A cold plug or one with a recessed firing electrode will not operate at low speeds without fouling.
- ☐ CDI unit or ECU defective. See Chapter 4A or 5.
- ☐ CDI pulse generator or crankshaft position sensor defective. See Chapter 4A or 5.
- ☐ Ignition coil defective. See Chapter 5.

Fuel/air mixture incorrect

- ☐ Pilot screw out of adjustment (Chapter 4).
- ☐ Pilot jet or air passage clogged (carbureted models). Remove and overhaul the carburetor (Chapter 4).
- ☐ Air bleed holes clogged (carbureted models). Remove carburetor and blow out all passages (Chapter 4).
- ☐ Air cleaner clogged, poorly sealed or missing.
- ☐ Air cleaner-to-carburetor boot poorly sealed (carbureted models). Look for cracks, holes or loose clamps and replace or repair defective parts.
- ☐ Float level too high or too low (carbureted models). Check and replace the float if necessary (Chapter 4).
- ☐ Fuel tank air vent obstructed. Make sure that the air vent passage in the filler cap is open.
- ☐ Carburetor or throttle body intake joint loose. Check for cracks, breaks, tears or loose clamps or bolts. Repair or replace the rubber boot and its O-ring (if equipped).

Compression low

- ☐ Spark plug loose. Remove the plug and inspect the threads. Reinstall and tighten to the specified torque (Chapter 1).
- ☐ Cylinder head not sufficiently tightened down. If the cylinder head is suspected of being loose, then there's a chance that the gasket and head are damaged if the problem has persisted for any length of time. The head nuts and bolts should be tightened to the proper torque in the correct sequence (Chapter 2).
- ☐ Improper valve clearance. This means that the valve is not closing completely and compression pressure is leaking past the valve. Check and adjust the valve clearances (Chapter 1).
- ☐ Cylinder and/or piston worn. Excessive wear will cause compression pressure to leak past the rings. This is usually accompanied by worn rings as well. A top end overhaul is necessary (Chapter 2).
- ☐ Piston rings worn, weak, broken, or sticking. Broken or sticking piston rings usually indicate a lubrication or carburetion problem that causes excess carbon deposits or seizures to form on the pistons and rings. Top end overhaul is necessary (Chapter 2).
- ☐ Piston ring-to-groove clearance excessive. This is caused by excessive wear of the piston ring lands. Piston replacement is necessary (Chapter 2).
- ☐ Cylinder head gasket damaged. If the head is allowed to become loose, or if excessive carbon build-up on the piston crown and combustion chamber causes extremely high compression, the head gasket may leak. Retorquing the head is not always sufficient to restore the seal, so gasket replacement is necessary (Chapter 2).
- ☐ Cylinder head warped. This is caused by overheating or improperly tightened head nuts and bolts. Machine shop resurfacing or head replacement is necessary (Chapter 2).
- ☐ Valve spring broken or weak. Caused by component failure or wear; the spring(s) must be replaced (Chapter 2).
- ☐ Valve not seating properly. This is caused by a bent valve (from over-revving or improper valve adjustment), burned valve or seat (improper carburetion) or an accumulation of carbon deposits on the seat (from carburetion, lubrication problems). The valves must be cleaned and/or replaced and the seats serviced if possible (Chapter 2).

Poor acceleration

- ☐ Carburetor leaking or dirty (carbureted models). Overhaul the carburetor (Chapter 4A).
- ☐ Timing not advancing. The CDI magneto or the CDI unit may be defective. If so, they must be replaced with new ones, as they can't be repaired.
- ☐ Engine oil viscosity too high. Using a heavier oil than that recommended in Chapter 1 can damage the oil pump or lubrication system and cause drag on the engine.
- ☐ Brakes dragging. Usually caused by debris which has entered the brake piston sealing boots, corroded wheel calipers or from a warped disc or bent axle. Repair as necessary (Chapter 7).
- ☐ Timing not advancing (fuel injected models). The crankshaft position sensor or ECU may be at fault (see Chapter 4B).

3 Poor running or no power at high speed

Firing incorrect

- ☐ Air cleaner restricted. Clean or replace element (Chapter 1).
- ☐ Spark plug fouled, defective or worn out. See Chapter 1 for spark plug maintenance.
- ☐ Spark plug cap or secondary (HT) wiring defective. See Chapters 1 and 5 for details of the ignition system.
- ☐ Spark plug cap not in good contact. See Chapter 5.
- ☐ Incorrect spark plug. Wrong type, heat range or cap configuration. Check and install correct plugs listed in Chapter 1. A cold plug or one with a recessed firing electrode will not operate at low speeds without fouling.
- ☐ CDI unit or CDI magneto defective. See Chapter 5.
- ☐ Ignition coil defective. See Chapter 5.

Fuel/air mixture incorrect (carbureted models)

- ☐ Pilot screw out of adjustment. See Chapter 4A for adjustment procedures.
- ☐ Main jet clogged. Dirt, water or other contaminants can clog the main jets. Clean the fuel tap strainer and in-tank strainer, the float bowl area, and the jets and carburetor orifices (Chapter 4A).
- ☐ Main jet wrong size. The standard jetting is for sea level atmospheric pressure and oxygen content. See Chapter 4A for high altitude adjustments.
- ☐ Throttle shaft-to-carburetor body clearance excessive. Refer to Chapter 4A for inspection and part replacement procedures.
- ☐ Air bleed holes clogged. Remove and overhaul carburetor (Chapter 4A).
- ☐ Air cleaner clogged, poorly sealed, or missing.
- ☐ Air cleaner-to-carburetor boot poorly sealed. Look for cracks, holes or loose clamps, and replace or repair defective parts.
- ☐ Float level too high or too low. Check float level and replace the float if necessary (Chapter 4A).
- ☐ Fuel tank air vent obstructed. Make sure the air vent passage in the filler cap is open.
- ☐ Carburetor intake joint loose. Check for cracks, breaks, tears or loose clamps or bolts. Repair or replace the rubber boots (Chapter 4A).
- ☐ Fuel tap clogged. Remove the tap and clean it (Chapter 1).
- ☐ Fuel line clogged. Pull the fuel line loose and carefully blow through it.

Fuel/air mixture incorrect (fuel injected models)

- ☐ Fuel tank vent hose or fitting obstructed.
- ☐ Fuel pump or pressure regulator faulty, or the fuel filter is blocked (see Chapter 4B).
- ☐ Fuel hose clogged. Remove the fuel hose (see Chapter 4B) and blow air through it.
- ☐ Fuel rail or injector clogged. Check the fuel pump. If the machine has been unused for several months, the fuel turns to a varnish-like liquid that can cause an injector needle to stick to its seat. Drain the tank and fuel system (see Chapter 4B).
- ☐ Intake air leak. Check for a loose connection between the throttle body and intake manifold, and check the intake air pressure sensor hose for leaks or a loose fit.
- ☐ Air filter clogged. Clean the air filter element or replace it with a new one (see Chapter 1).

Compression low

- ☐ Spark plug loose. Remove the plug and inspect the threads. Reinstall and tighten to the specified torque (Chapter 1).
- ☐ Cylinder head not sufficiently tightened down. If the cylinder head is suspected of being loose, then there's a chance that the gasket and head are damaged if the problem has persisted for any length of time. The head nuts and bolts should be tightened to the proper torque in the correct sequence (Chapter 2).
- ☐ Improper valve clearance. This means that the valve is not closing completely and compression pressure is leaking past the valve. Check and adjust the valve clearances (Chapter 1).
- ☐ Cylinder and/or piston worn. Excessive wear will cause compression pressure to leak past the rings. This is usually accompanied by worn rings as well. A top end overhaul is necessary (Chapter 2).
- ☐ Piston rings worn, weak, broken, or sticking. Broken or sticking piston rings usually indicate a lubrication or carburetion problem that causes excess carbon deposits or seizures to form on the pistons and rings. Top end overhaul is necessary (Chapter 2).
- ☐ Piston ring-to-groove clearance excessive. This is caused by excessive wear of the piston ring lands. Piston replacement is necessary (Chapter 2).
- ☐ Cylinder head gasket damaged. If a head is allowed to become loose, or if excessive carbon build-up on the piston crown and combustion chamber causes extremely high compression, the head gasket may leak. Retorquing the head is not always sufficient to restore the seal, so gasket replacement is necessary (Chapter 2).
- ☐ Cylinder head warped. This is caused by overheating or improperly tightened head nuts and bolts. Machine shop resurfacing or head replacement is necessary (Chapter 2).
- ☐ Valve spring broken or weak. Caused by component failure or wear; the spring(s) must be replaced (Chapter 2).
- ☐ Valve not seating properly. This is caused by a bent valve (from over-revving or improper valve adjustment), burned valve or seat (improper carburetion) or an accumulation of carbon deposits on the seat (from carburetion or lubrication problems). The valves must be cleaned and/or replaced and the seats serviced if possible (Chapter 2).

Knocking or pinging

- ☐ Carbon build-up in combustion chamber. Use of a fuel additive that will dissolve the adhesive bonding the carbon particles to the crown and chamber is the easiest way to remove the build-up. Otherwise, the cylinder head will have to be removed and decarbonized (Chapter 2).
- ☐ Incorrect or poor quality fuel. Old or improper grades of fuel can cause detonation. This causes the piston to rattle, thus the knocking or pinging sound. Drain old fuel and always use the recommended fuel grade.
- ☐ Spark plug heat range incorrect. Uncontrolled detonation indicates the plug heat range is too hot. The plug in effect becomes a glow plug, raising cylinder temperatures. Install the proper heat range plug (Chapter 1).
- ☐ Improper air/fuel mixture. This will cause the cylinder to run hot, which leads to detonation. Clogged jets or an air leak can cause this imbalance. See Chapter 4.

Miscellaneous causes

- ☐ Throttle valve doesn't open fully. Adjust the cable slack (Chapter 1).
- ☐ Clutch slipping. May be caused by improper adjustment or loose or worn clutch components. Refer to Chapter 1 for adjustment or Chapter 2 for clutch overhaul procedures.
- ☐ Timing not advancing.
- ☐ Engine oil viscosity too high. Using a heavier oil than the one recommended in Chapter 1 can damage the oil pump or lubrication system and cause drag on the engine.
- ☐ Brakes dragging. Usually caused by debris which has entered the brake piston sealing boot, or from a warped disc or bent axle. Repair as necessary.

4 Overheating

Engine overheats

- ☐ Coolant level low. Check and add coolant (see *Daily (pre-ride) checks* at the beginning of this manual)
- ☐ Leak in cooling system. Check cooling system hoses and radiator for leaks and other damage. Replace or repair parts as necessary (see Chapter 3).
- ☐ Defective thermostat. Check and replace if necessary (see Chapter 3).
- ☐ Bad radiator cap. Remove the cap and have it pressure tested.
- ☐ Coolant passages clogged. Drain, clean the passages and refill with fresh coolant (see Chapter 3).
- ☐ Water pump defective. Remove the pump and check the components (see Chapter 3).
- ☐ Clogged or damaged radiator fins (see Chapter 3).
- ☐ Faulty cooling fan, fan relay or fan switch (see Chapter 3).
- ☐ Engine oil level low. Check and add oil (Chapter 1).
- ☐ Wrong type of oil. If you're not sure what type of oil is in the engine, drain it and fill with the correct type (Chapter 1).
- ☐ Air leak at intake joint. Check and tighten or replace as necessary (Chapter 4).
- ☐ Fuel level low. Check and adjust if necessary (Chapter 4).
- ☐ Worn oil pump or clogged oil passages. Replace pump or clean passages as necessary.
- ☐ Clogged external oil line. Remove and check for foreign material (see Chapter 2).
- ☐ Carbon build-up in combustion chambers. Use of a fuel additive that will dissolve the adhesive bonding the carbon particles to the piston crown and chambers is the easiest way to remove the build-up. Otherwise, the cylinder head will have to be removed and decarbonized (Chapter 2).
- ☐ Operation in high ambient temperatures.

Firing incorrect

- ☐ Spark plug fouled, defective or worn out. See Chapter 1 for spark plug maintenance.
- ☐ Incorrect spark plug (see Chapter 1).
- ☐ Faulty ignition coil (Chapter 4).

Fuel/air mixture incorrect (carbureted models)

- ☐ Pilot screw out of adjustment (Chapter 4A).
- ☐ Main jet clogged. Dirt, water and other contaminants can clog the main jet. Clean the fuel tap strainer, the float bowl area and the jets and carburetor orifices (Chapter 4A).
- ☐ Main jet wrong size. The standard jetting is for sea level atmospheric pressure and oxygen content.
- ☐ Air cleaner poorly sealed or missing.
- ☐ Air cleaner-to-carburetor boot poorly sealed. Look for cracks, holes or loose clamps and replace or repair.
- ☐ Fuel level too low. Check fuel level and float level and adjust or replace the float if necessary (Chapter 4A).
- ☐ Fuel tank air vent obstructed. Make sure that the air vent passage in the filler cap is open.
- ☐ Carburetor intake manifold loose. Check for cracks or loose clamps or bolts. Check the carburetor-to-manifold gasket and the manifold-to-cylinder head O-ring (Chapter 4A).

Fuel/air mixture incorrect (fuel injected models)

- ☐ Fuel tank vent hose or fitting obstructed.
- ☐ Fuel pump or pressure regulator faulty, or the fuel filter is blocked (see Chapter 4B).
- ☐ Fuel hose clogged. Remove the fuel hose (see Chapter 4B) and blow air through it.
- ☐ Fuel rail or injector clogged. Check the fuel pump. If the machine has been unused for several months, the fuel turns to a varnish-like liquid that can cause an injector needle to stick to its seat. Drain the tank and fuel system (see Chapter 4B).
- ☐ Intake air leak. Check for a loose connection between the throttle body and intake manifold, and check the intake air pressure sensor hose for leaks or a loose fit.
- ☐ Air filter clogged. Clean the air filter element or replace it with a new one (see Chapter 1).

Compression too high

- ☐ Carbon build-up in combustion chamber. Use of a fuel additive that will dissolve the adhesive bonding the carbon particles to the piston crown and chamber is the easiest way to remove the build-up. Otherwise, the cylinder head will have to be removed and decarbonized (Chapter 2).
- ☐ Improperly machined head surface or installation of incorrect gasket during engine assembly.

Engine load excessive

- ☐ Clutch slipping. Can be caused by damaged, loose or worn clutch components. Refer to Chapter 2 for overhaul procedures.
- ☐ Engine oil level too high. The addition of too much oil will cause pressurization of the crankcase and inefficient engine operation. Check Specifications and drain to proper level (Chapter 1).
- ☐ Engine oil viscosity too high. Using a heavier oil than the one recommended in Chapter 1 can damage the oil pump or lubrication system as well as cause drag on the engine.
- ☐ Brakes dragging. Usually caused by debris which has entered the brake piston sealing boots (hydraulic front brakes), corroded wheel cylinders or calipers (hydraulic front brakes), sticking brake cam (mechanical front or all rear brakes) or from a warped drum, warped disc or bent axle. Repair as necessary (Chapter 7).

Lubrication inadequate

- ☐ Engine oil level too low. Friction caused by intermittent lack of lubrication or from oil that is overworked can cause overheating. The oil provides a definite cooling function in the engine. Check the oil level (Chapter 1).
- ☐ Poor quality engine oil or incorrect viscosity or type. Oil is rated not only according to viscosity but also according to type. Some oils are not rated high enough for use in this engine. Check the Specifications section and change to the correct oil (Chapter 1).
- ☐ Camshaft or journals worn. Excessive wear causing drop in oil pressure. Replace cam or cylinder head. Abnormal wear could be caused by oil starvation at high rpm from low oil level or improper viscosity or type of oil (Chapter 1).
- ☐ Crankshaft and/or bearings worn. Same problems as paragraph above. Check and replace crankshaft assembly if necessary (Chapter 2).

Miscellaneous causes

- ☐ Modification to exhaust system. Most aftermarket exhaust systems cause the engine to run leaner, which makes it run hotter. When installing an aftermarket exhaust system, always rejet the carburetor (if equipped).

5 Clutch problems

Clutch slipping

- ☐ Clutch friction plates worn or warped. Overhaul the secondary clutch assembly (Chapter 2).
- ☐ Clutch metal plates worn or warped (Chapter 2).
- ☐ Clutch spring(s) broken or weak. Old or heat-damaged spring(s) (from slipping clutch) should be replaced with new ones (Chapter 2).
- ☐ Clutch release mechanism defective. Replace any defective parts (Chapter 2).
- ☐ Clutch boss or housing unevenly worn. This causes improper engagement of the plates. Replace the damaged or worn parts (Chapter 2).
- ☐ Wrong type of engine oil. The friction modifiers in automotive engine oils can sometimes caused the clutch to slip. Use oil that meets JASO standard MA.

Clutch not disengaging completely

- ☐ Clutch improperly adjusted (see Chapter 1).
- ☐ Clutch plates warped or damaged. This will cause clutch drag, which in turn will cause the machine to creep. Overhaul the clutch assembly (Chapter 2).
- ☐ Sagged or broken clutch spring(s). Check and replace the spring(s) (Chapter 2).
- ☐ Engine oil deteriorated. Old, thin, worn out oil will not provide proper lubrication for the discs, causing the secondary clutch to drag. Replace the oil and filter (Chapter 1).
- ☐ Engine oil viscosity too high. Using a thicker oil than recommended in Chapter 1 can cause the secondary clutch plates to stick together, putting a drag on the engine. Change to the correct viscosity oil (Chapter 1).
- ☐ Clutch housing seized on shaft. Lack of lubrication, severe wear or damage can cause the housing to seize on the shaft. Overhaul of the clutch, and perhaps transmission, may be necessary to repair the damage (Chapter 2).
- ☐ Clutch release mechanism defective. Worn or damaged release mechanism parts can stick and fail to apply force to the pressure plate. Overhaul the release mechanism (Chapter 2).
- ☐ Clutch center nut. Causes housing and center misalignment putting a drag on the engine. Engagement adjustment continually varies. Overhaul the clutch assembly (Chapter 2).

6 Gear shifting problems

Doesn't go into gear or lever doesn't return

- ☐ Clutch not disengaging. See Section 5.
- ☐ Shift fork(s) bent or seized. May be caused by lack of lubrication. Overhaul the transmission (Chapter 2).
- ☐ Gear(s) stuck on shaft. Most often caused by a lack of lubrication or excessive wear in transmission bearings and bushings. Overhaul the transmission (Chapter 2).
- ☐ Shift drum binding. Caused by lubrication failure or excessive wear. Replace the drum and bearing (Chapter 2).
- ☐ Shift lever return spring weak or broken (Chapter 2).
- ☐ Shift lever broken. Splines stripped out of lever or shaft, caused by allowing the lever to get loose. Replace necessary parts (Chapter 2).
- ☐ Shift mechanism pawl broken or worn. Full engagement and rotary movement of shift drum results. Replace shaft assembly (Chapter 2).
- ☐ Pawl spring broken. Allows pawl to float, causing sporadic shift operation. Replace spring (Chapter 2).

Jumps out of gear

- ☐ Shift fork(s) worn. Overhaul the transmission (Chapter 2).
- ☐ Gear groove(s) worn. Overhaul the transmission (Chapter 2).
- ☐ Gear dogs or dog slots worn or damaged. The gears should be inspected and replaced. No attempt should be made to service the worn parts.

Overshifts

- ☐ Pawl spring weak or broken (Chapter 2).
- ☐ Shift cam stopper lever not functioning (Chapter 2).

7 Abnormal engine noise

Knocking or pinging

- ☐ Carbon build-up in combustion chamber. Use of a fuel additive that will dissolve the adhesive bonding the carbon particles to the piston crown and chamber is the easiest way to remove the build-up. Otherwise, the cylinder head will have to be removed and decarbonized (Chapter 2).
- ☐ Incorrect or poor quality fuel. Old or improper fuel can cause detonation. This causes the pistons to rattle, thus the knocking or pinging sound. Drain the old fuel (Chapter 4) and always use the recommended grade fuel (Chapter 1).
- ☐ Spark plug heat range incorrect. Uncontrolled detonation indicates that the plug heat range is too hot. The plug in effect becomes a glow plug, raising cylinder temperatures. Install the proper heat range plug (Chapter 1).
- ☐ Improper air/fuel mixture. This will cause the cylinder to run hot and lead to detonation. Clogged jets or an air leak can cause this imbalance. See Chapter 4A.

Piston slap or rattling

- ☐ Cylinder-to-piston clearance excessive. Caused by improper assembly. Inspect and overhaul top end parts (Chapter 2).
- ☐ Connecting rod bent. Caused by over-revving, trying to start a badly flooded engine or from ingesting a foreign object into the combustion chamber. Replace the damaged parts (Chapter 2).
- ☐ Piston pin or piston pin bore worn or seized from wear or lack of lubrication. Replace damaged parts (Chapter 2).
- ☐ Piston ring(s) worn, broken or sticking. Overhaul the top end (Chapter 2).
- ☐ Piston seizure damage. Usually from lack of lubrication or overheating. Replace the pistons and bore the cylinder, as necessary (Chapter 2).
- ☐ Connecting rod upper or lower end clearance excessive. Caused by excessive wear or lack of lubrication. Replace worn parts.

Valve noise

- ☐ Incorrect valve clearances. Adjust the clearances by referring to Chapter 1.
- ☐ Valve spring broken or weak. Check and replace weak valve springs (Chapter 2).
- ☐ Camshaft or cylinder head worn or damaged. Lack of lubrication at high rpm is usually the cause of damage. Insufficient oil or failure to change the oil at the recommended intervals are the chief causes.

Other noise

- ☐ Cylinder head gasket leaking.
- ☐ Exhaust pipe leaking at cylinder head connection. Caused by improper fit of pipe, damaged gasket or loose exhaust flange. All exhaust fasteners should be tightened evenly and carefully. Failure to do this will lead to a leak.
- ☐ Crankshaft runout excessive. Caused by a bent crankshaft (from over-revving) or damage from an upper cylinder component failure.
- ☐ Engine mounting bolts or nuts loose. Tighten all engine mounting bolts and nuts to the specified torque (Chapter 2).
- ☐ Crankshaft bearings worn (Chapter 2).
- ☐ Camshaft chain tensioner defective. Replace according to the procedure in Chapter 2.
- ☐ Camshaft chain, sprockets or guides worn (Chapter 2).

8 Abnormal driveline noise

Clutch noise

- ☐ Clutch housing/friction plate clearance excessive (Chapter 2).
- ☐ Loose or damaged secondary clutch pressure plate and/or bolts (Chapter 2).

Transmission noise

- ☐ Bearings worn. Also includes the possibility that the shafts are worn. Overhaul the transmission (Chapter 2).
- ☐ Gears worn or chipped (Chapter 2).
- ☐ Metal chips jammed in gear teeth. Probably pieces from a broken gear or shift mechanism that were picked up by the gears. This will cause early bearing failure (Chapter 2).
- ☐ Engine oil level too low. Causes a howl from transmission. Also affects engine power and clutch operation (Chapter 1).
- ☐ Chain not adjusted properly (see Chapter 1)
- ☐ Front or rear sprocket loose. Tighten fasteners (see Chapter 6).
- ☐ Sprockets and/or chain worn. Install new sprockets and chain (see Chapter 6).
- ☐ Rear sprocket warped. Install a new rear sprocket (see Chapter 6).

9 Abnormal chassis noise

Suspension noise

- ☐ Spring weak or broken. Makes a clicking or scraping sound.
- ☐ Steering shaft bearings worn or damaged. Clicks when braking. Check and replace as necessary (Chapter 6).
- ☐ Shock absorber fluid level incorrect. Indicates a leak caused by defective seal. Shock will be covered with oil. Replace shock (Chapter 6).
- ☐ Defective shock absorber with internal damage. This is in the body of the shock and can't be remedied. The shock must be replaced with a new one (Chapter 6).
- ☐ Bent or damaged shock body. Replace the shock with a new one (Chapter 6).

Brake noise

- ☐ Brake linings worn or contaminated. Can cause scraping or squealing. Replace the pads (Chapter 7).
- ☐ Brake linings warped or worn unevenly. Can cause chattering. Replace the linings (Chapter 7).
- ☐ Brake disc warped. Can cause chattering. Replace brake disc (Chapter 7).
- ☐ Loose or worn knuckle or rear axle bearings. Check and replace as needed (Chapter 6).

10 Coolant temperature indicator light comes on

Cooling system

- ☐ Coolant level low. Check and add coolant (see *Daily (pre-ride) checks* at the beginning of this manual)
- ☐ Leak in cooling system. Check cooling system hoses and radiator for leaks and other damage. Replace or repair parts as necessary (see Chapter 3).
- ☐ Defective thermostat. Check and replace if necessary (see Chapter 3).
- ☐ Bad radiator cap. Remove the cap and have it pressure tested.
- ☐ Coolant passages clogged. Drain, clean the passages and refill with fresh coolant (see Chapter 3).
- ☐ Water pump defective. Remove the pump and check the components (see Chapter 3).
- ☐ Clogged or damaged radiator fins (see Chapter 3).

Engine lubrication system

- ☐ High oil temperature due to operation in high ambient temperatures. Shut the engine off and let it cool.
- ☐ Engine oil level low. Inspect for leak or other problem causing low oil level and add recommended oil (Chapters 1 and 2).

Electrical system

- ☐ Coolant temperature sensor defective. Check the sensor according to the procedure in Chapter 5. Replace it if it's defective.
- ☐ Coolant temperature indicator light circuit defective. Check for pinched, shorted, disconnected or damaged wiring (Chapter 3).
- ☐ Cooling fan not working (Chapter 3).

11 Excessive exhaust smoke

White smoke

- ☐ Piston oil ring worn. The ring may be broken or damaged, causing oil from the crankcase to be pulled past the piston into the combustion chamber. Replace the rings with new ones (Chapter 2).
- ☐ Cylinders worn, cracked, or scored. Caused by overheating or oil starvation. If worn or scored, the cylinders will have to be rebored and new pistons installed. If cracked, the cylinder block will have to be replaced (see Chapter 2).
- ☐ Valve oil seal damaged or worn. Replace oil seals with new ones (Chapter 2).
- ☐ Valve guide worn. Perform a complete valve job (Chapter 2).
- ☐ Engine oil level too high, which causes the oil to be forced past the rings. Drain oil to the proper level (Chapter 1).
- ☐ Head gasket broken between oil return and cylinder. Causes oil to be pulled into the combustion chamber. Replace the head gasket and check the head for warpage (Chapter 2).
- ☐ Abnormal crankcase pressurization, which forces oil past the rings. Clogged breather or hoses usually the cause (Chapter 2).

Black smoke

- ☐ Air cleaner clogged. Clean or replace the element (Chapter 1).
- ☐ Main jet too large or loose. Compare the jet size to the Specifications (Chapter 4A).
- ☐ Choke stuck (carbureted models), causing fuel to be pulled through choke circuit (Chapter 4A).
- ☐ Fuel level too high (carbureted models). Check the fuel level and float level and adjust if necessary (Chapter 4A).
- ☐ Inlet needle held off needle seat (carbureted models). Clean the float chamber and fuel line and replace the needle and seat if necessary (Chapter 4A).
- ☐ Fuel injection system problem (2009 and later). See Chapter 4B.

Brown smoke

- ☐ Main jet too small or clogged. Lean condition caused by wrong size main jet or by a restricted orifice. Clean float chamber and jets and compare jet size to Specifications (Chapter 4A).
- ☐ Fuel flow insufficient. Fuel inlet needle valve stuck closed due to chemical reaction with old fuel. Float level incorrect; check and replace float if necessary. Restricted fuel line. Clean line and float chamber.
- ☐ Carburetor intake tube loose (Chapter 4A).
- ☐ Air cleaner poorly sealed or not installed (Chapter 1).

12 Poor handling or stability

Handlebar hard to turn

- ☐ Steering shaft nut too tight (Chapter 6).
- ☐ Lower bearing or upper bushing damaged. Roughness can be felt as the bars are turned from side-to-side. Replace bearing and bushing (Chapter 6).
- ☐ Steering shaft bearing lubrication inadequate. Causes are grease getting hard from age or being washed out by high pressure car washes. Remove steering shaft and replace bearing (Chapter 6).
- ☐ Steering shaft bent. Caused by a collision, hitting a pothole or by rolling the machine. Replace damaged part. Don't try to straighten the steering shaft (Chapter 6).
- ☐ Front tire air pressure too low (Chapter 1).

Handlebar shakes or vibrates excessively

- ☐ Tires worn or out of balance (Chapter 1 or 7).
- ☐ Swingarm bearings worn. Replace worn bearings by referring to Chapter 6.
- ☐ Wheel rim(s) warped or damaged. Inspect wheels (Chapter 7).
- ☐ Wheel bearings worn. Worn front or rear wheel bearings can cause poor tracking. Worn front bearings will cause wobble (Chapter 7).
- ☐ Wheel hubs installed incorrectly (Chapter 6 or Chapter 7).
- ☐ Handlebar clamp bolts or bracket nuts loose (Chapter 6).
- ☐ Steering shaft nut or bolts loose. Tighten them to the specified torque (Chapter 6).
- ☐ Motor mount bolts loose. Will cause excessive vibration with increased engine rpm (Chapter 2).

Handlebar pulls to one side

- ☐ Uneven tire pressures (Chapter 1).
- ☐ Frame bent. Definitely suspect this if the machine has been rolled. May or may not be accompanied by cracking near the bend. Replace the frame (Chapter 8).
- ☐ Wheel out of alignment. Caused by incorrect toe-in adjustment (Chapter 1) or bent tie-rod (Chapter 6).
- ☐ Swingarm bent or twisted. Caused by age (metal fatigue) or impact damage. Replace the swingarm (Chapter 6).
- ☐ Steering shaft bent. Caused by impact damage or by rolling the vehicle. Replace the steering stem (Chapter 6).

Poor shock absorbing qualities

- ☐ Too hard:
  - *a) Shock internal damage.*
  - *b) Tire pressure too high (Chapters 1 and 7).*
  - *c) Shock setting too hard for conditions (see Chapter 6).*
- ☐ Too soft:
  - *a) Shock oil insufficient and/or leaking (Chapter 6).*
  - *b) Shock springs weak or broken (Chapter 6).*

13 Braking problems

Front brakes are spongy, don't hold

- ☐ Air in brake line. Caused by inattention to master cylinder fluid level or by leakage. Locate problem and bleed brakes (Chapter 7).
- ☐ Linings worn (Chapters 1 and 7).
- ☐ Brake fluid leak. See first paragraph.
- ☐ Contaminated linings. Caused by contamination with oil, grease, brake fluid, etc. Clean or replace linings. Clean disc thoroughly with brake cleaner (Chapter 7).
- ☐ Brake fluid deteriorated. Fluid is old or contaminated. Drain system, replenish with new fluid and bleed the system (Chapter 7).
- ☐ Master cylinder internal parts worn or damaged causing fluid to bypass (Chapter 7).
- ☐ Master cylinder bore scratched by foreign material or broken spring. Repair or replace master cylinder (Chapter 7).
- ☐ Disc warped. Replace disc (Chapter 7).

Brake lever or pedal pulsates

- ☐ Axle bent. Replace axle (Chapter 6).
- ☐ Wheel warped or otherwise damaged (Chapter 7).
- ☐ Hub or axle bearings damaged or worn (Chapter 6).
- ☐ Brake disc warped. Replace brake disc (Chapter 7).

Brakes drag

- ☐ Master cylinder piston seized. Caused by wear or damage to piston or cylinder bore (Chapter 7).
- ☐ Lever balky or stuck. Check pivot and lubricate (Chapter 7).
- ☐ Wheel cylinder or caliper piston seized in bore. Caused by wear or ingestion of dirt past deteriorated seal (Chapter 7).
- ☐ Disc brake pads damaged. Lining material separated from pads. Usually caused by faulty manufacturing process or from contact with chemicals. Replace pads (Chapter 7).
- ☐ Pads improperly installed (Chapter 7).
- ☐ Rear brake pedal or lever free play insufficient (Chapter 1).

14 Electrical problems

Battery dead or weak

- ☐ Battery faulty. Caused by sulfated plates which are shorted through sedimentation or low electrolyte level. Also, broken battery terminal making only occasional contact (Chapter 5).
- ☐ Battery cables making poor contact (Chapter 5).
- ☐ Load excessive. Caused by addition of high wattage lights or other electrical accessories.
- ☐ Ignition switch defective. Switch either grounds internally or fails to shut off system. Replace the switch (Chapter 5).
- ☐ Regulator/rectifier defective (Chapter 5).
- ☐ Stator coil open or shorted (Chapter 5).
- ☐ Wiring faulty. Wiring grounded or connections loose in ignition, charging or lighting circuits (Chapter 5).

Battery overcharged

- ☐ Regulator/rectifier defective. Overcharging is noticed when battery gets excessively warm or boils over (Chapter 5).
- ☐ Battery defective. Replace battery with a new one (Chapter 5).
- ☐ Battery amperage too low, wrong type or size. Install manufacturer's specified amp-hour battery to handle charging load (Chapter 5).

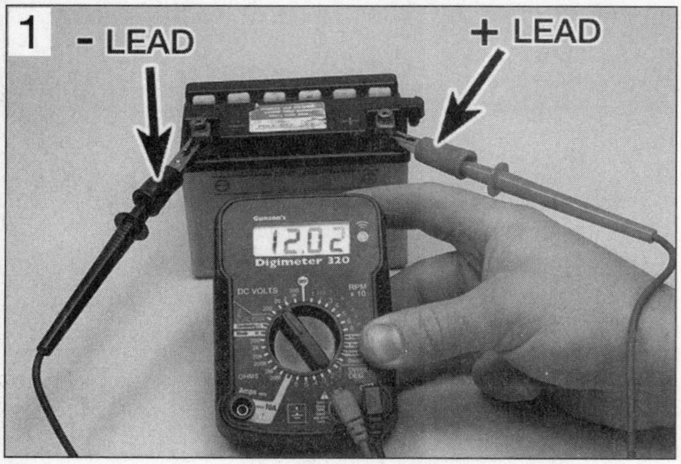

Measuring open-circuit battery voltage

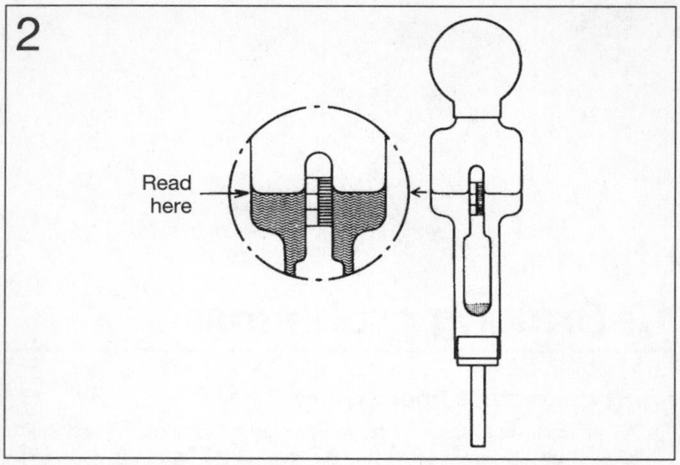

Float-type hydrometer for measuring battery specific gravity

Checking engine compression

- Low compression will result in exhaust smoke, heavy oil consumption, poor starting and poor performance. A compression test will provide useful information about an engine's condition and if performed regularly, can give warning of trouble before any other symptoms become apparent.
- A compression gauge will be required, along with an adapter to suit the spark plug hole thread size. Note that the screw-in type gauge/adapter set up is preferable to the rubber cone type.
- Compression testing procedures are described in Chapter 2.

Checking battery open-circuit voltage

> ***Warning: The gases produced by the battery are explosive - never smoke or create any sparks in the vicinity of the battery. Never allow the electrolyte to contact your skin or clothing - if it does, wash it off and seek immediate medical attention.***

- Before any electrical fault is investigated the battery should be checked.
- You'll need a dc voltmeter or multimeter to check battery voltage. Check that the leads are inserted in the correct terminals on the meter, red lead to positive (+), black lead to negative (-). Incorrect connections can damage the meter.
- A sound, fully-charged 12 volt battery should produce between 12.3 and 12.6 volts across its terminals (12.8 volts for a maintenance-free battery). On machines with a 6 volt battery, voltage should be between 6.1 and 6.3 volts.

1 Set a multimeter to the 0 to 20 volts dc range and connect its probes across the battery terminals. Connect the meter's positive (+) probe, usually red, to the battery positive (+) terminal, followed by the meter's negative (-) probe, usually black, to the battery negative terminal (-) **(see illustration 1)**.

2 If battery voltage is low (below 10 volts on a 12 volt battery or below 4 volts on a six volt battery), charge the battery and test the voltage again. If the battery repeatedly goes flat, investigate the vehicle's charging system.

Checking battery specific gravity (SG)

> ***Warning: The gases produced by the battery are explosive - never smoke or create any sparks in the vicinity of the battery. Never allow the electrolyte to contact your skin or clothing - if it does, wash it off and seek immediate medical attention.***

- The specific gravity check gives an indication of a battery's state of charge.
- A hydrometer is used for measuring specific gravity. Make sure you purchase one which has a small enough hose to insert in the aperture of an ATV battery.
- Specific gravity is simply a measure of the electrolyte's density compared with that of water. Water has an SG of 1.000 and fully-charged battery electrolyte is about 26% heavier, at 1.260.
- Specific gravity checks are not possible on maintenance-free batteries. Testing the open-circuit voltage is the only means of determining their state of charge.

1 To measure SG, remove the battery from the motorcycle and remove the first cell cap. Draw some electrolyte into the hydrometer and note the reading **(see illustration 2)**. Return the electrolyte to the cell and install the cap.

2 The reading should be in the region of 1.260 to 1.280. If SG is below 1.200 the battery needs charging. Note that SG will vary with temperature; it should be measured at 20°C (68°F). Add 0.007 to the reading for every 10°C above 20°C, and subtract 0.007 from the reading for every 10°C below 20°C. Add 0.004 to the reading for every 10°F above 68°F, and subtract 0.004 from the reading for every 10°F below 68°F.

3 When the check is complete, rinse the hydrometer thoroughly with clean water.

Checking for continuity

- The term continuity describes the uninterrupted flow of electricity through an electrical circuit. A continuity check will determine whether an **open-circuit** situation exists.
- Continuity can be checked with an ohmmeter, multimeter, continuity tester or battery and bulb test circuit **(see illustrations 3, 4 and 5)**.
- All of these instruments are self-powered by a battery, therefore the checks are made with the ignition OFF.
- As a safety precaution, always disconnect the battery negative (-) lead before making checks, particularly if ignition switch checks are being made.
- If using a meter, select the appropriate ohms scale and check that the meter reads

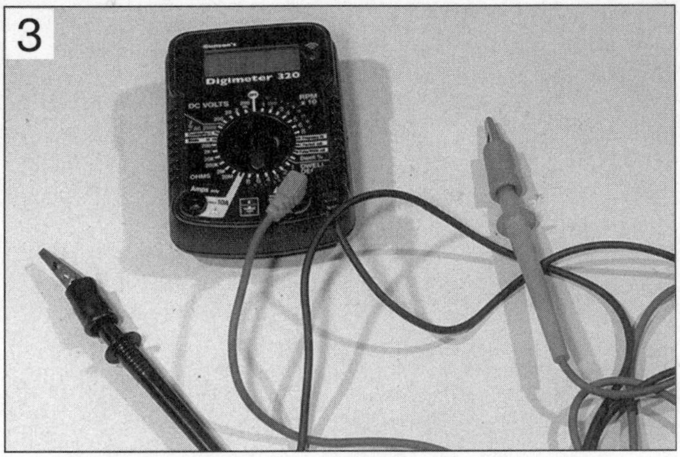

Digital multimeter can be used for all electrical tests

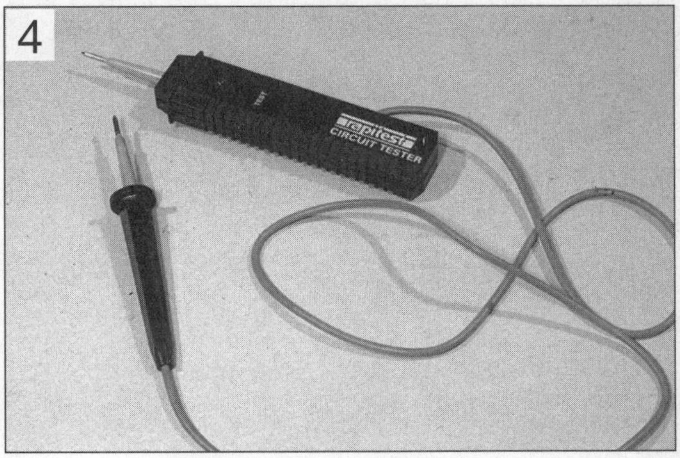

Battery-powered continuity tester

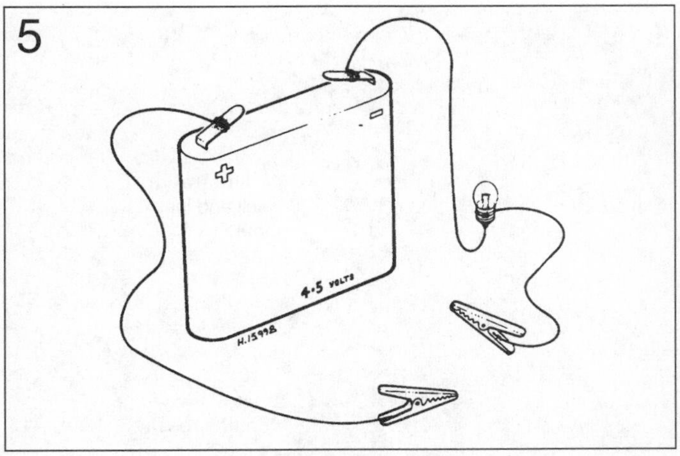

Battery and bulb test circuit

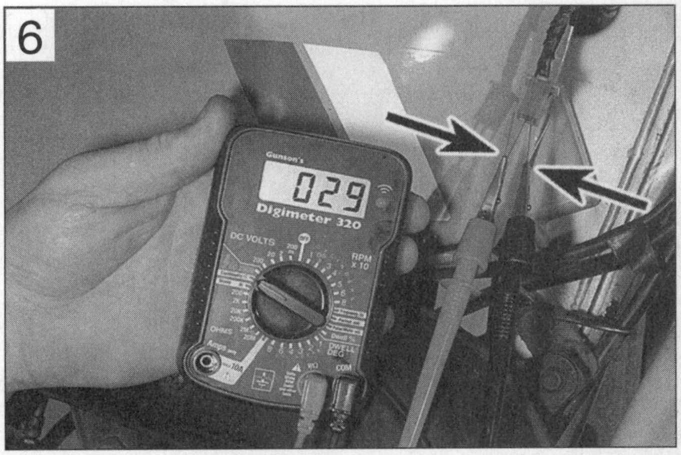

Continuity check of front brake light switch using a meter - note cotter pins used to access connector terminals

infinity (∞). Touch the meter probes together and check that meter reads zero; where necessary adjust the meter so that it reads zero.

● After using a meter, always switch it OFF to conserve its battery.

Switch checks

1 If a switch is at fault, trace its wiring up to the wiring connectors. Separate the wire connectors and inspect them for security and condition. A build-up of dirt or corrosion here will most likely be the cause of the problem - clean up and apply a water dispersant such as WD40.

2 If using a test meter, set the meter to the ohms x 10 scale and connect its probes across the wires from the switch **(see illustration 6)**. Simple ON/OFF type switches, such as brake light switches, only have two wires whereas combination switches, like the ignition switch, have many internal links. Study the wiring diagram to ensure that you are connecting across the correct pair of wires. Continuity (low or no measurable resistance - 0 ohms) should be indicated with the switch ON and no continuity (high resistance) with it OFF.

3 Note that the polarity of the test probes doesn't matter for continuity checks, although care should be taken to follow specific test procedures if a diode or solid-state component is being checked.

4 A continuity tester or battery and bulb circuit can be used in the same way. Connect its probes as described above **(see illustration 7)**. The light should come on to indicate continuity in the ON switch position, but should extinguish in the OFF position.

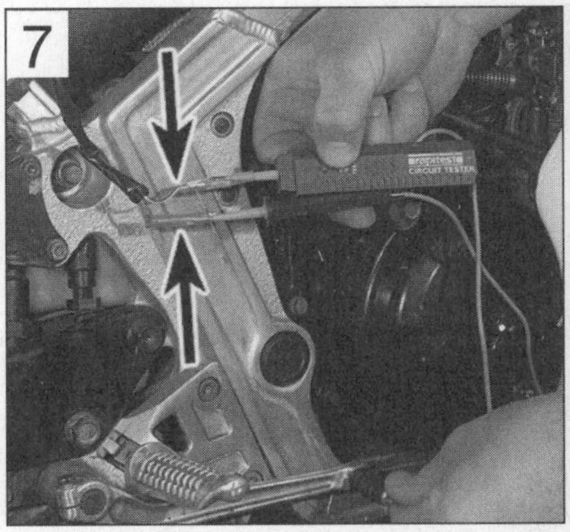

Continuity check of rear brake light switch using a continuity tester

Wiring checks

● Many electrical faults are caused by damaged wiring, often due to incorrect routing or chafing on frame components.

● Loose, wet or corroded wire connectors can also be the cause of electrical problems, especially in exposed locations.

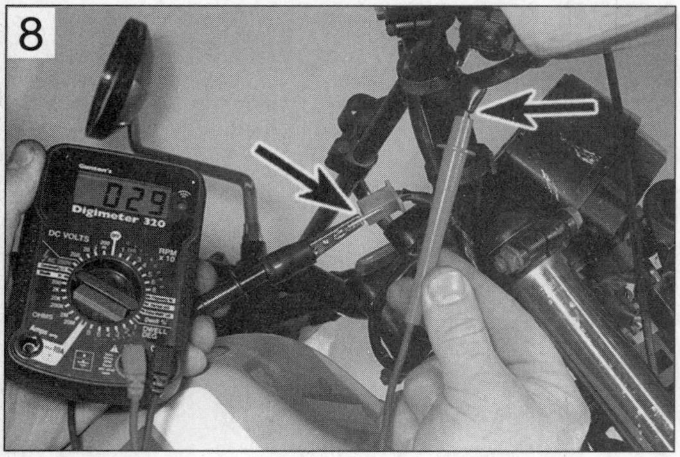

Continuity check of front brake light switch sub-harness

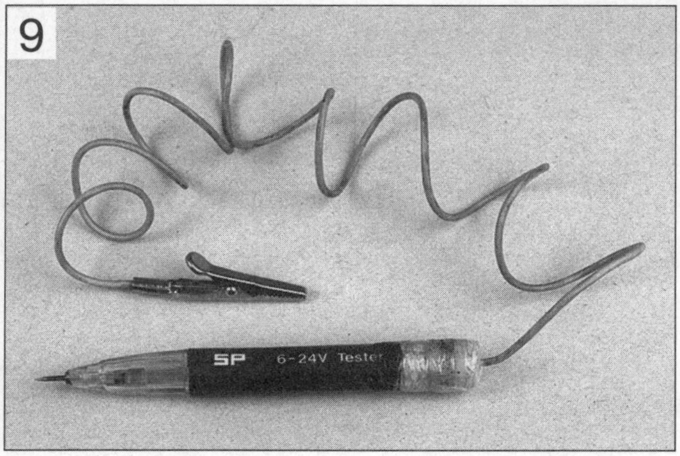

A simple test light can be used for voltage checks

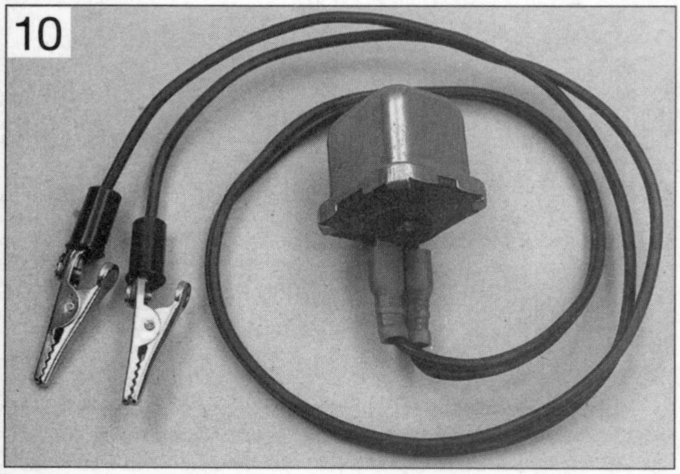

A buzzer is useful for voltage checks

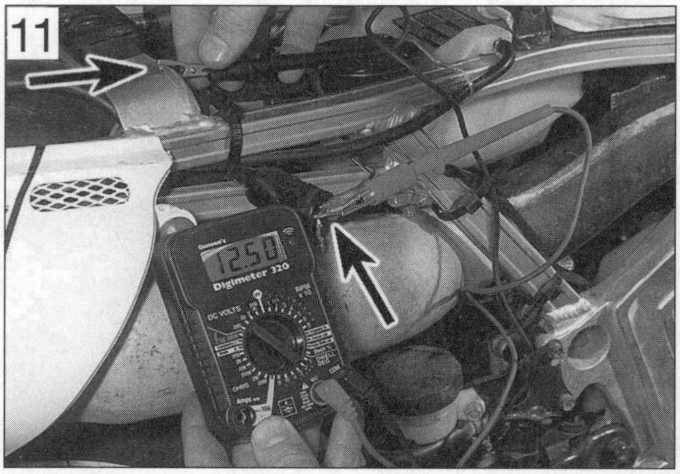

Checking for voltage at the rear brake light power supply wire using a meter . . .

1 A continuity check can be made on a single length of wire by disconnecting it at each end and connecting a meter or continuity tester across both ends of the wire **(see illustration 8)**.

2 Continuity (low or no resistance - 0 ohms) should be indicated if the wire is good. If no continuity (high resistance) is shown, suspect a broken wire.

Checking for voltage

- A voltage check can determine whether current is reaching a component.
- Voltage can be checked with a dc voltmeter, multimeter set on the dc volts scale, test light or buzzer **(see illustrations 9 and 10)**. A meter has the advantage of being able to measure actual voltage.
- When using a meter, check that its leads are inserted in the correct terminals on the meter, red to positive (+), black to negative (-). Incorrect connections can damage the meter.
- A voltmeter (or multimeter set to the dc volts scale) should always be connected in parallel (across the load). Connecting it in series will destroy the meter.
- Voltage checks are made with the ignition ON.

1 First identify the relevant wiring circuit by referring to the wiring diagram at the end of this manual. If other electrical components share the same power supply (ie are fed from the same fuse), take note whether they are working correctly - this is useful information in deciding where to start checking the circuit.

2 If using a meter, check first that the meter leads are plugged into the correct terminals on the meter (see above). Set the meter to the dc volts function, at a range suitable for the battery voltage. Connect the meter red probe (+) to the power supply wire and the black probe to a good metal ground on the motor-cycle's frame or directly to the battery negative (-) terminal **(see illustration 11)**. Battery voltage should be shown on the meter with the ignition switched ON.

3 If using a test light or buzzer, connect its positive (+) probe to the power supply terminal and its negative (-) probe to a good ground on the vehicle's frame or directly to the battery negative (-) terminal **(see illustration 12)**. With the ignition ON, the test light should illuminate or the buzzer sound.

4 If no voltage is indicated, work back towards the fuse continuing to check for voltage. When you reach a point where there is voltage, you know the problem lies between that point and your last check point.

12

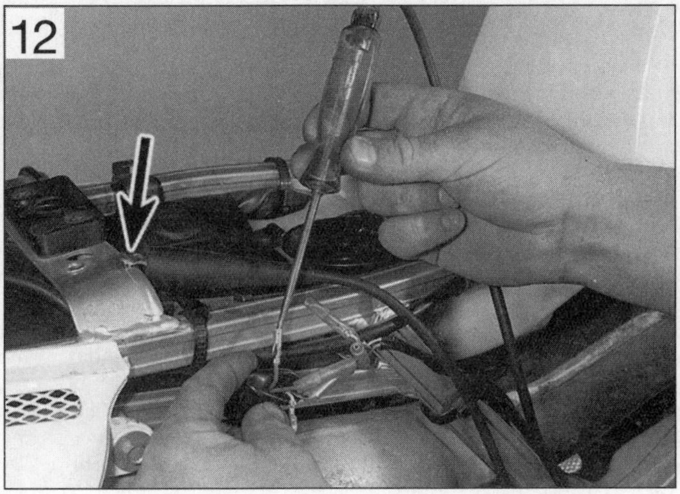

. . . or a test light - note the ground connection to the frame (arrow)

13

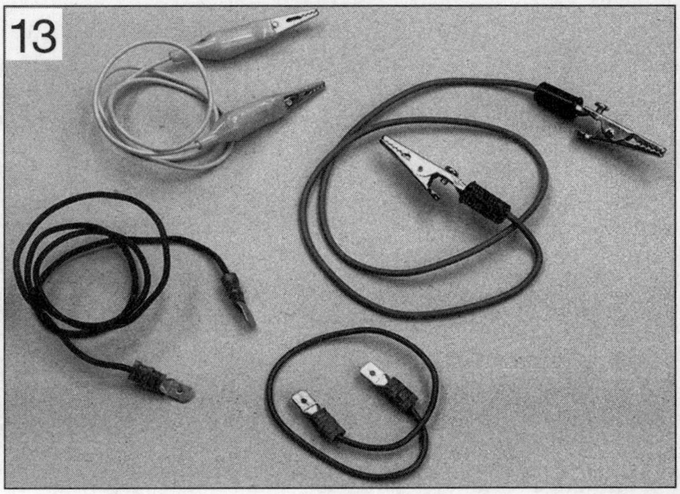

A selection of jumper wires for making ground checks

Checking the ground

● Ground connections are made either directly to the engine or frame (such as sensors, neutral switch etc. which only have a positive feed) or by a separate wire into the ground circuit of the wiring harness. Alternatively a short ground wire is sometimes run directly from the component to the vehicle's frame.

● Corrosion is often the cause of a poor ground connection.

● If total failure is experienced, check the security of the main ground lead from the negative (-) terminal of the battery and also the main ground point on the wiring harness. If corroded, dismantle the connection and clean all surfaces back to bare metal.

1 To check the ground on a component, use an insulated jumper wire to temporarily bypass its ground connection **(see illustration 13)**. Connect one end of the jumper wire between the ground terminal or metal body of the component and the other end to the vehicle's frame.

2 If the circuit works with the jumper wire installed, the original ground circuit is faulty. Check the wiring for open-circuits or poor connections. Clean up direct ground connections, removing all traces of corrosion and remake the joint. Apply petroleum jelly to the joint to prevent future corrosion.

Tracing a short-circuit

● A short-circuit occurs where current shorts to ground bypassing the circuit components. This usually results in a blown fuse.

● A short-circuit is most likely to occur where the insulation has worn through due to wiring chafing on a component, allowing a direct path to ground on the frame.

1 Remove any body panels necessary to access the circuit wiring.

2 Check that all electrical switches in the circuit are OFF, then remove the circuit fuse and connect a test light, buzzer or voltmeter (set to the dc scale) across the fuse terminals. No voltage should be shown.

3 Move the wiring from side to side while observing the test light or meter. When the test light comes on, buzzer sounds or meter shows voltage, you have found the cause of the short. It will usually shown up as damaged or burned insulation.

4 Note that the same test can be performed on each component in the circuit, even the switch.

ATV Chemicals and Lubricants

A number of chemicals and lubricants are available for use in motorcycle maintenance and repair. They include a wide variety of products ranging from cleaning solvents and degreasers to lubricants and protective sprays for rubber, plastic and vinyl.

- **Contact point/spark plug cleaner** is a solvent used to clean oily film and dirt from points, grim from electrical connectors and oil deposits from spark plugs. It is oil free and leaves no residue. It can also be used to remove gum and varnish from carburetor jets and other orifices.

- **Carburetor cleaner** is similar to contact point/spark plug cleaner but it usually has a stronger solvent and may leave a slight oily residue. It is not recommended for cleaning electrical components or connections.

- **Brake system cleaner** is used to remove brake dust, grease and brake fluid from the brake system, where clean surfaces are absolutely necessary. It leaves no residue and often eliminates brake squeal caused by contaminants.

- **Silicone-based lubricants** are used to protect rubber parts such as hoses and grommets, and are used as lubricants for hinges and locks.

- **Multi-purpose grease** is an all purpose lubricant used wherever grease is more practical than a liquid lubricant such as oil. Some multi-purpose grease is colored white and specially formulated to be more resistant to water than ordinary grease.

- **Gear oil** (sometimes called gear lube) is a specially designed oil used in transmissions and final drive units, as well as other areas where high friction, high temperature lubrication is required. It is available in a number of viscosities (weights) for various applications.

- **Motor oil** is the lubricant formulated for use in engines. It normally contains a wide variety of additives to prevent corrosion and reduce foaming and wear. Motor oil comes in various weights (viscosity ratings) from 0 to 50. The recommended weight of the oil depends on the season, temperature and the demands on the engine. Light oil is used in cold climates and under light load conditions. Heavy oil is used in hot climates and where high loads are encountered. Multi-viscosity oils are designed to have characteristics of both light and heavy oils and are available in a number of weights from 0W-20 to 20W-50.

- **Gasoline additives** perform several functions, depending on their chemical makeup. They usually contain solvents that help dissolve gum and varnish that build up on carburetor and inlet parts. They also serve to break down carbon deposits that form on the inside surfaces of the combustion chambers. Some additives contain upper cylinder lubricants for valves and piston rings.

- **Brake and clutch fluid** is a specially formulated hydraulic fluid that can withstand the heat and pressure encountered in break/clutch systems. Care must be taken that this fluid does not come in contact with painted surfaces or plastics. An opened container should always be resealed to prevent contamination by water or dirt.

- **Chain lubricants** are formulated especially for use on motorcycle final drive chains. A good chain lube should adhere well and have good penetrating qualities to be effective as a lubricant inside the chain and on the side plates, pins and rollers. Most chain lubes are either the foaming type or quick drying type and are usually marketed as sprays. Take care to use a lubricant marked as being suitable for O-ring chains.

- **Degreasers** are heavy duty solvents used to remove grease and grime that may accumulate on the engine and frame components. They can be sprayed or brushed on and, depending on the type, are rinsed with either water or solvent.

- **Solvents** are used alone or in combination with degreasers to clean parts and assemblies during repair and overhaul. The home mechanic should use only solvents that are non-flammable and that do not produce irritating fumes.

- **Gasket sealing compounds** may be used in conjunction with gaskets, to improve their sealing capabilities, or alone, to seal metal-to-metal joints. Many gasket sealers can withstand extreme heat, some are impervious to gasoline and lubricants, while others are capable of filling and sealing large cavities. Depending on the intended use, gasket sealers either dry hard or stay relatively soft and pliable. They are usually applied by hand, with a brush or are sprayed on the gasket sealing surfaces.

- **Thread locking compound** is an adhesive locking compound that prevents threaded fasteners from loosening because of vibration. It is available in a variety of types for different applications.

- **Moisture dispersants** are usually sprays that can be used to dry out electrical components such as the fuse block and wiring connectors. Some types an also be used as treatment for rubber and as a lubricant for hinges, cables and locks.

- **Waxes and polishes** are used to help protect painted and plated surfaces from the weather. Different types of pain may require the use of different types of wax polish. Some polishes utilize a chemical or abrasive cleaner to help remove the top layer of oxidized (dull) paint on older vehicles. In recent years, many non-wax polishes (that contain a wide variety of chemicals such as polymers and silicones) have been introduced. These non-wax polishes are usually easier to apply and last longer than conventional waxes and polishes.

A

ABS (Anti-lock braking system) A system, usually electronically controlled, that senses incipient wheel lockup during braking and relieves hydraulic pressure at wheel which is about to skid.

Aftermarket Components suitable for the motorcycle or ATV, but not produced by the manufacturer.

Allen key A hexagonal wrench which fits into a recessed hexagonal hole.

Alternating current (ac) Current produced by an alternator. Requires converting to direct current by a rectifier for charging purposes.

Alternator Converts mechanical energy from the engine into electrical energy to charge the battery and power the electrical system.

Ampere (amp) A unit of measurement for the flow of electrical current. Current = Volts ÷ Ohms.

Ampere-hour (Ah) Measure of battery capacity.

Angle-tightening A torque expressed in degrees. Often follows a conventional tightening torque for cylinder head or main bearing fasteners **(see illustration)**.

Angle-tightening cylinder head bolts

Antifreeze A substance (usually ethylene glycol) mixed with water, and added to the cooling system, to prevent freezing of the coolant in winter. Antifreeze also contains chemicals to inhibit corrosion and the formation of rust and other deposits that would tend to clog the radiator and coolant passages and reduce cooling efficiency.

Anti-dive System attached to the fork lower leg (slider) to prevent fork dive when braking hard.

Anti-seize compound A coating that reduces the risk of seizing on fasteners that are subjected to high temperatures, such as exhaust clamp bolts and nuts.

API American Petroleum Institute. A quality standard for 4-stroke motor oils.

Asbestos A natural fibrous mineral with great heat resistance, formerly used in the composition of brake friction materials. Asbestos is a health hazard and the dust created by brake systems should never be inhaled or ingested.

ATF Automatic Transmission Fluid. Often used in front forks.

ATU Automatic Timing Unit. Mechanical device for advancing the ignition timing on early engines.

ATV All Terrain Vehicle. Often called a Quad.

Axial play Side-to-side movement.

Axle A shaft on which a wheel revolves. Also known as a spindle.

B

Backlash The amount of movement between meshed components when one component is held still. Usually applies to gear teeth.

Ball bearing A bearing consisting of a hardened inner and outer race with hardened steel balls between the two races.

Bearings Used between two working surfaces to prevent wear of the components and a build-up of heat. Four types of bearing are commonly used on ATVs or motorcycles: plain shell bearings, ball bearings, tapered roller bearings and needle roller bearings.

Bevel gears Used to turn the drive through 90°. Typical applications are shaft final drive and camshaft drive **(see illustration)**.

BHP Brake Horsepower. The British measurement for engine power output. Power output is now usually expressed in kilowatts (kW).

Bevel gears are used to turn the drive through 90°

Bias-belted tire Similar construction to radial tire, but with outer belt running at an angle to the wheel rim.

Bleeding The process of removing air from a hydraulic system via a bleed nipple or bleed screw.

Bottom-end A description of an engine's crankcase components and all components contained therein.

BTDC Before Top Dead Center in terms of piston position. Ignition timing is often expressed in terms of degrees or millimeters BTDC.

Bush A cylindrical metal or rubber component used between two moving parts.

Burr Rough edge left on a component after machining or as a result of excessive wear.

C

Cam chain The chain which takes drive from the crankshaft to the camshaft(s).

Canister The main component in an evaporative emission control system (California market only); contains activated charcoal granules to trap vapors from the fuel system rather than allowing them to vent to the atmosphere.

Castellated Resembling the parapets along the top of a castle wall. For example, a castellated wheel axle or spindle nut.

Catalytic converter A device in the exhaust system of some machines which converts certain pollutants in the exhaust gases into less harmful substances.

Charging system Description of the

Cush drive rubber segments dampen out transmission shocks

components which charge the battery: the alternator, rectifer and regulator.

Clearance The amount of space between two parts. For example, between a piston and a cylinder, between a bearing and a journal, etc.

Coil spring A spiral of elastic steel found in various sizes throughout a vehicle, for example as a springing medium in the suspension and in the valve train.

Compression Reduction in volume, and increase in pressure and temperature, of a gas, caused by squeezing it into a smaller space.

Compression damping Controls the speed the suspension compresses when hitting a bump.

Compression ratio The relationship between cylinder volume when the piston is at top dead center and cylinder volume when the piston is at bottom dead center.

Connecting rod bearing The bearing in the end of the connecting rod that's attached to the crankshaft.

Continuity The uninterrupted path in the flow of electricity. Little or no measurable resistance.

Continuity tester Self-powered bleeper or test light which indicates continuity.

Cp Candlepower. Bulb rating commonly found on US motorcycles and ATVs.

Crossply tire Tire plies arranged in a criss-cross pattern. Usually four or six plies used, hence 4PR or 6PR in tire size codes.

Cush drive Rubber damper segments fitted between the rear wheel and final drive sprocket to absorb transmission shocks **(see illustration)**.

D

Degree disc Calibrated disc for measuring piston position. Expressed in degrees.

Dial gauge Clock-type gauge with adapters for measuring runout and piston position. Expressed in mm or inches.

Diaphragm The rubber membrane in a master cylinder or carburetor which seals the upper chamber.

Diaphragm spring A single sprung plate often used in clutches.

Direct current (dc) Current produced by a dc generator.

Decarbonization The process of removing carbon deposits - typically from the combustion chamber, valves and exhaust port/system.

Detonation Destructive and damaging explosion of fuel/air mixture in combustion chamber instead of controlled burning.

Diode An electrical valve which only allows current to flow in one direction. Commonly used in rectifiers and starter interlock systems.

Disc valve (or rotary valve) An induction system used on some two-stroke engines.

Double-overhead camshaft (DOHC) An engine that uses two overhead camshafts, one for the intake valves and one for the exhaust valves.

Drivebelt A toothed belt used to transmit drive to the rear wheel on some motorcycles. A drivebelt has also been used to drive the camshafts. Drivebelts are usually made of Kevlar. V-type (non-toothed) drivebelts are used in the transmissions of some ATVs.

Driveshaft Any shaft used to transmit motion. Commonly used when referring to the final driveshaft on shaft drive motorcycles or ATVs.

E

ECU (Electronic Control Unit) A computer which controls (for instance) an ignition system, or an anti-lock braking system.

EGO Exhaust Gas Oxygen sensor. Sometimes called a Lambda sensor.

Electrolyte The fluid in a lead-acid battery.

EMS (Engine Management System) A computer controlled system which manages the fuel injection and the ignition systems in an integrated fashion.

Endfloat The amount of lengthways movement between two parts. As applied to a crankshaft, the distance that the crankshaft can move side-to-side in the crankcase.

Endless chain A chain having no joining link. Common use for cam chains and final drive chains.

EP (Extreme Pressure) Oil type used in locations where high loads are applied, such as between gear teeth.

Evaporative emission control system Describes a charcoal filled canister which stores fuel vapors from the tank rather than allowing them to vent to the atmosphere. Usually only fitted to California models and referred to as an EVAP system.

Expansion chamber Section of two-stroke engine exhaust system so designed to improve engine efficiency and boost power.

F

Feeler blade or gauge A thin strip or blade of hardened steel, ground to an exact thickness, used to check or measure clearances between parts.

Final drive Description of the drive from the transmission to the rear wheel. Usually by chain or shaft, but sometimes by belt.

Firing order The order in which the engine cylinders fire, or deliver their power strokes, beginning with the number one cylinder.

Flooding Term used to describe a high fuel level in the carburetor float chambers, leading to fuel overflow. Also refers to excess fuel in the combustion chamber due to incorrect starting technique.

Free length The no-load state of a component when measured. Clutch, valve and fork spring lengths are measured at rest, without any preload.

Freeplay The amount of travel before any action takes place. The looseness in a linkage, or an assembly of parts, between the initial application of force and actual movement. For example, the distance the rear brake pedal moves before the rear brake is actuated.

Fuel injection The fuel/air mixture is metered electronically and directed into the engine intake ports (indirect injection) or into the cylinders (direct injection). Sensors supply information on engine speed and conditions.

Fuel/air mixture The charge of fuel and air going into the engine. See **Stoichiometric ratio**.

Fuse An electrical device which protects a circuit against accidental overload. The typical fuse contains a soft piece of metal which is calibrated to melt at a predetermined current flow (expressed as amps) and break the circuit.

G

Gap The distance the spark must travel in jumping from the center electrode to the side electrode in a spark plug. Also refers to the distance between the ignition rotor and the pickup coil in an electronic ignition system.

Gasket Any thin, soft material - usually cork, cardboard, asbestos or soft metal - installed between two metal surfaces to ensure a good seal. For instance, the cylinder head gasket seals the joint between the block and the cylinder head.

Gauge An instrument panel display used to monitor engine conditions. A gauge with a movable pointer on a dial or a fixed scale is an analog gauge. A gauge with a numerical readout is called a digital gauge.

Gear ratios The drive ratio of a pair of gears in a gearbox, calculated on their number of teeth.

Glaze-busting see **Honing**

Grinding Process for renovating the valve face and valve seat contact area in the cylinder head.

Ground return The return path of an electrical circuit, utilizing the vehicle's frame.

Gudgeon pin The shaft which connects the connecting rod small-end with the piston. Often called a piston pin or wrist pin.

H

Helical gears Gear teeth are slightly curved and produce less gear noise that straight-cut gears. Often used for primary drives.

Helicoil A thread insert repair system. Commonly used as a repair for stripped spark plug threads **(see illustration)**.

Installing a Helicoil thread insert in a cylinder head

Honing A process used to break down the glaze on a cylinder bore (also called glaze-busting). Can also be carried out to roughen a rebored cylinder to aid ring bedding-in.

HT (High Tension) Description of the electrical circuit from the secondary winding of the ignition coil to the spark plug.

Hydraulic A liquid filled system used to transmit pressure from one component to another. Common uses on motorcycles and ATVs are brakes and clutches.

Hydrometer An instrument for measuring the specific gravity of a lead-acid battery.

Hygroscopic Water absorbing. In motorcycle and ATV applications, braking efficiency will be reduced if DOT 3 or 4 hydraulic fluid absorbs water from the air - care must be taken to keep new brake fluid in tightly sealed containers.

I

Ibf ft Pounds-force feet. A unit of torque. Sometimes written as ft-lbs.

Ibf in Pound-force inch. A unit of torque, applied to components where a very low torque is required. Sometimes written as inch-lbs.

IC Abbreviation for Integrated Circuit.

Ignition advance Means of increasing the timing of the spark at higher engine speeds. Done by mechanical means (ATU) on early engines or electronically by the ignition control unit on later engines.

Ignition timing The moment at which the spark plug fires, expressed in the number of crankshaft degrees before the piston reaches the top of its stroke, or in the number of millimeters before the piston reaches the top of its stroke.

Infinity (∞) Description of an open-circuit electrical state, where no continuity exists.

Inverted forks (upside down forks) The sliders or lower legs are held in the yokes and the fork tubes or stanchions are connected to the wheel axle (spindle). Less unsprung weight and stiffer construction than conventional forks.

J

JASO Japan Automobile Standards Organization JASO MA is a standard for motorcycle and ATV oil equivalent to API SJ, but designed to prevent problems with wet-type motorcycle and ATV clutches.

Joule The unit of electrical energy.

Journal The bearing surface of a shaft.

K

Kickstart Mechanical means of turning the engine over for starting purposes.

Only usually fitted to mopeds, small capacity motorcycles and off-road motorcycles.

Kill switch Handebar-mounted switch for emergency ignition cut-out. Cuts the ignition circuit on all models, and additionally prevent starter motor operation on others.

km Symbol for kilometer.

kmh Abbreviation for kilometers per hour.

L

Lambda sensor A sensor fitted in the exhaust system to measure the exhaust gas oxygen content (excess air factor). Also called oxygen sensor.

Lapping see **Grinding**.

LCD Abbreviation for Liquid Crystal Display.

LED Abbreviation for Light Emitting Diode.

Liner A steel cylinder liner inserted in an aluminum alloy cylinder block.

Locknut A nut used to lock an adjustment nut, or other threaded component, in place.

Lockstops The lugs on the lower triple clamp (yoke) which abut those on the frame, preventing handlebar-to-fuel tank contact.

Lockwasher A form of washer designed to prevent an attaching nut from working loose.

LT Low Tension Description of the electrical circuit from the power supply to the primary winding of the ignition coil.

M

Main bearings The bearings between the crankshaft and crankcase.

Maintenance-free (MF) battery A sealed battery which cannot be topped up.

Manometer Mercury-filled calibrated tubes used to measure intake tract vacuum. Used to synchronize carburetors on multi-cylinder engines.

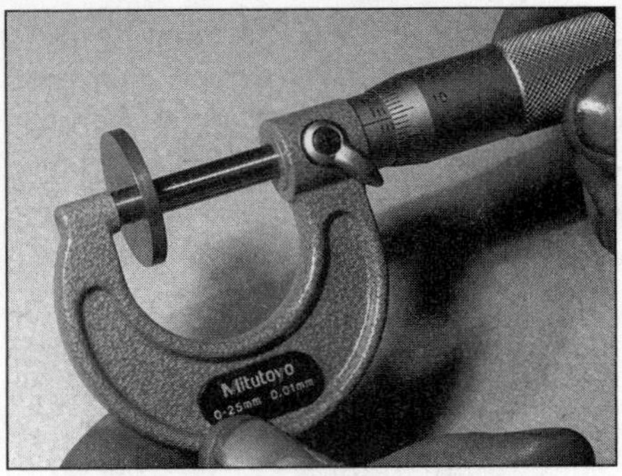

Tappet shims are measured with a micrometer

Micrometer A precision measuring instrument that measures component outside diameters **(see illustration)**.

MON (Motor Octane Number) A measure of a fuel's resistance to knock.

Monograde oil An oil with a single viscosity, eg SAE80W.

Monoshock A single suspension unit linking the swingarm or suspension linkage to the frame.

mph Abbreviation for miles per hour.

Multigrade oil Having a wide viscosity range (eg 10W40). The W stands for Winter, thus the viscosity ranges from SAE10 when cold to SAE40 when hot.

Multimeter An electrical test instrument with the capability to measure voltage, current and resistance. Some meters also incorporate a continuity tester and buzzer.

N

Needle roller bearing Inner race of caged needle rollers and hardened outer race. Examples of uncaged needle rollers can be found on some engines. Commonly used in rear suspension applications and in two-stroke engines.

Nm Newton meters.

NOx Oxides of Nitrogen. A common toxic pollutant emitted by gasoline engines at higher temperatures.

O

Octane The measure of a fuel's resistance to knock.

OE (Original Equipment) Relates to components fitted to a motorcycle or ATV as standard or replacement parts supplied by the manufacturer.

Ohm The unit of electrical resistance. Ohms = Volts ÷ Current.

Ohmmeter An instrument for measuring electrical resistance.

Oil cooler System for diverting engine oil outside of the engine to a radiator for cooling purposes.

Oil injection A system of two-stroke engine lubrication where oil is pump-fed to the engine in accordance with throttle position.

Open-circuit An electrical condition where there is a break in the flow of electricity - no continuity (high resistance).

O-ring A type of sealing ring made of a special rubber-like material; in use, the O-ring is compressed into a groove to provide the sealing action.

Oversize (OS) Term used for piston and ring size options fitted to a rebored cylinder.

Overhead cam (sohc) engine An engine with single camshaft located on top of the cylinder head.

Overhead valve (ohv) engine An engine with the valves located in the cylinder head, but with the camshaft located in the engine block or crankcase.

Oxygen sensor A device installed in the exhaust system which senses the oxygen content in the exhaust and converts this information into an electric current. Also called a Lambda sensor.

P

Plastigage A thin strip of plastic thread, available in different sizes, used for measuring clearances. For example, a strip of Plastigage is laid across a bearing journal. The parts are assembled and dismantled; the width of the crushed strip indicates the clearance between journal and bearing.

Polarity Either negative or positive ground, determined by which battery lead is connected to the frame (ground return). Modern motorcycles and ATVs are usually negative ground.

Pre-ignition A situation where the fuel/air mixture ignites before the spark plug fires. Often due to a hot spot in the combustion chamber caused by carbon build-up. Engine has a tendency to 'run-on'.

Pre-load (suspension) The amount a spring is compressed when in the unloaded state. Preload can be applied by gas, spacer or mechanical adjuster.

Premix The method of engine lubrication on some gasoline two-stroke engines. Engine oil is mixed with the gasoline in the fuel tank in a specific ratio. The fuel/oil mix is sometimes referred to as "petrol".

Primary drive Description of the drive from the crankshaft to the clutch. Usually by gear or chain.

PS Pferdestärke - a German interpretation of BHP.

PSI Pounds-force per square inch. Imperial measurement of tire pressure and cylinder pressure measurement.

PTFE Polytetrafluoroethylene. A low friction substance.

Pulse secondary air injection system A process of promoting the burning of excess fuel present in the exhaust gases by routing fresh air into the exhaust ports.

Q

Quartz halogen bulb Tungsten filament surrounded by a halogen gas. Typically used for the headlight **(see illustration)**.

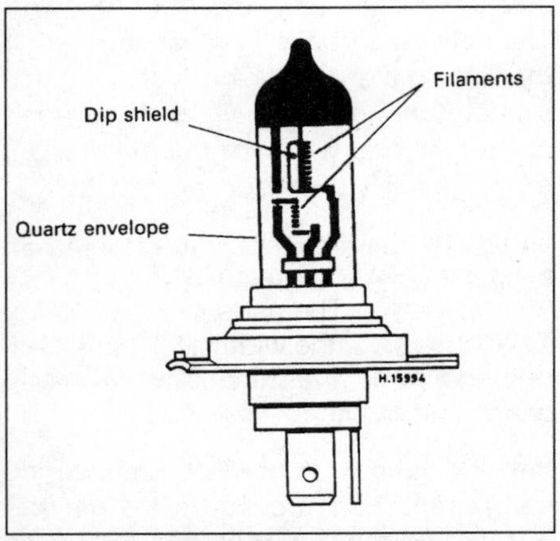

Quartz halogen headlight bulb construction

R

Rack-and-pinion A pinion gear on the end of a shaft that mates with a rack (think of a geared wheel opened up and laid flat). Sometimes used in clutch operating systems.

Radial play Up and down movement about a shaft.

Radial ply tires Tire plies run across the tire (from bead to bead) and around the circumference of the tire. Less resistant to tread distortion than other tire types.

Radiator A liquid-to-air heat transfer device designed to reduce the temperature of the coolant in a liquid cooled engine.

Rake A feature of steering geometry - the angle of the steering head in relation to the vertical **(see illustration)**.

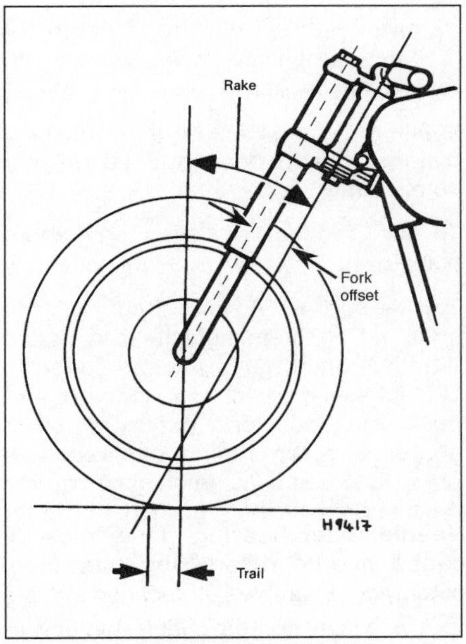

Steering geometry

Rebore Providing a new working surface to the cylinder bore by boring out the old surface. Necessitates the use of oversize piston and rings.

Rebound damping A means of controlling the oscillation of a suspension unit spring after it has been compressed. Resists the spring's natural tendency to bounce back after being compressed.

Rectifier Device for converting the ac output of an alternator into dc for battery charging.

Reed valve An induction system commonly used on two-stroke engines.

Regulator Device for maintaining the charging voltage from the generator or alternator within a specified range.

Relay A electrical device used to switch heavy current on and off by using a low current auxiliary circuit.

Resistance Measured in ohms. An electrical component's ability to pass electrical current.

RON (Research Octane Number) A measure of a fuel's resistance to knock.

rpm revolutions per minute.

Runout The amount of wobble (in-and-out movement) of a wheel or shaft as it's rotated. The amount a shaft rotates "out-of-true." The out-of-round condition of a rotating part.

S

SAE (Society of Automotive Engineers) A standard for the viscosity of a fluid.

Sealant A liquid or paste used to prevent leakage at a joint. Sometimes used in conjunction with a gasket.

Service limit Term for the point where a component is no longer useable and must be replaced.

Shaft drive A method of transmitting drive from the transmission to the rear wheel.

Shell bearings Plain bearings consisting of two shell halves. Most often used as connecting rod and main bearings in a four-stroke engine. Often called bearing inserts.

Shim Thin spacer, commonly used to adjust the clearance or relative positions between two parts. For example, shims inserted into or under tappets or followers to control valve clearances. Clearance is adjusted by changing the thickness of the shim.

Short-circuit An electrical condition where current shorts to ground bypassing the circuit components.

Skimming Process to correct warpage or repair a damaged surface, such as brake discs or drums.

Slide-hammer A special puller that screws into or hooks onto a component such as a shaft or bearing; a heavy sliding handle on the shaft bottoms against the end of the shaft to knock the component free.

Small-end bearing The bearing in the upper end of the connecting rod at its joint with the gudgeon pin.

Snap-ring A ring-shaped clip used to prevent endwise movement of cylindrical parts and shafts. An internal snap-ring is installed in a groove in a housing; an external snap-ring fits into a groove on the outside of a cylindrical piece such as a shaft. Also known as a circlip.

Spalling Damage to camshaft lobes or bearing journals shown as pitting of the working surface.

Specific gravity (SG) The state of charge of the electrolyte in a lead-acid battery. A measure of the electrolyte's density compared with water.

Straight-cut gears Common type gear used on gearbox shafts and for oil pump and water pump drives.

Stanchion The inner sliding part of the front forks, held by the yokes. Often called a fork tube.

Stoichiometric ratio The optimum chemical air/fuel ratio for a gasoline engine, said to be 14.7 parts of air to 1 part of fuel.

Sulphuric acid The liquid (electrolyte) used in a lead-acid battery. Poisonous and extremely corrosive.

Surface grinding (lapping) Process to correct a warped gasket face, commonly used on cylinder heads.

T

Tapered-roller bearing Tapered inner race of caged needle rollers and separate tapered outer race. Examples of taper roller bearings can be found on steering heads.

Tappet A cylindrical component which transmits motion from the cam to the valve stem, either directly or via a pushrod and rocker arm. Also called a cam follower.

TCS Traction Control System. An electronically-controlled system which senses wheel spin and reduces engine speed accordingly.

TDC Top Dead Center denotes that the piston is at its highest point in the cylinder.

Thread-locking compound Solution applied to fastener threads to prevent loosening. Select type to suit application.

Thrust washer A washer positioned between two moving components on a shaft. For example, between gear pinions on gearshaft.

Timing chain See **Cam Chain**.

Timing light Stroboscopic lamp for carrying out ignition timing checks with the engine running.

Top-end A description of an engine's cylinder block, head and valve gear components.

Torque Turning or twisting force about a shaft.

Torque setting A prescribed tightness specified by the manufacturer to ensure that the bolt or nut is secured correctly. Undertightening can result in the bolt or nut coming loose or a surface not being sealed. Overtightening can result in stripped threads, distortion or damage to the component being retained.

Torx key A six-point wrench.

Tracer A stripe of a second color applied to a wire insulator to distinguish that wire from another one with the same color insulator. For example, Br/W is often used to denote a brown insulator with a white tracer.

Trail A feature of steering geometry. Distance from the steering head axis to the tire's central contact point.

Triple clamps The cast components which extend from the steering head and support the fork stanchions or tubes. Often called fork yokes.

Turbocharger A centrifugal device, driven by exhaust gases, that pressurizes the intake air. Normally used to increase the power output from a given engine displacement.

TWI Abbreviation for Tire Wear Indicator. Indicates the location of the tread depth indicator bars on tires.

U

Universal joint or U-joint (UJ) A double-pivoted connection for transmitting power from a driving to a driven shaft through an angle. Typically found in shaft drive assemblies.

Unsprung weight Anything not supported by the bike's suspension (ie the wheel, tires, brakes, final drive and bottom (moving) part of the suspension).

V

Vacuum gauges Clock-type gauges for measuring intake tract vacuum. Used for carburetor synchronization on multi-cylinder engines.

Valve A device through which the flow of liquid, gas or vacuum may be stopped, started or regulated by a moveable part that opens, shuts or partially obstructs one or more ports or passageways. The intake and exhaust valves in the cylinder head are of the poppet type.

Valve clearance The clearance between the valve tip (the end of the valve stem) and the rocker arm or tappet/follower. The valve clearance is measured when the valve is closed. The correct clearance is important - if too small the valve won't close fully and will burn out, whereas if too large noisy operation will result.

Valve lift The amount a valve is lifted off its seat by the camshaft lobe.

Valve timing The exact setting for the opening and closing of the valves in relation to piston position.

Vernier caliper A precision measuring instrument that measures inside and outside dimensions. Not quite as accurate as a micrometer, but more convenient.

VIN Vehicle Identification Number. Term for the vehicle's engine and frame numbers.

Viscosity The thickness of a liquid or its resistance to flow.

Volt A unit for expressing electrical "pressure" in a circuit. Volts = current x ohms.

W

Water pump A mechanically-driven device for moving coolant around the engine.

Watt A unit for expressing electrical power. Watts = volts x current.

Wet liner arrangement

Wear limit see **Service limit**

Wet liner A liquid-cooled engine design where the pistons run in liners which are directly surrounded by coolant **(see illustration)**.

Wheelbase Distance from the center of the front wheel to the center of the rear wheel.

Wiring harness or loom Describes the electrical wires running the length of the vehicle and enclosed in tape or plastic sheathing. Wiring coming off the main harness is usually referred to as a sub harness.

Woodruff key A key of semi-circular or square section used to locate a gear to a shaft. Often used to locate the alternator rotor on the crankshaft.

Wrist pin Another name for gudgeon or piston pin.

Trail rules

Just when you're ready to have some fun out in the dirt you get slapped with more rules. But by following these rules you'll ensure everyone's enjoyment, not just your own. It's important that all off-roaders follow these rules, as it will help to keep the trails open and keep us in good standing with other trail users. Really, these rules are no more than common sense and common courtesy.

- **Don't ride where you're not supposed to.** Stay off private property and obey all signs marking areas that are off limits to motorized vehicles. Also, as much fun as it might be, don't ride in State or Federal wilderness areas.

- **Leave the land as you found it.** When you've left the area, the only thing you should leave behind are your tire tracks. Stay on the trails, too. There are plenty of trails to ride on without blazing new ones. Be sure to carry out all litter that you create (and if you want to do a good deed, pick up any litter that you come across). Be sure to leave gates as you found them, or if the gate has a sign on it, comply with whatever the sign says (some people don't close gates after passing through them. Others may close gates when the landowner actually wants to keep them open).

- **Give other trail users the right-of-way.** There has been an ongoing dispute amongst trail users as to who belongs there and who doesn't. If the off-roading community shows respect and courtesy to hikers and equestrians, we stand a far better chance of being able to enjoy our sport in the years to come, and to keep the trails open for our children. When you ride up behind hikers or horses, give them plenty of room and pass slowly so as not to startle them. When you approach an equestrian from the opposite direction, stop your machine when the horse nears you so it won't get frightened and bolt.

- **Don't scare the animals!** Whether it be horses, cattle or wild animals like deer, rabbits or coyotes, leave them alone. Remember, you're visiting their home, so treat them with respect. Besides, startling animals can be dangerous. Loud noises or your sudden appearance can trigger an animal's defensive instinct, which could mean bad news for you.

- **Don't ride "over your head."** Sometimes the trails start to resemble ski runs, with a few irresponsible riders going so fast that they're barely able to maintain control of their vehicles. They'd never be able to stop to avoid another trail user if they had to. Most collisions on the trail are caused by such individuals and the results are occasionally tragic. You should only ride fast in areas where you can clearly see a good distance ahead - never on trails with blind corners or rises high enough that prevent you from seeing what's on the other side.

- **Be prepared.** Carry everything you think you may need to make minor repairs should your machine break down. Know how to make basic repairs and keep your vehicle in good mechanical condition to minimize the chances of becoming stranded. Always let someone know where you're going, and ride with a friend whenever possible.

Note: *References throughout this index are in the form, "Chapter number"•"Page number"*